the Young child

reviews of research, volume 3

Editors

Shirley G. Moore, University of Minnesota
Catherine R. Cooper, University of Texas

A 1981–82 Comprehensive Membership Benefit

National Association for the Education of Young Children
Washington, D.C.

Cover photograph: Sandy Felsenthal
Cover design: Rebecca Miller

National Association for the Education of Young Children
1834 Connecticut Avenue, N.W.
Washington, DC 20009

Library of Congress Catalog Card Number: 67-24993
ISBN Catalog Number: #0-912674-78-4
NAEYC #206

Printed in the United States of America.

Contents

Cluster III: Children's social relationships: process and consequences   135

Cluster IV: Biological factors in development: the issue of malleability   191

Cluster V: Special needs of children: labels, prediction, and intervention   231

Preface

This volume contains an introductory chapter on the use of research by practitioners, and 13 reviews of the most recent research findings in selected areas of child development. The reviews are on topics of particular concern to practitioners in education, child care, and health and psychological services and are appropriate for post-secondary, college-level, and graduate students, as well as for practicing professionals and parent educators.

The volume is by no means exhaustive as to topics reviewed, nor is the coverage of each review exhaustive. Although the work presented is of contemporary interest and significance to the target audience, care has been taken not to distort the essence of an area of study by the selection of research presented.

In contrast to Volumes I and II of this series, each of the chapters has been written solely for inclusion here. The authors of the reviews are leading contributors to research in their respective areas and share, with us, a commitment to the dissemination of child development information to those responsible for services to children and their families. Their knowledge of the research and their perspectives on its implications for practice make this volume somewhat unique among child development reviews of research.

The 13 reviews are clustered under five general topics; Socioemotional beginnings, Language and thinking, Children's social relationships, Biological factors in development, and Special needs of children. Each of the five clusters is preceded by a brief overview of the cluster content and a commentary on the major themes recurring in the cluster. It is hoped that the cluster comments will help the reader to find the links between chapters and, in the process, see the forest as well as the trees. Readers whose appetites are whetted by this book may also wish to explore other series of research reviews under the titles *Review of Child Development Research*, *Advances in Child Development and Behavior*, *Minnesota Symposia on Child Psychology*, and *Carmichael's Manual of Child Psychology* (the most recent of which will be published in 1983).

Acknowledgments

We would like to express our sincere gratitude to our chapter authors for their extraordinary efforts in contributing their work to this volume for the National Association for the Education of Young Children. We also would like to thank Jan Brown, Director of Publications at NAEYC, for her able counsel and assistance along the way, and Melanie Rose White, Publications Manager, for her contribution to the final product.

Shirley G. Moore
Minneapolis, Minnesota

Catherine R. Cooper
Austin, Texas

Shirley G. Moore
Catherine R. Cooper

1 Personal and scientific sources of knowledge about children

Children's behavior has been a perennial source of fascination for adults from the beginning of time, and the focus of scientific investigation for many decades. As objects of study, children are complex, to say the least. A child brings to every experience a biological integrity, a physical state of well-being, a history of past experiences with people, and a predisposition to respond in particular ways to particular events. Adults have a keen sense of responsibility for children's welfare whether in the role of parent, as a teacher in a day care center or after-school program, as a pediatrician, or indirectly as a lawyer in a child custody suit. To be helpful, however, we need a clear sense of what to expect of children of different ages and an understanding of the experiences and relationships that affect their development. We must also appreciate that children, in turn, influence the events and people around them by their appearance, their behavior, and their attitudes.

This volume is a collection of research reviews that are on topics pertinent to those who work with children, and that are designed to help the reader interpret a wide variety of research findings. We will introduce you to the material that follows by discussing, in this chapter, the research enterprise itself and the nature of research knowledge. Research is just one of the sources of information that is available to us about child development; other sources are our own observations and experiences, and the observations and experiences of those who share them with us, including children themselves. Most of us have implicit confidence in our own experiences, as indeed we should. Our personal observations are based on things that we have witnessed; we know them to be true in the instances of which we speak. Our confidence in research, however, is frequently another matter. One can hardly imagine a question that receives a greater variety of answers from the practitioner than the question: "What can child development research do for you?" For some practitioners, research is the key to ultimate truths about children, elegant in its conception and design, flawless in its execution, and exhaustive in its revelations. For others, it is irrelevant; it seems to them to have been based on the whims of the researcher and carried out in isolated laboratory situations unrelated to real life. We will attempt to present a perspective about research, and the information it yields, that will serve the needs of the practitioner, and that is more discerning than either of the sweeping generalizations above. To do this we will first discuss the more salient features of research as a method of inquiry—as an approach to the gathering of information about children—and then comment on the use of research by the practitioner.

Research: a method of inquiry

The methods of child study used by researchers and practitioners to obtain information about children will be compared first. Two issues will be given special attention: the use of the laboratory setting in research, and the researcher's approach to questions about the causes of behavior.

How does research evidence differ from our personal knowledge?

Our personal observations and experiences are an integral part of each of us as individuals; they are, in some respects, not very different from the observations of the researcher. We move around in the world observing children in natural settings, watching them interact with others, and interacting with them ourselves. Our personal observations are unique and private events from which we develop our own implicit theories about child behavior—drawing conclusions about normative development, about the needs of children, and about the effects of significant events on children's lives. This personal knowledge is essential to our understanding of child development and is the foundation for much of our expertise as practitioners.

One characteristic of personal knowledge, however, is that we each must necessarily construct it out of our own experience, and we cannot completely share the data base of that experience with others. We can describe generally the kinds of experiences we have had with children, and the settings in which those experiences have taken place, but we cannot specify the exact nature of the observations from which our personal knowledge about children has evolved. One consequence of this state of affairs is that when we do not agree with one another about some aspect of development, we can only guess at the source of our disagreement. We do not know, for example, whether differences in our impressions about children are due to actual differences in the behavior of the children with whom we have each had contact, or to differences in our interpretations of the same, or similar, behaviors. One of us might call a given behavior timidity, while another calls the very same behavior sensitivity, or one calls a behavior assertive, and another, aggressive.

In contrast to our personal knowledge, the sources of scientific knowledge are necessarily explicit and open to scrutiny and examination by others. Each aspect of the information gathering process in research must be described in detail, including who was observed (for example, middle-socioeconomic status [SES] four-year-old White children, suburban children, inner-city Black three-year-olds) and in what setting the observations took place (in a rural Head Start center, in the maternity ward of a city hospital, in homes, in a university laboratory). If a researcher concludes from such observations that children in one school setting are more helpful and less selfish with their companions than the children in another, the behaviors that the researcher calls *helpful* and *selfish* must be specifically defined. It must also be demonstrated that, using these definitions, different observers watching the same child at the same time can agree that the child did, or did not, show the behaviors. If the observers cannot agree, let us say, at least 80 percent of the time, the definitions of the terms are improved and made more explicit. Other investigators must be able to repeat the study if they desire to do so, by observing children of the same general description in a similar setting and recording the same categories of behavior. It is in this sense that research information is public; it must be replicable. Still other researchers might wish to extend our knowledge of the behavior under investigation by using the same observation instrument to compare other populations of children (e.g., rural vs. urban) or other settings (e.g., home vs. school) to see if similar results are obtained. If findings from the original research are not confirmed in repetitions of the study, or in extensions of it to other populations of children or settings, we must try to resolve the discrepancies or await further study of the area to see if, in time, a consensus will emerge.

A second way in which research differs from personal observations is that the observations of the researcher are expressed in numerical terms. The general impressions of an observer concerning the incidence of a behavior—in the case described above, helpfulness and selfishness in different school settings—is not enough. The number of helpful and selfish behaviors recorded in the different settings must be compared with the use of statistical procedures. Differences that are too small to be considered statistically significant are assumed to have arisen by chance and are not considered reliable. Although the researcher's method of observation does not offer a panacea that will solve all of our problems as students of child behavior, it does allow us to compare observations made in different settings, with different children, using the same or different observational instruments.

So far our comments about research methods have involved observations of children's spontaneous behavior. As will be clear from the chapters that follow, however, researchers use many other measurement techniques, including tests or tasks designed by the experimenter to stimulate the child to engage in the particular behavior of interest (such as the four-year-old's use of the concept *because,* toddlers' preferences for sex-typed toys, children's recall of novel vs. conventional objects) or to measure the effects of an experimental intervention (changes in perspective-taking abilities following training, the effects of peer models on altruism). From time to time, standardized tests (to measure IQ, personality structure, or school readiness, for example) are used as well as interviews, surveys, and behavioral ratings. In fact, researchers often use more than one method of inquiry in a given study, especially a combination of observational and other methods. Regardless of the methods used, researchers have an obligation to describe their procedures and data in detail so they can be compared with those used by other investigators and replicated if necessary.

The laboratory as an aid to research

Although much of the research you will read about in this volume has been conducted in the natural settings in which children are born, live, play, and are cared for, researchers frequently use especially prepared environments or laboratory settings for conducting research. One of the major reasons for this is to control factors in the environment that affect the behavior being studied in ways that interfere with the purposes of the investigation. If, for example, we wish to study the effects of different types of toys on the play of boys compared with girls, we will want to control the kinds of toys that are presented to the children, and be certain that the same selection is available to both sexes. Such a requirement could not be left to the chance availability of toys in a typical playroom or home setting.

A second example will help to highlight another reason why a particular research project might be conducted outside of the natural setting; to answer questions about the *causes* of behavior. Many of our most pressing research questions are causal ones. For example, we might ask, what is the effect on children's vocabulary of a particular program of language instruction? Under what conditions does success have a positive effect on self-concept? Does violence on television cause aggression in children?

Although we speculate about the causes of behavior based on our personal observations, intuitions, and hunches, we rarely can establish causal relationships unequivocally in the natural environment where so many variables are interacting at once. We notice sequences of events (a change in the physical composition of the playroom is followed by more cooperative play among the children) or the co-occurrence of events (frequent family reading sessions go hand in hand with precocious vocabulary development) but we usually cannot be certain that one of these events actually caused the occurrence of the other. To confirm a causal relationship in research we must do more than just observe sequences or co-occurrence. We must actually *recreate* a cause-effect relationship by manipulating one or more of the causal factors, recording the effects of the manipulation on children's behavior, and comparing the behavior of those children with that of children who have not been exposed to the manipulation. It is in this way that the researcher establishes causal relationships in which we can have a high degree of confidence.

A hypothetical example of a research study designed to answer a causal question will demonstrate the process. Suppose that an investigator wishes to test the hypothesis that TV violence causes high levels of aggression in the play of four-year-old children compared with nonviolent TV. To answer this question, a sample of children would probably be randomly assigned to one of two viewing conditions, an aggressive TV condition and a nonaggressive TV condition. Random assignment is important because it can be relied upon, when one is dealing with sizable numbers of children, to distribute the aggressive and the nonaggressive children more or less evenly between the viewing groups. The groups of children would then view television, perhaps two or three 15-minute segments, according to their respective conditions, after which they would be observed in free play. Instances of aggressive and nonaggressive play would be recorded and the groups would be compared.

In designing a study of this kind, some of the important factors that could cause play-session differences in the two kinds of viewers would clearly have to be kept comparable in the play groups. We know, for example, that boys generally are more aggressive than girls, consequently the proportion of boys in each kind of viewing group would need to be equal. Also, the selection of toys and materials available during play would need to be identical, or nearly so, since these things vary in the extent to which they elicit aggression. One can see at a glance how difficult it would be to establish the comparability of children and settings in the natural environment where so many important factors are operating—factors that, if allowed to vary in such a way as to bias the results, could either produce differences in aggression between the groups, or mask differences that, in fact, are there.

It will be clear, as you read the chapters in this volume, that research conducted in laboratory settings, or in natural settings where the experimenter can maintain a high degree of control over significant variables, can be particularly helpful to the practitioner in confirming causal relationships that we can only guess at from our informal observations as we watch and interact with children.

Causes and correlations: an important distinction

As consumers of research, it is important that we maintain the distinction between studies that establish causal relationships (in which the experimenter has actually recreated the effect) and studies that describe correlated events that may or may not be causal. In correlational data, the researcher assesses the extent to which variables appear to be related in some systematic way. Although there are many different kinds of correlational relationships, the two most common in the research literature are *positive relationships* (as in the case of children's height and weight—as height *increases,* so does weight *increase*) and *negative relationships* (as in the case of children's age and their crying—as age *increases,* the frequency of crying *decreases*). It will help to realize that perfect correlations are virtually unheard of in the study of child development. In the case of height and weight, for example, rarely will a group of children who are ordered on the basis of their height fall in exactly the same order on the basis of weight; some children who are relatively short will almost certainly be heavier than some of their taller companions. A correlation is determined to be statistically significant by an investigator if the relationship between variables is clearly greater than would occur by chance even though it might be far from perfect. In interpreting correlational data, therefore, we must be careful not to assume that the relationship does not exist for groups simply because we can point to individual exceptions.

It bears emphasizing here that although correlations often do involve variables that are causally related, *correlations themselves do not establish causes*. To know, for example, that friendliness and peer acceptance are positively correlated does not tell us that the friendliness *caused* the acceptance. It is just as reasonable to hypothesize that acceptance by peers caused the friendliness, or that both the friendliness and the peer acceptance were caused by still a third variable (an easygoing disposition, for example). As a matter of fact, all three things could be true.

Before leaving the topic of correlations, something should be said about the dilemma posed by having to settle for correlational evidence when important causal questions are being asked. There are many issues about which causal information would be enlightening but, for ethical reasons, it is not available. Catastrophic events are of this kind. Such events are often negatively correlated with thriving in children, yet we rarely have clear evidence of a causal kind regarding them because we simply do not do experiments in which we deliberately produce conditions that we suspect will interfere with a child's normal development. For example, we do not *create* conditions of malnutrition in children to study its effect on cognitive development. We do not deprive children of an enriched childrearing environment in order to get causal evidence of the effects of such an environment, nor do we randomly assign parents and children to a *parental hostility* condition to see if there is a causal link between hostility and childhood aggression, or hostility and self-concept. We can find children who experience such conditions in the normal course of events—for example, children whose parents show high levels of hostility in childrearing—but we cannot be certain that such groups do not differ from other groups on many other dimensions as well, any or all of which could be the cause of the negative outcomes in their children. In fact, it is generally the case that natural groups *do* vary from other groups on many related dimensions; for example, parents who are hostile to their children also have more marital problems, and experience more (general) family stress which could also affect their children's aggression or self-concept. To establish causal relationships in such matters would require randomly assigning children to catastrophic conditions—one condition at a time, controlling for the others—an outlandish idea, to be sure.

Ironically, it is precisely in this area of negative, even catastrophic, behavioral outcomes that researchers are criticized the most by practitioners for providing only correlational evidence where causal evidence is needed. An example will help to highlight the dilemma for researchers. There has been much speculation concerning the effects of a regular diet of TV violence on the commission of acts of violence (even murders) during middle childhood and adolescence. Lawyers, parents, and media analysts all want proof one way or the other—does it, or does it not cause such acts? Yet, unambiguous causal evidence will not be forthcoming because we will never deliberately create the conditions to test that hypothesis, isolated from all of the other suspected causes of such events. We will never, for example, randomly assign children to long-term viewing of especially violent TV and monitor the outcome to see if they commit more than their share of violent crimes as they mature. Random assignment would be critical to an investigation of causes since "volunteers" would produce a group of viewers of violence who already have a more-than-ordinary taste for such acts; later violence could be due to differences that were there before viewing. We do know, from research studies on TV viewing (similar to our hypothetical study of children's aggression), that relatively innocuous levels of aggressive TV, the kind to which most children are exposed in the course of any normal week, tend to inspire aggressive activity in a significant number of children. We can extrapolate from these data and suspect that more intense levels of viewing over longer periods of time might have a significant effect on more extreme acts of violence. We might, of course, be wrong, and we must weigh the consequences of both kinds of errors that we could be making. We can ignore the implications of TV violence in childhood aggression and risk its possible negative consequences, or we can put pressure on decision makers and risk having indicted violence on TV unjustly. The one thing we cannot have is unambiguous causal evidence on this issue; for sound and justifiable ethical reasons, we will never have it.

The application of research to practice

Practitioners have every reason to expect that research findings will be informative and have applications to practice, especially research on behaviors that are of direct concern to practitioners. We will now consider some issues to keep in mind as you reflect upon the research you will be reading about, and as you incorporate the new knowledge it offers into your frame of reference.

The search for the perfect variable

When we identify a causal factor in research, or suspect it from correlational data, it is tempting for the practitioner to think of it as the only cause of the behavior under consideration rather than one of several causes. We long for behavior to be simpler and more easily understood than it is, but it is helpful for the practitioner to keep in mind that most of the significant behaviors of interest to us have multiple causes, not single ones. The researcher isolates causes in order to study each one independent of the others, but causes rarely function in isolation in the natural environment. Generally we can identify from research at least three or four factors that are likely candidates as major causes of such outcomes as school success, peer acceptance, obedience, cooperativeness, aggression, delinquency, honesty, and altruism. To yearn for the single predictor of such complex behavioral domains leads to simplistic conceptions of the behavior itself and of the solutions to problems related to it. Hence we hear "if only" arguments: if only parents would do such and such, or if only schools would do thus and so; as though if such prescriptions were followed, all of our problems as practitioners would be solved.

Even when we can order variables on the basis of their importance in predicting behavior, to ignore all but the most impressive one is to reduce the extent of our understanding of child behavior. Ironically, the debate over which are the most important sources of influence often involves pairs of factors both of which can be demonstrated from our research to have profound effects on child behavior; for example, home/school, parents/peers, heredity/environment, and early years/later childhood.

The research contribution: norms of behavior

Although many researchers are interested in the study of individual differences in children, most research is directed at establishing norms and general laws of behavior—what is true for *most* of the children *most* of the time; what we can *expect* of a child of a given age; what is *likely* to happen to a behavior under a particular condition of reinforcement; what is *probably* the cause, or one of several causes, of a particular behavior. Because generalizations from research do not fit all children under all circumstances, practitioners are sometimes inclined to question their validity or usefulness. We should keep in mind, however, that although our contacts are with individuals, many of our most important decisions as practitioners are made on the basis of what we know about children in general. The preparation of a child care environment, the selection of a school curriculum, the application of principles of reinforcement to a learning situation, the espousal of a philosophy of discipline and child management, or the decision to worry about a child or feel encouraged by her or his development, is based largely on our knowledge of groups of children, including what we know about individual differences in development typical at any given age. Having a grasp of developmental norms and the major sources of influence on child behavior will certainly enhance the validity of our decisions about individual children.

The importance of a general knowledge of children is reflected in the value we place on *experience* with them. We know that having encountered many different children under a variety of circumstances gives us a broader perspective of what children are like than we would otherwise have. We will never again encounter a child exactly like Michael Weber or Jennifer Anderson, but having known them helps us understand others. Our research knowledge then, can complement our personal experiences by adding to our knowledge of normative development and improving our perspectives about children in general.

When does research have something to offer the practitioner?

Generally the practitioner will find reviews of research more useful and informative than individual research studies because authors of reviews attempt to present a *consensus* of what is known in an area of study with different investigators, populations of children, and measures. The findings of an individual research study, no matter how carefully done, or how relevant to practice, should not be given excessive weight by the practitioner. It is not until we have at least four or five studies, ideally more, all of which address the same general research question and suggest the same general conclusion, that we can have confidence in the statements to be made about behavior from our research. Even when research findings are not totally consistent across studies, a consensus in which we can be reasonably confident often emerges despite the occasional contradiction, due possibly to population or measurement differences.

In the process of refining and extending our generalizations about child development, researchers often test the limits of our knowledge. They ask—under what conditions do generalizations *fail* to hold up? Practitioners find this aspect of the research enterprise frustrating because it seems to imply that previous research findings about which we had consensus are no longer credible. Although current work does sometimes contradict work done in the past and cause us to revise our perceptions about children, much of what appears to be contradictory is, in fact, a refinement or extension of what we know, and should not shake our confidence in what we thought we knew. An example can be drawn from the work on invulnerable children. A number of psychologists are now studying children who, by all criteria, should be failing to thrive, but are doing just fine. Identifying some of the common denominators in the lives of these children (such as having one strong, stable parent despite poverty, family stress, health problems, and family mobility) can help us to understand resiliency in children as well as vulnerability. But to conclude from this work that high levels of adversity are good for children is not justified; we should not lose sight of the more common finding that children who seem to have the cards stacked against them are *less* likely to thrive than others, not *more* likely.

Finally, as practitioners, we should require an extraordinarily persuasive body of research literature before concluding that our collective wisdom and folklore about children is faulty or invalid. It is heartening to realize that our common knowledge and our research knowledge often lead us to the same generalizations about children's behavior and development. Despite the confidence we can have in our common knowledge, however, we should question that knowledge when it conflicts with research, and we should keep an open mind on those issues that do not lend themselves to ready consensus.

Conclusions

To do justice to the task of providing for children, we need the benefit of our current research knowledge as well as our personal observations and experience. The chapters that follow address aspects of child behavior of relevance and interest to practitioners. For this reason, we sincerely hope that the material in them will be a help to you in refining and extending your implicit theories of child development, and in innovating and experimenting on your own as you accommodate to the needs of children and their families. In the future, we certainly will know more about child development than we do today, but we cannot put today's children on the shelf while we wait. We must work with the knowledge we have.

The clusters: an introduction

This book is divided into five clusters that group chapters according to the common issues they consider:

Socioemotional beginnings: the significance of relationships
Language and thinking: understanding children's understanding
Children's social relationships: process and consequences
Biological factors in development: the issue of malleability
Special needs of children: labels, prediction, and intervention

Opening each cluster is a brief overview of its distinctive themes. Before proceeding to the clusters themselves, however, we will discuss four larger themes which recur across chapters and clusters. For the most part, these pervasive themes represent new ways of viewing young children, as well as new approaches to the scientific study of developmental process and outcomes.

The first major theme concerns a new awareness of *children as an active influence on the people and events in their lives* as well as being influenced by those people and events. For example, a child's physical characteristics—being attractive, handicapped, or unusually coordinated—influence other people to respond in special ways, talking more frequently to a cute baby, sending a deaf child to a special drama program, or allowing a talented young gymnast to turn cartwheels indoors. In other words, socialization or childrearing is not a one-way process, but rather it is a unique collaboration, with the adult's responsiveness to the special needs of the individual child in turn encouraging the child's continued, active involvement in the developmental process.

A second overall theme of this book highlights *competencies in young children that we had not fully appreciated in the past*. Recent studies of young children, conducted under conditions that allow them to display their abilities, have revealed many such competencies. Although young children still have a long way to go in the development of their skills and abilities, reports of parent-infant interactions, child-child interactions in the preschool years, and many aspects of the development of language, cognition, and social skills, indicate that young children may be more able than we previously thought.

A third theme concerns the increased attention researchers are giving to identifying *the significant events in children's lives that alter the course of future development and allow us to predict future competencies from early assessments.* More complex approaches to prediction are especially important in assessing the developmental potential of high-risk or handicapped children. Sources of inaccuracy in prediction that are caused by bias in our observations are also a recurring concern, and we are increasingly sensitive to the errors we might make in predicting future behavior by our use of convenient but misleading labels, such as *special education, minority, only child, disadvantaged,* or *hyperactive.*

Finally, we now recognize to a greater extent than we did previously that children are biological organisms as well as social ones, and that *biological factors provide the context within which socialization occurs.* Rather than viewing the nature-nurture issue as a question of how much influence each has, discussion centers on the constraints that biological factors impose on development, and ways these factors can be overcome by learning and socialization, especially with handicapped children. Both biological factors and environmental experiences are seen not only as potential sources of vulnerability, but also as sources of resilience for children.

The chapters in this volume illustrate how much the goals of researchers—to assess, predict, and enhance development—are similar to those of practitioners. We hope this volume offers an opportunity to examine the scientific consensus on issues of interest and concern to you.

Cluster I

Socioemotional beginnings: the significance of relationships

Individual development is influenced not only by physical factors such as nutrition, but also by the social world into which the child is born. The three chapters in this cluster illustrate the progress being made in understanding how the quality of children's relationships affects later thriving. We now view the infant as both vulnerable—sensitive to deprivation, and resilient—capable of mobilizing compensatory resources and recovering from insult, each to some extent and in different ways. Thus, predicting the path of development for a given child must take into account sources of both vulnerability and resiliency, present and future.

Horowitz introduces the theme of prediction by tracing the variety of factors that are associated with thriving. The difficulty of prediction is a testimonial to how diverse the developmental paths may be for different children from infancy to early and later childhood. As Horowitz notes, the interweaving of prenatal and birth experiences, nutrition, and interpersonal factors is now being linked to the varied patterns of later thriving.

The meshing and fine tuning of reciprocal patterns of interaction between infant and caregiver are hallmarks of the early months of life, and Goldberg traces how the elements of these first relationships originate in biologically given behaviors—not only single behaviors such as crying, but also social responsiveness itself. This more specific approach to describing how infants and caregivers accrue experience with one another helps us appreciate how individual histories evolve into distinctive relationships and attachments, and also illuminates the adaptive significance of parent-infant interaction.

As children enter their preschool years, their learning of the social and intellectual skills of mature members of their culture is expected to be enhanced by parents, teachers, and other socializing agents. Radin extends our understanding of the mutual influence of parents and children. Her taxonomy of indirect and direct influences illustrates the diversity of these processes. Discussion of the process of identification, and of sex role and cognitive socialization, illustrate the power of the social system of which children and parents are a part, as well as the role of other sources of socialization.

Certainly these chapters provide cause for optimism, but also concern. As children grow older, the influences on them become increasingly complex. Yet research findings continue to demonstrate that adults do have powerful influences on their children, so abdication to others, or the choice of temporary substitutes such as group or family day care, schools, or older siblings merits thoughtful consideration.

Frances Degen Horowitz

2 The first two years of life: factors related to thriving

The normal human infant spends approximately 38 to 40 weeks growing in the relatively protected environment of the uterus. Birth is an eruptive event that thrusts the infant dramatically out into the world. The drama is no less than the miracle of development that has resulted in a normal, healthy newborn infant who is, at birth, prepared to undergo the physiological adjustments required for independent respiration, temperature control, nutrient intake, and elimination. We used to believe that the newborn infant's abilities beyond physiological functioning were largely limited to being able to engage in reflexive behavior—responding automatically to certain stimuli such as rooting to a touch on the cheek and sucking on a nipple. But a revolution has occurred in our knowledge over the last 30 years: in addition to the physiological competence of the newborn infant, we now know more about infants' behavioral competence. The normal newborn infant is capable of reacting to visual, auditory, olfactory, and tactile stimuli; the newborn infant can sustain brief to moderate durations of interaction with caregivers; the newborn infant cries and sleeps but also has periods of alertness and engages in brief visual exploration of the environment. It is possible to observe these behaviors in the context of well-controlled experiments (Lipsitt 1979) and under the less controlled conditions of neurological and behavioral assessments (Self and Horowitz 1979).

The initial behavioral repertoire of the newborn infant will undergo rapid changes and elaboration during the first two years of life in motor, cognitive, and language development, and social interaction (Appleton, Clifton, and Goldberg 1975; Osofsky 1979). The major milestones of this development are depicted in Tables 2.1 and 2.2 for each of these areas. The developmental course that normal, healthy infants follow along an approximate time schedule is shown. Most infants exhibit such development; some do not. Those infants who move along the developmental course according to expectations are said to be thriving; those who do not are said to be developmentally delayed. This chapter examines the factors we know relate to or seem to account for thriving, and conversely,

Table 2.1. Major milestones in development, age birth to 12 months.

Age in months (approximately)

Area of development	Birth	1	2	3	4	5	6	7	8	9	10	11	12
Motor	exhibits reflex head turn	lifts chin when prone		lifts chest; has head erect when held	shows first directed reaching	turns from side to back	holds head steady; transfers object, reaching improves	sits with support; sits alone	sits steadily	stands with help		crawls; pulls to standing position	walks with support
Cognitive	demonstrates reflexes		shows primary circular reactions (repetitive acts involving bodily activity: finger sucking, vocalization, touching)				shows secondary circular reactions (repetitive acts maintaining change in environment: shaking, striking)			coordinates actions to solve simple problems; achieves object permanence (awareness that an object exists when out of sight)			
Language	responds to auditory stimulation	recognizes voices and other sounds	responds to tones; exhibits differentiated crying	coos			babbles	shows increasing discrimination of language; makes vowel-like cooing sounds		attempts to imitate sounds	imitates sounds	says first word	
Social	begins bonding process	participates in mutual gazing; responds to face and voice		exhibits spontaneous social smiling		vocalizes moods	discriminates in social smiling	shows stranger wariness, fear, anxiety	lifts arms in greeting		clings	demonstrates attachment	
Personality		shows distress, excitement, and delight decreases crying		shows anticipation			discriminates self and mother in mirror	smiles at mirror image		rejects confinement		repeats behavior if applauded	expresses more discrete emotions

Table 2.2. Major milestones in development, age 13 to 24 months.

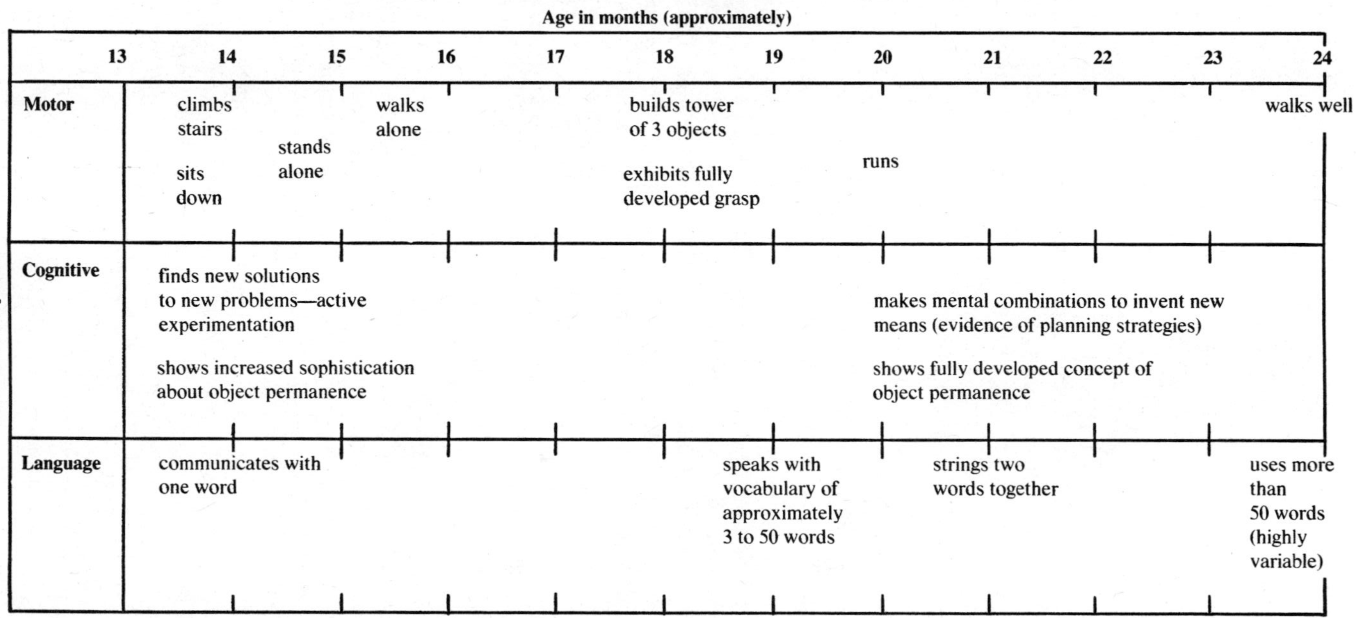

Area of development	13	14	15	16	17	18	19	20	21	22	23	24
Motor		climbs stairs / sits down	stands alone	walks alone			builds tower of 3 objects / exhibits fully developed grasp		runs				walks well
Cognitive		finds new solutions to new problems—active experimentation / shows increased sophistication about object permanence								makes mental combinations to invent new means (evidence of planning strategies) / shows fully developed concept of object permanence			
Language		communicates with one word						speaks with vocabulary of approximately 3 to 50 words		strings two words together			uses more than 50 words (highly variable)

what we currently know about the factors that seem to interfere with thriving during the first two years of life.

If we believe that growth and development are the result of many factors working together, we can ask what those factors are and how they interact. Because so many children seem to thrive under diverse caregiving arrangements and environments, it is easy to think that development occurs automatically. But, what seems to be automatic is, in fact, the result of very complex processes that involve biological, hereditary, and environmental variables. Our description of early development is, at this point, far more complete than our understanding of the factors that affect it. Nevertheless, we shall attempt, in this chapter, to provide the reader with an overview of those factors that recent research has led us to believe in part relate to early development. Factors related to both *thriving* and *vulnerability* during the early months of life will be discussed. Attention will be given to the prediction of later development from early status and experience.

In the beginning: development before birth

To discuss the beginning of the infant's life in terms of birth, and to refer to the relatively protected environment of the uterus is somewhat misleading because birth is not the beginning of either life or development. The developmental journey begins about nine months previous to birth—with conception—and that journey is not totally insulated from external events (Annis 1978). At the moment of conception, hereditary characteristics carried in the genes are laid down and a blueprint of development is set. Sex is determined and factors such as eye and hair color are established. Some characteristics that will become apparent only in later years (such as the mature development of primary and secondary sex characteristics) are also determined at the time of conception. But whether and how the fetus thrives after conception depends upon the adequacy of the uterine environment, the physiological functioning of the mother, and the behavior of the mother (Lubchenko 1976). In this sense, the only pure moment of genetic influence is at conception.

At birth the attending physician will assign a status to the infant—normal, abnormal, or at-risk. That status reflects observations about the infant's weight, length, physical appearance, and ability to sustain independent respiration. It also reflects observations about the infant's ability to feed, eliminate, and show a certain amount of behavioral organization. Whether the infant is considered normal and healthy at birth is dependent upon a lot of factors that have occurred prior to birth. The infant is more likely to be classified as normal at birth if the following factors have been true during the mother's pregnancy: the mother sought prenatal care early in her pregnancy; the mother did not smoke, ate a well-balanced diet, was not below 20 years of age nor above 35 years of age, did not use drugs or consume alcohol, and did not become pregnant when she was underweight or of poor nutritional status. The absence of pregnancy complications like high blood pressure and retention of fluids also affects the probabilities of whether or not the infant at birth will be normal and healthy (Kopp and Parmelee 1979; Lubchenko 1976). These factors do not guarantee the absence or presence of problems for the infant. Rather, they are factors that research has shown increase the probability of problems.

There are many factors related to thriving in utero that are important but are not yet fully understood. Among these is the relative *degree* of vulnerability to stressful events. We do not know what is involved in differential vulnerability, but we do know that it seems to exist (Kopp and Parmelee 1979). For example, boys are more vulnerable than girls. It is estimated that there are 130 to 150 males conceived for every 100 females, but at birth the ratio is about 106 males to every 100 females, and by the end of the first year of life the ratio is 100 males to 100 females. By five years of age the survival ratio actually favors females. Male embryos and fetuses are more likely to die in utero or be aborted before term; male newborns are more likely to have problems, and when problems exist males are less likely to weather them well. If two newborn infants exhibit the same difficulties and one is male, the female infant has a better chance of overcoming the problems. Why males are more vulnerable than females is a mystery. There is no commonly accepted explanation for the phenomenon.

While vulnerability is related to the sex of the infant, sex does not account for all of the difference. We shall return to this concept and the issue of vulnerability at the end of this chapter.

The newborn infant

When the process of giving birth moved from the home to the hospital, it was considered an advance for modern society. The benefits to the health and welfare of both the mother and infant were indisputable: maternal and infant mortality declined, and help was available to combat complications and emergencies. New practices became part of the routine: the use of obstetrical medication helped remove or lessen childbirth pain; formula-feeding as an alternative to breast-feeding allowed mothers more freedom and permitted special food formulation when needed; and separation of mothers, restricted visiting, and fixed feeding schedules seemed to insure an initial period of rest for the new mother.

Questions have now arisen concerning the value of some of these practices, and some changes have occurred. Rigid hospital schedules have been relaxed as much or more in response to consumer demand than from research evidence at no obvious reduction in either the health or welfare of mothers and infants. But the question of separation, especially in the first hours after birth, has been the focus of a great deal of interest in the last several years. In 1976, Klaus and Kennell published their controversial claim that the period immediately after birth is an especially sensitive period for fostering the attachment or social bond between the infant and mother. They also proposed that failure to permit the infant and mother to room in, and to be in skin-to-skin contact with one another during this period may have profound effects on the development of attachment between the two. They have reported beneficial effects on infant development when infants have been permitted to be in extended contact with their mothers beyond normal hospital routine during the first few days of life in the hospital. Others (Leiderman 1978) have claimed that the beneficial effects of extended contact are more likely to be seen in single parent and low-income populations, and that contact, per se, in the hospital may not make much difference when circumstances involve a middle-SES family. It has been argued that middle-SES mothers are more likely to look forward to the birth of their babies, and hence form bonds or become attached to their infants by fantasizing about them during pregnancy. More research is needed to provide conclusive evidence on this matter. While the work of Klaus and Kennell has been an important influence in changing attitudes of both new parents and medical personnel with regard to frequency and duration of mother-infant contact in the hospital, practitioners have probably overinterpreted the data, causing unnecessary fear and anxiety in mothers who have not had such an experience.

The practice of using medications during labor and delivery to ease the pain associated with childbirth has come under serious question in recent years. While natural childbirth has had its advocates since the introduction of obstetrical medication, it has only been in the last few years that extensive evidence has been marshalled claiming deleterious effects on the infant as a result of the use of analgesic and anesthetic preparations during labor and delivery (Brackbill 1979). Heavy medication appears to have depressive effects upon the infant. It is not clear whether these effects are largely short-term or long-term. Although all medication has some effect on the physiological functioning of the infant, relatively light levels of medication may not have even short-term effects on the observable behaviors of the newborn (Horowitz et al. 1977). Nevertheless, as a result of the issues that have been raised concerning the effects of medication on the infant, the amount of routine obstetrical medication used in labor and delivery rooms has declined over the last few years.

The challenge of prediction

Methods for establishing the status of the newborn infant have been the object of intensive research over the last 20 years. Some of this effort has been directed at the question of whether or not it was possible to predict which newborn infants would develop poorly and which would develop well. In the case of conditions such as prematurity, low birth weight, and respiratory distress that might require intensive care during the neonatal period, the research indicates that, barring direct evidence of brain damage, the accurate prediction of subsequent development is not possible without some knowledge about the nature of the environment into which the child will go. Infants with the same initial problems who live in two very different environments will often show different developmental outcomes. Further, even in the case of more extreme conditions such as Down syndrome or phenylketonuria (PKU) that are associated with subsequent mental retardation, it is possible, through the use of special environmental training programs for Down syndrome infants or special diets for infants who are shown to have PKU, to reduce the degree of retardation that occurs (Berman, Waisman, and Graham 1966; Bedder, Bryant, and Gray 1975).

An interest in determining whether improved evaluation of the status of the newborn infant would permit better prediction of later status has motivated the development of a number of newborn assessment instruments (Self and Horowitz 1979). Research on two of the instruments, Prechtl and Beintema's (1964) *The Neurological Examination of the Full-Term Newborn Infant* and Rosenblith's Graham/Rosenblith Scale (Rosenblith 1979) has been used to demonstrate that evaluation during the first few days of life does permit some prediction of subsequent neurological and developmental status. The Prechtl/Beintema Scale can be used with full-term infants in combination with factors such as the presence or absence of obstetrical complications to predict neurological problems at two, four, and eight years of age (Prechtl 1965; 1967). The examination is, however, long and detailed and not easily used for general clinical purposes. A shorter screening version has been developed and can be employed as part of a general clinical procedure.

The Graham/Rosenblith Scale (Rosenblith 1979) also has resulted in the demonstration of some predictive capability. It is shorter than the Prechtl/Beintema Scale and different in that it samples mainly nonreflexive behaviors (visual, auditory, and motor behavior) whereas the Prechtl/Beintema Scale is largely a neurological assessment based upon reflex behaviors. Rosenblith has reported that selected scores on the scale predict some developmental outcomes at eight months of age and at four years of age with poorer performance on the scale at birth related to poorer development at later ages. However, neither the Prechtl/Beintema nor the Graham/Rosenblith Scale permits accurate enough prediction of later development for individual infants.

The most widely used neonatal assessment technique, called the Neonatal Behavior Assessment Scale (NBAS), was designed by T. Berry Brazelton and his co-workers. The scale was not designed to predict later developmental status but rather to describe in a systematic manner the nature of the newborn infant's response to visual and auditory stimuli and to evaluate the infant's interactive abilities (Sameroff 1978; Brazelton et al. 1979). In its original design the NBAS examiner was instructed to score only the infant's *best* response to social interactions and to nonsocial auditory and visual stimuli. Brazelton and his colleagues were aware of the fact that with some extra and skilled effort on the part of the examiner it was often possible to elicit the infant's response at a higher level than without that extra effort and without the skills of the trained examiner. They felt that extra effort procedure provided the most useful index of a child's developmental level. Some recent modifications and additions (resulting in the NBAS-K, Neonatal Behavioral Assessment Scale with Kansas Supplements) that evaluate both the *best* and *modal* (typical—not necessarily *best*) behavior of the infant (Horowitz, Sullivan, and Linn 1978) and that provide for a subjective rating of how much the examiner liked the infant, show promise for helping describe what the infant brings to the interaction with people to facilitate the infant's own development (Lancioni, Horowitz, and Sullivan 1980a; Linn 1979). The evidence indicates that examiners like infants who are high in responsiveness to visual and auditory stimuli, who show strong social interaction with the examiner, and who are not irritable during the exam. These same characteristics may make an infant a fuller partner in reciprocal interactions with caregivers.

The infant who is born prematurely, with birth weight lower than expected for gestational age, or who is ill, is considered at risk for normal development. However, as has been noted, whether or not the infant has subsequent developmental problems seems to depend, in large part, upon the nature and adequacy of the caregiving environment to which the infant goes (Kopp and Parmelee 1979; Sameroff and Chandler 1975). Even for the infant who is born at term and who appears normal, subsequent developmental status seems to depend to a considerable extent upon the nature and adequacy of the infant's caregiving environment (see Weissbourd and Musick 1981). Let us now turn to a discussion of the factors in that environment that appear to contribute to thriving during the first two years of life.

The caregiving environment

Tables 2.1 and 2.2 describe the time line of the expected progression of behaviors during the first two years of life. An infant who exhibits such behavioral development is said to be developing normally. As was noted earlier, because a large percentage of infants living in very diverse kinds of environments and under a variety of caregiving conditions show normal development, it is sometimes assumed that normal development happens automatically and that no special efforts need to be made to foster development. But, in fact, the natural environment in which the infant is developing can be thought of as a configuration of conditions which, in interaction with the biological characteristics and individual differences of the infant, result in normal development—or not. What are these conditions?

Adequate nutrition

Adequate nutrition is considered the single most important factor affecting physical growth and development in the young child. Breast milk is considered the natural food for full-term infants in the first few months of life, though modern formulas appear to provide adequate nutritional substitutes. While the psychological benefits of breast-feeding for both mother and infant have been proclaimed, there is no extensive body of research evidence that documents particular advantages of one or the other practice in our society. However, in developing societies, where refrigeration is not readily available and hygienic conditions do not insure proper preparation of formula, the failure to breast-feed can have life-threatening consequences to young infants.

The most beneficial time for the introduction of solid foods into the infant's diet has been the subject of some discussion. While solid foods are often given as early as three to six weeks of age, there is no evidence that indicates solid foods need to be introduced much before three to four months of age (Laupus 1975). When solid foods do become a significant part of the infant's diet, specific deficiencies in nutrient intake can occur with respect to such things as iron and protein. Such deficiencies have been associated with effects on early and later physical development and some have concomitant effects on cognitive and social development. The consumption of adequate amounts of good quality protein is especially essential for early thriving. Kwashiorkor is the clinical manifestation of inadequate protein nutrition. In its severe forms it is associated with significant physical and mental retardation and with death. It is the most frequently occurring form of malnutrition in the world at the present time and is especially prevalent in strife-ridden societies (Barness 1975).

Severe general malnutrition is also associated with physical and mental retardation and can occur because of conditions of poverty or in the context of what has become known as the failure to thrive syndrome. Although failure to thrive can be caused by specific metabolic problems (such as malabsorption of nutrients) or obstructions that prevent adequate utilization of nutrients (such as a blocked intestinal tract), it is generally thought of as a syndrome when basic physical causes for the failure to thrive have been eliminated and it would appear that caregiver neglect exists, including failure to provide adequate food even when food is generally available. After ruling out physical causes, the usual test for failure to thrive is to remove the child from the home and provide an adequate diet and loving social interactions. If the child begins to gain weight and to show an increased alertness, the failure to thrive that had occurred is attributed to psycho-social causes reflected in general caregiver neglect (Barbero and McKay 1975; Smith and Berenberg 1970). Failure to thrive is considered a form of child abuse by many investigators (Helfer and Kempe 1976). Its frequent occurrence in premature and high-risk infants suggests that these infants may be more difficult to care for or less reinforcing to caregivers. Untreated failure to thrive can result in severe physical and mental retardation and sometimes death.

Although malnourished infants, when tested, exhibit poorer test performance than comparison infants who are not malnourished, subsequent performance once good nutritional status has been restored is not necessarily depressed if the malnutrition has not occurred over a very extended period of time. Further, extreme caution is urged in considering any claim that malnutrition is the *direct* cause of delayed mental development (Latham 1974); in many studies disease and psychological trauma co-exist with poor nutritional status so it is not possible to conclude that nutritional factors alone are responsible for mental retardation (Lloyd-Still 1976).

The physical effects of specific vitamin, mineral, and iron deficiencies on infant development have received considerable study but concomitant effects in the domains of social and cognitive development are not yet clear. There is some recent evidence that remediation of iron deficiencies produces improved performance on the Bayley Scales of Infant Development (Honig and Oski 1978) though the specific causes of the better performance are unknown (Honig and Oski 1979; Pollitt, Greenfield, and Leibel 1978).

Responsive social caregiving and the development of social attachments

It is now obvious that the infant, from the first day of life, is not only capable of interacting with caregivers but can initiate and terminate episodes of mutual gazing (Stern 1974). The opportunity to engage in this behavior and the opportunity for close physical contact with the mother have, as discussed previously, been claimed as the basis for the initial establishment of the social bond between the mother and infant immediately after birth (Klaus and Kennell 1976). Whether the period directly after birth is a particularly sensitive period for the development of social attachments between mother and infant is not conclusively known. But we do know that the quality of social interactions and of social attachment between the mother and the infant can predict something about the later functioning of the infant and of the infant's future interactions with the mother and others.

Until recently the nature of the earliest social attachments has not been considered seriously (Parke 1979). However, new evidence points to the importance of early interactions. Cohen and Beckwith (1979) studied social transactions of premature infants at one, three, and eight months of age and reported that the quality of these interactions as early as one month of age was as related to the infant's competence (as measured by developmental level, language ability, and mental ability) at two years of age as were the infant's interactions observed at two years of age. The finding suggests that a constellation of characteristics about the mother and infant interacting begins to have a very early influence on the infant's development.

Sroufe and his colleagues (Arend, Gove, and Sroufe 1979; Matas, Arend, and Sroufe 1978; Waters, Wippman, and Sroufe 1979) have reported that measurements of early infant attachment relate to later infant competence. For example, in one population of children the quality of the infant's attachment at 15 months was related to the infant's personal and interpersonal competence at 3½ years of age. In another sample infants rated as securely attached at 18 months of age were rated as more effective and autonomous at 2 years and as having greater ego control and ego resiliency at 4 and 5 years of age compared with insecurely attached infants. The quality of early infant attachment appears to predict across situations, across age, and across behaviors to general competence at later ages. However, it should be kept in mind that these findings reflect significant trends in the data for groups of infants and do not permit individual predictions. The most we can say is that infants who are evaluated as securely attached in the first year-and-a-half of life are more likely to show the strengths that have been described at later ages.

There has been much less work done on the interactions between fathers and their infants. Parke and his colleagues (Parke and O'Leary 1976; Parke 1978; 1979) have reported that fathers engage in similar kinds of interactions with their newborn infants as do mothers. At the present time a great deal of research on father-infant interaction is being carried out and we can expect our understanding of this important area of infant experience to increase over the next few years.

The descriptions of the relationships between early secure attachment and later competence do not tell us exactly what elements of the securely attached relationship are responsible for later competence although the quality of mothering is presumably one of those elements. Clarke-Stewart (Clarke-Stewart, VanderStoep, and Killian 1979) has reported finding that 2-year-olds who were judged to be competent were more likely to have mothers who were positive and responsive in their interactions with the child and who directed more language to the child. Similarly, Main, Tomasini, and Tolan (1979) found that infants who were judged securely attached at 12 months of age had mothers at 21 months of age who were more sensitive, accepting, and expressive of affect. Conversely, infants who were not securely attached had mothers who were more angry.

The relationships between infant attachment and maternal responsiveness may be quite complex. As was noted earlier, infant examiners like newborn infants who are more responsive and less irritable (Lancioni, Horowitz, and Sullivan 1980b). It was suggested that such infants may be more responsive in their interactions with the mother as well. Bradley, Caldwell, and Elardo (1979) have reported that more capable children at 6 to 12 months of age appear to elicit higher levels of maternal interaction that, in turn, appear to result in more capable children between 12 and 24 months of age. The nature of these mutually reinforcing interactions may involve an infant who stimulates the caregiver to look at, play, and talk with the infant who, in turn, responds with more behavior that is stimulating to the caregiver. Thus, a cycle of good interactions begins that may account for the consistency of the relationships that are being reported in a number of the studies cited here.

There is some evidence that atypical infants and their mothers do not engage in the same kind of interactions as do typical infants and mothers (Greenberg 1971). There is also some evidence that developmentally delayed infants tend to be involved in more noncontingent interactions with their mothers (i.e., where the infant's behavior is not followed immediately by a relevant behavior from the mother) than developmentally normal infants (Vietze et al. 1978). These findings may be due to the fact that the developmentally delayed infants are less reinforcing to parents as a function of a subdued or minimal behavioral repertoire. Remember that Lancioni, Horowitz, and Sullivan (1980b) found that the behaviors that contributed to the ratings of babies scored as more likeable on the NBAS-K involved higher scores on visual and auditory orientation (looking and responding more to objects, sounds, and faces) and lower general irritability. By one month of age the same relationships existed but, by then, general irritability was much more a factor in affecting the examiner's rating. Developmentally delayed, abnormal, and physically unattractive infants may be less reinforcing (likeable) to caregivers and thus compound risk for normal development.

Stimulating environments

As we have come to appreciate the complexity of the behavioral competence of the infant in the social domain, we have also achieved a much better perspective about the competence that develops in the cognitive domain over the first two years of life. The basic description of that cognitive development has come from Piaget's observations of infants (Brainerd 1978; Flavell 1977) and is represented by the behaviors in this domain as shown in Tables 2.1 and 2.2. Piaget describes the first two years of life as the period of sensorimotor development or the period of sensorimotor intelligence involving the increasing ability of the infant to touch, reach, and manipulate things in the environment so as to make things happen. He considers the development of sensorimotor intelligence as a universal characteristic of the human species, with individual differences regarded as minor variations of rate that occur because of biological differences in infants.

The evidence that has been gathered generally supports the progression of behaviors Piaget describes as constituting sensorimotor intelligence, but there is much less consensus concerning both the origins of individual differences and the implications of different rates of cognitive development for later intellectual and cognitive achievements. On the one hand, there are claims that all normal infants achieve all the milestones of the sensorimotor period despite extensive variations in environments; individual differences in rates of achievement are regarded as minor variations on a theme of no long-lasting significance (Scarr-Salapatek 1976). On the other hand, there is evidence of extreme differences in the achievement of such milestones as object permanence (the ability of the infant to know an object exists when it is no longer in view) for infants reared in very different environments with the implication that such differences have long-term significance in affecting cognitive outcome (Hunt et al. 1975); there is also evidence that environmental differences with respect to the quality, variety, and contingency of stimulation are related to performance on such developmental indexes as the Bayley Scales (Yarrow, Rubenstein, and Pedersen 1975).

We have discussed the importance of positive contingent mother-infant interactions for good developmental outcome, and now we are calling attention to the importance of stimulating environments. In one sense effective mother-infant interactions are part of a stimulating environment, but there is also stimulation provided by the nonsocial environment that involves things to look at, hear, and manipulate. An understanding, among developmental theorists, of the relationship between early experience and later cognitive development has relied heavily upon a model originally proposed by Hebb (1949). He talks about the importance of adequate early intellectual and cognitive development for later learning ability. Hunt (1961) elaborates the model further in his claim that environmental experience could account for individual differences in achievement, and that by increasing the amount, variety, and quality of environmental stimulation in the first two years of life, subsequent intellectual development could be aided. These analyses became the basis for extensive social intervention programs with respect to the importance of early stimulation on the development of intelligence and subsequently on school achievement (Horowitz and Paden 1973; Horowitz 1980).

Many questions have been raised about the continuity between relationships of early development and later development. Some doubt the validity of Hebb's original model (Clarke and Clarke 1976). Others claim there is little continuity between early and later development. The emerging evidence about the relationships between early mother-child attachment and later competence that we have already discussed seems to contradict claims for discontinuity between early and later periods. It is not clear if the contradictions are a function of the possibility that continuity in social-emotional development is different from continuity in cognitive development. It is possible that only when we have a better understanding of the degree to which social-emotional development and cognitive development are separate or interrelated domains of development will the current claims and counter claims be better understood. In summary, at the present time the evidence (Gollin 1981; Osofsky 1979) seems to support the notion that both social and nonsocial experiences are important factors in thriving in the first two years of life; positive, contingent responsiveness on the part of caregivers *and* stimulating physical environments result in good social-emotional and cognitive development. However, it is also clear that these general statements do not fit every individual case and only more research will help us unravel these continuing puzzles.

Variations in caregiving

As has been noted, good developmental outcomes are found in a variety of environments. This is especially true if one considers caregiving arrangements that are alternatives to infants being reared entirely in the home with a single primary caregiver. There is no evidence that group day care has any direct relationship to the development of the infant (Brookhart and Hock 1976); quality day care is neither better nor worse than home care (Kagan 1978), nor do such extreme variations as communal rearing as practiced in the kibbutzim in Israel result in better or poorer infant development (Kohen-Raz 1968).

It should be noted that virtually all the different caregiving arrangements that have been studied involved adequate environments replete with positive evidence of the factors we have cited as being related to good infant development. When caregiving arrangements involve institutions such as orphanages with one or more of the following negative factors present—high staff turnover, relatively inconsistent caregiving figures and/or the absence of a primary caregiver, and minimal social and nonsocial stimulation—then adverse effects on infant development have been documented (Casler 1961; Skodak and Skeels 1949; Yarrow 1961). It would appear that the key determinant of adequate developmental progress in young infants is the presence of important factors and not the arrangements in which their presence is made available to infants.

Individual resiliency or vulnerability

On several occasions in the preceding discussions we have alluded to the fact that similar circumstances do not have identical outcomes for different infants, and that the ability of an infant to thrive may, in part, be a function of the relative vulnerability of the organism to environmental impact. Figure 2.1 depicts a schema that may become more useful as a developmental model (Horowitz 1978).

From the diagram in Figure 2.1 it can be seen that the developmental outcome (the upper surface of the model) is the result of a contribution of the individual's vulnerability (or resiliency) in combination with the adequacy of the environment in terms of its being facilitative or nonfacilitative of development. As can be seen from the model, an infant who happens to be born with high resiliency (low vulnerability) will do well even in a moderately nonfacilitating environment, but an infant who is more vulnerable or more affected by the inadequacies of the environment will not do well in that same (nonfacilitating) environment.

Figure 2.1.
Model of organism-environment relationships and developmental outcome*

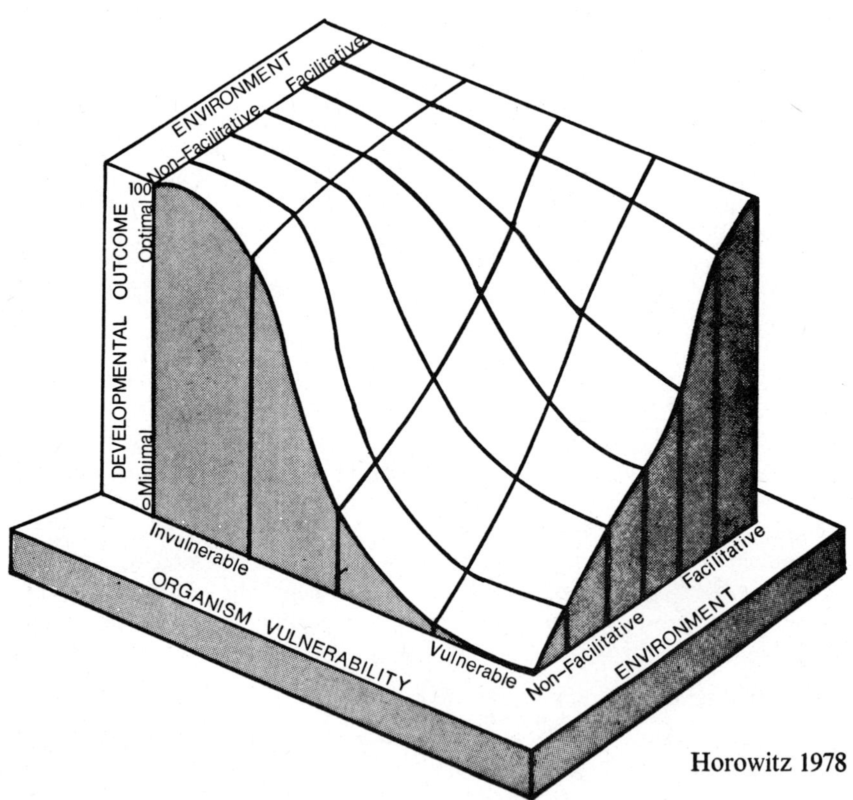

*Adapted from Gowen (1952) (as shown in Williams 1956)

The question of vulnerability and its place in determining developmental outcomes has a long history. It is reflected in the research on coping behavior (Murphy and Moriarty 1976), temperament (Thomas and Chess 1977), and individuality (Tyler 1978). Individual differences in vulnerability could account for a variety of developmental outcomes, but the picture of the functional interactions between child characteristics and environments is not a simple one. The characteristics of resiliency in one developmental domain may not generalize to other domains. For example, in a review of the continuity of social and emotional behavior, Beckwith (1979) concludes from a number of studies that there is some evidence for continuity of social-emotional characteristics; that is, sociability may be a characteristic that determines the infant's vulnerability to circumstances that adversely affect social-emotional stability with more sociable infants being less influenced by nonoptimal social conditions than less sociable infants. Yet sociability may not be relevant to cognitive and intellectual development. For cognitive development, the significant element may lie in the infant's ability to make use of environmental information or stimulation. Thus, infants who are very efficient in using even minimal information or inconsistent stimulation may be less affected by unstimulating environments than infants who are not efficient in their use of information from the environment. Such individual differences in relative vulnerability, functioning differently in different domains, probably underlie the complexity of some aspects of development. Until our research is influenced by models of development that account for this level of complexity, the evidence may seem very contradictory. In addition to the recent literature cited here, such orientations as those that focus on the effects of the infant on the caregiver (Lewis and Rosenblum 1977) and on individual differences (Westman 1973) are contributing to more complex reformulations aimed at our understanding of why some infants thrive and others do not under similar circumstances. It is also possible that an environment is adequate for a child at one stage in development, but that same environment may not be adequate for another period. Our full understanding of this awaits further research.

Conclusions

Thriving in the first two years of life is the result of many factors functioning in complex interactions. We have begun to develop an understanding of what some of the factors are, but we have only a minimal account of how these factors function individually and in combination. The factors that determine whether or not an infant thrives begin with conception, and are strongly influenced by prenatal events and the course of pregnancy. Following birth we have cited nutrition, various characteristics of the caregiving environment, and individual vulnerability as being important determinants of developmental outcome. Some of these will be touched upon again and some will be discussed in more detail in other chapters.

How the factors we have cited operate to facilitate or hinder development is not always clear. Opportunities to learn and repeated circumstances of exposure probably combine in complex ways with the given and developing biological characteristics of the child. It will remain for future research to unravel the specific functions involved in the interactions of these factors. In the meantime we have made enormous progress in our appreciation of infants' competence and of the kinds of environments that are likely to contribute to the thriving of infants.

References

Annis, L. F. *The Child before Birth*. Ithaca, N.Y.: Cornell University Press, 1978.

Appleton, T.; Clifton, R.; and Goldberg, S. "The Development of Behavioral Competence in Infancy." In *Review of Child Development Research. Vol. 4*, ed. F. D. Horowitz. Chicago: University of Chicago Press, 1975.

Arend, R.; Gove, F. L.; and Sroufe, L. A. "Continuity of Early Adaptation: From Attachment in Infancy to Resiliency and Curiosity at Age Five." Unpublished manuscript, 1979.

Barbero, G. J., and McKay, R. J. "Failure to Thrive." In *Nelson Textbook of Pediatrics*. 10th ed., ed. V. C. Vaughn and R. J. McKay. Philadelphia: Saunders, 1975.

Barness, L. A. "Nutritional Disorders." In *Nelson Textbook of Pediatrics*. 10th ed., ed. V. C. Vaughn and R. J. McKay. Philadelphia: Saunders, 1975.

Beckwith, L. "Prediction of Emotional and Social Behavior." In *Handbook of Infant Development*, ed. J. D. Osofsky. New York: Wiley, 1979.

Bedder, R. T.; Bryant, G.; and Gray, D. P. "Benefits for Down's Syndrome Children Through Training Their Mothers." *Archives of Diseases in Childhood* 50 (1975): 383–386.

Berman, P. W.; Waisman, H. A.; and Graham, F. K. "Intelligence in Treated Phenylketonuric Children—A Developmental Study." *Child Development* 37 (1966): 731–747.

Brackbill, Y. "Obstetrical Medication and Infant Behavior." In *Handbook of Infant Development*, ed. J. D. Osofsky. New York: Wiley, 1979.

Bradley, R. H.; Caldwell, B. M.; and Elardo, R. "Home Environment and Cognitive Development in the First Two Years: A Cross-Lagged Panel Analysis." *Developmental Psychology* 15 (1979): 246–250.

Brainerd, C. *Piaget's Theory of Intelligence*. Englewood Cliffs, N.J.: Prentice-Hall, 1978.

Brazelton, T. B. *Neonatal Behavioral Assessment Scale*. London: Heinemann Medical Books, 1973.

Brazelton, T. B.; Als, H.; Tronick, E.; and Lester, B. "Specific Neonatal Measures: The Brazelton Neonatal Behavioral Assessment Scale." In *Handbook of Infant Development*, ed. J. D. Osofsky. New York: Wiley, 1979.

Brookhart, J., and Hock, E. "The Effects of Experimental Context and Experimental Background on Infants' Behavior Toward Their Mothers and a Stranger." *Child Development* 47 (1976): 333–360.

Casler, L. "Maternal Deprivation: A Critical Review of the Literature." *Monographs of the Society for Research in Child Development* 26 (1961). Serial No. 80.

Clarke, A. M., and Clarke, A. D. B. *Early Experience: Myth and Evidence*. New York: Free Press, 1976.

Clarke-Stewart, K. A.; VanderStoep, L. P.; and Killian, G. A. "Analysis and Replication of Mother-Child Relations at Two Years of Age." *Child Development* 50 (1979): 777–793.

Cohen, S. E., and Beckwith, L. "Preterm Infant Interaction with the Care Given in the First Year of Life and Competence at Age Two." *Child Development* 50 (1979): 767–776.

Flavell, J. H. *Cognitive Development*. Englewood Cliffs, N.J.: Prentice-Hall, 1977.

Gollin, E., ed. *Developmental Prestigity*. New York: Academic Press, 1981.

Greenberg, N. H. "A Comparison of Infant-Mother Interactional Behavior in Infants with Atypical Behavior." *Exceptional Infant: Studies in Abnormalities. Vol. 2*, ed. J. Hellmuth. New York: Brunner/Mazel, 1971.

Hebb, D. O. *The Organization of Behavior*. New York: Wiley, 1949.

Helfer, R. E., and Kempe, C. H. *Child Abuse and Neglect*. Cambridge, Mass.: Ballinger, 1976.

Honig, A. S., and Oski, F. A. "Developmental Scores of Iron Deficient Infants and the Effects of Therapy." *Infant Behavior and Development* 1 (1978): 168–176.

Honig, A. S., and Oski, F. A. "Reply to Pollitt Et Al." *Infant Behavior and Development* 2 (1979): 239–240.

Horowitz, F. D. "Toward a Functional Analysis of Individual Differences." Presidential address to the Division of Developmental Psychology, American Psychological Association meetings, Toronto, 1978.

Horowitz, F. D. "Intervention and Its Effects on Early Development: What Model of Development Is Appropriate?" In *Life-Span Developmental Psychology: Intervention*, ed. R. R. Turner and H. W. Reese. New York: Academic Press, 1980.

Horowitz, F. D.; Ashton, J.; Culp, R. E.; Gaddis, E.; Levin, S.; and Reichmann, B. "The Effect of Obstetrical Medication on the Behavior of Israeli Newborns and Some Comparisons with American and Uruguayan Infants." *Child Development* 48 (1977): 1607–1623.

Horowitz, F. D., and Paden, L. Y. "The Effectiveness of Environmental Intervention Programs." In *Review of Child Development Research. Vol. 3*, ed. B. M. Caldwell and H. N. Ricciuti. Chicago: University of Chicago Press, 1973.

Horowitz, F. D.; Sullivan, J. W.; and Linn, P. "Stability and Instability in the Newborn Infant: The Quest for Elusive Threads." In *Organization and*

Stability of Newborn Behavior: A Commentary on the Brazelton Neonatal Behavioral Assessment Scale. Monographs of the Society for Research in Child Development 43 (1978): 29–45.

Hunt, J. McV. *Intelligence and Experience.* New York: Ronald Press, 1961.

Hunt, J. McV.; Paraskevopoulos, J.; Schickedanz, D.; and Uzgiris, I. "Variations in Mean Ages of Achieving Object Permanence under Diverse Conditions of Rearing." In *Exceptional Infant. Vol. 3,* ed. B. Friedlander, G. Sterrit, and G. Kirk. New York: Brunner/Mazel, 1975.

Kagan, J. *Infancy.* Cambridge, Mass.: Harvard University Press, 1978.

Klaus, M., and Kennell, J. *Maternal-Infant Bonding.* St. Louis: Mosby, 1976.

Kohen-Raz, R. "Mental and Motor Development of Kibbutz, Institutionalized and Home Reared Infants in Israel." *Child Development* 39 (1968): 489–504.

Kopp, C. B., and Parmelee, A. H. "Prenatal and Perinatal Influences on Infant Behavior." In *Handbook of Infant Development,* ed. J. D. Osofsky. New York: Wiley, 1979.

Lancioni, G.; Horowitz, F. D.; and Sullivan, J. "NBAS-K I. A Study of Its Stability and Structure over the First Month of Life." *Infant Behavior and Development* 3 (1980a): 341–359.

Lancioni, G.; Horowitz, F. D.; and Sullivan, J. "NBAS-K II. Reinforcement Value of the Infant's Behavior." *Infant Behavior and Development* 3 (1980b): 361–366.

Latham, M. C. "Protein-Calorie Malnutrition in Children and Its Relation to Psychological Development and Behavior." *Physiology Review* 54 (1974): 541–565.

Laupus, W. E. "Feeding of Infants." In *Nelson Textbook of Pediatrics.* 10th ed., ed. V. C. Vaughn and R. J. McKay. Philadelphia: Saunders, 1975.

Leiderman, H. "The Critical Period Hypothesis Revisited: Mother to Infant Social Bonding in the Neonatal Period." In *Early Developmental Hazards: Predictors and Precautions,* ed. F. D. Horowitz. Boulder, Col.: Westview Press, 1978.

Lewis, M., and Rosenblum, L. A., eds. *Interaction, Conversation, and the Development of Language.* New York: Wiley, 1977.

Linn, P. L. "Newborn Environments and Mother-Infant Interactions." University of Kansas, doctoral dissertation, 1979.

Lipsitt, L. P. "The Newborn As Informant." In *Infants at Risk: Assessment of Cognitive Functioning,* ed. R. B. Kearsley and I. Sigel. Hillsdale, N.J.: Lawrence Erlbaum Associates, 1979.

Lloyd-Still, J. D. "Clinical Studies on the Effects of Malnutrition During Infancy and Subsequent Physical and Intellectual Development." In *Malnutrition and Mental Development,* ed. J. D. Lloyd-Still. Littleton, Mass.: Publishing Sciences Group, 1976.

Lubchenko, L. *The High Risk Infant.* Philadelphia: Saunders, 1976.

Main, M.; Tomasini, L.; and Tolan, W. "Differences among Mothers of Infants Judged to Differ in Security." *Developmental Psychology* 15 (1979): 472–473.

Matas, L.; Arend, R. A.; and Sroufe, L. A. "Continuity of Adaptation in the

Second Year: The Relationship Between Quality of Attachment and Later Competence." *Child Development* 49 (1978): 547–556.

Murphy, L. B., and Moriarty, A. E. *Vulnerability, Coping and Growth*. New Haven, Conn.: Yale University Press, 1976.

Osofsky, J. D. *Handbook of Infant Development*. New York: Wiley, 1979.

Parke, R. D. "Parent-Infant Interaction: Progress, Paradigms and Problems." In *Observing Behavior. Vol. 1*, ed. G. P. Sackett. Baltimore, Md.: University Park Press, 1978.

Parke, R. D. "Perspectives on Father-Infant Interaction." In *Handbook of Infant Development*, ed. J. D. Osofsky. New York: Wiley, 1979.

Parke, R. D., and O'Leary, S. E. "Father-Mother Infant Interaction in the Newborn Period: Some Findings, Some Observations and Some Unresolved Issues." In *The Developing Individual in a Changing World*, ed. K. Riegel and J. Meacham. The Hague: Mouton, 1976.

Pollitt, E.; Greenfield, D.; and Leibel, R. "Significances of Bayley Scale Score Changes Following Iron Therapy." *Journal of Pediatrics* 92 (1978): 177–178.

Prechtl, H. F. R. "Prognostic Value of Neurological Signs in the Newborn Infant." *Proceedings of the Royal Society of Medicine* 58 (1965): 3–4.

Prechtl, H. F. R. "Neurological Sequelae of Prenatal and Perinatal Complications." *British Medical Journal* 4 (1967): 763–767.

Prechtl, H., and Beintema, D. *The Neurological Examination of the Full-Term Newborn Infant*. London: Heinemann Medical Books, 1964.

Rosenblith, J. F. "The Graham/Rosenblith Behavioral Examination for Newborns: Prognostic Value and Procedural Issues." In *Handbook of Infant Development*, ed. J. D. Osofsky. New York: Wiley, 1979.

Sameroff, A. J., ed. "Organization and Stability of Newborn Behavior: A Commentary on the Brazelton Neonatal Behavioral Assessment Scale." *Monographs of the Society for Research in Child Development* 43 (1978). Serial No. 177.

Sameroff, A., and Chandler, M. "Reproductive Risk and the Continuum of Caretaking Casualty." In *Review of Child Development Research. Vol. 4*, ed. F. D. Horowitz. Chicago: University of Chicago Press, 1975.

Scarr-Salapatek, S. "An Evolutionary Perspective on Infant Intelligence Species Patterns and Individual Variations." In *Origins of Intelligence*, ed. M. Lewis. New York: Plenum, 1976.

Self, P. A., and Horowitz, F. D. "Neonatal Assessment: An Overview." In *Handbook of Infant Development*, ed. J. D. Osofsky. New York: Wiley, 1979.

Skodak, M., and Skeels, H. M. "A Final Follow-Up Study of One Hundred Adopted Children." *Genetic Psychology* 75 (1949): 85–125.

Smith, C. A., and Berenberg, W. "The Concept of Failure to Thrive." *Pediatrics* 46 (1970): 661–662.

Sroufe, L. A. "Socioemotional Development." In *Handbook of Infant Development*, ed. J. D. Osofsky. New York: Wiley, 1979.

Stern, D. N. "Mother and Infant at Play: The Dyadic Interaction Involving Facial, Vocal and Gaze Behaviors." In *The Effect of the Infant on Its Caregiver*, ed. M. Lewis and L. A. Rosenblum. New York: Wiley, 1974.

Thomas, A., and Chess, S. *Temperament and Development*. New York: Brunner/Mazel, 1977.

Tyler, L. E. *Individuality*. San Francisco: Jossey-Bass, 1978.

Vietze, P. M.; Abernathy, S. R.; Ashe, M. L.; and Faulstich, G. "Contingent Interaction Between Mothers and Their Developmentally Delayed Infants." In *Observing Behavior. Vol. 1*, ed. G. P. Sackett. Baltimore, Md.: University Park Press, 1978.

Waters, E.; Wippman, J.; and Sroufe, L. A. "Attachment, Positive Affect and Competence in the Peer Group: Two Studies in Construct Validation." *Child Development* 50 (1979): 821–829.

Weissbourd, B., and Musick, J., eds. *Infants: Their Social Environments*. Washington, D.C.: National Association for the Education of Young Children, 1981.

Westman, J. C., ed. *Individual Differences in Children*. New York: Wiley, 1973.

Yarrow, L. J. "Maternal Deprivation: Toward an Empirical and Conceptual Re-Evaluation." *Psychological Bulletin* 58 (1961): 459–490.

Yarrow, L. J.; Rubenstein, J. L.; and Pedersen, F. A. *Infant and Environment*. New York: Wiley, 1975.

Susan Goldberg

3 Some biological aspects of early parent-infant interaction

Biology is the study of living things. The study of behavior therefore falls within the province of biology. Oddly enough, while studies of animal behavior are often carried out in university departments of biology, those of human behavior are typically reserved for departments of anthropology, psychology, sociology, and human development. This tradition has served to erect an arbitrary boundary between what is biological and what is social in human behavior.

All behavior, social or not, has a biological basis: the form, extent, and limits of behavioral capacities in any species are defined by anatomical structure and physiological functioning. Human babies, for example, are carried by their mothers in one way, baboon babies in another, and baby birds not at all. All female mammals are capable of nursing their young; female amphibians are not. Human babies have the opportunity to view their mothers' faces when in the feeding position, but baby calves do not.

Within this context, the capacity for a specific behavior does not guarantee its occurrence, especially in any particular situation. Some human infants are carried very little. Some are wheeled in carriages or carried in cloth slings or sacks. Both human and other mammalian infants can be bottle fed. The schedule on which a particular mother offers nourishment, or an infant solicits it, as well as the length of time spent feeding, can vary considerably. While the capacity for behavior, and its developmental schedule for emergence, is determined by the gene pool of the species, this need not lead to fixed behavior patterns. While it is true that some species are characterized by relatively fixed behavior patterns (e.g., ants), others, particularly higher primates, including humans, are characteristically flexible, enabling them to adapt to a variety of living conditions.

The traditional nature-nurture debate is not appropriate in this conception of behavior and biology. All behavior is 100 percent inherited. Unless capacities for behavior are inherited, a behavior can never occur (e.g., chimpanzees will never talk regardless of what experiences are provided). But all behavior is also 100 percent determined by experience because the actual occurrence of behavior depends on appropriate experience (e.g., a human infant will not learn to speak without hearing the speech of others).

The description of human adult-infant interaction in this chapter highlights biologically determined behavioral capacities (species-characteristic patterns) shared by all adult-infant dyads. However, biological factors can also play a role in individual differences between dyads. This is illustrated in examples of biological stress that threaten physical health and/or growth in ways that influence infant social behavior. Examples of such stresses include genetic defects, illness, and malnutrition. Notice that while these stresses are indeed biological, their distribution in current populations can be traced to social conditions such as mating and childbearing patterns, living conditions, and access to medical care. Thus, the distinction between what is biological and what is social is again an arbitrary one.

The above examples are all of deleterious effects in which biological stress interferes with normal behavior and/or development. But biological conditions can also facilitate normal behavior and development. There are many examples that demonstrate that acquisition of behavior occurs most easily during states of optimal physiological readiness. Factors that influence such states of readiness may be transient (such as patterns of wakefulness and sleep) or of longer duration (such as neurophysiological maturation). Infants, for example, are most ready for social interaction when they are in quiet alert states. Developmental changes depending on maturation of the visual system allow newborns to discriminate faces from other stimuli, yet they generally do not discriminate and respond differentially to facial expressions until after five months of age. There is some evidence that suggests that physiological changes during pregnancy and birth produce a maternal state of optimal readiness to form an attachment to an infant. Once again, such biological states are not independent of social conditions. Culturally proscribed customs surrounding pregnancy, delivery, and infant care can influence the timing and duration of such states.

In the first section of this chapter, a dynamic model of parent-infant interaction will be presented in which it is assumed that parent and infant share important biological goals: infant survival, infant growth and development, and infant protection. The behavioral skills of adults and infants that allow a dyad to address these goals will be described. In the second section, biological influences on three important behavioral domains (infant crying, infant social responsiveness, and mother-to-infant bonding) will be surveyed. In the concluding section, the adult-infant dyad is discussed within the larger perspective of the family and society.

A dynamic model of parent-infant interaction

For much of the short time that researchers have been studying parent-infant relationships, we have had a rather narrow view of the enterprise. We have looked primarily at overt behavior in a static mechanical fashion. Both parent and infant were considered to have a relatively fixed repertoire of behaviors that served as stimuli and responses to each other in chains of turn-taking. At first, we thought of the infant as a relatively passive participant who was acted upon by adults so as to mold and shape immature behavior into its adult form. Later, we recognized (along with all the parents who spent sleepless nights tending to their crying infants) that the infant is an active and often controlling participant in the interaction process. But even in the 1960s and 1970s when we gave infants full credit for their interactive skills, the basic model of interaction was the chains-of-turn-taking one.

A more complex dynamic model is presented here. It is one that is increasingly popular among developmental psychologists and seems to be closer to the everyday experiences of parents and infants. There are two lines of theory and research that have influenced the acceptance of this more dynamic model. The first is more detailed observation of parent-infant interactions. With the advent of sophisticated recording techniques such as film and video equipment we have been able to view a particular interaction sequence many times at reduced speeds or even frame by frame. Detailed observations of this type (e.g., Brazelton, Koslowski, and Main 1974; Stern 1974) have allowed us to study social interactions that are regulated and organized in a fashion that goes beyond chains in which each participant responds only to the partner's previous act. Both parents and infants react to each other and modify their behavior so rapidly that they appear to be sharing a program, much like two partners in a dance, rather than reacting independently as in a turn-taking game (Stern 1977).

The other major impetus for a change in our conception of the parent-infant dyad was the theoretical and empirical work of Bowlby and his followers (e.g., Ainsworth 1973; Sroufe and Waters 1977). In his influential volume on attachment, Bowlby (1969) describes the parent-infant relationship as a behavioral system that evolves to serve biologically important functions. It is within this context that we will consider parent-infant interactions in this chapter.

Biological goals of the parent-infant dyad

In our highly complex industrialized society, it is easy to lose sight of the biological functions of the parent-infant relationship because they are taken for granted so readily, yet it is clear that in humans, as in most mammalian species, the care of an adult is essential for the survival of the young. A behavioral system that has evolved to serve the function of physical survival must guarantee that adults will be willing and able to make changes in their lives to accommodate to the care of an infant. Infants must be able, from birth, to solicit care from adults and adults must be able to recognize and respond appropriately to these infant signals. Thus, it is not surprising that crying is a behavior that is widespread among newborn mammals and that prompt responses to cries by adults are equally common. Few adult humans can listen to a young infant crying for any length of time without feeling impelled to do something.

Beyond the conditions of physical survival, the parent-infant relationship serves at least two additional functions. The first is to establish the conditions that promote the growth and development of the infant. Studies of infants reared in institutions have made it clear that physical care alone is not enough to ensure adequate growth and development. Human infants, like the young of other species in which flexible rather than fixed behavior is the rule, need to explore and learn from the environment in order to develop normally. It has been suggested that one of the important functions of the caregiver is to support the development of a motive to explore and practice new skills (Lewis and Goldberg 1969) without which infants can become listless and apathetic and fail to thrive.

Second, in all species where the period of immaturity is prolonged, the infant and caregiver must establish a relationship that will endure as long as is necessary to supervise and protect the infant. Thus, in humans, as in many other higher primates, we would expect the parent-child interaction system to be organized in a way that guarantees not only caregiving but social interactions that form the basis for such an ongoing relationship.

When an infant cries, the predominant human response is to pick the baby up for cuddling. Not surprisingly, Korner and Grobstein (1966) found that of several interventions administered to crying babies, this was the most effective in terminating crying. Furthermore, holding a baby upright at the shoulder usually elicits visual alertness and scanning. Thus, while infant crying is the most effective way to get attention, the adult's typical response effectively terminates crying and produces a reward for the caregiver as the baby moves into a quiet alert state that signals readiness for social exchange. This is one example of the way in which typical caregiving interactions of adults and infants have a high probability of leading to rewarding social interactions.

Social skills and the goals of adult-infant dyads

The previous section outlined three functions of the parent-infant interaction system: infant survival, promotion of infant growth and development, and the formation of a lasting protective social bond. What are the characteristic infant and adult behaviors that enable adult-infant dyads to achieve these goals? Those who have studied infants and adult-infant interactions repeatedly note the extent to which the adult behavior toward infants and infant behavior and skills complement each other in almost ideal fashion.

First, the appearance of young infants seems to be very attractive to adults. Lorenz (1943) was the first to suggest that infants of all species share certain features (such as an enlarged head, flattened nose, broad cheeks, relatively large eyes, and smooth, soft body surfaces) that appeal to adults. In fact, cartoonists often use exaggeration of these features to draw appealing characters (see Gould 1979). A number of recent studies report that across a wide age range, pictures of infants attract more attention than those of adults (e.g., Feldman and Nash 1978, 1979; Fullard and Reiling 1976) and this is especially true when the features identified by Lorenz are exaggerated (Sternglanz, Grey, and Murakami 1977).

Second, although a large part of the newborn infant's repertoire consists of reflex behaviors, many of these have adaptive functions in interactions with caregivers. Rooting and sucking are obviously important in feeding, but other reflexes that first appear meaningless can be understood when we remember that before the invention of cribs, carriages, and modern housing, babies were carried by adults for most of the day, as they still are in many societies (see Leiderman, Tulkin, and Rosenfeld 1977). In this context, it appears that reflexes such as head lifting and turning, stepping movements, crawling, and grasping allow the infant to make postural adjustments when being carried by a moving adult.

Third, even in the infant's limited repertoire, there are a few behaviors that have powerful effects upon adults. We have already mentioned crying as the infant's most effective means of getting adult attention. After the first few weeks, as infants begin to make eye contact and smile, this becomes another means of capturing the adult's attention. Undoubtedly we have all seen or found ourselves engaged in otherwise embarrassing performances for the sake of seeing a baby smile.

Fourth, as we learn more about the perceptual skills of infants, we find that the human adult is difficult to surpass as the most successful attention-getting device in the infant's world. Studies of visual perception in young infants indicate that infants are most likely to look at visual displays that include movement (e.g., a light that blinks in a different location each time rather than one that goes on and off in the same place) (Haith 1966); borders of high contrast (e.g., black and white stripes rather than a solid color) (Fantz 1965); and a moderately complex design (e.g., a figure with 10 rather than 5 angles) (Hershenson, Munsinger, and Kessen 1965). In fact, even newborns visually follow a drawing of a face longer than other face-like stimuli (Jirari 1970; Goren, Sartz, and Wu 1975). This does not necessarily mean they recognize faces but only that faces embody many of the stimulus properties that attract infants' visual attention. When adults present their faces to infants, it is usually with a lot of head nodding and exaggerated facial expression (Stern 1974). Thus, adults spontaneously capitalize on exactly those features that are most likely to attract the infant.

Studies of infants' auditory skills indicate that they quiet and listen or show more heart rate change to tones in the human voice range, especially its higher pitches (Eisenberg 1976), notice tonal changes and rhythms (Kaplan and Kaplan 1971), and can discriminate some of the sounds unique to speech (Eimas 1975). When adults talk to infants they tend to raise the pitch of their voices and to slow and exaggerate articulation and tonal changes (Stern 1974), thus enhancing the attention-getting features of human speech.

Perhaps even more remarkable, humans are constructed so that a baby can only be held and carried in a limited number of positions and each of these provides stimulation in some sensory modality (visual, auditory, tactile, kinesthetic) or combination of modalities, in a fashion that is considered optimal for soothing, alerting, or precipitating social interaction.

Beyond these initial predispositions, both infants and adults seem to be capable of matching the pacing and rhythms of each other's behavior (Brazelton,

Koslowski, and Main 1974; Condon and Sander 1974) and making adjustments that are self-correcting for the interaction system. One example of this is the normal nursing process where the infant's sucking stimulates release of milk and the emptying of the breast stimulates further production of milk. Thus, although the infant's nutritional needs are changing with growth and addition of other foods to the diet, the milk supply is regulated by the infant's demand for it.

It appears that both infant and adult characteristics and behavior have evolved to guarantee that there will be mutually rewarding and pleasurable social interactions. However, as we all know, the description thus far is to real life as the smiling Gerber baby is to the one you live with. While we seem to be predisposed toward successful adult-infant interactions, what happens when something goes wrong? One of the features of a successful system is that there is more than one way to achieve a given result; when one part of the system fails or functions improperly, corresponding adjustments are made so that the system as a whole can continue to operate. Thus, many institutions have a backup generator in case of power failures. Is there any evidence of such backup features in the parent-infant interaction system?

Recent studies of parents with atypical infants suggest that there are. Goldberg (1978) reviewed studies that compared parent-infant interaction in dyads with preterm infants and their full-term counterparts. Typically the preterm infants were less responsive, alert, and attentive than the full-term babies. Although most studies reported that in the newborn period the preterm parent-infant dyads interacted less actively and enthusiastically than full-term dyads, the reverse was true with older infants. Parents of preterm infants observed one or more months after hospital discharge were found to exert *more* time and effort in interacting with their babies than parents of full-term infants of the same age (e.g., Brown and Bakeman 1979; Field 1977; Brachfeld, Goldberg, and Sloman 1980). Similar phenomena have been described in families with blind infants (Fraiberg 1977), Down syndrome infants (Jones 1980), and hearing-impaired infants (Anderson 1979; Wedell-Monnig and Lumley 1980).

These examples suggest that adults make efforts to compensate for the limited skills of their infant partner when interacting with a handicapped infant. Although parents seem to experience difficulties in their initial experiences with such infants, they eventually become more familiar with behaviors and needs of their infants and can make efforts to adjust to them. These more extreme examples may in fact be exaggerations of the subtle adjustments caregivers make when normal babies are unresponsive or inattentive.

Given the infant's limited repertoire, we would expect that the burden of such adjustments normally falls upon the adult member of the dyad. Nevertheless, Tronick and his colleagues (Tronick et al. 1978) found that when face to face with a mother who has been instructed not to respond, infants make repeated efforts to engage the mother before finally withdrawing from social interaction. There are also many clinical examples of infants, whose handicapped parents are unable to respond normally, developing unusual and effective modes of communication with their parents and showing otherwise normal development.

For example, hearing infants with deaf parents interact with both their parents and with hearing adults. They learn spoken language and are able to maintain two different modes of interacting with adults, one with their parents that does not depend on sound and another for other adults that includes sound.

These few illustrations suggest, as we would expect, that a system as biologically important as the parent-infant dyad includes many alternatives to back up the normally optimal modes of interaction and development. Apparently both infants and adults are able to initiate repeated and varied bids for attention at times when their partners are unable (or unwilling) to respond immediately. Of course, there will be limits to the capacities of the interaction system for coping with stress, but it is likely that in many cases self-correcting mechanisms will compensate for threats to the integrity of the dyad.

Biological influences on social interactions

We have only begun to explore the nature of atypical interactions, the stresses they place on the system, and the range of coping strategies available to infants and adults. The effects of four biological stressors (Down syndrome, nutritional problems, obstetric conditions, and premature birth) on two areas of infant behavior have already been identified as important to caregivers; *crying* and *responsiveness to potential social stimuli* will be discussed here. In addition, because there has been much controversy in the popular media as well as the research community about the importance of early *mother-to-infant bonding,* some of the evidence for a sensitive or optimal period for the initiation of maternal behavior will be reviewed.

Infant cries

Crying has already been mentioned as one of the most important behaviors in the repertoire of young infants. An infant whose cries are particularly aversive or one whose cries do not sound urgent enough to bring caregiver attention can be problematic for the normal functioning of the interactive system. It is now possible, with the use of spectrograms, to do careful analyses of the acoustic and temporal features of cries. Sounds produced during cries can be described in terms of the predominant pitch (fundamental frequency), number and kinds of other pitches present (harmonics), tonal variation (changes in pitch), and timing of vocalizations (time to onset, period between cries). In addition, investigators have studied the amount of stimulation necessary to elicit a cry. In most studies mentioned, the cries analyzed were pain cries elicited by snapping a rubber band on the sole of the infant's foot. A growing body of research indicates that the acoustic properties of infant cries are affected by many types of biological stress and that adults can hear the difference in the cries of stressed and normal infants (Lester and Zeskind 1979). Some examples of the kinds of biological stressors that produce these qualitative changes in cry sounds follow.

Down syndrome. Down syndrome, a genetically caused form of mental retardation, affects 1 in 600 infants. Analysis of the cries of Down syndrome infants (Fisichelli and Karelitz 1963; Karelitz and Fisichelli 1962; Lind et al. 1970) indicates that more stimulation is needed to elicit cries and that cries are characterized by longer periods of onset, lower pitch, and less tonal variation than those of normal control children. Adults who listened to infant cries judged those of infants with Down syndrome less aversive and less in need of attention than those of normal infants (Freudenberg, Driscoll, and Stern 1978).

Nutritional status. Infants who are born at term weighing significantly less than normal birth weights have been inadequately nourished during their prenatal development. Newborn behavioral assessments indicate that full-term but small-for-date babies are more irritable and difficult to console than their full-weight counterparts (Als et al. 1976; Lester and Zeskind 1979). Lester and Zeskind (1979) analyzed the cries of a sample of small-for-date infants and found that in comparison with normal neonates, their cries were of shorter duration, higher pitched, and had a more complex pitch structure. Some of these same features were also found to characterize the cries of malnourished one-year-olds (Lester 1976).

Obstetric conditions. A variety of stressful events during pregnancy and delivery are known to increase the probability that an infant will encounter subsequent developmental problems even when no known abnormality is identified in the newborn period. Some examples of such complications include maternal illnesses or drug addiction, premature rupture of membranes, unusually long labor, and drugs given during delivery. A review by Brackbill (1979) summarizes the findings of a large number of studies that examined the effects of obstetric medication on infant behavior and found that among the most frequent short-term effects were influences on newborn alertness and irritability. Few of these studies, however, actually examined effects on parent-infant interaction. Though four papers reported such effects, Brackbill feels that the evidence was not strong enough to be conclusive.

There now exist extensive findings on the subsequent development of babies from less than optimal pregnancies and deliveries, and this information has been used to develop scales that estimate the degree of risk for subsequent problems in a particular infant from obstetric information (e.g., Lubchenco 1976; Littman 1979; Prechtl 1968). Zeskind and Lester (1978) used a scale developed by Prechtl to form two groups of normal appearing newborns: one considered to be a high-risk group (five to nine risk conditions) and one considered to be a low-risk group (zero to two risk conditions). The cries of the the high-risk babies were found to differ from those at low risk in having longer latencies, requiring more stimulation, having a higher pitch, and shorter duration. When adults listened to the cries of these same infants, they judged those of the high-risk group to be more "urgent, grating, sick, arousing, piercing, discomforting, aversive, and distressing" than those of the low-risk group.

Premature birth. Premature birth is generally included as an important obstetric complication. Because it is the most common birth abnormality (affecting 5 to 7 percent of births), it has been extensively studied. Infants are considered premature if they are born after fewer than 37 weeks gestation and weigh less than

2500 grams.

Assessments of the crying behavior of preterm and full-term infants in the hospital indicate that preterm infants cry less often, with less intensity, and longer latencies than full-term infants (DiVitto and Goldberg 1979; Field et al. 1978; Lester and Zeskind 1979; Sostek, Quinn, and Davitt 1979). In addition, Lester and Zeskind (1979) find that shortened gestation is associated with cries of higher fundamental frequencies and shorter duration than those of the typical full-term infant, a finding similar to that found with small-for-date and high-risk babies.

The effectiveness of the preterm infant's cries in compelling adult attention was investigated by Frodi and her colleagues (Frodi et al. 1978). Parents of infants were shown videotapes of preterm and full-term infants in crying or quiet states. A dubbed sound track was used to allow the sound and picture to be paired in various combinations. This allowed the experimenters to assess the independent effects of the *appearance* of the baby and the *sound* of the cry. Changes in heart rate, skin resistance, and blood pressure were measured as indexes of physiological arousal in the adults. The cry of the preterm infant elicited more physiological changes in adults than that of the full-term infant regardless of which picture appeared on the videotape. However, of the two situations (full-term or preterm picture) in which the preterm cry was played, it was most arousing when paired with the picture of the preterm infant. In addition, the cries of the preterm baby were verbally judged to be more aversive than those of the full-term infant.

Infant social responsiveness

Unlike crying, which is a readily specified behavior, social responsiveness is a global category that can include a variety of behaviors and characteristics. For the purpose of this discussion, it will include the frequency and ease with which infants can achieve and maintain alert states, responsiveness to visual and auditory stimulation, and emotional expression, particularly smiling. This group of behaviors is important to the development of the parent-infant interaction system because it includes the infant's contribution to those social interactions that are the basis for long-term parent-child relationships. In addition, it includes many of the behaviors of young infants that are pleasurable and rewarding for caregivers. In the face of the many frustrations involved in the care of very young infants, a caregiver's willingness and ability to be responsive may depend upon receiving at least some minimal amount of pleasurable interaction. An infant who is unable to reward caregivers in this fashion makes extraordinary demands upon the caregiver that can compromise the development of normal parent interaction (Goldberg 1977).

Some of the studies to be described below have used a standardized instrument for evaluating newborn behavior designed by Brazelton and his colleagues (Brazelton 1973). The Brazelton Neonatal Behavioral Assessment Scale includes items assessing visual and auditory responses, quality of alertness, irritability, and ease of consoling the infant. In addition, a combined score based upon selected items can be derived as a more global estimate of the infant's attentive and social interactive skills. This score includes responses to visual and auditory stimulation (including the face of the examiner) and the ability to maintain alertness and to be cuddled and consoled by the examiner. The items upon which this score is based suggest that the scales may be tapping the social responsiveness of newborns. Studies of infants with a variety of biological problems or handicaps suggest that most biological stressors have consequences for the social responsiveness of infants. As examples, let us consider the same conditions discussed in the section on infant cries.

Down syndrome. In an extensive study of Down syndrome infants, Cicchetti and Sroufe (1976, 1978) found that the infants' emotional expression is muted and less intense than that of normal infants at the same developmental stage. This is true for both positive and negative emotions and is related to poor muscle tone (hypotonia) that prevents the Down syndrome infants from building up the level of muscle tension associated with similar emotional expression in normal individuals. Emde and his colleagues (Emde, Katz, and Thorpe 1978) report similar data.

In addition, as part of the generally slower development of the Down syndrome infants, smiling to particular stimuli occurs at later ages than for normal infants. Thus, the parents of these infants wait longer for the rewards of smiles, may find them less captivating when they occur, and may find it somewhat difficult to read and interpret the emotional expressions that confront them. Indeed Emde and his colleagues (Emde, Katz, and Thorpe 1978) report that for the parents of Down syndrome infants, the muted quality of the first smiles are often the first confirmation of the infant's atypical development. Instead of becoming the joyous occasion that it is for parents of normal infants, the emergence of these less rewarding smiles is often the occasion for grief.

When facial expressions in photographs of normal and Down syndrome infants were rated, the latter were judged as expressing less intense emotions. However, those mothers who were familiar with Down syndrome and recognized that some photographs were not of normal infants were more likely to judge these low-intensity expressions as signals for caregiving. Mothers lacking this awareness regarded the same expressions as signals for nonintervention (Sorce and Emde 1980).

Nutritional status. Full-term but small-for-date infants obtain poorer social responsiveness scores than their full-weight peers on the Brazelton Scales (Als et al. 1976). Furthermore, on follow-up, mothers of small-for-date babies were more likely to report sleeping and feeding problems and to describe their baby as difficult to care for than mothers of full-weight controls (Als et al. 1976).

Obstetric conditions. Earlier, we noted that one of the most ubiquitous effects of medications given during labor and delivery is decreased alertness (Brackbill 1979). Numerous studies have tried to determine the extent to which drugs given during labor and delivery are related to items assessed on the Brazelton Scales (see Sameroff 1978). The findings have not always been consistent, with some reports of little effect (e.g., Tronick et al. 1976) and some reports of effects lasting up to 28 days after birth (Aleksandrowicz and Aleksandrowicz 1974). The kind of items most frequently involved in these reports are those related to social responsiveness (such as attention to visual and auditory stimulation) and those related to changes in state (frequency of changes to and from alert states). Factors associated with obstetric risks, such as the Apgar Score that indicates the physical condition of the infant at birth, are also associated with performance on the same kind of items (Lester et al. 1976).

Premature birth. Studies that have assessed preterm infants in the hospital with the Brazelton Scales found that the infants obtained poorer social responsiveness scores (DiVitto and Goldberg 1979; Field 1977; Sostek, Quinn, and Davitt 1979), and were more difficult to rouse and keep in alert states than full-term controls. In addition, DiVitto and Goldberg (1979) found that those infants who had been unresponsive as neonates received more functional stimulation (e.g., more position changes, jiggles of the bottle) from parents during feedings both as newborns and four months later. Field (1977) reports that neonatal social responsiveness scores on the Brazelton Scales were predictive of mother-infant face-to-face play at three-and-one-half months; those who obtained poor scores as neonates were, at three-and-one-half months, less attentive and more restless during face-to-face play, and their mothers were more active than was the case for infants with more optimal neonatal scores.

Summary. These examples suggest that biologically stressed infants are likely to present problematic behavior to caregivers. Such infants are less ready to be social partners as a consequence of spending less time alert or being more irritable than normal infants. In addition, their responses to visual and auditory stimuli are often poorer than those of normal infants. Finally, conditions involving developmental delays (such as prematurity or Down syndrome) confront parents with a prolonged period of immaturity during which the rewards of positive signs of growth and increased social responsiveness are not forthcoming.

With the exception of Down syndrome infants whose cries are less aversive and compelling than those of normal infants (and might therefore be problematic by eliciting *less* caregiver attention than appropriate), the studies analyzing cries and adult responses present a consistent picture. The cries of the stressed infants are more difficult to elicit but acoustically more unpleasant (e.g., higher pitched) and judged as such by adults. This suggests that these cry features can serve an adaptive function in compelling attention to the infant who is in need of more intensive care. However, when an adult is unable to terminate particularly aversive cries, the caregiving situation will be an unpleasant and stressful one for both infant and caregiver.

Young children with developmental disabilities are often found to be overrepresented in statistics on child abuse and neglect (Gil 1973; Elmer and Gregg 1967). From the above summary, it is easy to see why life with an infant who has a handicap, illness, or physical limitation can be frustrating for parents. However, it is important to remember that the majority of infants, even those with severe handicaps, *do* receive adequate care. Thus, the majority of parent-infant dyads do successfully adapt to the stress of an infant's problems. As we will suggest in the final section of this chapter, breakdowns in the parent-infant relationship are most likely to occur when a fragile parent-infant dyad is additionally stressed by the absence of support from the family and surrounding community.

Maternal-infant bonding

Thus far, the discussion has been concerned with infant interactions with adult caregivers, whether mothers, fathers, other relatives, or unrelated adults. This section will focus more specifically on mothers, for whom the biological aspects of nurturant behavior are more clearly defined and have been more extensively studied. Many of the factors discussed above as influences upon the behaviors of infants also influence the behavior of mothers during the neonatal period. For example, drugs administered during delivery leave the mother as well as the infant in a state that is not conducive to social exchanges. Mothers who have had Caesarean deliveries are physically uncomfortable, less mobile, and stay in the hospital longer than mothers who have had vaginal deliveries. Specific illness (e.g., diabetes) is frequently associated with complications of pregnancy and delivery as well as a prolonged need for medical care following birth. Thus, this section could present a series of examples of biological influences on mothers that would parallel the discussion of such influences on infants.

However, because there is a great deal of public controversy concerning the concept of a critical period for maternal behavior, attention will be given to the origins of this notion and the evidence available to evaluate it. In their much publicized book, Klaus and Kennell (1976) state: "There is a sensitive period in the first minutes and hours of life during which it is necessary that the mother and father have close contact with their neonate for later development to be optimal" (p. 14).

Interpretations of this statement and the research reviewed in Klaus and Kennell's book often take a more extreme position than the authors intended, a position that assumes what Klaus (1978) calls the epoxy theory of parent-infant bonding. This approach assumes that there is a very brief period immediately following birth when parents are malleable and the formation of an attachment or emotional bond to the baby can occur. After this period, the glue, so to speak, hardens and if the participants have been fortunate enough to have had the right experiences, they are inextricably glued together. If they have had the wrong experiences, they are frozen in a separated or nonbonded condition. This view had led to a great deal of consumer pressure for early parent-infant contact. Hospitals have responded by offering parents the opportunity for mother, father, and baby to have an extended period of social interaction in the delivery room. While this experience is enjoyed by many families, the inability to have such an experience (e.g., because of delivery complications) leads many new parents to feel that they have failed in a way that may be injurious to their infant's development. Are such feelings warranted? Is the time immediately after birth a critical period for parent-infant bonding?

Origins of the critical period concept. The concept of a critical period originated in embryology and refers to periods during which specific organs or organ systems undergoing rapid development are vulnerable to interfering influences. For example, a number of years ago it was painfully discovered that the drug thalidomide taken by women in the early months of pregnancy can interfere with normal development of limbs, leaving the infant with stumps rather than fully developed limbs. However, once the limbs are formed, they cannot be damaged by thalidomide.

This concept of a critical period was originally intended to refer to structural changes, as in the above example, that were irreversible. It has since been applied to more clearly psychological phenomena such as language acquisition, infant-to-mother attachment, and the initiation of maternal behavior. In all of these cases, there is the implicit notion of the original concept that (a) there are underlying physiological processes that mark the critical period and (b) the effects of trauma or deprivation during these critical periods produce irreversible deficits.

Applications of the concept to maternal behavior. There are, of course, extensive physiological changes preceding the first extrauterine-mother-infant contact and continuing well into the infant's first year (depending partially upon duration of breast-feeding). For the most part, we know very little about the role that these changes play in the development of postnatal maternal behavior. Although animal studies can only be suggestive, extensive work by Rosenblatt and his colleagues (see Rosenblatt 1969, 1975; Trause, Klaus, and Kennell 1976 for summaries) points to the possible significance that one class of physiological events, hormonal changes, may have for the initiation of maternal behavior.

In one series of studies in which rat males, virgin females, and females at various stages of pregnancy and parturition were repeatedly exposed to newborn rats, Rosenblatt (1969) showed that hormones influence the ease with which maternal behavior is initiated. While males and virgin females required many days of exposure before crouching, licking, and retrieving infants, females close to and following delivery responded to infants almost immediately. Further studies showed that the latency (the time that elapses before a response) for rat maternal behavior decreases from the eleventh day of pregnancy on and that a hormone (estradiol), that rises rapidly during pregnancy and just before birth, does stimulate maternal behavior (Rosenblatt 1975). Thus, hormonal changes during pregnancy in the rat (and possibly the human) serve to bring the mother to a state of maximal responsiveness to infants at the time of birth.

Of course, without direct evidence from humans, we cannot conclude that hormones are equally important in the experience of human mothers. In fact, given the greater flexibility of the human species, hormonal condition is probably of lesser importance for humans. Pregnancy and childbirth represent periods of dramatic psychological change as well, and the fact that fathers and others who may be present at deliveries in different hormonal states anecdotally report the formation of strong attachments to the baby suggests that psychological factors are also operating for humans.

Further studies with infra-human species indicate that in some cases, removal of young immediately after birth interferes with the initiation of maternal behavior. Perhaps the most dramatic example occurs in goats, where females will not accept their young if they have been removed after birth for more than one hour (Collias 1956; Klopfer 1971). However, as little as five minutes of contact immediately after birth is sufficient to enable goat mothers to reaccept their young after as much as three hours of separation. Although there are wide variations in the presence or absence of such a critical period and its duration across species (and there are many species for which we have no data), studies such as these stimulate interest in the possibility that humans might also be maximally responsive to their young shortly after birth.

Studies of early contact and separation in humans. In the United States most births occur in hospitals where mothers and infants are routinely separated after the birth. For the three to five days spent in the hospital, their main contact occurs during the 20 to 30 minute feedings scheduled every four hours. In one of the first attempts to vary this routine experimentally, 14 mothers of first-borns in a Cleveland hospital were given their infants in bed for one hour during the first two hours of life and for five extra hours on each of the next three days. They were compared to 14 mothers who experienced the routine hospital treatment. Mothers who agreed to participate were assigned randomly to the experimental or control group. A month later, when all of the mothers returned for their infant's routine checkups, interviews revealed that the mothers with extra contact were more reluctant to leave their babies. They stayed closer to their infants during the physical examination and spent more time face to face and fondling their babies during a feeding than the controls (Klaus et al. 1972). Follow-ups at a year showed that the extra contact group again stayed closer to their infants during the examination (Kennell et al. 1974). At two years, five mothers in each group were selected at random for follow-up. The extended-contact mothers asked more questions, used more words, more adjectives, and fewer commands than the control mothers (Ringler et al. 1975).

Studies by other investigators, though they have not produced long-term follow-up data, show that mothers with extra contact also are more likely to establish successful breast-feeding, breast-feed longer, have infants who show more optimal growth, and spend more time in affectionate interactions than controls (e.g., deChateau 1980).

A second group of studies, carried out at Case Western Reserve and Stanford University Medical Centers, allowed extra contact to mothers of preterm infants who are routinely separated even more thoroughly and for longer periods of time than normal infants. In these studies, mothers in the experimental groups were allowed to visit and care for their infants in the intensive care nursery while the mothers in the control groups experienced the routine separations. Otherwise, nursery procedures at any given time were uniform for all families. In both centers, the extra-contact groups of mothers demonstrated some effects of their experience. In the Case Western Reserve sample, the extra-contact mothers spent more time looking at their infants during two feeding observations (Kennell and Klaus 1976). In the Stanford study, mothers without extra contact, especially if they were mothers of first-borns, scored lower on an assessment of self-confidence and were initially less skillful in handling their infants (Seashore et al. 1973). However, subsequent follow-ups in the first months, at one year, and at five to eight years revealed few differences between groups (Leiderman 1981). An unexpected finding was that there were more divorces among families in the routinely treated control group than in the contact group (Leifer et al. 1972; Leiderman 1981). This finding was a statistically significant one that could not be explained by any obvious differences in initial group composition. We have already suggested that the presence of an infant who has been biologically stressed and is therefore a difficult social partner can be frustrating and stressful for parents. For those whose marriage is also problematic, a difficult baby can exacerbate marital problems. Possibly the advantage of early contact in the above study was that it did facilitate parent-infant relationships and alleviate some of the stresses of caring for a difficult baby. This may have allowed the early contact group to devote more effort to potentially troublesome marriages or to have a less stressed family unit. While this interpretation is highly speculative, it is consistent with other interpretations of the early contact literature (Leiderman 1981; Lozoff 1977).

Although all of these studies have shown short-term effects of early contact on maternal behavior, they are less consistent about long-term effects and there is little evidence to suggest that such early experiences are critical for maternal behavior. First, there is the overwhelming evidence that millions of mothers have adequately cared for children after routine hospital treatment. Second, children can be adopted and adequately cared for at all ages.

Within the confines of the experimental data, there has been little effort to relate behavioral effects of early bonding to underlying physiological events such as hormonal changes in mothers, or mothers' physical recovery. Without such data, it is impossible to determine what specific processes bonding entails. Do physiological changes in the mother affect her ability or inclination to respond to infant behavior or appearance? Some literature suggests that, in early adolescence, stages of pubertal development in females are related to response to pictures of infants (Chandler 1977; Goldberg, Blumberg, and Kriger, in press). Girls who were more advanced in pubertal development made more choices of infant pictures in a preference task than those of the same age who were less physically mature. Differences were apparently not due to infant caregiving experiences, interest in motherhood, or sophistication about the relation between puberty and childbearing since these factors were unrelated to picture choices. These findings indicate at least one point in the childbearing cycle where physiological changes are related to sensitivity to the physical features of infants.

It has also been suggested that for a brief period after delivery the nondrugged baby is in an especially alert state, that may be more rewarding to adults than the subsequent period of recovery from the effects of delivery. It is also possible that the effects of early contact are more tied to psychological than to physiological states of mother or baby. Birth is a rather dramatic and stressful experience that is the culmination of a period of changing roles and expectations. To experience a period of rewarding contact may enhance the parents' commitment because it makes the previous months and hours worth it. In order to fully understand the effects of early contact, there is a need for much more information (see Klaus and Kennell 1976, pp. 67–80, for other speculations about processes).

Thus far there has been little agreement as to what are the appropriate measures of maternal behavior. While the repertoire of maternal behavior in rats and goats can be exhausted by a list of five or six activities, this is not the case for humans. Thus it is not surprising that there is little agreement as to which aspects of maternal attitude and behavior should be assessed in follow-up studies of early contact.

In a review of these studies, Leiderman (1981) points out that those that report long-term effects typically studied lower-SES families, while those finding only short-term effects generally studied middle-SES families. He suggests, as does Lozoff (1977), that when environmental conditions are not conducive to optimal care, the hours and days after birth may assume special importance. While early contact is not a necessity for human maternal care, it enhances the mother's early experiences and may help to maintain maternal behavior at optimal levels even when environmental pressures threaten to prevent adequate care. Thus, when there are no serious medical complications, it is advantageous to make birth a more rewarding human experience for parents and infants. When medical interventions necessary for the health of the mother or infant prevent early contact, however, all is not lost. Human maternal care does not depend on a single brief precisely timed event. This is another example of the systemlike organization of dyadic interaction. Under most circumstances one missed opportunity can be overcome by many other opportunities.

Larger perspectives

Although the previous section raised the issue of the lasting effects of early experiences, this chapter for the most part has discussed the parent-infant dyad only within its own narrow framework, during a short period of time. In this section, early parent-infant interaction will be viewed in a broader context.

While the emphasis has been on the parent-infant dyad as an interactive system, it is, of course, a subsystem within the larger context of the family. The family in turn is a subsystem within an expanding network of systems that make up the neighborhood, the community, and society. The success of the dyad in fulfilling its basic functions of supporting infant development and well-being depends on both internal and external conditions (Jameson 1978). The dyad may be stressed from within its system (e.g., by infant handicap or difficult behavior, by maternal physical or emotional limitations) or by external forces (e.g., marital discord, poverty, the school problems of a sibling). Similarly, resources for meeting the challenge of stress exist within the dyad (e.g., self-correcting tendencies discussed previously) as well as externally (support from family, friends, professionals).

A well-functioning parent-infant dyad generates confidence and competence in its members (Goldberg 1977; Lewis and Goldberg 1969) that become resources for coping with new challenges. In contrast, a poorly functioning dyad creates its own internal stress, will be more vulnerable to external stress, and will have fewer resources for meeting threats to its integrity. Nevertheless, a fragile parent-infant dyad may be energized or buffered against such threats by support from the larger social systems that surround it. For example, the availability of more than one caregiver can prevent any one individual from an overdose of the frustrations that an unrewarding infant can arouse. Assistance with other family problems from a professional source may enable a parent to devote more time and energy to a difficult relationship with an infant than would be otherwise available. The knowledge that tomorrow her baby will spend two hours in a day care center may enable an overworked or emotionally unstable mother to cope with today's difficult feeding. Under normal conditions, the interactive dyad is in dynamic equilibrium with the surrounding social network.

With this broader context in mind, it is now easier to understand why we have been unable to make very many long-term predictions about parent-child relationships or developmental outcomes from single events or measures. A stressful event such as premature birth or a complicated delivery that presents problems for parent and infant individually also challenges the interactive dyad, the family, and the larger social network. In addition to the subsequent medical course of infant and/or mother, we need to know how the dyad copes with these early problems, how the family does or does not support the dyad, and how the family is or is not supported by the larger social system, before we can make refined predictions about outcome.

A few events may be sufficiently powerful to override self-correcting mechanisms in the dyadic or family system and to overwhelm a network of coping resources. But generally, the effects of a single event, like the ripples moving outward from a stone dropped in water, will be observable in the short run, but will eventually be subdued. However, conditions that endure over a long time period, whether they are biological or social, are likely to have an enduring effect (Sameroff and Chandler 1975). Since the parent-infant dyad at the heart of the caregiving environment generally *is* one of the ever-present influences on the child, it has the potential within its biosocial context for relatively powerful influences on development.

References

Ainsworth, M. D. S. "The Development of Infant-Mother Attachment." In *Review of Child Development Research. Vol. 3*, ed. B. Caldwell and H. Ricciuti. Chicago: University of Chicago Press, 1973.

Aleksandrowicz, M. K., and Aleksandrowicz, D. R. "Obstetrical Pain-Relieving Drugs As Predictors of Infant Behavior Variability." *Child Development* 45 (1974): 935–945.

Als, H.; Tronick, E.; Adamson, L.; and Brazelton, T. B. "The Behavior of the Full Term But Underweight Newborn." *Developmental Medicine and Child*

Neurology 18 (1976): 590–602.

Anderson, B. J. "Parents' Strategies for Achieving Conversational Interactions with Their Young Hearing Impaired Children." In *Parent-Infant Intervention: Communication Disorders,* ed. A. S. Martin and D. R. Calvert. New York: Grune & Stratton, 1979.

Bowlby, J. *Attachment and Loss, Vol. 1: Attachment.* New York: Basic Books, 1969.

Brachfeld, S.; Goldberg, S.; and Sloman, J. "Parent-Infant Interaction in Free Play at 8 and 12 Months: Effects of Prematurity and Immaturity." *Infant Behavior and Development* 3 (1980): 289–305.

Brackbill, Y. "Obstetric Medication and Infant Behavior." In *Handbook of Infant Development,* ed. J. D. Osofsky. New York: Wiley, 1979.

Brazelton, T. B. "Neonatal Behavioral Assessment Scale." *Clinics in Developmental Medicine No. 50.* Philadelphia: Lippincott, 1973.

Brazelton, T. B.; Koslowski, B.; and Main, M. "The Origins of Reciprocity: The Early Mother-Infant Interaction." In *The Effect of the Infant on Its Caregiver,* ed. M. Lewis and L. A. Rosenblum. New York: Wiley, 1974.

Brown, J. V., and Bakeman, R. "Relationships of Human Mothers with Their Infants During the First Year of Life." In *Maternal Influences and Early Behavior,* ed. R. W. Bell and W. P. Smotherman. Jamaica, N. Y.: Spectrum, 1979.

Chandler, J. "Sex Differences in the Nurturant Responses of Adolescent Children." Unpublished doctoral dissertation, University of Denver, 1977.

Cicchetti, D., and Sroufe, L. A. "The Relationship Between Affective and Cognitive Development in Down's Syndrome Infants." *Child Development* 47 (1976): 920–929.

Cicchetti, D., and Sroufe, L. A. "An Organizational View of Affect: Illustration from the Study of Down's Syndrome Infants." In *The Development of Affect,* ed. M. Lewis and L. A. Rosenblum. New York: Plenum, 1978.

Collias, N. E. "The Analysis of Socialization in Sheep and Goats." *Ecology* 37(1956): 228–239.

Condon, W., and Sander, L. "Synchrony Demonstrated Between Movements of the Neonate and Adult Speech." *Child Development* 45 (1974): 456–462.

deChateau, P. "Effects of Hospital Practice on Synchrony in the Development of the Infant-Parent Relationship." In *Parent Infant Relationships,* ed. P. M. Taylor. New York: Grune & Stratton, 1980.

DiVitto, B., and Goldberg, S. "The Development of Parent-Infant Interaction As a Function of Newborn Medical Status." In *Infants Born at Risk,* ed. T. Field et al. Jamaica, N.Y.: Spectrum, 1979.

Eimas, P. D. "Speech Perception in Early Infancy." In *Infant Perception,* ed. L. B. Cohen and P. Salapatek. New York: Academic Press, 1975.

Eisenberg, R. B. *Auditory Competence in Early Life: The Roots of Communicative Behavior.* Baltimore, Md.: University Park Press, 1976.

Elmer, E., and Gregg, G. S. "Developmental Characteristics of Abused Children." *Pediatrics* 40 (1967): 596–602.

Emde, R. N.; Katz, E. L.; and Thorpe, J. K. "Emotional Expression in Infancy: II.—Early Deviations in Down's Syndrome." In *The Development of Affect*, ed. M. Lewis and L. A. Rosenblum. New York: Plenum, 1978.

Fantz, R. L. "Visual Perception from Birth As Shown by Pattern Selectivity." *Annals of the New York Academy of Science* 118 (1965): 793–814.

Feldman, S. S., and Nash, S. C. "Interest in Babies During Young Adulthood." *Child Development* 49 (1978): 617–622.

Feldman, S. S., and Nash, S. C. "Sex Differences in Responsiveness to Babies among Mature Adults." *Developmental Psychology* 15 (1979): 430–436.

Field, T. "Effects of Early Separation, Interactive Deficits and Experimental Manipulation on Mother-Infant Interaction." *Child Development* 48 (1977): 763–771.

Field, T. M.; Hallock, N.; Ting, G.; Dempsey, J.; Dabiri, C.; and Shuman, H. H. "A First Year Followup of High Risk Infants: Formulating a Cumulative Risk Index." *Child Development* 49 (1978): 119–131.

Fisichelli, V., and Karelitz, S. "The Cry Latencies of Normal Infants and Those with Brain Damage." *Journal of Pediatrics* 62 (1963): 724–734.

Fraiberg, S. *Insights from the Blind*. New York: Basic Books, 1977.

Freudenberg, R. P.; Driscoll, J. W.; and Stern, G. S. "Reactions of Adult Humans to Cries of Normal and Abnormal Infants." *Infant Behavior and Development* 1 (1978): 224–227.

Frodi, A.; Lamb, M.; Leavitt, L.; Donovan, C. F.; Neff, C.; and Sherry, D. "Fathers' and Mothers' Responses to the Faces and Cries of Normal and Premature Infants." *Developmental Psychology* 14 (1978): 490–498.

Fullard, W., and Reiling, A. M. "An Investigation of Lorenz's 'Babyness.'" *Child Development* 47 (1976): 1191–1193.

Gil, D. *Violence Against Children*. Cambridge, Mass.: Harvard University Press, 1973.

Goldberg, S. "Social Competence in Infancy: A Model of Parent-Infant Interaction." *Merrill-Palmer Quarterly* 23 (1977): 164–177.

Goldberg, S. "Prematurity: Effects on Parent-Infant Interaction." *Journal of Pediatric Psychology* 3 (1978): 137–144.

Goldberg, S.; Blumberg, S. L.; and Kriger, A. "Menarche and Interest in Infants: Biological and Social Influences." *Child Development*, in press.

Goren, G. G.; Sartz, M.; and Wu, P. Y. K. "Visual Following and Pattern Discrimination of Face-Like Stimuli in Newborn Infants." *Pediatrics* 56 (1975): 544–549.

Gould, S. J. "Mickey Mouse Meets Konrad Lorenz." *Natural History* 88 (1979): 30–36.

Haith, M. "The Response of the Human Newborn to Visual Movement." *Journal of Experimental Child Psychology* 3 (1966): 235–243.

Hershenson, M.; Munsinger, H.; and Kessen, W. "Preference for Shapes of Intermediate Variability in the Human Newborn." *Science* 147 (1965): 630–631.

Jameson, J. C. "Vulnerable Mother-Child Dyads: Findings from an Epidemiological Interview and Observational Study." Qualifying paper, Harvard University Graduate School of Education, 1978.

Jirari, C. "Form Perception, Innate Form Preferences and Visually Mediated Head-Turning in Human Neonates." Unpublished doctoral dissertation, Committee on Human Development, University of Chicago, 1970. (Cited in Freedman, D. *Human Infancy*. Hillsdale, N.J.: Lawrence Erlbaum Associates, 1974.)

Jones, O. H. M. "Prelinguistic Communication Skills in Down's Syndrome and Normal Infants." In *High Risk Infants and Children: Interactions with Adults and Peers*, ed. T. Field, S. Goldberg, D. Stern, and S. Sostek. New York: Academic Press, 1980.

Kaplan, E., and Kaplan, G. "The Prelinguistic Child." In *Human Development and Cognitive Processes*, ed. J. Eliot. New York: Holt, Rinehart & Winston, 1971.

Karelitz, S., and Fisichelli, V. R. "The Cry Thresholds of Normal Infants and Those with Brain Damage." *Journal of Pediatrics* 61 (1962): 679–685.

Kennell, J.; Jerauld, R.; Wolfe, H.; Chesler, D.; Kreger, N. C.; McAlpine, W.; Steffa, M.; and Klaus, M. H. "Maternal Behavior One Year After Early and Extended Post-Partum Contact." *Developmental Medicine and Child Neurology* 16 (1974): 172–179

Kennell, J. H., and Klaus, M. H. "Caring for Parents of a Premature or Sick Infant." *Maternal-Infant Bonding*, ed. M. H. Klaus and J. H. Kennell. St. Louis: Mosby, 1976.

Klaus, M. H. Invited address to the International Conference on Infant Studies. Providence, Rhode Island, March 1978.

Klaus, M. H.; Jerauld, R.; Kreger, N.; McAlpine, W.; Steffa, M.; and Kennell, J. H. "Maternal Attachment: Importance of the First Post-Partum Days." *New England Journal of Medicine* 286 (1972): 460–463.

Klaus, M. H., and Kennell, J. H. "Human Maternal and Paternal Behavior." In *Maternal-Infant Bonding*, ed. M. Klaus and J. H. Kennell. St. Louis: Mosby, 1976.

Klaus, M. H., and Kennell, J. H. *Maternal-Infant Bonding*. St. Louis: Mosby, 1976.

Klopfer, P. "Mother Love: What Turns It On?" *American Scientist* 49 (1971): 494–497.

Korner, A., and Grobstein, R. "Visual Alertness As Related to Soothing in Neonates: Implications for Maternal Stimulation and Early Deprivation." *Child Development* 37 (1966): 867–876.

Leiderman, P. H. "The Critical Period Hypothesis Revisited: Mother to Infant Social Bonding in the Neonatal Period." In *Issues in Behavioral Development: The Bielefeld Interdisciplinary Conference*, ed. K. Immelman et al. Cambridge: Cambridge University Press, 1981.

Leiderman, P. H.; Tulkin, S. R.; and Rosenfeld, A., eds. *Culture and Infancy: Variations in the Human Experience*. New York: Academic Press, 1977.

Leifer, A. D.; Leiderman, P. H.; Barnett, C. R.; and Williams, J. A. "Effects of

Mother-Infant Separation on Maternal Attachment Behavior." *Child Development* 43 (1972): 1203–1218.

Lester, B. M. "Spectrum Analysis of the Cry Sounds of Well-Nourished and Malnourished Infants." *Child Development* 47 (1976): 237–241.

Lester, B. M.; Emory, E. K.; Hoffman, S. L.; and Eitzman, D. V. "A Multivariate Study of the Effects of High Risk Factors on the Brazelton Neonatal Assessment Scale." *Child Development* 47 (1976): 515–517.

Lester, B. M., and Zeskind, P. "The Organization and Assessment of Crying in the Infant at Risk." In *Infants Born at Risk*, ed. T. Field et al. Jamaica, N.Y.: Spectrum, 1979.

Lewis, M., and Goldberg, S. "Perceptual-Cognitive Development in Infancy: A Generalized Expectancy Model As a Function of Mother-Infant Interaction." *Merrill-Palmer Quarterly* 15 (1969): 81–100.

Lind, J.; Vuorenkoski, V.; Rosberg, G.; Partanen, T. J.; and Wasz-Hockert, O. "Spectrograph Analysis of Vocal Response to Pain Stimuli in Infants with Down's Syndrome." *Developmental Medicine and Child Neurology* 12 (1970): 478–486.

Littman, B. "The Relationship of Medical Events to Infant Development." In *Infants Born at Risk*, ed. T. Field et al. Jamaica, N.Y.: Spectrum, 1979.

Lorenz, K. Z. "Die Angeborenen Formen Moglicher Erfahrung." *Zeitschrift Tierpsychologie* 5 (1943): 235–409. (Cited in Hess, E. "Ethology and Developmental Psychology." In *Carmichael's Manual of Child Psychology*. 3rd ed., ed. P. H. Mussen. New York: Wiley, 1977.

Lozoff, B. "The Sensitive Period: An Anthropological View." Paper presented at the Symposium on the Ecology of Maternal Infant Bonding, Society for Research in Child Development, New Orleans, March 1977.

Lubchenco, L. *The High Risk Infant*. Philadelphia: Saunders, 1976.

Prechtl, H. F. R. "Neurological Findings in Newborn Infants After Pre- and Paranatal Complication." In *Aspects of Prematurity and Dysmaturity: A Nutrica Symposium*, ed. J. Jonix, H. Visser, and J. Troelstra. Leiden: Stenfert & Kroese, 1968.

Ringler, N. M.; Kennell, J. H.; Jarvella, R.; Navajosky, B. J.; and Klaus, M. H. "Mother-to-Child Speech at 2 Years: Effects of Early Postnatal Contact." *Journal of Pediatrics* 86 (1975): 141–144.

Rosenblatt, J. S. "The Development of Maternal Responsiveness in Rats." *American Journal of Orthopsychiatry* 39 (1969): 36–56.

Rosenblatt, J. S. "Prepartum and Post Partum Regulation of Maternal Behavior in Rats." In *Parent-Infant Interaction, CIBA Foundation Symposium. Vol. 33*. New York: Elsevier, 1975.

Sameroff, A. J. "Organization and Stability of Newborn Behavior: A Commentary on the Brazelton Neonatal Behavior Assessment Scale." *Monographs of the Society for Research in Child Development* 43 (1978). Serial No. 177.

Sameroff, A. J., and Chandler, M. J. "Reproductive Risk and the Continuum of Caretaking Casualty." In *Review of Child Development Research. Vol. 4*, ed. F. Horowitz. Chicago: University of Chicago Press, 1975.

Seashore, M. J.; Leifer, A. D.; Barnett, C. R.; and Leiderman, P. H. "The Effects of Denial of Early Mother-Infant Interaction on Maternal Self-Confidence." *Journal of Personality and Social Psychology* 26 (1973): 369–375.

Sorce, J. F., and Emde, R. N. "The Meaning of Infant Emotional Expression: Regularities in Caregiving Responses to Normal and Down's Syndrome Infants." Submitted for publication, 1980.

Sostek, A. M.; Quinn, P. O.; and Davitt, M. K. "Behavior Development and Neurologic Status of Premature and Full Term Infants with Varying Medical Complications." *Infants Born at Risk*, ed. T. Field. Jamaica, N.Y.: Spectrum, 1979.

Sroufe, L. A., and Waters, E. "Attachment As an Organizational Construct." *Child Development* 48 (1977): 1184–1199.

Stern, D. "Mother and Infant at Play: The Dyadic Interaction Involving Facial, Vocal, and Gaze Behaviors." In *The Effect of the Infant on its Caregiver*, ed. M. Lewis and L. A. Rosenblum. New York: Wiley, 1974.

Stern, D. *The First Relationship: Infant and Mother*. Cambridge, Mass.: Harvard University Press, 1977.

Sternglanz, S. M.; Grey, J. H.; and Murakami, M. "Adult Preferences for Infant Facial Features: An Ethological Approach." *Animal Behavior* 25 (1977): 108–115.

Trause, M. A.; Klaus, M. H.; and Kennell, J. H. "Maternal Behavior in Mammals." In *Maternal-Infant Bonding*, ed. M. H. Klaus and J. H. Kennell. St. Louis: Mosby, 1976.

Tronick, E.; Als, H.; Adamson, L.; Wise, S.; and Brazelton, T. B. "The Infant's Response to Entrapment Between Contradictory Messages in Face-to-Face Interaction." *Journal of the American Academy of Child Psychiatry* 17 (1978): 1–13.

Tronick, E.; Wise, S.; Als, H.; Adamson, L.; Scanlon, J.; and Brazelton, T. B. "Regional Obstetric Anesthesia and Newborn Behavior: Effect over the First 10 Days of Life." *Pediatrics* 58 (1976): 94–100.

Wedell-Monnig, J., and Lumley, J. "Child Deafness and Mother-Child Interaction." *Child Development* 51 (1980): 766–774.

Zeskind, P. S., and Lester, B. M. "Acoustic Features and Auditory Perceptions of the Cries of Newborns with Prenatal and Perinatal Complications." *Child Development* 49 (1978): 580–589.

Norma Radin

4 The unique contribution of parents to childrearing: the preschool years

Discussing parental influence on young children is much like selecting two connected knots in an enormous fishnet and giving them careful scrutiny while ignoring the dozens of remaining knots. It can be done, but one loses a great deal of information if the goal is to understand all the forces pulling on just one of those intersections. However, one must start somewhere in any effort to comprehend a complex structure, and it is helpful to start with the parents if one wants to begin to understand the child. This approach is reasonable provided we do not forget that the parents and the child are interlinked with many other individuals and that there are many other forces tugging upon all three.

Before analyzing the parental influences upon young children, two limitations must also be recognized. First, the child is not infinitely malleable, since genetic and congenital factors account for significant aspects of human behavior. Second, the child's influence upon the parent is as great as the parent's influence upon the child. This chapter will open with a brief summary of some major findings concerning the bidirectionality of parent-child interaction that have relevance for understanding the childrearing literature. A more focused discussion of parental influences on young children will ensue, beginning with a delineation of six key processes through which mothers and fathers influence their children. This will be followed by a discussion of the process of parental identification, an analysis of parental influences on their children's sex-role identification, and finally, an overview of parental influence techniques on their young children's cognitive development. A brief summary will conclude the chapter.

The influence of children on parents

One of the first investigators in the past two decades to highlight the influence of children upon parents was Bell, whose classic analysis (1968) reinterpreted a number of studies that had been accepted as demonstrating parental shaping of their children's behavior. The reinterpretation involved taking the same data and providing logical reasons for concluding that it was just as likely that children, by virtue of their temperament and constitution, influenced the behavior of their parents as that parents influenced their children. For example, Bandura and Walters (1959) had found more physical punishment by parents of 15–16-year-old male repeat offenders than by parents of nondelinquents, and concluded that physical punishment by parents leads to delinquent behavior. Bell offers an alternative explanation that congenital assertiveness of hyperactivity in the boys elicits parental control efforts and that these control efforts escalate to physical punishment.

Bell also questioned the interpretation offered for a positive correlation obtained between a demanding and intrusive mother-child relationship and higher scores by their children in the verbal (language) area compared to the quantitative (mathematical) area. According to Bing (1963), these findings confirm her hypothesis that verbal ability in children is fostered by a close relationship with a somewhat intrusive mother. Bell (1968) poses the alternative explanation that children high in person orientation but low in assertiveness may reinforce maternal social responses. The resultant interactions, in turn, enhance the child's verbal expression because language is the primary channel of communication. Further, because these children are low in assertiveness, their mothers may attempt to stimulate their behaviors by being demanding and intrusive. Bell refers to these eliciting maternal behaviors as *lower-limit* control responses in contrast to the *upper-limit* control responses made by parents to reduce hyperactive behavior, as discussed above.

Bell (1974) observed that there is a balance between the influence of the child on parents and the influence of parents on the child. Parents may have planfulness or intention on their side of the equation but the child has the sheer volume of interactions initiated and the compelling nature of these behaviors. For example, sustained distress reactions of infants in the form of aversive crying shapes their mothers' behavior to prevent the cries since they are so disturbing, while infant babbling and smiling will entice mothers to enter into games with children, smiling at them and tickling them. Above all, by modifying their behaviors, that is, by learning, even infants show mothers that they matter, and responsive social interaction is thereby maintained.

Bell is not the only researcher to study the impact of the child upon the adult. Goldberg (1977) concludes from her longitudinal study of parents and infants that the less predictable, less readable, and less responsive infant has the potential of generating, in initially responsive parents, feelings of failure and helplessness. In contrast, the more predictable, readable, and responsive infant has the potential for capturing even the initially less responsive parent into cycles of effective interactions by generating parental feelings of efficacy.

The role of temperament

Perhaps most well-known of all the investigators exploring the direction of influence from child to parent are Thomas, Chess, and Birch, who studied the interplay of inborn temperament and environment in shaping behavior. They conducted a number of studies of parenting, including an intensive longitudinal study of 141 middle-SES children starting when the children were three months of age and continuing until they were 14 years old (Thomas, Chess, and Birch 1968; 1970). The parents of the children in the study were interviewed regularly and were asked to keep logs; the children were observed periodically, and, as the children became older, they were tested and their teachers were interviewed. Thomas, Chess, and Birch (1970) conclude that there are nine stable characteristics of children that could be scored reliably over the years and are discernible by the time the children reach three months of age: Level and extent of motor activity; regularity of biological functions such as sleeping and eating; response to a new object or person; adaptability to changes in the environment; sensitivity to stimuli; intensity of responses; disposition such as cheerful or cranky; distractability; and span of attention and persistence.

These nine characteristics cluster into three groups and describe three types of children: the *easy* children, 40 percent of their sample; the *difficult* children, 10 percent of their sample; and *slow-to-warm-up* children, 15 percent of their sample. The remaining 35 percent of the children were of mixed types belonging to no one cluster. The easy children were delineated as having a positive disposition, were regular in bodily function, adaptable, and had a positive approach to new situations. The difficult children had irregular bodily functions, withdrew from new stimuli, were slow to adapt to change, and were negative in disposition. The slow-to-warm-up children withdrew in the face of new stimuli, had a low activity level, and were slow to adapt to change.

These three types of children placed different demands upon their caregivers, with the easy children responding favorably to various childrearing styles and the difficult children requiring unusually painstaking handling to function well. If the parents were inconsistent, impatient, or punitive, the difficult child was likely to react negatively and have a problematic course of development. The slow-to-warm-up child was moderately difficult to rear, for if pressured to move quickly to a new situation, the child was likely to withdraw and have limited opportunities for new experiences. As evidence that the children's temperaments (behavioral styles or intrinsic characteristics), observable from the first months of life, are predictive of their future functioning, Thomas, Chess, and Birch (1970) report that 70 percent of the difficult children developed behavioral problems of varying degrees of severity compared with only 18 percent of the easy children.

Thomas and his colleagues stress the fact that the children showed distinct individuality in temperament from infancy, seemingly independent of the parents' handling or personality style, and these characteristics persisted in most children over the years. Thus it was important to relieve parents of the guilt they may have felt if their difficult child was a trial and unpleasant to rear. However, Thomas, Chess, and Birch (1968) also emphasize the fact that by recognizing a child's temperament and modifying childrearing practices to harmonize with the child's characteristics, parents could prevent many problems and foster healthy development. For example, children who are slow to adapt to change may need support and extra preparation when faced with a new situation. According to Thomas, Chess, and Birch, temperament in and of itself does not produce behavior disorders; these emerge in response to environmental circumstances and patterns of care to which the children are exposed. It is, however, acknowledged that certain types of temperaments are more likely to result in behavior disorders than others. Although these investigators do not commit themselves to any point of view about the origins of temperament, Thomas and Chess (1977) do suggest that the weight of the data favors a genetic explanation for the difficult temperament of some children.

Brazelton's work (1969; 1973; 1977) fills the gap left by Thomas, Chess, and Birch concerning the period prior to the first three months of life. He concludes from his observations that neonates differ in the extent to which they possess three basic characteristics: the ability to shut off disturbing stimuli, that is, to shut down or habituate; the ability to orient toward positive stimuli or give alerting responses; and the ability to control their states of arousal, that is, to control and comfort themselves. Like Thomas, Chess, and Birch, Brazelton uses the information he collected to counsel parents about the importance of knowing their infants and responding in a way so as to mesh with the infants' basic predispositions (Brazelton 1974).

> We have found significant differences in feeding and interactional behavior between mothers and infants at 1 month, and significantly better performances on the Bayley exams at one year when mothers are alerted to their infants' individual behaviors. They say, ''You've shown me what I need to know to mother this baby.'' (Brazelton 1977, pp. 14–15)

Brazelton suggests that the development of at-risk infants might be fostered if mothers could be provided with this information, and he implies that the incidence of child abuse might thereby be reduced.

Other investigators emphasize the circular or transactional nature of parent-child influence, suggesting that it is virtually impossible to understand the impact of children on mothers and fathers or the impact of mothers and fathers on children in isolation; both sets of interactions must be considered (Clarke-Stewart 1978; Osofsky 1976; Sameroff 1977).

The influence of parents on children

The nonbiological or social influence that parents exert on their children for the most part is encompassed in the term *socialization*. Although the word has been used to refer to the *goal* of childrearing, more typically it describes the *process* involved. Socialization in this sense has been defined in various ways, for example, as the process by which an individual develops through transaction with others, her or his specific patterns of socially relevant behaviors (Zigler and Child 1969) or as the process by which individuals acquire their knowledge, skills, attitudes, values, and cultural patterns that shape their adaptation to the setting in which they live (Inkeles 1973). Although socialization continues throughout life for individuals who live in complex societies, it most frequently refers to the process by which children are oriented and trained as members of an established adult community (Hess 1970). Authors who write about socialization focus on the broad array of means by which individuals learn to fill roles in society, and authors highlight the fact that virtually everything parents do contributes to socialization whether the influence on the child is intentional or not, whether direct or indirect. In view of the breadth of the term, little is gained simply by stating that parents socialize their children. Consideration of the specific processes by which change in the child is brought about is needed for an understanding of how parental influence operates.

Direct and indirect influence

Parents contribute to children's development in both an *indirect* and *direct* manner. In direct influence, the parent does or says something and the effect is felt by the child; in the indirect influence the parent does or says something to someone other than the child, and, in turn, that individual exerts influence on the child. A common type of indirect influence occurs when one spouse affects the other, who then interacts with the child in a different way because of this experience. There are a number of illustrations of such indirect influence in the research literature. For example, fathers' long-term and short-term academic expectations, as assessed by questionnaires, were positively and significantly correlated with measures of girls' cognitive functioning although fathers' *observable behaviors* were not (Radin 1976). It was hypothesized that a father's future expectations for his daughter may have been communicated to his wife, who may have then altered her own expectations and behaviors with their daughter. Independent evidence in the study showed that this had occurred. Fathers may also influence children indirectly by the kind of relationship they have with their wives, that affects the way the women interact with their offspring. This type of indirect influence is reported to have an effect on a child's cognitive style (Dyk and Witkin 1965) and moral development (Hoffman 1970). Hoffman's work on moral development suggests that fathers who experience very little power in the occupational sphere tend to assert power over their wives at home, who then use power-assertive strategies in interactions with their children. The frequent use of power assertion by mothers is associated, in turn, with weak moral development in children.

Indirect paternal influence may also operate in families with a working mother. A study of middle-SES families shows that a mother's positive feelings about her job were linked to the satisfaction she felt with parenting discussions between herself and her spouse and with her spouse's involvement in child care

(Radin 1981). It is likely that her satisfaction with her occupational role influenced her performance of the parent role, for the many roles played by working women appear to be interdependent (Radin 1981).

Another form of indirect parental influence is evidenced when mothers and fathers put their young children in contact with other individuals who then exert influence on the boys and girls. The potency of such contacts is highlighted by Cochran and Brassard (1979), who discuss the many ways in which infants and young children are influenced by their parents' personal social network, that is, people outside of the household who engage in activities and exchanges with members of the immediate family. Such people can introduce children to new modes of interaction, and to experiences and activities substantially different from those engaged in by parents. In addition, members of the parents' social network can serve as models; as they are visibly rewarded or punished for their activities, they provide opportunities for vicarious learning by the children. Cochran and Brassard also describe ways in which members of the personal network can modify a parent's childrearing practices, thereby offering support for the view expressed early in this chapter that parents and children form part of an enormous influence network.

Six key processes of direct parental influence

Research has shown that direct parental influence is exerted through at least six different processes: modeling, use of sanction or rewards, giving direct instructions, stating expectations of desired behaviors, employing cognitive modification techniques, and providing a specific physical setting for the child. This taxonomy will now be discussed and examples offered from the research literature on socialization.

Parental modeling, or (from the child's perspective) learning from observation or imitation, has been associated with the child's sex-role development by social learning theorists, but its applicability as a direct parent influence is much broader. In general, children tend to imitate people who are available, powerful, and nurturant, and since most parents possess these qualities from their child's point of view, the conditions promoting imitation of parents by children are amply present (Maccoby 1980). For example, Hetherington (1967) found that children of both sexes tend to imitate and have personality characteristics that are similar to the parent who is dominant, regardless of the parent's sex.

The use of rewards, verbal or physical, for approved behaviors and the use of **punishment,** verbal or physical, for disapproved behaviors dates back to Biblical times. The admonition that sparing the rod is spoiling the child is part of ancient folklore. In recent years numerous books have been written instructing parents on the use of behavior modification techniques to achieve desired child behaviors (Patterson and Guillon 1968; Wittes and Radin 1969). Publications have also appeared on how to train parents to be more effective in their use of sanctions, such as Rose (1974) and Patterson, Shaw, and Ebner (1969). Parental use of sanctions when children engage in unacceptable behavior is illustrated in the research of Langlois and Downs (in Maccoby 1980). They asked young children to play with sex-typed toys the way a child of the opposite sex would do and then ushered mothers or fathers into the room. It was evident that fathers reacted more negatively to their son's sex-inappropriate play than to their daughter's, for example, by showing expressions of disgust or disapproval. Fathers also reacted more negatively to this deviant behavior than mothers.

Direct instruction or explicit training is often associated with the academic sphere of development or with physical safety ("Don't go into the street," or "Don't cross when the light is red.") although there is more research in the former area than the latter. For example, it was shown that fathers who are extensively involved in caring for preschool children in two-parent families spend more time than traditional fathers in direct instructional activities with their children, particularly with their sons, such as teaching them colors (Radin, in press).

Stating expectations of desired behaviors has been studied more often in relation to teachers than parents. However one book on instructions for parents uses *to state the rule* as its most important guideline (Smith and Smith 1966). The authors suggest that a rule be repeated without emotion on several occasions when it is being violated, and if this does no good, to use negative sanctions. In a more historic vein, one can cite the Ten Commandments as statements of expectations.

The use of cognitive modification strategies, defined as such, is more recent, although once again folk wisdom in this area is ancient, such as labeling children to bring them under control (bad boy). The term *cognitive modification* has been popularized by Meichenbaum (1977) who uses it to refer to a particular type of therapeutic treatment, but it is equally useful as a term to categorize the following influence techniques used by parents.

(a) *Highlighting the discrepancy* between a child's actions and her or his values or attitudes in order to bring about change in one or the other. According to cognitive dissonance theory, discomfort is experienced when two cognitions or ideas held by an individual are inconsistent; the individual is motivated to change one or the other to relieve the tension. Numerous studies have been performed to show that when such dissonance does exist, attitudes do change. For example, when students willingly participated in a dull experiment, and were then asked to tell another subject the task was interesting, the students subsequently rated the experiment as more interesting and exciting than students in a control group who did not engage in the counter-attitudinal behavior (Festinger and Carlsmith 1959).

(b) *Labeling the child* to alter her or his self-perception and subsequent behavior. Thus far, research has demonstrated this effect with teachers, although not yet with parents. Dweck and her colleagues (Dweck 1975; Dweck and Gilliard 1975; Dweck and Reppucci 1973) have shown that when children attribute their failure to stable, uncontrollable factors within themselves such as *lack of ability*, their performance deteriorates after failure. However, if they believe that their failure was due to *lack of effort*, they often show increased effort and better performance. Dweck found that girls more often receive messages from their teachers that their poor work is attributable to stable, internal factors, while boys receive the message that poor work is due to lack of effort, fooling around, or poor attention, that are unstable, correctable factors. Thus girls are more likely to suffer from *learned helplessness* ("I just can't do it.") than boys, who tend to say "I could do it if I tried." The implications for parents appear to be that helping a child become aware of lack of effort—a controllable quality—is more likely to lead to subsequent good performance than offering sympathy for lack of ability.

(c) *Arousing the child's empathy or guilt* by describing the unhappy plight of the victim. Among the investigations of parental behaviors that facilitate empathy and helping in young children is that of Yarrow and Waxler (1978), who conducted an intensive study using both home observations and laboratory tests with mothers and their one-and-one-half-year-old children. Mothers who frequently used explanations linking the child's behavior with its consequences for the victim had children who were more likely to try to help a victim when they caused harm. For example, a mother might say "John is crying because you pushed him." Maternal tactics such as physical restraint or arbitrary, unexplained prohibitions are not as effective in fostering altruism (Hetherington and Parke 1979). Perhaps the strategy of describing the plight of the victim is powerful because it fosters affective role taking (Iannotti 1975; Rubin and Schneider 1973).

(d) *Reasoning or using rational persuasion* to change a child's behavior. This strategy is similar to the discipline strategy Hoffman (1970) calls *induction*. After conducting numerous studies on maternal childrearing practices, Hoffman concludes that induction and affection are associated with the most advanced moral development in children as seen in their resisting temptation, confessing and accepting blame, and feeling guilt following transgressions.

Providing physical materials and settings for the child can result in opportunities to engage in certain types of activities, such as exploring the environment, reading, and manipulating objects. (It should be noted that this influence process can be considered indirect since it is not the parent who influences the child, but it has been categorized among the direct influences since no other person intervenes.) It has been shown that a major factor in sex-typed behavior is the distinctive environment parents provide for their children. For example, parents give their boys and girls different toys and clothing and decorate their rooms differently (Rheingold and Cook 1975).

The many specific influence techniques parents use have been conceptualized in terms of three underlying, independent dimensions: a *control* dimension varying from high to low; an *affect* dimension ranging from very warm to cold; and a *demand* dimension, extending from having no expectations to having high expectations of the child. The control and affect dimensions have been studied and described by Schaefer (1961) and the demand dimension by Roe and Siegelman (1963). Baumrind (1967) focuses on the demand factor in her delineation of the *authoritative* parent who seems to elicit mature, independent behavior by being both warm and demanding. The demand concept also is discussed earlier in relation to the explanations offered by Bing (1963) and Bell (1968) for the association between verbal precociousness in children and demanding characteristics in mothers.

Parental influences and the concept of identification

The process of parental identification is considered by many developmental psychologists to be the hallmark of the preschool period in the socioemotional realm, just as attainment of object permanence is the hallmark of the sensorimotor period in the cognitive realm. The term *identification* has been used in two ways: To refer to the end product of a developmental process by which children acquire their characteristic behaviors (such as, "He has achieved identification with his uncle during his father's absence.") and to refer to the process itself. Identification, as used in this discussion, will refer to the process by which children come to think, feel, and behave as though the characteristics of another person belong to them, or in which the child comes to act as if she or he *were* the other individual. Because this is an internal process it can never be assessed directly but only inferred from observable behaviors. For example, when a little girl puts on her mother's lipstick and high heels it is commonly believed that she is expressing her identification with her mother, but one cannot be certain. In spite of the fact that behaviors believed to reflect identification with a parent have not been found to intercorrelate highly (Sears, Rau, and Alpert 1965), the construct is so useful in explaining much of the young child's behavior and in integrating seeming diverse responses that it continues to be widely used in the child development literature.

Although identification is often used to refer to the internalization of behaviors appropriate to one's sex—that is, sex-role identification—parental identification refers to the broader process through which the child internalizes many of the behaviors, attitudes, and social values of the parent. An analysis of the process of identification, as it is described by social learning theorists, will help to bring the concept into focus. Two versions of social learning theory are postulated to account for identification in children, *a responsive conditioning model* and an *operant conditioning model.*

In responsive conditioning, a pleasurable stimulus, such as *food* to a hungry baby, is constantly associated with another stimulus, the caregiver who feeds the baby. (Although there may be more than one primary caregiver, and the caregiver need not be the mother, the process will be described using the mother as the prototype.) Because of the constant pairing of the mother with pleasure, she takes on special meaning to the baby. Babies come into the world with some strong biological needs that are met by human adults. The most obvious, of course, is the need to be fed. There are other needs too, however, that are either innate or emerge in the first months of life, including a need to be touched, rocked, fondled, and kept warm. Experiences in which the pain of hunger, or the pleasure of being caressed are constantly associated with the presence of mothers and other caregivers predispose the child to attend to caregivers and to seek their nurturance. While at first a child's pleasure in maternal behaviors is focused on feeding and other physical care functions that lead to gratification, in time the mother's presence per se leads to gratification—apart from the caregiving situations from which it began. The child will gradually feel at ease and in a state of well-being in the presence of the mother, and unhappy or unsatisfied in her absence. Since the mother cannot be with the child all of the time, the child will attempt to behave like the mother—to identify with her—so that aspects of the mother-present situation can be recreated in her absence. For example, when alone, babies might produce some of the sensations involved in maternal caregiving by patting their own cheeks and making soft vocal sounds resembling those made by their own mothers. Children thus become their own source of consolation and reinforcement.

It has been suggested that the more loving and nurturant the parent, the greater the feeling of loss in the absence of the caregiver, and hence the greater the identification. According to most of those who support this view of identification, such as Kagan (1958), Mussen and Rutherford (1963), and Sears (1953), the degree of identification with the parent depends on two other variables as well, the parent's power and the parent's similarity to the child. Because the powerful person controls resources and masters the environment, the child who identifies with the powerful parent gains similar feelings of control and mastery. The importance of the similarity of the model to the child is highlighted in the tendency of girls to identify with mothers and boys to identify with fathers. The responsive conditioning model proposes that as a consequence of identifying with the similar parent, children come to identify with their own gender.

The second model of social learning theory, the *operant conditioning model*, is also helpful in explaining the phenomenon of identification. This model suggests that behaviors that are approved of and rewarded by caregivers will be maintained and those that are disapproved of or punished will be less likely to occur. Since parents take pleasure in seeing their children imitate the behaviors of the caregiver, particularly the same-sex caregiver, it is these behaviors that are reinforced. The end result of the process is similar—the child begins to behave like significant caregivers—but in the operant conditioning model it is the *consequences* of the child's behavior (the approval and rewards) that are critical, not the associations made with a nurturant caregiver. Thus, according to the proponents of this theory, sex-role identification is acquired through social rewards for sex-appropriate behaviors, and their acquisition can be described by the same principles used to account for the learning of any other aspect of an individual's behavior (Mischel 1970). If the child is reinforced consistently for sex-appropriate behavior, both parental identification (or imitation) and sex-role identification (or imitation) should occur simultaneously. It is important to note that the responsive conditioning model and the operant conditioning model are not mutually exclusive; both probably operate in the same childrearing setting to produce identification with parents—especially with the same-sex parent.

Before leaving the topic of identification, two other theoretical perspectives should be mentioned that have special implications for sex-role identification, a *cognitive* theory and a *role* theory. The major theorist who proposes that sex-role identification originates in cognitive development is Kohlberg (1966); his theory is supported by the research of Emmerich and his colleagues (1976). Kohlberg views sex-role identification as evolving out of the child's acquisition of constancy of identity, the understanding that an object or person maintains the same identity in spite of variations in appearance, for example, that a girl will remain a girl even if her hair is cut very short. This understanding is acquired between three and seven years of age. Children develop a conception of themselves as having an unchanging identity through the same process by which they develop the conception of the constancy of physical objects; it is a part of their cognitive growth. Thus, variations in children's sex-role identity are seen as related for the most part to differences in age and intellectual maturity. Once the child's sexual identity is cognitively stabilized, it is extremely difficult to change. The boy *knows* he was a boy yesterday, is a boy today, and will be a boy tomorrow. In Kohlberg's view, identification with the same-sex parent is the result of the child's basic sexual identity, for the child will value objects and activities consistent with her or his gender identity as a result of the human tendency toward cognitive consistency (Abelson and Rosenberg 1958; Festinger 1957). The young boy thus says, "I am a boy and will always be one. Therefore, I want to do boy things. Doing boy things is rewarding." The child is then motivated to seek an individual who is most like herself or himself and to use that individual for a model. Some aspects of parent identification thus emerge from sexual identification and the child's active selection of models to imitate. Kohlberg (1966) summarizes his theory by stating that although identification with a like-sex person and the formation of sex-role values may be facilitated by appropriate same-sex parental behavior, the process seems to take place without the presence of the same-sex parent and under a variety of childrearing conditions.

One of the first theorists to use role theory to explain the origin of sex-role identification is Parsons (1955), who defines identification as the internalization of a reciprocal role relationship. He proposes that children learn at a very early age the sex role they are to play, as well as the reciprocal (opposite sex) role. Through the socialization process in which parents use the strategies discussed earlier to influence children's behaviors, boys are taught to play the instrumental role, that of disciplinarian, dispensing rewards and punishments, being competent and powerful, and a manipulator of the environment. Girls are taught to play the expressive role, being affectionate, conciliatory, supportive, passive, interpersonally sensitive. In interactions with both mothers and fathers, boys and girls learn each sex role by identifying with the same-sex parent, and at the same time learn the reciprocal or complementary role. Thus, one learns how to give orders partially by learning what is expected of the individual who takes orders; one learns to dispense affection partially by learning what is expected of the recipient of the affection.

Parsons's theory is expanded and elaborated by Johnson (1977), who postulates that it is primarily the father who teaches children their sex role. Fathers do this by treating boys and girls differently; mothers do not. Mothers give noncontingent love to boys and girls and by being nurturant, socialize both to be caring human beings. This nurturance also fosters an initial (asexual) identification with mothers. Heterosexual roles and a heterosexual identification are learned through interactions with fathers who give girls affection for being attractive but give boys rewards for being instrumentally competent. Fathers are more punishing and contingent with boys, treating them more as trainees who must develop initiative and independence. In contrast, fathers' attitudes toward girls have been called "appreciative" (Johnson 1977).

The importance of role theory in sex-role identification is also indicated in the work done by Money and his associates (Ehrhardt and Baker 1977; Money and Ehrhardt 1972; Money and Tucker 1975). These researchers conclude from their investigations of hermaphrodites (children whose physiological sex was ambiguous) that the sex role assigned to the child by the parents at birth determines the child's sex-role identification. Further, by two-and-one-half-years of age, the sexual self-concept is so firmly established that it is extremely difficult to change, even if the parents are initially in error in their role assignment. Money and Tucker refer to this as the closed gate phenomenon. In role terminology one could refer to the process as role assignment, or even altercasting. Parents determine the sex roles children shall play at their birth, and then proceed to interact with them appropriately as reciprocal role partners, thereby firmly establishing the sexual identity of the children. According to Money and Ehrhardt (1972), biological factors are not sufficient to determine gender identity. Rather, the variable that holds the balance of power appears to be the consistency of the experiences of being reared as a male or a female, especially in the early years.

Parental influence techniques used in the development of children's sex-role identification. When we examine the theories of sex-role identification in terms of our taxonomy of parental influence processes, we can see that different processes are emphasized, or at least implicated, in each theoretical approach. Social learning theorists emphasize modeling children's vicarious learning as they observe models being rewarded for behaving according to cultural norms of male and female behaviors, and parents' use of rewards and punishments, especially by fathers. In cognitive developmental theory, the use of reasoning and provision of space for exploratory behavior, both of which are believed to foster cognitive development (Goldschmid 1968; Radin 1972; White 1975), and hence sex-role identification, are important. Finally, in role theory the use of physical materials, such as toys and clothes appropriate for each sex, stating expectations of desired behavior, and direct instruction are each implicated. Evidence exists that men are particularly upset at feminine behavior in their sons (Goodenough 1957; Maccoby 1980), and teach them that men do not cry, or it is a man's job to fight for his country. In addition, fathers give instruction to their sons in skills considered to be masculine, such as playing baseball or football. Similarly, mothers often give daughters instruction in activities women are traditionally expected to perform, such as cooking, sewing, or knitting. The role of direct instruction in these sex-linked activities is so strong that parents are sometimes accused of neglecting their obligations when their offspring are deficient in these spheres. Of course, much indirect instruction also occurs, such as a father not including his daughter in a football game, or a mother not teaching her son to sew.

Before leaving the topic of sex-role identification it should be noted that new family forms may lead to new knowledge about the socialization process in this area of development. For example, recent research with families in which parents have partially reversed the traditional sex roles promises to shed considerable light on how parents influence sex-role development in their children. One of the first investigations of intact families in which the father is the primary caregiver and the mother works or attends school indicates that the sex-role orientation of the preschool-aged children involved is *not* different from that of children raised in traditional families (Radin 1978; 1980; in press). These findings suggest that more than mere parental modeling is responsible for the children's sex-role identification. One could speculate that these findings support a cognitive development theory in which the child's sex-role development is seen as relatively independent of parents' behavior. However, when a similar study was performed in Israel, the results were slightly different: here the girls in the partially role-reversed families had lower feminine scores, although still in the feminine range (Radin and Sagi, in press; Sagi, in press; Sagi and Reshef 1981). For boys there was no difference between those raised in traditional or nontraditional homes. The data offer some support for Johnson's (1977) reciprocal role theory of children's sex-role development. It appears that the nontraditional men may not have been treating their daughters as traditional females and thus the girls' sex-role development was somewhat different from that of daughters of more stereotyped fathers. Perhaps the difference in the U.S. and Israeli findings can be explained in terms of the sex-role orientations of the men in the two countries. In America, the caregiver-fathers were as masculine as their traditional peers. Although the Israeli nontraditional fathers were not assessed directly, there were indications that they more closely resembled their counterparts in Australia, who have been reported as *less* masculine than men whose wives reared children (Russell 1978). If so, these Israeli fathers may have elicited less feminine behavior from their daughters. Further research is much needed to clarify these complex issues.

Parental influence on children's cognitive development

Numerous studies have shown that parental reinforcement or nurturance correlates significantly with the intellectual functioning and growth of the preschool child (Bayley and Schaefer 1964; Bradley and Caldwell 1976; Radin 1970; 1971). It is theorized that parental warmth fosters identification with the parent, according to social learning theory, and hence increases the likelihood that the child will imitate the adult's problem-solving strategies and vocabulary as well as other behaviors. Through such modeling, cognitive development may be stimulated. It is also postulated that positive responses from parents may lead young children to perceive the environment as generally reinforcing, and this belief may foster children's tendency to explore the world about them. Such investigative activities should foster children's intellectual growth, according to Piagetian theory (Goldschmid 1968; Piaget 1972). Supportive of the identification hypothesis of cognitive development are the findings that maternal warmth is particularly relevant to the cognitive growth of preschool-aged girls, and paternal warmth to preschool-aged boys (Epstein and Radin 1975; Jordan, Radin, and Epstein 1975; Radin 1972; Radin and Epstein 1975).

It has also been found (Baumrind 1967) that nurturance accompanied by demands for mature, independent behavior fosters competence in preschool-aged children and at three and four years of age, this competence is highly correlated with intelligence. As discussed earlier, Baumrind uses the term *authoritative* to describe parents who combine positive reinforcement with a willingness to direct the child. She confines the term *authoritarian* to parents who are primarily restrictive and intrusive. In Baumrind's studies (Baumrind 1967; 1971), as well as those of other researchers (Bayley and Schaefer 1964; Radin 1970; 1972; Radin and Epstein 1975; Radin and Glasser 1972), parental authoritarianism, restrictiveness, or punitiveness is found to hinder the development of intellectual competence in young children, especially in lower-SES families. For example, in a study of 180 White families with preschool-aged children it was found that for lower-class boys, the only father behavior associated with cognitive measures of the children was verbal restrictiveness, and the relationship was negative (Radin and Epstein 1975). For working-class and middle-class boys however, various paternal behaviors reflective of nurturance were positively linked with cognitive competence in the children. In contrast, some paternal abrasiveness was found by Baumrind (1979) to foster self-direction or effectiveness in young girls, since it stimulated assertive interaction with the environment too often missing in young females. According to Baumrind, biology and society conspire to emphasize passivity in young girls.

In several studies, parental explaining of restrictions, a process similar to reasoning, and parental consulting with the child, another appeal to reason, were associated with the intellectual development of the preschooler (Baumrind 1967; Epstein and Radin 1975; Radin 1970). This suggests that the parental strategy of rationality as well as the use of sanctions and stating expectations to the child influence cognitive development. There is also evidence that the presence of stimulating materials in the home is associated with enhanced mental functioning of the preschool child, particularly in lower-SES families (Bradley and Caldwell 1976; Elardo, Bradley, and Caldwell 1975; Radin 1969). In addition, at least one investigation suggests that explicit training of boys by their fathers in the academic realm has a positive impact on the child's subsequent performance on intelligence tests (Radin 1973).

Although one could debate whether watching TV should be labeled a vicarious learning experience specifically instigated by parents, it has been found that children who watched *Sesame Street* at least two times per week displayed significant gains on a verbal intelligence test, the Peabody Picture Vocabulary Test (Ball and Bogartz 1977). It is suggested by the investigators that the effects could be even more dramatic if mothers were to watch the programs with the children

and discuss the content with them afterward. Perhaps
tivities by both parents would serve to add reinforceₙ.
vicarious learning experience.

Summary

In sum, we have ample evidence that parents influence their young children, but we still have much to learn about the particular processes by which this influence is transmitted. It is apparent that different processes affect the various aspects of the child's functioning in different ways. Why this is so is not always clear. We also have much to learn about how the effects of each socialization technique may differ for children with particular types of temperaments. For example, is modeling, a rather nondirective strategy, as effective with the difficult child as with the easy child? Does the slow-to-warm-up child require more than a physical setting conducive to exploration to start investigating the environment? Thomas, Chess, and Birch (1968) suggest that mere exposure to an opportunity may be insufficient for these children. And do difficult children elicit negative sanctions more often than positive reinforcement as a consequence of their generally negative disposition? Bell (1968) implies that this is likely.

Clearly we are just beginning to untangle the influence of activities by parents and the influence of their own personality characteristics on their offspring. We are also becoming increasingly aware of the need to consider the influence of the societal context on the family's functioning. As a result of both factors, research in child development in the coming decade may look very different from that which has been conducted in the past 50 years.

References

Abelson, R. P., and Rosenberg, M. J. "Symbolic Psycho-Logic: A Model of Attitude Cognition." *Behavioral Science* 3 (1958): 1–13.

Ball, S., and Bogartz, G. A. "Research on Sesame Street: Some Implications for Compensatory Education." In *Comtemporary Readings in Child Psychology,* ed. E. M. Hetherington and R. D. Parke. New York: McGraw-Hill, 1977.

Bandura, A., and Walters, R. H. *Adolescent Aggression.* New York: Ronald Press, 1959.

Baumrind, D. "Childcare Practices Anteceding Three Patterns of Preschool Behavior." *Genetic Psychology Monographs* 75 (1967): 43–88.

Baumrind, D. "Current Patterns of Parental Authority." *Developmental Psychology Monographs* 4 (1971): 1–103.

Baumrind, D. "Current Issues in Socialization." Paper presented at meetings of the Society for Research in Child Development, San Francisco, March 16, 1979.

Bayley, N., and Schaefer, E. S. "Correlations of Maternal and Child Behaviors with the Development of Mental Abilities: Data from the Berkeley Growth Study." *Monographs of the Society for Research in Child Development* 29 (1964). Serial No. 97.

Bell, R. Q. "A Reinterpretation of the Direction of Affects in Studies of Socialization." *Psychological Review* 75 (1968): 81–95.

Bell, R. Q. "Contributions of Human Infants to Caregiving and Social Interaction." In *The Effect of the Infant on Its Caregiver,* ed. M. Lewis and L. A. Rosenblum. New York: Wiley, 1974.

Bing, E. "The Effect of Childrearing Practices on Development of Differential Cognitive Abilities." *Child Development* 34 (1963): 631–648.

Bradley, R. H., and Caldwell, B. M. "The Relation of Infants' Home Environment to Mental Test Performance at Fifty-Four Months: A Follow-Up Study." *Child Development* 47 (1976): 1172–1174.

Brazelton, T. B. *Infants and Mothers: Differences in Development.* New York: Dell, 1969.

Brazelton, T. B. "Neonatal Behavioral Assessment Scale." *Clinics in Developmental Medicine. No. 50.* Philadelphia: Lippincott, 1973.

Brazelton, T. B. *Toddlers and Parents.* New York: Dell, 1974.

Brazelton, T. B. "Importance of New Techniques of Neonatal Assessment." Paper presented at The American Association for the Advancement of Science Meeting, Denver, February 22, 1977.

Clarke-Stewart, K. A. "Interaction Between Mothers and Their Young Children: Characteristics and Consequences." *Monographs of the Society for Research in Child Development* 38 (1973). Serial No. 153.

Clarke-Stewart, K. A. "And Daddy Makes Three: The Father's Impact on the Mother and Young Child." *Child Development* 49 (1978): 466–478.

Cochran, M. M., and Brassard, J. A. "Child Development and Personal Social Networks." *Child Development* 50 (1979): 601–616.

Dweck, C. S. "The Role of Expectations and Attributions in the Alleviation of Learned Helplessness." *Journal of Personality and Social Psychology* 31 (1975): 674–685.

Dweck, C. S., and Gilliard, D. "Expectancy Statements As Determinants of Reactions to Failure: Sex Differences in Persistence and Expectancy Change." *Journal of Personality and Social Psychology* 32 (1975): 1077–1084.

Dweck, C. S., and Reppucci, N. D. "Learned Helplessness and Reinforcement Responsibility in Children." *Journal of Personality and Social Psychology* 25 (1973): 109–116.

Dyk, R. B., and Witkin, H. A. "Family Experiences Related to the Development of Differentiation in Children." *Child Development* 36 (1965): 21–55.

Ehrhardt, A. A., and Baker, S. W. "Fetal Androgens, Human Central Nervous System Differentiation, and Behavior Sex Differences." In *Contemporary Readings in Child Psychology,* ed. E. M. Hetherington and R. D. Parke. New

York: McGraw-Hill, 1977.

Elardo, R.; Bradley, R.; and Caldwell, B. M. "The Relation of Infants' Home Environments to Mental Test Performance from Six to Thirty-Six Months: A Longitudinal Analysis." *Child Development* 46 (1975): 71–76.

Emmerich, W.; Goldman, K. S.; Kirsh, B.; and Sharabany, R. *Development of Gender Constancy in Economically Disadvantaged Children.* Report of the Educational Testing Service, Princeton, N.J., 1976.

Epstein, S., and Radin, N. "Motivational Components Related to Father Behavior and Cognitive Functioning." *Child Development* 46 (1975): 831–839.

Festinger, L. A. *A Theory of Cognitive Dissonance.* Evanston, Ill.: Row, Peterson, 1957.

Festinger, L. A., and Carlsmith, J. "Cognitive Consequences of Forced Compliance." *Journal of Abnormal and Social Psychology* 58 (1959): 202–210.

Gold, D., and Andres, D. "Comparisons of Adolescent Children with Employed and Non-Employed Mothers." *Merrill-Palmer Quarterly* 24 (1978): 243–254.

Goldberg, S. "Social Competence in Infancy: A Model of Parent-Infant Interaction." *Merrill-Palmer Quarterly* 23 (1977): 163–177.

Goldschmid, M. L. "The Relation of Conservation to Emotional and Environmental Aspects of Development." *Child Development* 39 (1968): 579–589.

Goodenough, E. W. "Interest in Persons As an Aspect of Sex Difference in the Early Years." *Genetic Psychology Monographs* 55 (1957): 287–323.

Hess, R. D. "Social Class and Ethnic Influences upon Socialization." In *Carmichael's Manual of Child Psychology. Vol. II.* 3rd ed., ed. P. H. Mussen. New York: Wiley, 1970.

Hetherington, E. M. "The Effects of Familial Variables in Sex Typing, on Parent-Child Similarity and on Imitation in Children." In *Minnesota Symposium on Child Psychology. Vol. I,* ed. J. P. Hill. Minneapolis: University of Minnesota Press, 1967.

Hetherington, E. M., and Parke, R. D. *Child Psychology: A Contemporary Viewpoint.* 2nd ed. New York: McGraw-Hill, 1979.

Hoffman, M. L. "Moral Development." In *Carmichael's Manual of Child Psychology. Vol. II.* 3rd ed., ed. P. H. Mussen. New York: Wiley, 1970.

Iannotti, R. J. "The Many Faces of Empathy." Paper presented at the biennial meeting of the Society for Research in Child Development, Denver, April 1, 1975.

Inkeles, A. "Society, Social Structure, and Child Socialization." In *Socialization and Society,* ed. J. A. Clausen. Boston: Little, Brown, 1973.

Johnson, M. M. "Fathers, Mothers and Sex Typing." In *Contemporary Readings in Child Psychology,* ed. E. M. Hetherington and R. D. Parke. New York: McGraw-Hill, 1977.

Jordan, B.; Radin, N.; and Epstein, A. S. "Paternal Behavior and Intellectual Functioning in Preschool Boys and Girls." *Developmental Psychology* 11 (1975): 407–408.

Kagan, J. "The Concept of Identification." *Psychological Review* 65 (1958): 296–305.

Kohlberg, L. "A Cognitive-Developmental Analysis of Children's Sex Role Concepts and Attitudes." In *The Development of Sex Differences*, ed. E. Maccoby. Stanford, Calif.: Stanford University Press, 1966.

Maccoby, E. *Social Development, Psychological Growth, and Parent-Child Relations*. New York: Harcourt Brace Jovanovich, 1980.

Meichenbaum, D. *Cognitive-Behavior Modification*. New York: Plenum, 1977.

Mischel, W. "Sex-Typing and Socialization." In *Carmichael's Manual of Child Psychology. Vol. II*. 3rd ed., ed. P. H. Mussen. New York: Wiley, 1970.

Money, J., and Ehrhardt, A. A. *Man and Woman, Boy and Girl*. Baltimore, Md.: Johns Hopkins University Press, 1972.

Money, J., and Tucker, P. *Sexual Signatures*. Boston: Little, Brown, 1975.

Mussen, P., and Rutherford, E. "Parent-Child Relations and Parental Personality in Relation to Young Children's Sex Role Preferences." *Child Development* 34 (1963): 589–607.

Osofsky, J. D. "Neonatal Characteristics and Mother-Infant Interaction in Two Observational Situations." *Child Development* 47 (1976): 1138–1147.

Parsons, T. "Family Structure and the Socialization of the Child." In *Family Socialization and Interaction Process*, ed. T. P. Parsons and R. F. Bales. New York: Free Press, 1955.

Patterson, G. R., and Guillon, E. M. *Living with Children*. Champaign, Ill.: Research Press, 1968.

Patterson, G. R.; Shaw, D. A.; and Ebner, M. J. "Teachers, Peers, and Parents As Agents of Change in the Classroom." In *Modifying Deviant Social Behaviors in Various Classroom Settings*, ed. F. A. M. Benson. Eugene: University of Oregon, 1969.

Piaget, J. "Development and Learning." In *Readings in Child Behavior and Development*. 3rd ed., ed. C. S. Lavatelli and F. Stendler. New York: Harcourt Brace Jovanovich, 1972.

Radin, N. "The Impact of a Kindergarten Home Counseling Program." *Exceptional Children* 36 (1969): 251–256.

Radin, N. "Childrearing Antecedents of Cognitive Development in Lower-Class Preschool Children." *Dissertation Abstracts International* 30 (1970): 4364B. (University Microfilms No. 70–4170)

Radin, N. "Maternal Warmth Achievement Motivation, and Cognitive Functioning in Lower-Class Preschool Children." *Child Development* 42 (1971): 1560–1565.

Radin, N. "Father-Child Interaction and the Intellectual Functioning of Four-Year-Old Boys." *Developmental Psychology* 6 (1972): 353–361.

Radin, N. "Observed Paternal Behaviors As Antecedents of Intellectual Functioning in Young Boys." *Developmental Psychology* 8 (1973): 369–376.

Radin, N "Observed Maternal Behavior with Four-Year-Old Boys and Girls in Lower-Class Families." *Child Development* 45 (1974): 1126–1131.

Radin, N. "The Role of the Father in Cognitive/Academic and Intellectual Development." In *The Role of the Father in Child Development*, ed. M. E. Lamb. New York: Wiley, 1976.

Radin, N. "Childrearing Fathers in Intact Families with Preschoolers." Paper presented at the annual meeting of the American Psychological Association, Toronto, September 1978.

Radin, N. "Childrearing Fathers in Intact Families: An Exploration of Some Antecedents and Consequences." Paper presented at a study group on "The Role of the Father on Child Development, Social Policy, and the Law." Sponsored by the Society for Research in Child Development and the University of Haifa, Haifa, Israel, July 14, 1980.

Radin, N. "Wives of Childrearing Men." Paper presented at the biennial meeting of the Society for Research in Child Development, Boston, April 1981.

Radin, N. "Rolesharing Fathers and Preschoolers." In *Non-Traditional Families: Parenting and Child Development*, ed. M. E. Lamb. Hillsdale, N. J.: Lawrence Erlbaum Associates, in press.

Radin, N., and Epstein, A. S. "Observed Paternal Behavior and the Intellectual Functioning of Preschool Boys and Girls." Paper presented at meetings of the Society for Research in Child Development, Denver, April 1975.

Radin, N., and Glasser, P. "The Utility of the Parental Attitude Research Instrument for Intervention Programs with Low-Income Families." *Journal of Marriage and the Family* 34 (1972): 448–458.

Radin, N., and Sagi, A. "Childrearing Fathers in Intact Families in Israel and the U.S.A." *Merrill-Palmer Quarterly*, in press.

Rheingold, H. L., and Cook, K. U. "The Contents of Boys' and Girls' Rooms As an Index of Parents' Behavior." *Child Development* 46 (1975): 459–463.

Roe, A., and Siegelman, M. "A Parent-Child Relations Questionnaire." *Child Development* 34 (1963): 355–369.

Rose, S. D. "Group-Training of Parents As Behavior Modifiers." *Social Work* 19 (1974): 156–162.

Rubin, K. H., and Schneider, F. W. "The Relationships Between Moral Judgement, Egocentrism and Altruistic Behavior." *Child Development* 43 (1973): 661–665.

Russell, G. "The Father Role and Its Relation to Masculinity, Femininity, and Androgyny." *Child Development* 49 (1978): 1174–1181.

Sagi, A. "Antecedents and Consequences of Various Degrees of Paternal Involvement in Childrearing: The Israeli Project." In *Non-Traditional Families: Parenting and Child Development*, ed. M. E. Lamb. Hillsdale, N. J.: Lawrence Erlbaum Associates, in press.

Sagi, A., and Reshef, R. "Degrees of Paternal Involvement in Childrearing in Intact Families in Israel: Antecedents and Effects." Paper presented at the biennial meeting of the Society for Research in Child Development, Boston, April 1981.

Sameroff, A. J. "Early Influences on Development: Fact or Fancy?" In *Contemporary Readings in Child Psychology*, ed. E. M. Hetherington and R. D. Parke. New York: McGraw-Hill, 1977.

Schaefer, E. S. "Converging Conceptual Models for Maternal Behavior and for Child Behavior." In *Parental Attitudes and Child Behavior*, ed. J. Glidewell.

New York: Charles C. Thomas, 1961.

Sears, P. S. "Childrearing Factors Related to the Playing of Sex-Typed Roles." *American Psychologist* 8 (1953): 431.

Sears, R. R.; Rau, L.; and Alpert, R. *Identification and Childrearing*. Stanford, Calif.: Stanford University Press, 1965.

Smith, J. M., and Smith, E. P. *Child Management: A Program for Parents*. Ann Arbor, Mich.: Ann Arbor Publishers, 1966.

Thomas, A., and Chess, S. *Temperament and Development*. New York: Brunner/Mazel, 1977.

Thomas, A.; Chess, S.; and Birch, H. G. *Temperament and Behavior Disorders in Children*. New York: New York University Press, 1968.

Thomas, A.; Chess, S.; and Birch, H. G. "The Origin of Personality." *Scientific American* 223 (1970): 102–109.

White, B. L. "Critical Influences in the Origins of Competence." *Merrill-Palmer Quarterly* 21 (1975): 243–266.

Wittes, G., and Radin, N. *Helping Your Child to Learn: The Reinforcement Approach*. San Rafael, Calif.: Dimensions Publishing, 1969.

Yarrow, M. R., and Waxler, C. Unpublished manuscript, National Institute of Mental Health, 1978.

Zigler, E., and Child, I. L. "Socialization." In *The Handbook of Social Psychology. Vol. III*. 2nd ed., ed. G. Lindzey and E. Aronsen. Reading, Mass.: Addison-Wesley, 1969.

Cluster II

Language and thinking: understanding children's understanding

<table>
<tr><td rowspan="2" style="font-size:3em">5</td><td>**Adults' talk and children's language development**</td></tr>
<tr><td>*Frances Fuchs Schachter and Amy A. Strage*</td></tr>
<tr><td rowspan="2" style="font-size:3em">6</td><td>**Social perspective-taking in young children**</td></tr>
<tr><td>*Kenneth H. Rubin and Barbara Everett*</td></tr>
<tr><td rowspan="2" style="font-size:3em">7</td><td>**The foundations of knowledge: concept development in the young child**</td></tr>
<tr><td>*Henry M. Wellman*</td></tr>
</table>

everal new themes are highlighted in this group of chapters. One is a
sharpening of our understanding of how adults can assist children in
their learning. Schachter and Strage demonstrate how parents, other
caregivers, and even other children, adapt their language to the linguistic level of the child learning to talk. We also see how effective
caregivers update their style of interaction in response to the changing skills of
the child.

Despite the importance of other people in this process of language learning,
research on the complexity of the child's achievement also shows that children
must construct their own system for producing and comprehending language
and other cognitive functions. Rubin and Everett emphasize the skillfulness of
the young child in constructing these systems of knowledge in the areas of social
perspective-taking. Whereas traditional accounts of this development emphasize the dramatic improvements in skill that are seen with increasing age, recent
research points to how competent even very young children are, leading us to
supplement our previous inventories of young children's lack of skills with an
appreciation of their abilities. As Rubin and Everett note, this new view has
developed in part because of our increasing sophistication in assessment.

Wellman also illustrates this new view of the competent child, actively constructing both physical and social knowledge—sometimes with the help of
adults, but often through her or his own efforts. He reports too on our greatly
increased awareness of the significance of children's thinking *about* thinking,
sometimes called *metacognition*. But young children only gradually acquire the
ability to plan their own behavior ("What can I tell my friend so he'll feel better?") or reflect on past events ("Did I understand that question?"), or think
about the thoughts of others.

All three chapters emphasize how children's social interactions with both
peers and adults provide a context for intellectual development, while acknowl-
edging how individual an accomplishment each child's learning must be.

Frances Fuchs Schachter
Amy A. Strage

5 Adults' talk and children's language development

Until the past decade, research on language development has focused on what children say, paying scant attention to the other half of the conversation, to what it is that others say to children. At times, it seemed as if the children developed language in a social vacuum, with no assistance from others. In recent years this other half of the conversation has come under intensive investigation as researchers have begun to focus their tape recorders on parents, teachers, and even older children as they talk to the young child developing language. For example, by 1977, this area of research had matured sufficiently to warrant compilation of a major book, *Talking to Children* (Snow and Ferguson 1977). Research on this topic bears directly on the question of how caregivers might help foster young children's language learning.

We talk in a special way to young children—altering our ordinary speech—and this special way of talking may contribute significantly to the child's language development. It may even be that children cannot learn to talk without it.

When linguists identify a special way of speaking, they call it a linguistic code. We all hear and use many different linguistic codes. For example, newscasters have a special way of speaking, as do preachers. The linguistic code we use when chatting with friends is different from the one we use when talking with a group of strangers. There is evidence that children as young as age four have begun to acquire some code-switching skills.

Linguists call the code we use in talking to young children *baby talk,* but we will use *talk-to-young-children* (TYCh) for the following reasons: First, the word *baby* commonly refers to infants, not to toddlers and preschoolers, yet most of the research on talk-to-young-children has centered on children who range in age from one to three years. The toddler phase is the time of the most rapid language development (by the time children are three or four they have generally mastered the basic rules of their language) and it is in speech to toddlers that we are most likely to use the special features of talk-to-young-children. Second, although *baby talk* is a technical term, it is commonly used, so most people have some preconceptions about its meaning, and for some the term may even carry negative connotations. For example, some caregivers express concern that using baby talk rather than ordinary speech may retard rather than facilitate the young child's language development.

Although talk-to-young-children occurs throughout the world, it is used in large part without people being aware of it except for a few of its salient features, like talking in a high-pitched voice or saying words like *tummy* instead of *stomach*. More than 100 ways that we alter our ordinary speech when we talk to the young language-learning child have been identified by researchers (Brown 1977).

The procedure used to detect these distinct characteristics of talk-to-young-children is to observe someone, such as a mother, talking to a language-learning child. This same speaker is then observed talking with an older child or adult. Those features that appear far more often in talk to the language-learning child than they do in talk to others are viewed as distinct features of the talk-to-young-children code.

This code has been observed in use by mothers and fathers (Gleason 1975); by teachers, whether experienced or not (Schachter et al. 1976); by parents and nonparents (Snow 1972); and even among older children talking to younger ones (Shatz and Gelman 1973). Four-year-olds use features of talk-to-young-children when they are speaking to toddlers, and they use more of its features when talking to younger toddlers than to older toddlers. Further, children without siblings are as adept as those with brothers or sisters. That children as well as adults use this linguistic code is important because there are cultures where children, often older siblings, assume the major responsibility for childrearing.

Although young children seem to elicit the talk-to-young-children code from almost everyone, most of the research has been done with mothers or other adult caregivers. In some work the code has been described as "Motherese" (Newport 1976). Although we will refer to the speakers of talk-to-young-children as adults or caregivers, the reader should keep in mind that the use of this linguistic code is not limited to these adults.

Theories of language development

Investigators have long been intrigued by the uncanny ability of children to learn to speak and understand their native tongue in just a few short years. Think of how difficult it is to learn a second language in adulthood, and then consider a two-year-old who is cheerfully acquiring language at a dazzling speed while developing so many other skills at the same time.

Many theories of language acquisition have been proposed to explain this phenomenon, from the *environmental* position of behaviorists (Skinner 1957), who assign the key role in language learning to adult teaching, to the *nativist* view of some linguists (e.g., Chomsky 1965) who question whether parents and teachers contribute anything significant to language acquisition while attributing the key forces to inborn capacities of the child. For the behaviorist, language learning is no different from learning any other behavior. Language is simply verbal behavior, and learning, as always, depends on imitation of adult models, successive approximation to adult forms, and reinforcement. Preschool language intervention programs like those of Bereiter and Engelmann (1966) or Becker, Engelmann, and Thomas (1971) typify this behaviorist approach. In such programs, teachers use traditional strategies of direct instruction, including modeling (for example, "This is a box."), eliciting imitations of the model ("Say, 'This is a box.' "), test questions ("What color is this?"), reinforcement of successes, and correction of mistakes.

Linguists and developmental psycholinguists—psychologists who study language development—question the behavioristic view on the grounds of both theory and research. They argue that language is not like many other behaviors because it is *rule-governed*. We are all familiar with many of the rules of grammar, for example, that the past tense of many words is formed by adding *ed*. But there are many other grammatical rules that we may not be aware of, such as that it is proper to say *a book,* but improper to say *a water.* Apart from these rules of grammar there are many others, such as rules for combining sounds and rules for making conversations. Linguists argue that the heart of the language-learning process involves discovering and mastering these abstract or general rules, not merely imitating those particular sounds that have been heard or of being rewarded for particular utterances. Only through such rules can it be explained how the child comes to be able to speak and understand an infinite number of sentences, most of which have never been said or heard before.

Considerable evidence has accumulated to support the linguistic view as accounting for the central achievements of language acquisition. Probably the most convincing evidence that language learning is fundamentally a matter of learning rules comes from the observations of overgeneralization of these rules. Often when children are learning a particular grammatical rule, they will apply it even in cases where their language makes an exception to the rule. Thus, for example, English-speaking children learning the past tense rule for adding *ed* will often say *goed,* instead of the exception to the rule *went;* or they will say *breaked* instead of the exception *broke.* Since words like *goed* and *breaked* are never used by adult speakers, we are certain that children cannot have learned them either by explicit reinforcement from adults or by more informal imitation of adult speech. Instead, children create these words on the basis of overgeneralizing the rules they are learning. Only later do they learn that such words as *went* and *broke* are exceptions to these rules.

Other evidence casts doubt on the behavioristic position as the best account of language learning. If reinforcement were the key factor in language learning, then we would expect to be able to hear parents of young children approving of good grammar and correcting or disapproving of incorrect grammar. In fact, they seem to ignore the child's grammar altogether; and when they do correct, they attend to the content of what the child is saying instead, especially its accuracy or truthfulness. Schachter's (1979) study of 24,000 utterances in mothers' everyday talk to their toddlers showed only one grammatical correction; the child said "tooths" and the mother corrected saying "teeth." Many other investigators have reported similar findings (Brown, Cazden, and Bellugi 1969). Parents rarely correct their children's grammar; yet somehow children learn the rules of grammar, and do so in large part before entering first grade.

Some have suggested that children learn proper linguistic usage because they are more likely to be understood and thus more apt to get what they want. In fact, when children are learning language, they talk primarily about the *here and now*, about what they are doing at the moment or what is around them, so that the meaning of what they say is usually obvious from the context. Relying on context, caregivers are very good at deciphering what their children are saying regardless of how well formed the utterance is. For example, when the child says "mi" while reaching for the bottle, mothers react as if the child has said "I want some milk." As Slobin (1975) has pointed out, mothers are apparently too involved in interacting with their children to pay much attention to the linguistic form of their utterances.

What about the role of imitation? Imitation obviously contributes to language acquisition; French children learn French and Chinese children learn Chinese. Children whose physical capacity to speak is so impaired that they are unable to imitate have learned to understand language (Lenneberg 1962). Thus direct imitation (at least in a form visible to others) does not seem essential for language learning. Further, when normal children do imitate, they generally reduce the utterance they have heard to their own level of mastery. For example, when children at the stage of two-word sentences imitate "Throw the red ball to me," they will usually say "Throw ball." Research suggests that children cannot be forced to imitate; they do so when they are ready. Especially in the early phases of mastery of a language skill, the particular context influences how much a child will imitate (Bloom, Hood, and Lightbown 1974).

If language acquisition is an active process of discovering the rules of language, does this imply that it is wholly dependent on inborn biological mechanisms, that parents and teachers contribute little or nothing to the process? Although nativists acknowledge that children need to hear speech to learn to talk, they claim that adult speech is so flawed that no child could learn the general rules of language merely by listening to it.

This argument has been questioned by language development researchers. Developmental psycholinguists have documented that speech addressed to young children is not flawed as is some talk to adults. On the contrary, when they talk to young children, adults make a vast number of alterations in their speech and, most important, many of these alterations are exactly of the kind that might help the child learn language.

Talk-to-young-children seems to assist the child's language development in three basic ways.

(1) The adult's use of talk-to-young-children is correlated with the pace of language development in the child. As noted earlier, adults use it most in talk to

toddlers ages one to three, when the child's language acquisition is most rapid. Table 5.1 summarizes the rapid pace of language development during these early years. As the child's rate of language development slackens, most of the modifications of talk-to-young-children begin to disappear from the adult's speech and those that do persist tend to occur to a far lesser degree. For example, the rate of adults' talk-to-young-children (during free play) is much slower than in their ordinary talk to adults. Adult speech is significantly slower in talk to toddlers (69.2 words per minute), than to five-year-olds, (86.2 words per minute). Adults' talk to other adults is twice as fast as talk to toddlers (132.0 words per minute) (Broen 1972).

(2) Not only do adults make gross adjustments in their speech that can be observed in comparing their talk to toddlers and to five-year-olds, but they also make fine adjustments (Schachter 1979). For example, as toddlers progress from one- to three-word sentences, adults talk to them in longer and longer sentences. Also as toddlers' language comprehension improves, adults are less likely to

Table 5.1.
Development of language.

Age in months	Characteristics of vocalization and language
4	Coos and chuckles.
6–9	Babbles; duplicates common sounds; produces sounds such as "ma" or "da."
12–18	A small number of words; follows simple commands and responds to no; uses expressive jargon.
18–21	From about 20 words at 18 months to about 200 words at 21; points to many more objects; comprehends simple questions; forms 2-word phrases.
24–27	Vocabulary of 300 to 400 words; has 2- to 3-word phrases; uses prepositions and pronouns.
30–33	Fastest increase in vocabulary; 3- to 4-word sentences are common; word order, phrase structure, and grammatical agreement approximate the language of surroundings, but many utterances are unlike anything an adult would say.
36–39	Vocabulary of 1000 words or more; well-formed sentences using complex grammatical rules, although certain rules have not yet been fully mastered; grammatical mistakes are much less frequent; about 90 percent comprehensible.

Adapted from Lenneberg (1966).

repeat themselves (Cross 1977).

If the adult's use of these speech adjustments are to assist in learning language, they must be finely tuned to the child's progress in language mastery. Were adult speech too simple, children might hear nothing new to learn. Were adult speech too advanced, children might not be ready to benefit from it.

(3) Many of the special characteristics of talk-to-young-children appear to be plausible teaching strategies. As researchers have identified each of these characteristics, they have speculated on how each might serve to assist language development. As we describe these characteristics of TYCh, the reader is asked to keep in mind that all of these characteristics are not applied to all young children all of the time. Caregivers use different degrees and patterns of adjustment of their speech depending on the age and linguistic stage of the child (Cross 1977; Schachter 1979).

Characteristics of talk-to-young-children

The sounds of TYCh: prosody and phonology

Probably the most noticeable features of talk-to-young-children are its high pitch and the wider range of pitch from high to low (Garnica 1977). TYCh is also much slower than ordinary speech, as we have noted. There is a tendency to pause at the end of sentences in TYCh, whereas pauses are far more unpredictable in talk to adults (Broen 1972).

How could these characteristics of TYCh help the child learn language? The higher pitch could attract the child's attention by signaling that the utterance is meant for the child, not for others, and variations in pitch might maintain the child's attention. The slower speed of delivery may serve to ensure that the information the child needs to absorb is transmitted at a manageable rate. The placement of pauses can help the child segment the flow of speech into analyzable grammatical units.

Just as the general pitch and rhythm of TYCh are different from ordinary speech, so are the specific sounds or phonemes (Ferguson 1977). Not only do adults use a restricted set of phonemes in TYCh, but they tend to pronounce each sound more clearly (Newport 1976). Further, when the sounds are complex, adults tend to simplify them. For example, in such typical TYCh words as *tummy* (instead of *stomach*) or *s'eepy* (instead of *sleepy*), adults omit one of the two initial consonants. All of these restrictions and simplifications seem to present children with clearer, more manageable material as they try to decipher the rules of their language.

The grammar of TYCh: syntax

The grammar of TYCh is also simplified. Many studies have shown that adults speak in shorter sentences to the language-learning child than to other adults. The average length of sentence (mean length of utterance) is widely viewed as an overall index of grammatical complexity. Many examples of grammatical simplification in TYCh have been noted. Sentences contain fewer clauses. There are also fewer words before the main verb so that the subject of the sentence is easier to keep in mind as the child tries to understand the entire sentence (e.g., "Jamie is coming over today," rather than "Your friend Jamie is coming over today."). Moreover, the grammar of TYCh is not only simpler, but it is also more correct. The incidence of ungrammatical sentences is much lower than in speech to adults (Newport 1976; Phillips 1973; Snow 1972).

What is the possible advantage for the child of these grammatical adjustments? The shorter sentences probably help maintain the child's attention. The grammatical simplification makes it possible for the child to deal with a limited number of rules at any one time. The lower incidence of ungrammatical sentences provides the child with a "cleaner" sample from which to extract grammatical rules.

The content of TYCh: semantics

Adults use a limited vocabulary and repeat words more often when they talk to the language-learning child. They also tend to avoid words that change in meaning, like the pronouns *I* or *you*. These pronouns are relative terms; their meaning depends upon who is talking. By contrast, names are absolute terms. To avoid using complicated relative pronouns, adults often refer to people by name, for example, as in "Mommy's making lunch," rather than "I'm making lunch" (Phillips 1973).

The topic of conversation is also limited. Like the talk of young children itself, adult's talk-to-young-children is concerned with what is happening at the moment, not with the past or the future, the far away, or the abstract. Few adults, for example, would talk to a toddler about the last presidential election or about a trip to the moon. Even fantasy play involves pretending real objects are present. Adults also tend to express the same sort of meanings as children spontaneously express, such as the possessive ("That's Daddy's") or the locative ("It's over there") (Snow 1977a).

If children are to extract the rules of their language from the talk that is addressed to them, it seems crucial that they understand what is being said. These findings on the content of talk-to-young-children indicate that adults make every effort to be understood. They appear to adjust their talk to the cognitive level of the child, using words and expressing meaning at the child's level of comprehension.

Communication and conversation in TYCh: discourse

Adults' conversations with young children differ in both form and function from their conversations with other adults. In form, TYCh is highly repetitive and interlaced with questions. Adults repeat their own utterances as well as those of the child. The incidence of these features in talk to toddlers is high, about 18 percent for repetitions of oneself, 10 percent for repetitions of the child, and 30 percent for questions (Newport 1976; Schachter 1979; Snow 1972).

Adults may provide either partial or complete repetitions, as well as para-

phrases of their previous statements, such as "Let's go now. . . . Come on."
Exact repetitions may assist children who miss a grammatical element the first
time the utterance is said. Partial repetitions may assist the child in breaking the
sentence into its grammatical parts, as did a mother recorded by Snow (1972):
"Put the red truck in the box now. The red truck. No, the red truck. In the box."
Paraphrasing demonstrates that the same meaning can be expressed in many
different ways, a fundamental feature of all languages and a characteristic all
children must learn. It may even be that when we express the same thought in
two or more ways, one way is more linguistically advanced than the other(s) and
shows the child how to express the same thought with more mature language
(Cross 1977).

Beside their self-repetition, adults' repetition and paraphrasing of the child's
utterances might also facilitate language learning. Often adults *expand* the
child's short utterances by adding parts of speech that the child has omitted. For
example, the child might say, "Dolly sleeping" and the mother might respond
"Dolly is sleeping in her bed." These expansions might call attention to what the
child has yet to learn. It is interesting to note that adult's expansions have been
the subject of more research than any other feature of TYCh, possibly because
they were one of the first such features identified (Brown and Bellugi 1964). Yet
the efficacy of expansions has not been proven definitely. Field studies suggest
that expansion may foster development (Brown 1973; Snow et al. 1976), whereas
experimental studies (Cazden 1965; Nelson, Carskaddon, and Bonvillian 1973)
have produced conflicting results.

Adult's conversations with young children not only differ in form from those
with other adults, but they also appear to differ in the functions they serve.
Speech is used to convey a variety of intentions or communication functions,
such as requesting, refusing, commanding, and reporting. These communication
aspects of language are far more difficult to study than formal aspects like grammar or repetition, because they entail a variety of complex socioemotional and
motivational factors. Researchers have only recently begun to study conversation and communication in TYCh. Nevertheless, a consistent picture is beginning to emerge. A number of investigators suggest that the urge to communicate
with children seems so fundamental that when children are incapable of carrying
on a conversation by themselves, adults seem to speak *for* them (Bruner 1978;
Gleason 1977; Schachter 1979; Snow 1977b).

This pattern of speaking for the child has been studied in ritualized language
games and in spontaneous conversations. Many early conversations, such as
peekaboo, are ritualized with prescribed patterns of alternating turns and re-
versible roles. In peekaboo, either the mother can hide, reappear, and ask
"Where's Mummy?" or the baby can. Developmental studies indicate that in
the earliest stages, adults both initiate these games and take all the turns themselves, the child's as well as their own. Gradually, the children begin to initiate
these language games themselves and assume their own roles. Eventually, they
learn to manage all of the interchangeable roles themselves.

In spontaneous conversations, patterns of speaking for the child are more complex and subtle. Very young children (under age three) use speech mainly for two purposes, to express their own desires ("Drink, Mommy") or to report their own activities or experiences ("I run"). Older preschoolers also constantly ask for things and report on their own activities (the latter make up the bulk of Piaget's *egocentric speech*), but these older children usually succeed in making themselves understood. They generally speak for themselves, and they also begin to use language for many other purposes. For example, they begin to boast and to use collaborative speech as they play with peers (Schachter et al. 1974).

In the case of the desire requests and reports of children under age three, adults tend to adopt the role of speaking for the child (Schachter 1979). Adults often restate or reformulate the child's desire requests to make sure they have understood them. For example, in response to "Drink, Mommy," the mother might say "Do you want some juice?" or "Do you want some more?" Adults often try to engage the child in conversation by eliciting reports on the child's activities ("What are you doing?" "What are you making?"). When the child fails to respond, many adults will report for the child, answering their own question (e.g., "Are you baking? Oh, you're making pancakes."). As adults speak for the young child, they often seem to ask if they have said what the child meant to say. For example, they seem to ask, *Is this what you meant to say you want?* or *Is this what you meant to say you are doing?* These are, indeed, special kinds of conversations where adults assume the conversational role of their children, and constantly check to make sure that they are playing their role adequately.

How can this pattern of speaking for the child help in language acquisition? Some suggest that it may assist the child in learning conversation rules such as how to take turns. Others are interested in the nature of this kind of assistance. Bruner (1978) uses the metaphor of a scaffold to describe how adults provide the conversational framework and children insert their utterances into the framework. Cazden (1979) points out that it is "a very special kind of scaffold that self-destructs gradually as the (child's) need lessens, and is then replaced by a new structure for a more elaborate construction" (p. 11). Still others suggest that this pattern of speaking for the child may account for many of the other features of TYCh, for example, many of the questions may derive from the question-and-answer sequences that adults use when speaking for the child.

Social class differences in adults' speech

Although talk-to-young-children has been studied in many languages, there are only two studies comparing samples of families from different social classes, a study of Dutch toddlers by Snow et al. (1976), and a study of Black and White New York toddlers by Schachter (1979) in which she found almost no differences between the early verbal environments of Black and White toddlers when controlling for social class. Although all features of TYCh were not examined in these two studies, no striking social class differences were found. Snow's analysis of 34 features covering grammar, repetitions, and communication functions, showed only four significant differences. Furthermore, the differences that have been found sometimes favor one social class, sometimes another. For example, both Snow and Schachter found that high-education, high-income mothers produce more repetitions of the child's speech (including expansions), whereas low-education, low-income mothers produce more exact repetitions of their own speech. Since both kinds of repetitions are characteristic of TYCh and are presumed to be beneficial to language learning, it could be that adults in different social classes adopt different formal features of TYCh with the overall number of these features remaining the same.

If the social class differences in the features of TYCh are neither striking nor readily interpretable, are there other class differences in the early verbal environment that may have implications for language learning? There appear to be. Whereas the pattern of speaking *for* the child seems useful in distinguishing talk-to-young-children from talk to adults, patterns of speaking *to* and speaking (responsively) *with* the child appear to be useful in contrasting the talk of low- and high-education/income mothers of young children. This contrast may indirectly affect the learning process by impinging on the motivation for learning.

Speaking *to* the child is the more familiar pattern. We tend to think of talking as a process of speaking to others, perhaps especially so in the case of communicating with children. This pattern of speaking to children consists mainly of directives and of direct instruction. In Schachter's (1979) category system for the talk of mothers and teachers to young children, directives include *dos* (*Let's have story-time now*), *don'ts* (*No pushing*), and refusals (*Not now*); and direct instruction consists mainly of providing new knowledge (*This is wet and this is dry*) and asking test questions (*What do we call this?*). These types of communication, directives and direct instruction, seem to characterize the speech of low-education/income mothers of young children. For example, Schachter (1979) found that 50 percent of the speech of low-education mothers of toddlers consists of directives, and 25 percent consists of *don'ts*. While directives are indeed very common in talk-to-young-children, they comprise about 30 percent of the speech of high-education/income mothers and *don'ts* comprise only about an additional 10 percent. Teachers of young children also tend to use directives about 30 percent of the time (Schachter et al. 1976). The relatively higher percent of directives in the speech of less-educated mothers may even serve to account for the higher incidence of exact self-repetitions in their speech since these repetitions often occur in association with directives (Schachter 1979).

Whereas low-education/income mothers tend to use directives, high-education/income mothers tend to speak responsively *with* their children. Sometimes caregivers will initiate a new topic of conversation, as when they suggest a new activity for the child, and sometimes they will respond to a prior communication of the child, usually continuing the topic the child has introduced (e.g., the child might say "Up we go" and the caregiver might say "Right, up and down you go" or ask "Sheryl's going up the slide?" The latter statements are classified as adult responsive speech. While mothers in both social classes initiate about the same amount of speech to their toddler, educated mothers produce three times more speech in response to a prior communication of the child (Schachter 1979). This responsive style could easily explain why these mothers show more repetitions of the child's speech. As one comments on or questions the prior statement of the child one often uses the same words as the child, as in the previous example in which the caregiver repeats the topic of the child's conversation, "going up."

It is important to note that these social class differences do not suggest that the verbal environment of the low-income child is cognitively deficient. In fact, instructional talk has been found to comprise about 10 percent of the speech of mothers, regardless of their social class. Nor are low-education mothers less talkative than high-education mothers when it comes to initiating conversations. It is only in responsive speech that the social-class difference appears. Low-education mothers tend to speak *to* their children; high-education mothers tend to speak responsively *with* their children.

How might this distinction between speaking to and speaking with children bear on language learning. If language development is an active process, wherein children attempt to extract the rules of their language from the everyday speech addressed to them, their motivation to pursue and persist in this demanding task is of major importance. Active learning requires self-confidence and faith in one's own efforts. The responsive style of high-education mothers would seem to support the growing autonomy and independence of the language-learning child and engender the kind of self-confidence that active learning requires. That is, social-class differences in the socioemotional and motivational aspects of the early verbal environment may be far more significant for development than differences in the cognitive sphere.

Educational implications

Caution is warranted whenever we derive practical implications from basic research, because there is always so much that we do not yet know. Although many of our leading developmental psycholinguists feel that the special way we talk to young children may contribute to the child's language development, most feel that language learning also relies at least in part on inborn capacities in children, and some remain committed to Chomsky's extreme nativist position. Even when we conclude that the evidence justifies an important role for talk-to-young-children, there are still many questions to be answered. For example, are some modifications of adult speech more helpful in learning certain aspects of child language? Simplifying the sounds of speech may be especially helpful during the phase when children are mastering the basic sounds of their language, whereas expanding the child's short utterances may be especially helpful later when the child begins to learn grammar. It may even be that the traditional behavioristic techniques—imitating a model, eliciting imitations, asking questions, approving success, and correcting mistakes—are helpful in teaching certain aspects of language. For example, some have suggested that vocabulary learning may benefit from correcting the child's mistakes (deVilliers and deVilliers 1979; Moerk 1977).

Despite all that we do not know, research on talk-to-young-children leads to some potentially useful teaching strategies. When people consciously try to teach children language, they tend to adopt traditional behavioristic strategies. They say things like "That's a double-decker bus" or "How many is that?"; they praise children for their successes and correct their mistakes. Few people are aware that, in their naturally occurring talk to children, they may also be using many other strategies that contribute just as much or perhaps much more, to the child's language development. Research on TYCh has made us aware of these potentially useful, naturally occurring strategies. To summarize, these strategies can be classified as follows:

(1) Attracting and maintaining the child's attention, as when the adult speaks in a high-pitched voice or addresses questions to the child.

(2) Simplifying one's speech with regard to sounds, meanings, grammar, and conversational patterns.

(3) Repeating and rephrasing one's speech. "This process is so 'natural' . . . that speakers are only barely aware of using it" (Ferguson 1977, p. 223).

(4) Repeating or rephrasing the child's speech, as when the caregiver expands the child's short utterances.

(5) Mapping words onto the child's experiences as when the adult speaks in the present, and describes the child's desires or ongoing activities.

(6) Speaking *for* the child, as when caregivers assume the child's role in the conversation, as well as their own role (for instance, when they answer their own questions).

(7) Speaking responsively *with* the child, as when caregivers continue the topic of conversation initiated by the child rather than introducing a new topic of their own.

Some readers may note that a number of these strategies are similar to the techniques Blank has recommended for helping older preschool children when they give inadequate answers to a teacher's questions (Blank, Rose, and Berlin 1978). Blank's list of teaching techniques is based on her analysis of teacher talk in a tutorial program for cognitive stimulation of preschoolers ages three to five, not on studies of the special linguistic code we use in talking to the language-learning child, ages one to three. The similiarity between some of Blank's teaching strategies and those based on research on this linguistic code suggests that these speech strategies may be helpful in a variety of teaching settings and throughout the early years.

Why are some adults reluctant to use TYCh? Sometimes when people talk to young children, they imitate the child's mistakes, such as errors in pronunciation. They might say *twuck* instead of *truck* or *widdle* instead of *little*. Here it is important to distinguish between mistakes and simplification. The word *tummy* simplifies the initial consonant sound of *stomach,* but the word *twuck* does not simplify the initial consonant of *truck*. It merely replaces one double consonant *(tr)* for another *(tw)*.

Researchers have found that simplifications are very common in TYCh but that mistakes are not. In fact, as we have noted, adults use clearer pronunciation and make fewer grammatical mistakes in talking to young children than in talking to adults. Further, it may be that the adult's occasional imitation of the child's mistakes does little harm. These imitated mistakes could be one aspect of assuming the child's role in the conversation, in which case they might help the child learn the rules of making conversations. Making intentional mistakes may also be one of the ways we have for expressing our affection toward the child. In any case, simplifications and not mistakes are a prominent feature of the picture of TYCh that has emerged from research.

Some people express concern about talking down to the child, speaking in such a simple, babyish fashion that the child hears nothing new to learn. Yet, although TYCh is a simplified version of ordinary talk to adults, it is much more than that. Simplification is only one of seven kinds of major TYCh strategies. Moreover, there is considerable evidence TYCh is finely tuned to the child's progress. We do not yet understand how and why this fine-tuning occurs, but there has been considerable speculation (and some controversy) on the subject among researchers in this area; see, for example, Cross (1977) vs. Newport, Gleitman, and Gleitman (1977). Adults appear to adjust their use of some TYCh strategies in response to particular aspects of the child's progress in language development. For example, adults do not need to continue to expand children's utterances when children begin to use long utterances themselves. Nor do adults need to assume the child's role in the conversation as children speak more and more for themselves. For other strategies, the child's cognitive development may signal to the caregiver that the child is ready to hear a new linguistic form. For example, the child may begin to talk about some future event, such as taking a bike to the park, without yet knowing how to construct a sentence in the future tense. A child might say "Ride bike" as the mother starts dressing her for the park. The mother might then ask "Are you going to ride your bike in the park?" thus providing her with the linguistic form to describe a future event—one that she understands but cannot yet express in mature language (Snow 1977a).

In some cases, the child's emotional development may signal the readiness to hear more advanced language. Mahler, Pine, and Bergman (1975) describe the first three years of life as the time of the psychological birth of the child, the time when "separation and individuation" begin as the child emerges from the original "oneness" with the mothering figure. In that connection, Schachter et al. (1974) have found that children begin to boast at around age three, as they become aware of themselves as separate people. There is no one so self-satisfied as the just-turned four-year-old proudly holding up four fingers, and announcing "I'm four." It is doubtful whether this use of language could ever occur in children who have not yet developed a strong sense of a separate self. The child's use of the pronouns *I* and *you*, that begins at the toddler age, probably depends on at least some elementary degree of development of a sense of self separate from other people, and it is likely that adults do not use these pronouns in their speech until children signal their capacity to understand them. That adults speak for children during their early years of childhood probably also reflects the oneness between the self and the other. The adult speaker seems to be the child's "alter ego" until the child develops her or his own separate ego (Schachter 1979).

In summary, language learning seems to be a complex process intimately related both to the development of what the child knows—because we cannot talk about what we do not understand—and intimately related to the development of the self—because *I* and *you* are so often the subject or the object of our sentences. To assist language development, caregiver speech must be finely tuned to the child's language development and also to these related developments in the cognitive and socioemotional spheres. As caregivers try to communicate with children, to understand them and to be understood, they no doubt search constantly for subtle signals from the child to help them know whether they are communicating successfully and to guide them in adjusting their speech to the proper range of difficulty for the child. Being a good listener is probably just as important for a caregiver as being an effective talker.

Research on talk-to-young-children may have a direct bearing on the central question of early language education, the question of how to structure children's language environments.

> One decision about the language program which preschool teachers must make is to what extent encounters should be preplanned with children, and how much they can rely on responding or initiating spontaneously as they watch and listen to the children at work and at play. (Cazden 1981, p. 10)

As many of you know, there are two major conflicting views on language education for preschoolers, the direct-instruction approach and the child development or active-learning approach. The direct-instruction approach advocates adult-directed, preplanned lessons, while the child development approach relies on naturally occurring adult-child communication in the classroom with the teacher often responding to the child's initiations. The direct-instruction approach is perhaps best represented by the DISTAR program (Becker, Engelmann, and Thomas 1971) that draws on the behavioristic formulations of Bereiter and Engelmann (1966). The child development approach is best exemplified by the developmental-interaction approach of Bank Street College (Biber 1977), based on the theories of Dewey, Freud, and Piaget.

In direct-instruction programs, the teacher's role is clearly defined in terms of the strategies of teaching and the content to be taught. Teachers use behavioristic strategies and the content of the language curriculum usually centers on vocabulary or grammar. By contrast, child development programs are consistent with current theory and research on language development that reveals that most children seem to learn language in the context of the natural flow of everyday communication. Probably the best advice for facilitating this natural flow is summarized by Brown (1977):

> . . . seek, above all, to communicate. To understand and be understood. To keep your minds fixed on the same target. In doing that, you will, without thinking about it, make 100 or maybe 1000 alterations in your speech and action. Do not try to practice them as such. There is no set of rules of how to talk to a child that can even approach

what you unconsciously know. If you concentrate on communicating, everything else will follow. (p. 26)

References

Becker, W. C.; Engelmann, S.; and Thomas, D. R. *Teaching: A Course in Applied Psychology*. Chicago: Science Research Associates, 1971.

Bereiter, C., and Engelmann, S. *Teaching Disadvantaged Children in Preschool*. Englewood Cliffs, N.J.: Prentice-Hall, 1966.

Biber, B. "A Developmental-Interaction Approach: Bank Street College of Education." In *The Preschool in Action: Exploring Early Childhood Programs*, ed. M. C. Day and R. K. Parker. Boston: Allyn & Bacon, 1977.

Blank, M. B.; Rose, S.; and Berlin, L. *The Language of Learning: The Preschool Years*. New York: Grune & Stratton, 1978.

Bloom, L.; Hood, L.; and Lightbown, P. "Imitation in Language Development: If, When, and Why." *Cognitive Psychology* 6 (1974): 380–420.

Broen, P. "The Verbal Environment of the Language Learning Child." *Monograph of the American Speech and Hearing Association*, no. 17, 1972.

Brown, R. *A First Language*. Cambridge, Mass.: Harvard University Press, 1973.

Brown, R. "Introduction." In *Talking to Children: Language Input and Acquisition*, ed. C. E. Snow and C. A. Ferguson. Cambridge: Cambridge University Press, 1977.

Brown, R., and Bellugi, U. "Three Processes in the Acquisition of Syntax." *Harvard Educational Review* 34 (1964): 133–151.

Brown, R.; Cazden, C. B.; and Bellugi, U. "The Child's Grammar from 1 to 3." In *Minnesota Symposia on Child Psychology. Vol. 2*, ed. J. Hill. Minneapolis, Minn.: University of Minnesota Press, 1969.

Bruner, J. S. "The Role of Dialogue in Language Acquisition." In *The Child's Conception of Language*, ed. A. Sinclair, R. J. Jarvella, and W. J. M. Levelt. New York: Springer-Verlag, 1978.

Cazden, C. B. "Environmental Assistance to the Child's Acquisition of Grammar." Unpublished doctoral dissertation, Harvard University, 1965.

Cazden, C. B. "Peekaboo As an Instructional Model: Discourse Development at Home and at School." Keynote address at the Stanford Child Language Research Forum, Stanford University, Stanford, California, 1979.

Cazden, C. B., ed. *Language in Early Childhood Education, Rev. ed.* Washington, D.C.: National Association for the Education of Young Children, 1981.

Chomsky, N. *Aspects of the Theory of Syntax*. Cambridge, Mass.: MIT Press, 1965.

Cross, T. G. "Mother's Speech Adjustments: The Contribution of Selected

Child Listener Variables." In *Talking to Children: Language Input and Acquisition*, ed. C. E. Snow and C. A. Ferguson. Cambridge: Cambridge University Press, 1977.

deVilliers, P. S., and deVilliers, J. G. *Early Language*. Cambridge, Mass.: Harvard University Press, 1979.

Ferguson, C. A. "Baby-Talk As a Simplified Register." In *Talking to Children: Language Input and Acquisition*, ed. C. E. Snow and C. A. Ferguson. Cambridge: Cambridge University Press, 1977.

Garnica, O. "Some Characteristics of Prosodic Input to Young Children." In *Talking to Children: Language Input and Acquisition*, ed. C. E. Snow and C. A. Ferguson. Cambridge: Cambridge University Press, 1977.

Gleason, J. B. "Fathers and Other Strangers: Men's Speech to Young Children." In *Georgetown University Round Table on Language and Linguistics*, ed. D. P. Dato. Washington, D.C.: Georgetown University Press, 1975.

Gleason, J. B. "Talking to Children: Some Notes on Feedback." In *Talking to Children: Language Input and Acquisition*, ed C. E. Snow and C. A. Ferguson. Cambridge: Cambridge University Press, 1977.

Kamii, C. K. "An Application of Piaget's Theory to the Conceptualization of a Preschool Curriculum." In *The Preschool in Action: Exploring Early Childhood Programs*, ed. R. K. Parker. Boston: Allyn & Bacon, 1972.

Lenneberg, E. H. "Understanding Language Without Ability to Speak: A Case Report." *Journal of Abnormal and Social Psychology* 65 (1962): 419–525.

Lenneberg, E. H. "The Natural History of Language." In *The Genesis of Language*, ed. F. Smith and G. Miller. Cambridge, Mass.: MIT Press, 1966.

Mahler, M.; Pine, F.; and Bergman, A. *The Psychological Birth of the Human Infant: Symbiosis and Individuation*. New York: Basic Books, 1975.

Moerk, E. L. *Pragmatic and Semantic Aspects of Early Language Development*. Baltimore, Md.: University Park Press, 1977.

Nelson, K.; Carskaddon, G.; and Bonvillian, J. "Syntax Acquisition: Impact of Experimental Variation in Adult Verbal Interaction with the Child." *Child Development* 44 (1973): 497–504.

Newport, E. "Motherese: The Speech of Mothers to Young Children." In *Cognitive Theory II*, ed. N. Castellan, D. Pisoni, and G. Potts. Hillsdale, N.J.: Lawrence Erlbaum Associates, 1976.

Newport, E. L.; Gleitman, H.; and Gleitman, L. " 'Mother, I'd Rather Do It Myself': Some Effects and Non-Effects of Maternal Speech Style." In *Talking to Children: Language Input and Acquisition*, ed. C. E. Snow and C. A. Ferguson. Cambridge: Cambridge University Press, 1977.

Phillips, J. "Syntax and Vocabulary of Mothers' Speech to Children: Age and Sex Comparisons." *Child Development* 44 (1973): 182–185.

Piaget, J. *The Language and Thought of the Child*. 3rd ed. New York: Humanities Press, 1959. (Originally published, 1926)

Schachter, F. F.; Fosha, D.; Stemp, S.; Brotman, N.; and Ganger, S. "Everyday Caretaker Talk to Toddlers Vs. Threes and Fours." *Journal of Child Language* 3 (1976): 221–245.

Schachter, F. F.; Kirshner, K.; Klips, B.; Friedricks, M.; and Sanders, K. "Everyday Preschool Interpersonal Speech Usage: Methodological, Developmental and Sociolinguistic Studies." *Monographs of the Society for Research in Child Development* 39 (1974). No. 3, Serial No. 156.

Schachter, F. F., with Marquis, R. E.; Shore, E.; Bundy, C. L.; and McNair, J. H. *Everyday Mother Talk to Toddlers: Early Intervention*. New York: Academic Press, 1979.

Shatz, M., and Gelman, R. "The Development of Communication Skills: Modifications in the Speech of Young Children As a Function of Listener." *Monographs of the Society for Research in Child Development* 38 (1973). No. 5, Serial No. 152.

Skinner, B. F. *Verbal Behavior*. New York: Appleton-Century-Crofts, 1957.

Slobin, D. "On the Nature of Talk to Children." In *Foundations of Language Development,* ed. E. H. Lenneberg and E. Lenneberg. New York: Academic Press, 1975.

Snow, C. E. "Mothers' Speech to Children Learning Language." *Child Development* 43 (1972): 549–565.

Snow, C. E. "Mothers' Speech Research: From Input to Interaction." In *Talking to Children: Language Input and Acquisition,* ed. C. E. Snow and C. A. Ferguson. Cambridge: Cambridge University Press, 1977a.

Snow, C. E. "The Development of Conversation Between Mothers and Babies." *Journal of Child Language* 4 (1977b): 1–22.

Snow, C. E.; Arlman-Rupp, A.; Hassing, Y.; Jobse, J.; Joosten, J.; and Vorster, J. "Mothers' Speech in Three Social Classes." *Journal of Psycholinguistic Research* 5 (1976): 1–20.

Snow, C. E., and Ferguson, C. A., eds. *Talking to Children: Language Input and Acquisition*. Cambridge: Cambridge University Press, 1977.

Kenneth H. Rubin
Barbara Everett

6 Social perspective-taking in young children

When the first volume of *The Young Child: Reviews of Research* was published, Flavell (1967) noted that we knew far more about children's knowledge of the physical world than we did about their knowledge of the social world. During the 1960s studies of conservation, seriation, and classification of physical entities abounded while efforts to understand social knowledge were negligible. The one-sided focus on the nonsocial, perhaps more academically oriented skills mirrored the North American tempo of the times. Following the Russian launching of the first earth-orbiting satellite, and in response to the newly declared War on Poverty, parents and teachers expressed concern with the training of children's cognitive skills earlier and better than before.

In recent years, psychologists and educators have turned to the work of Piaget (1970), who was convinced that the growth of knowledge concerning the social-personal and the physical worlds was linked by similar, if not the same, cognitive operations. Now researchers are investigating how young children conceptualize the figurative (i.e., the thoughts, emotions, and intentions) and the literal (physical and spatial) viewpoints of others.

The significance of this new research is suggested by both theory and data indicating the importance of children's abilities to think about their social worlds (or to engage in *social cognizing*). For example, it appears as if the ability to understand that others may have perspectives or views of the world different from one's own may determine the extent to which the child evinces altruistic, socially responsible, cooperative, and appropriately competitive behaviors. *Cognitive perspective-taking,* or the ability to consider others' thoughts and intentions, would most certainly appear beneficial when attempting to organize a game cooperatively (agreeing upon game rules) and when attempting to compete in it. After all, how could one possibly play games like hide-and-seek or chess successfully without considering what the opponent is thinking?

97

Affective perspective-taking, or the ability to take into account others' feelings or emotions is of significance in situations calling for prosocial behavior. For example, despite feeling relatively happy and at ease in a given situation, a child may realize that a friend is unhappy and ill-at-ease in the same setting. Such a realization may spur the child to discover that the friend's unhappiness stems from the desire to play with an object for which she is reluctant to ask. The affective perspective-taker may consequently provide some form of aid to the playmate. In a similar situation, the child who cannot take others' perspectives may be less likely to aid the peer in need.

Spatial perspective-taking, or the ability to consider others' literal, physical views of the world, seems important in many everyday social situations as well. For example, a child may realize that, because of some visual barrier, a playmate cannot see a small stepladder that will enable her to reach a desired object. Consequently, the child points out the existence of the stepladder. The inability to take others' spatial perspectives would not have enabled the altruistic act to occur. Similarly, in games of tag, a child who sees the person who is it approach a friend who is unaware of the pending catch may produce a signal that will aid the playmate.

In short, the study of perspective-taking would appear to be a most important area of inquiry. It provides the researcher, educator, and parent with clues about why children of the same age behave with different degrees of competence in similar social situations. Recently, researchers have begun to consider the relevance of perspective-taking in school settings. For example, Shure and Spivack (1978) have found cognitive and language deficits in children who are socially maladjusted in the classroom. Among the deficits identified by these authors is the inability to take others' perspectives. Many would not only agree with Shure and Spivack's position with regard to the importance of perspective-taking, but would extend the implications of their data by contending that socially competent young children are more likely than their less competent age-mates to view the entire academic milieu as pleasant and rewarding. Such positive affect could itself provide the child with a head start toward academic success.

In this chapter we will first assess the traditional view of the young child as egocentric, or lacking perspective-taking skills. We begin with a brief review of theory and research centering on the concept of perspective-taking and considering the relationship between perspective-taking and various other indexes of social skill such as altruism and communicative development. Finally, experiences that appear to play a causal role in the development of perspective-taking will be discussed and some implications for parents and teachers will be presented.

How egocentric are young children?

The study of perspective-taking emanates from the early work of Piaget (1926) concerning the concept of egocentrism. To Piaget, egocentrism refers to the state of being so immersed in one's own point of view as to be incapable of imagining any other perspective. His initial assumption was that young children are highly egocentric and that they become less so with age.

Support for the Piagetian position stemmed from research that indicated that young children had difficulty in predicting how an object would appear to a person who was looking at that same object from a different position. The typical egocentric response was the child's assertion that the other person saw the object exactly as she or he did.

Further manifestations of egocentrism were found during situations in which children were called upon to infer the knowledge, thoughts, intentions, or emotions of others. For example, Piaget noted that much preschool speech uttered in social settings was egocentric in that it was comprehensible only to the self; a preschooler might ask a question about an incident not witnessed by the listener, leaving the listener confused and uninformed—or use ambiguous referents to describe objects to a listener and then become perplexed at the listener's lack of comprehension. For example, the following incident took place between the first author and his then three-year-old daughter:

> Dad: "Amy, what are you doing upstairs?"
> Amy: "This."
> Dad: "Amy, you know that I can't see what you are doing! What is it you are up to?"
> Amy: "I'm doin' this!" (in a louder voice).

As for *why* children were found to be egocentric, psychologists turned to the Piagetian cognitive function of adaptation and its complementary faces—*assimilation* and *accommodation*. At every point in a person's life, there must be adaptation to the environment in order to satisfy one's needs. Take, for example, the case of a child facing a social situation or event that is novel. Such situations engender a state of cognitive imbalance, confusion, or conflict within the child. To regain a sense of cognitive balance, the child either "adjusts incoming information in a manner that is congruent with . . . [her or his] current level of cognitive structure" (Brainerd 1978) or changes the cognitive structure in reaction to the incoming information. The former process is labeled assimilation while the latter is referred to as accommodation. As an example of assimilation, take the situation in which a child is known to have an elementary cognitive concept of *dog*. Joshua then is introduced, for the first time, to a cat. Noting the similarity between the animals (both are four-legged, furry animals allowed to pad about in peoples' houses) the assimilator distorts certain dissimilar features (lack of whiskers on dogs) and labels the cat a doggy. Such a distortion of external features to the whims of the ego does not require cognitive reorganization. On the other hand, when Joshua comes to realize (through further experience and conversations with others) that the match between the perceived environment (in this case, the cat) and the available cognitive concept (dog) is a poor one, he may form a new concept (cat) to *accommodate* the lack of the adequate match. The concept *cat* will be understood to refer to those house pets with whiskers and distinctive facial and body features who use litter boxes. According to Piaget (1970), during the early years of life there appears to be a primacy of assimilation over accommodation. As such, the young child tends to interpret new events egocentrically, fitting them into already established concepts thereby altering the properties of objects and situations to suit the child's own conceptual structures.

How, then, does Piaget account for the decline of egocentric thought? One way, certainly, is through exchanges of information with other people. Piaget suggests that children are socially motivated from birth. Such motivations typically lead the child into social situations with adults and with other children in which the various participants may not share similar points of view and cognitive structures. The child then must reconcile the two discrepant perspectives. Such situations are illustrated in the work of Matthews (1977), who finds that in smoothly functioning dramatic play dyads, preschool children are likely to assume specific familiar sex roles (e.g., mother and father). In those cases dramatic play can be viewed as assimilative in that the children's similar perceptions of their respective roles offer no challenge to their cognitive structures. In other dyads, however, disagreements ensue concerning the sex-role appropriateness of each partner's behaviors (mothers *can* be employed; fathers *can* cook dinner). For these children, conflicts, when resolved, lead to a broader recognition of sex-appropriate behavior as exemplified by changes or compromises in their fantasy play following the settling of such conflicts. In short, Matthews reveals the accommodative function of social conflict and peer interaction. Her findings support Piaget's view that the decline of childhood egocentrism is caused, in part, by the incidence of peer conflict (Damon 1977).

Do all three dimensions of perspective-taking, be they physical/spatial, cognitive (knowledge of what the other is thinking), or affective (knowledge of how the other is feeling) emerge simultaneously at some specifiable age? Researchers do not provide support for the notion that egocentrism is a unitary trait. Measures of egocentrism in each of the three domains are not necessarily positively correlated with those in the others (see Ford 1979, for a review of this work). Moreover, even *within* a given domain of perspective-taking (e.g., affective), children of the same age may have difficulty on some tasks and yet may find others extremely easy.

There are two likely explanations for the lack of consistent relationships of children's performances on perspective-taking tasks (Rubin 1978). First, it appears as if the research methods employed across tasks differ (i.e., some tasks require verbal responses). Second, it may be that the measures tap different levels of difficulty in perspective-taking. Taken together, both of these possibilities could make it unlikely that all measures of perspective-taking would correlate highly with one another.

A closer look: assessing children's spatial, cognitive, and affective perspective-taking skills

In the following section some of the literature that reveals how children of different ages perform on many of the various perspective-taking tests will be reviewed. Two possible explanations for the seemingly inconsistent performance of young children within and across the different areas of perspective-taking will be considered.

Spatial perspective-taking

One of the earliest investigations of spatial perspective-taking is Piaget and Inhelder's (1956) classic three mountains study. In this task, the child is seated in front of a model of three mountains that are of different colors and have different objects on them. One mountain, for example, has a small stream running down its side; another is topped by a small red cross. A doll is placed at various positions around the model, and the child's task is to identify the doll's view of the mountains from each of the positions by (a) selecting from a group of photographs the one that best represents the doll's view, (b) using three pieces of cardboard shaped like the mountains to reconstruct the photograph that could be taken of them from the doll's positions, or (c) selecting one of the photographs and deciding which position the doll would have to be in in order to see that view.

Piaget and Inhelder conclude that perspective-taking ability develops in three sequential stages. In the first, that extends through about age six, children tend to be not only inaccurate, but also egocentric, i.e., when asked to identify the doll's perspective, they typically respond with their own. Between the ages of seven and eight, children continue to be inaccurate, but they now seem to know that the doll will not share their perspective. During this stage, however, children are unable to imagine exactly what it is the doll sees despite their realization that it does not share their own viewpoint. Finally, at about age nine or ten, children become both accurate and nonegocentric.

In recent years researchers have simplified the original spatial task and, in so doing, have demonstrated that three- and four-year-olds are capable of perspective-taking to some degree. One representative study is that of Borke (1975), who, like Piaget and Inhelder, presented children with the task of identifying a doll's perspective of a three-dimensional display from a number of viewing positions, but unlike Piaget and Inhelder, used displays that contained familiar toy objects (e.g., a lake with a sailboat). Moreover, the children were asked to indicate their awareness of the doll's perspective by rotating a movable replica of the display so that the children themselves were looking at the display in the same way as the doll. Borke found that three- and four-year-old children responded correctly on her simplified spatial tasks between 80 percent and 93 percent of the time. She attributed the preschoolers' seeming lack of egocentrism to the more familiar scenes and to the simplification of the task.

Flavell (1978) proposes that much of the observed variation in children's performance on various spatial tasks may be attributed to the existence of two different perspective-taking levels. At the first level the child can recognize that others *may* see objects differently from the self and can identify *what* objects the other sees. These skills appear to be available to three-year-olds. The second level involves not only recognizing *what* the other sees, but also *how* the other views the objects or events; that is, the exact position of objects or order of events. This latter skill appears to develop during the later preschool years, at least when the content is familiar and the task is not too complex.

Cognitive perspective-taking

In the study of the child's conceptions of what others are *thinking*, experimental procedures are more varied than those in the area of spatial perspective-taking. Procedures used successfully with school-aged children include having the child make up a story about a picture and then retell it from the points of view of its various characters (Feffer 1970); asking the child questions about the perspectives of characters seen in a filmstrip (Selman and Byrne 1974); and asking the child to infer another's interpretation of an event about which the other has only part of the information that is available to the child (Chandler and Greenspan 1972). Another testing approach has been to involve the child in a game situation with a second person and to assess perspective-taking abilities on the basis of the competitive strategies employed by the child (DeVries 1970).

As with spatial perspective-taking, recent efforts to simplify the tasks, making them more appropriate for preschool children, have involved using more familiar content and requiring less verbal explanation. For example, Marvin, Greenberg, and Mossler (1976) would ask a mother and her child to sit in a circle with an experimenter. Each of the three participants covered their eyes in turn, while the other two had to decide which of two toys was going to be their secret. Perspective-taking ability was assessed in terms of the extent to which the child understood which of the participants did or did not know the secret. In another procedure, Mossler, Marvin, and Greenberg (1976) asked children to watch a videotaped film of an event with an audio portion that contained information about the reasons for the actions of the story character. The children were then asked to watch while their mothers were shown the same film *without* the audio portion. For example, one character was a child who was described in the film as about to enter his grandmother's house for a particular purpose. Perspective-taking ability was assessed by the extent to which children understood that their mothers could not know those reasons, since they had not heard them.

Unlike the results of the more difficult perspective-taking tasks of Feffer (1970), Selman and Byrne (1974), and Chandler and Greenspan (1972), that indicate the onset of some aspects of perspective-taking to occur during the early elementary school years at best, competent cognitive role-taking has been found in preschool-aged children when simplified tasks such as those described above have been employed (Brandt 1978; Marvin, Greenberg, and Mossler 1976).

As with spatial perspective-taking, different levels of cognitive role-taking skill have been described. One of the more creative hierarchical conceptions of such skill is that of Selman (1976), who argues that cognitive perspective-taking first emerges when children are approximately three years of age and continues to develop until the adolescent years. Support for Selman's model emanates from analyses of children's responses to structured interview questions about the perspectives of various story characters (Selman 1976). Selman classifies the verbal responses according to five stages: At *Stage 0* (three to six years), *egocentric role-taking*, the child can understand that others may have distinctive thoughts and feelings but cannot distinguish between one's own perspective and those of others who share a common experience. Instead the child judges that all others will view this shared experience in the same way as the self.

At *Stage 1* (six to eight years), *subjective role-taking*, the child makes the distinction between self-centered and other-centered viewpoints of the same social situation but cannot interpret either her or his own or the *other's* actions or thoughts from the *other's* viewpoint. At *Stage 2* (eight to ten years), *self-reflective role-taking*, the child has the ability to think that others think of the self in particular ways. Moreover, the child comes to realize that another person's perspective of her or him can have implications for how that person behaves toward the self. As Flavell (1977, p. 133) writes, "The fundamental insight of Level 2 may come down to this: I know I could conceivably tune in on your cognitive perspective because we are both subjects or persons rather than objects; I also know that you could do the same to me for the same reason; it follows that you may be doing so at the very moment I am and that your tuning may therefore pick up my tuning. Such an insight, whenever it comes, must represent a giant step in the development of social cognition."

While Stage 2 does represent a major advance in perspective-taking skills, it still denies the child the ability to step outside of a two-person relationship and view it as a third person would (e.g., "Jeffrey knows that Maureen and I think of each other as friends."). At *Stage 3* (10–12 years), *mutual role-taking*, simultaneous consideration of viewpoints is possible from the third-person perspective. However, only by *Stage 4* (12–15 years), *societal role-taking*, can the child conceptualize how a society or generalized other would perceive of a given social situation. It is at this latter stage that a mature understanding of social conventions is reached (Selman 1976).

As mentioned earlier, a number of researchers present evidence that cognitive perspective-taking develops at younger ages than Selman's stages would suggest. For example, the findings of Marvin, Greenberg, and Mossler (1976) and Mossler, Marvin, and Greenberg (1976) that children as young as four years old can differentiate perspectives appears consistent with *Stage 1* thought, presumably characteristic of six- to eight-year-olds. As with the lack of strong relationships among measures of perspective-taking, at least two explanations exist for the discrepant findings regarding when children learn to perspective-take cognitively. First, social-cognitive competencies are found to appear earlier when assessment requires minimal verbal proficiency (Brandt 1978). Second, the presence of concrete, physically present cues with which to evaluate a given social situation (as in actually seeing that a co-participant had closed eyes vs. having been *told* that the person did not see the event, Marvin, Greenberg, and Mossler 1976) allows earlier detection of role-taking skills than when the cues are less salient. Thus, when one must infer perspectives by recognizing what the other has *not* experienced (as in the privileged information paradigms of Chandler and Greenspan 1972) *and* further when that information is not physically available in the experimental situation (as it was to Marvin, Greenberg, and

Mossler's 1976 subjects), the ability to take others' perspectives appears to emerge at later ages.

Such explanations for the discrepant ages reported for the onset of role-taking skills should not suggest that researchers will soon discover the more advanced role-taking skills in preschool-aged children. Rather, we are suggesting that new methodological wrinkles may alter, somewhat, the age ranges that Selman proposes as normative for his hierarchical model. We shall discuss this possibility further in a later section of the chapter.

Affective perspective-taking

Typical of the affective perspective-taking studies is that of Burns and Cavey (1957). Children were shown cartoons depicting a child whose facial expression suggested an emotion that either was or was not appropriate to a given situation (e.g., a child smiling vs. frowning at a birthday party). The children were then asked how they thought the story character was feeling. The authors reported that three-year-olds typically responded in terms of how one would ordinarily feel in that given situation (e.g., happy at a birthday party), thereby disregarding the facial cues of the story characters. By the ages of five and seven years, children were more likely to disregard the situational context (a birthday party) and to base their judgments on the character's facial expression.

Rothenberg (1970), in asking children to infer affective perspectives (e.g., happiness, anger) from audiotaped conversations between two adults, found that ten-year-olds performed better than eight-year-olds. Borke (1971) simplified the task by visually presenting familiar situations involving child characters and asked preschoolers to choose from a series of face drawings how the characters felt (e.g., "X is at a party. Choose the picture that shows how X feels."). Borke thus employed a procedure that did not require a verbal explanation from the child, that centered on the feelings of children rather than those of adults, and that presented stories visually as opposed to auditorily (as in Rothenberg's study). This task simplification led Borke to conclude that preschool children were not so egocentric as had been proposed earlier, since they could consistently identify situations in which story characters typically would be expected to feel happy and sad.

Others, however, challenge Borke's interpretation by claiming that successful performance on her task need only involve children asking themselves how *they* would feel in the depicted situation, and that while such a response represents a very primitive level of perspective-taking, genuine perspective-taking involves the ability to infer a perspective that *differs* from one's own. While some researchers support this criticism of Borke, others, employing tasks in which story characters are known to have differing affective perspectives from the subjects, show evidence that children as young as three-and-one-half years are capable of appropriate empathic responses (Dickstein, Lieber, and McIntyre 1976).

In summary, studies within each of the three perspective-taking domains do not provide a clear answer concerning when children's egocentrism wanes (Black 1981). Some cite variation in testing procedures as the principal cause for discrepancies in data on egocentrism, suggesting that children as young as three show some elementary level of perspective-taking skills depending on the methods of assessment. Others cite the possibility that different tasks assess various levels or stages of perspective-taking skill. Suffice it to say that both explanations seem reasonable. Since perspective-taking seems to be a skill with several distinctive components, it seems likely that different aspects may develop at different times.

The role of perspective-taking in social skills

Is there any reason to believe that children who are good at perspective-taking behave any better than others? Over the years, psychologists have suggested that perspective-taking skill is a prerequisite to the development of prosocial behaviors and social competence (Hartup 1970). Although findings concerning these hypothesized relationships are not totally consistent (Feshbach and Feshbach 1969), a body of supportive evidence is accruing that reveals significant positive relationships between measures of affective and cognitive perspective-taking and indexes of altruism (Buckley, Siegel, and Ness 1979; Rubin and Schneider 1973), cooperation (Marcus, Telleen, and Roke 1979), peer popularity (Gottman, Gonso, and Rasmussen 1975), and the ability to influence a listener (Rubin 1979).

While these studies do indicate some link between social cognitive competence and behavior, their correlational nature does not allow us to comment on the direction of causality. However, a number of experiments in which children have been trained or provided a school curriculum in role-taking skills have resulted in increases in prosocial behaviors (Iannotti 1978; Staub 1971) and decreases in antisocial acts (Chandler 1973) suggesting a causal link between the two. One of the more interesting preschool curricular developments is the previously mentioned work of Spivack and Shure (1974). These psychologists believe that perspective-taking is one of the necessary skills underlying the growth of social competence. Their studies show that when small groups of lower-SES preschoolers were led by adults in role-play (using a nondirective Socratic method), they were more likely to improve their social problem-solving skills (e.g., obtaining a desired object from a peer through constructive means) and to become better adjusted socially than their nontrained age-mates. While Spivack and Shure's findings, as well as those reports from similar large-scale curricular projects, are most promising, it must be noted that their program is not solely concerned with training sensitivity to feelings, thoughts, and intentions. The small-group instruction provided to teach social skills also addresses the use of relational terms (*same/different*) important in problem solving of all kinds, social and nonsocial. Tutoring the child in these more general cognitive concepts may contribute in some unknown way to improvements in behavior following training. In any case, one should not be quick to accept training in perspective-taking as the answer for the remediation or acceleration of prosocial behaviors. It is but one educational procedure that appears to have some impact. Other procedures, designed to influence the desired behaviors directly, such as providing the child with appropriately acting child or adult models, or coaching the child in the desired social behaviors may prove just as effective in producing socially competent children (see Chapter 8).

Experiences contributing to growth in perspective-taking

How does perspective-taking develop and what experiences facilitate it? As mentioned earlier, Piaget suggests that peer interaction plays a causal role in the development of perspective-taking skills. He notes that peer play allows children to interact with individuals whose social and cognitive capacities are similar to their own. Such egalitarian relationships give children opportunities to assert themselves, to present their own views of the world, and to argue freely with peers concerning different social-cognitive viewpoints. Such conflicts and interactions may ultimately help children to understand that others may have different thoughts, feelings, and perspectives than their own. Adult-child relationships, however, would hardly be construed as egalitarian, at least in the child's mind. Young children may be reticent to be assertive, aggressive, or argumentative when in the company of "all-knowing" adults.

Indirect support for the position that peer interaction plays a causal role in social-cognitive development may be gleaned from Rubin's (1976) finding that children who both initiate and with whom other children initiate active interchanges are less egocentric than their less socially active preschool age-mates.

Nahir and Yussen (1977) predicted that the greater amount of peer interaction experienced by first and fifth grade children in an Israeli kibbutz vs. those in a city environment would lead to better performance on role-taking tasks by the former group. The results support their prediction. Similarly, Hollos and Cowan (1973) found that seven- to nine-year-old Norwegian children who lived in a fairly isolated farm community performed more poorly on perspective-taking tasks than their age-mates who resided in a village or in a town. These latter groups were purported to have greater opportunities for peer interaction. Unfortunately, neither study provided quantitative data descriptive of the quality of parent-child and sibling interaction for the contrasting groups of children. As a result, it may well be that factors other than peer interaction account for the different levels of perspective-taking skills.

Given that peer relations play a role in determining social-cognitive growth, a number of psychologists have begun to ask about the particular forms of interaction that are likely to be most significant in development. One such form identified by Smilansky (1968) is sociodramatic play, that allows children to get figuratively outside themselves, thereby gaining a reflection of the self as different from, but related to, others. Sociodramatic play presumably evokes decentration skills that help the child to regard behaviors from one's own role perspective and from the perspectives of one's peers simultaneously.

Recent training studies provide some support for the causal role of sociodramatic play with peers in inducing change in perspective-taking skills. Rosen

(1974), Smith and Syddall (1978), and Burns and Brainerd (1979) among others find that small group instruction of preschoolers in dramatic play leads to improved performance on perspective-taking tasks. Typically, the training procedure involves having an adult leading small groups of children in acting out fairy tales (thematic play) or everyday events such as going to a doctor's office (sociodramatic play). The tutor introduces the play theme, encourages the children to select given characters, and, if needed, initiates discussion as to how the drama should proceed. In so doing, the adult may call attention to the differing perspectives of the story characters or ask the children leading questions about who is responsible for what action and why.

While sociodramatic play training with peers seems to produce gains in perspective-taking skill, it is important to note that most of the studies have involved an active adult tutor who interacts with the children to a significant degree. As Rubin (Rubin 1980; Rubin and Pepler 1980) points out, and as Smith (Smith, in press; Smith and Syddall 1978) empirically shows, simply interacting with a responsive adult might be as responsible for the social-cognitive gains as is the fantasy play experience with peers.

Despite the acknowledged contributions of adult tutors, a related possible explanation for the beneficial effects of sociodramatic play is that social-cognitive growth occurs during conflicts and conversations between peers when, in the course of their play, they slip out of the fantasy play frame (Rubin 1980). It is common practice for children who are engaged in fantasy play to interrupt their actions and to discuss or debate the roles or rules of the drama and its characters. For example, Matthews (1977), in studying same-sex, preschool-aged dyads engaged in fantasy play found that children often stopped their dramatic activities to discuss differing viewpoints concerning character roles. Once such discussions of discrepant perspectives started, the children could no longer be considered to be role-playing. The conflicts themselves, when resolved through discussion, led not only to a resumption of sociodramatic activity but also to new knowledge concerning roles and perspectives. As such, these data support the original Piagetian hypothesis expressed earlier that a key causal variable to social-cognitive growth is peer conflict and its resolution.

Given the Piagetian view that children learn best by acting upon their environments, it should not be surprising that role-play, social conflict, and peer interaction in general (three forms of *social action*) all serve to promote perspective-taking to some degree. Within the spatial domain, it has further been suggested that *motoric action* or kinaesthesis, serves a didactic function. For example, Priddle and Rubin (1977) found that preschoolers who were led in movement games (e.g., creating statues with right or left appendages) by an adult who provided spatial labels for them performed better on outcome measures of spatial perspective-taking than their counterparts who either (a) listened to an adult explain spatial labels (left-right) with the aid of visual cue cards or (b) who received no tutoring whatsoever. These data corroborate those of Shantz and Watson (1971) who found that children allowed to move around a spatial display were better able to spatially decenter than those children who remained stationary. In short, the training research suggests the significance of active rather than passive learning experiences for developing perspective-taking skills.

Finally, it appears sensible to assume that childrearing practices contribute somewhat to social-cognitive development. Surprisingly, however, few researchers have studied this most important area. Bearison and Cassel (1975) found that mothers who used person-oriented and inductive persuasive appeals (e.g., gave reasons and explained consequences for various actions) had children who were less communicatively egocentric than those mothers who used status-oriented tactics (e.g., "Do it because I told you to."). Similarly, Hoffman (1963) found that person-oriented mothers who stressed the consequences of their children's behaviors for others had children who were more considerate of others in their school settings, a behavior that would appear to require perspective-taking (Rubin and Schneider 1973).

Parents may also model a perspective-taking behavioral style in their interactions with their children. Keller (1976) reports that preadolescent children who rated their parents as being warm and supportive were themselves better cognitive perspective-takers than children who perceived their parents as being unresponsive and severe. Finally, Shure and Spivack (1978) indicate that a training program designed to teach mothers to deal more flexibly with their children led not only to the child's improved social problem-solving skills and social adjustment, but also to an improvement in the social problem-solving skills of their mothers. In explaining the rationale for their parent-training program, Shure and Spivack make clear the connection between childrearing practices and the development of maternal as well as child perspective-taking: ". . . when a parent helps a child think about [her or] his own and others' feelings, and how to consider the effects of . . . [one's] own actions on others, the parent also thinks about feelings and what he or she does affects other adults as well as the child" (1978, p. 41).

New perspectives on perspective-taking

In this chapter we have considered the development of perspective-taking and its social correlates. We have demonstrated how the various forms of perspective-taking (i.e., spatial, cognitive, and affective) may be measured and that evidence of competence may be found even in preschool-aged children—a decidedly anti-Piagetian discovery. This finding is one of the major insights of the past decade derived from the perspective-taking literature.

It would now appear appropriate to discuss some of the new directions that investigators of perspective-taking are heading toward in the 1980s. First, recent attempts are being made to identify more clearly the functional relationships between the various perspective-taking domains. To address this issue, Abrahams (1979) recently developed a single task by which spatial, cognitive, and affective perspective-taking skills could be simultaneously assessed. She had preschool-aged children view a three-dimensional scene that showed a boy and a dog running away from a bear and asked the child what the boy was *seeing, thinking,* and *feeling.* In this way she was able to control for measurement problems (such as differences in stimulus characteristics) and response requirements of role-taking tasks that have plagued the earlier literature. To get a "third person" perspective, Abrahams also asked the children what another person, sitting at a different position and who could not see the bear, would think the boy saw, thought, and felt.

The results clearly indicate that children succeed at the spatial perspective-taking tasks prior to attaining success at the cognitive and affective tasks, and that both of the latter two skills develop simultaneously. The data suggest that children must be able to identify those objects and events seen by another person before they are able to infer how the other might feel or what the other thinks about those events.

Abrahams's study represents somewhat of a turning point for the laboratory examination of perspective-taking skills. There is, however, a growing movement to examine social cognition in the natural setting (e.g., Damon 1977). Rubin and Pepler (1980) have attempted to demonstrate how Selman's (1976) different levels of perspective-taking may be inferred from observations of children at play. For example, one form of play that is common from about age six to eight years is the simple, competitive game with rules. As Sutton-Smith (1971) notes, in the competitive games of this age group, the sides or roles chosen are transitory and winning is episodic. That is, the games do not have ultimate or fixed winners. The games of dodge ball and frozen tag are typical of this age and require an understanding of reciprocity and role-reversibility both of which are *Stage 2* (self-reflective) perspective-taking skills. However, one need not simultaneously consider points of view from a third-person perspective to engage in such early competitive games. One is only required to keep in mind that "When you are it, I have to flee," and "When I am it, you have to flee." Furthermore, there is little need to speculate about strategies based on recursive thought processes ("If I do this, she will do that, so I had better do. . . . "). Such skills of strategy do appear to be necessary for games like checkers or chess or organized sports (e.g., football, unless the coach is the signal caller) that are probably reflective of simultaneous, *Stage 3* perspective-taking skills, and that effectively develop in behavioral form at around nine or ten years of age.

We should also note that children between the ages of six and ten years have difficulty planning attack and defense game strategies simultaneously (Sutton-Smith 1971). Instead the focus is on attack *or* defense while considering the prospective actions of the self and the other. Such behavioral strategies are reflective of the perspective-taking skills of Selman's *Stage 2* children while *Stage 3* children might be expected to consider both attack *and* defense simultaneously.

Implications

In summary, we now know that young children are not nearly as social-cognitively unsophisticated as they were once thought to be. Moreover, we are beginning to gain some knowledge concerning how changes in perspective-taking skills occur in children. In a nutshell, training studies indicate that a principal variable in the development of cognitive, affective, and spatial perspective-taking is the direct *action* of the child on the environment. With regard to the development of cognitive and affective perspective-taking, actions including role-play, social conflict, and general interactions with peers all seem important. With regard to growth in the visual domain, spatial knowledge appears to be learned best through movement (Priddle and Rubin 1977). These recent findings have implications for teachers of young children. If one goal of educational programs is to encourage the development of all perspective-taking domains, then process-oriented, small group actions and interactions are most effective.

It is also important for teachers and parents to realize that certain forms of adult-child interaction encourage the development of role-taking skills. Thus when discussing events or when requesting that a child carry out an action, parents and teachers might do well to employ person- rather than status-oriented statements (Bearison and Cassel 1975; Hoffman 1963), thereby taking into account the *child's* own feelings and thoughts.

Finally, it is important that parents and teachers realize that the older, perhaps more traditional expectations that young children cannot learn to cooperate, or that they communicate ineffectively *because* of their egocentric views of the world are outmoded. Such perceptions may have led those who live with or teach children to believe that preschoolers and kindergarteners are not yet ready to behave in more socially mature ways. Given the findings of recent laboratory studies and given those inferences concerning perspective-taking skill that can be gleaned from naturalistic observations, it is clear that young children do enter preschool and kindergarten with a fairly sophisticated social-cognitive repertoire. As such, the encouragement of such skills should now find a meaningful place in the curriculum goals of the teachers of young children.

References

Abrahams, B. "An Integrative Approach to the Study of the Development of Perspective-Taking Abilities." Doctoral dissertation, Stanford University, 1979.

Bearison, D. J., and Cassel, T. Z. "Cognitive Decentration and Social Codes: Communicative Effectiveness in Young Children from Differing Family Contexts." *Developmental Psychology* 11 (1975): 29–36.

Black, J. K. "Are Young Children Really Egocentric?" *Young Children* 36, no. 6 (September 1981): 51–55.

Borke, H. "Interpersonal Perception of Young Children: Egocentrism or Empathy?" *Developmental Psychology* 5 (1971): 263–269.

Borke, H. "Piaget's Mountains Revisited: Changes in the Egocentric Landscape." *Developmental Psychology* 11 (1975): 240–243.

Brainerd, C. J. *Piaget's Theory of Intelligence.* New York: Prentice-Hall, 1978.

Brandt, M. "Relations Between Cognitive Role-Taking Performance and Age, Task Presentation, and Response Requirements." *Developmental Psychology* 14 (1978): 206–213.

Buckley, N.; Siegel, L. S.; and Ness, S. "Egocentrism, Empathy, and Altruistic Behavior in Young Children." *Developmental Psychology* 15 (1979): 329–330.

Burns, N., and Cavey, L. "Age Differences in Empathic Ability among Children." *Canadian Journal of Psychology* 11 (1957): 227–230.

Burns, S. H., and Brainerd, C. J. "Effects of Constructive and Dramatic Play on Perspective-Taking in Very Young Children." *Developmental Psychology* 15 (1979): 512–521.

Chandler, M. "Egocentrism and Antisocial Behavior: The Assessment and Training of Social Perspective-Taking Skills." *Developmental Psychology* 9 (1973): 326–332.

Chandler, M. J., and Greenspan, S. "Ersatz Egocentrism: A Reply to H. Borke." *Developmental Psychology* 7 (1972): 104–106.

Damon, W. *The Social World of the Child.* San Francisco: Jossey-Bass, 1977.

DeVries, R. "The Development of Role-Taking as Reflected by Behavior of Bright, Average, and Retarded Children in a Social Guessing Game." *Child Development* 41 (1970): 759–770.

Dickstein, E. B.; Lieber, L. E.; and McIntyre, C. W. "The Development of Cognitive, Affective, and Perceptual Role-Taking Skills in Early Childhood." Unpublished manuscript, Southern Methodist University, 1976.

Feffer, M. H. "A Developmental Analysis of Interpersonal Behavior." *Psychological Review* 77 (1970): 197–214.

Feshbach, N. D., and Feshbach, S. "The Relationship Between Empathy and Aggression in Two Age Groups." *Developmental Psychology* 1 (1969): 102–107.

Flavell, J. H. "Role-Taking and Communication Skills in Children." In *The Young Child: Reviews of Research. Vol. 1,* ed. W. W. Hartup and N. L. Smothergill. Washington, D.C.: National Association for the Education of Young Children, 1967.

Flavell, J. H. *Cognitive Development.* New York: Prentice-Hall, 1977.

Flavell, J. H. "The Development of Knowledge about Visual Perception." In *Nebraska Symposium on Motivation,* ed. C. B. Keasey. Lincoln, Nebr.: University of Nebraska Press, 1978.

Ford, M. E. "The Construct Validity of Egocentrism." *Psychological Bulletin* 86 (1979): 1169–1188.

Gottman, J. M.; Gonso, J.; and Rasmussen, B. "Social Interaction, Social Competence, and Friendship in Children." *Child Development* 46 (1975): 709–718.

Hartup, W. W. "Peer Interaction and Social Organization." In *Carmichael's Manual of Child Psychology. Vol. II,* ed. P. H. Mussen. New York: Wiley, 1970.

Hoffman, M. "Parent Discipline and the Child's Consideration for Others." *Child Development* 34 (1963): 573–588.

Hollos, M., and Cowan, P. "Social Isolation and Cognitive Development: Logical Operations and Role-Taking Abilities in Three Norwegian Social Settings." *Child Development* 44 (1973): 630–641.

Iannotti, R. J. "Effect of Role-Taking Experiences on Role-Taking, Empathy, Altruism, and Aggression." *Developmental Psychology* 14 (1978): 119–124.

Keller, M. "Development of Role-Taking: Social Antecedent and Consequences for School Success." Unpublished manuscript, University of Heidelberg, 1976.

Marcus, R. F.; Telleen, S.; and Roke, E. J. "Relation Between Cooperation and Empathy in Young Children." *Developmental Psychology* 15 (1979): 346–347.

Marvin, R. S.; Greenberg, M. T.; and Mossler, D. G. "The Early Development of Conceptual Perspective-Taking: Distinguishing among Multiple Perspectives." *Child Development* 47 (1976): 511–514.

Matthews, W. S. "Sex Role Perception, Portrayal, and Preference in the Fantasy Play of Young Children." Paper presented at the biennial meeting of the Society for Research in Child Development, New Orleans, 1977.

Mossler, D. G.; Marvin, R. S.; and Greenberg, M. T. "Conceptual Perspective-Taking in 2- to 6-year-old Children." *Developmental Psychology* 12 (1976): 85–86.

Nahir, H. T., and Yussen, S. R. "The Performance of Kibbutz- and City-Reared Israeli Children on Two Role-Taking Tasks." *Developmental Psychology* 13 (1977): 450–455.

Piaget, J. *The Language and Thought of the Child*. London: Routledge & Kegan Paul, 1926.

Piaget, J. "Piaget's Theory." In *Carmichael's Manual of Child Psychology. Vol. I*, ed. P. H. Mussen. New York: Wiley, 1970.

Piaget, J., and Inhelder, B. *The Child's Conception of Space*. London: Routledge & Kegan Paul, 1956.

Priddle, R. E., and Rubin, K. H. "A Comparison of Two Methods for the Training of Spatial Cognition." *Merrill-Palmer Quarterly* 23 (1977): 57–65.

Rosen, C. "The Effects of Sociodramatic Play on Problem-Solving Behavior among Culturally Disadvantaged Preschool Children." *Child Development* 45 (1974): 920–927.

Rothenberg, B. "Children's Social Sensitivity and the Relationship to Interpersonal Competence, Intrapersonal Comfort, and Intellectual Level." *Developmental Psychology* 2 (1970): 335–350.

Rubin, K. H. "Social Interaction and Communicative Egocentrism in Preschoolers." *Journal of Genetic Psychology* 129 (1976): 121–124.

Rubin, K. H. "Role-Taking in Childhood: Some Methodological Considerations." *Child Development* 49 (1978): 428–433.

Rubin, K. H. "Social Cognition and Communicative Development in Young Children." Invited address, Society for Research in Child Development Institute on the Origins and Growth of Communication, University of Delaware, June 1979.

Rubin, K. H. "Fantasy Play: Its Role in the Development of Social Skills and Social Cognition." In *Children's Play: New Directions for Child Development,* ed. K. H. Rubin. San Francisco: Jossey-Bass, 1980.

Rubin, K. H., and Pepler, D. J. "The Relationship of Child's Play to Social-Cognitive Growth and Development." In *Friendship and Childhood Relationships,* ed. H. Foot, T. Chapman, and J. Smith. London: Wiley, 1980.

Rubin, K. H., and Schneider, F. W. "The Relationship Between Moral Judgment, Egocentrism, and Altruistic Behavior." *Child Development* 44 (1973): 661–665.

Selman, R. L. "Social-Cognitive Understanding: A Guide to Educational and Clinical Practice." In *Moral Development and Behavior,* ed. T. Lickona. New York: Holt, Rinehart & Winston, 1976.

Selman, R. L., and Byrne, D. "A Structural-Developmental Analysis of Levels of Role-Taking in Middle Childhood." *Child Development* 45 (1974): 803–806.

Shantz, C. U., and Watson, J. "Spatial Abilities and Spatial Egocentrism in the Young Child." *Child Development* 42 (1971): 171–181.

Shure, M. B., and Spivack, G. *Problem-Solving Techniques in Childrearing.* San Francisco: Jossey-Bass, 1978.

Smilansky, S. *The Effects of Sociodramatic Play on Disadvantaged Preschool Children.* New York: Wiley, 1968.

Smith, P. K. "A Comparison of Fantasy Play Tutoring and Skills Tutoring in Nursery Games." *Child Development,* in press.

Smith, P. K., and Syddall, S. "Play and Non-Play Tutoring in Preschool Children: Is It Play or Tutoring That Matters?" *British Journal of Educational Psychology* 48 (1978): 315–325.

Spivack, G., and Shure, M. B. *Social Adjustment of Young Children.* San Francisco: Jossey-Bass, 1974.

Staub, E. "The Use of Role Playing and Induction in Children's Learning of Helping and Sharing Behavior." *Child Development* 42 (1971): 805–816.

Sutton-Smith, B. "A Syntax for Play and Games." In *Child's Play,* ed. R. R. Herron and B. Sutton-Smith. New York: Wiley, 1971.

Henry M. Wellman

7 The foundations of knowledge: concept development in the young child

Consider the world as described by physicists—a reality made up of atoms and molecules, of waves and frequencies, of forces and resistances. Then consider the world as it appears to us—a world of color, of number, of people and things, of plants and animals, of friends and enemies. How does the human mind transform events that have a physical reality of the first sort into the familiar world of the second sort? One crucial process in this transformation is the process of conception—the organization of information presented to the mind into an intricate array of *concepts*.

Concepts are the cognitive categories that allow people to group together perceptually distinct information, events, or items. My concept of *red* allows me to treat distinctly different colors (magenta and carmine) as similar in some ways, and also as distinct from blue or green. My concept of *chair* allows me to recognize a chair when I see one, even a new unfamiliar design. Individual concepts are further compounded and linked together. There are different colors and even different reds, all captured in a larger conceptual system of similarities and differences. These in turn are related to other concepts that carve the world into different sizes, shapes, items, and types. The term *concept* is used in several related fashions to refer to discrete, particular concepts (concepts of chair), to concepts of a more general level (the concept of furniture), and to large conceptual systems (concepts of number, of time).

The concepts possessed by the average adult are immense in scope and number. They include all the knowledge that the person uses to organize, interpret, and reason about the world. In general, concepts can be considered in two large overlapping sets. There are concepts that aid in the understanding of the *physi-*

cal world and there are those specific to an understanding of the *social world*. Concepts of the physical world include ideas of number and amount, causes and effects, concepts of time, spatial relations, length, and weight. Also included are concepts of plants and animals, and physical systems such as weather, the seasons, gravity, and electricity. Concepts in this domain are represented in many areas of curricula—mathematics, science, music, art. Concepts of the social world, however, include the world of self, others, and social interaction. There are concepts of the variety of human behaviors (aggression, flirting, helping, competing), knowledge of a multitude of human states (fatigue, anger, dreaming, love, illness), and abilities (intelligence, creativity, retardation, memory, reasoning). In this domain would be included concepts of social roles (doctor, lawyer, boss, teacher), of the relationships between persons (friends, parents, classmate, bully), and larger social categories and institutions (races, nations, religions, and customs). Concepts of the social world also figure prominently in current curricula. All of social studies (history, civics, economics) concerns such knowledge; as does affective education (encompassing awareness and knowledge of feelings and values), moral or ethical education (utilizing concepts of good, bad, equitable, fair), and multicultural education (concerned with concepts of others, differences, tolerance).

Obviously these domains, the physical and the social, overlap, and many concepts cross-cut the two. Concepts of life and death, for example, apply to animals and plants as well as to self and others. Conceptual systems of classification apply to the physical world (e.g., biological taxa) and the social world (e.g., kinship classes). The self can be considered as a physical entity (the body) and as a social entity (the psyche).

Of course not all of these concepts and categories are possessed by the young child; much of what the adult knows must be accumulated over a long course of development. However, even the youngest children organize their world into concepts and conceptual systems. The focus of this chapter is the concepts of the young child, specifically the conceptual acquisitions of the preschooler. These early concepts are particularly important since they lay the foundation for all later knowledge and for conceptual development.

To illustrate concept development in young children, I will take as examples the development of two different conceptual systems in preschoolers. These are the child's concepts of *number* and the child's concepts of *human thinking*. Why focus on the development of these two systems? As outlined above, a list of concepts acquired by children would be immense, so any sampling of concepts must be selective. These two concepts were selected in accordance with a set of general considerations that have shaped this chapter.

The first consideration is that not all concepts are equally important or fundamental. The child's concept of *dessert* is likely to develop early, but it does not seem essential to later important developments. However, a child's conception of number is generally thought of as a crucial conceptual acquisition. Since it provides a basis for mathematics learning, it is a typical and central content in curricula for preschool children. Furthermore, number games ("One, two, buckle my shoe") are spontaneously played and invented by children themselves. A similar argument can be made for the importance of the child's conceptions of thinking. Concepts of thinking include a knowledge of human memory, dreams, reasoning, and other mental workings. Human beings are creatures whose immediate acts and behavior are products of such internal mental processes. Thus children's knowledge of how humans reason, remember, and imagine—their knowledge of thinking broadly defined—must be an integral and major part of their larger concepts of themselves and of others.

A second consideration is that these two conceptual systems represent distinctly different types of concepts. Concepts of number are an instance of concepts of the physical world, similar to time, weight, volume, distance, and speed. In contrast, conceptions of human thinking are more related to an understanding of the social world of people, human behavior and, ultimately, society.

Finally, these two concepts are particularly rich; discussion of their development facilitates a discussion of larger issues. Perhaps the most important of these issues concerns a description of the general conceptual competence of the preschool child. All too often, preschool children have been described in negative terms. That is, studies illustrate what the child does not know or cannot do that the older elementary school child does. In Piaget's theory, for example, preschool children's conceptual systems are termed preoperational. Essentially, this stresses that they are deficient in comparison to the later, operational child. As Gelman (Gelman 1978; Gelman and Gallistel 1978) argues, such a description obscures an understanding of preschoolers in their own right. For both the concepts considered here, there is recent research that allows us to paint a more comprehensive picture of the young child's knowledge.

The concept of number in the young child

Consider the standard, and now famous, number conservation task devised by Piaget (1952). A child sees two identical rows of about seven or eight marbles and correctly judges that there are the same number of marbles in each row. Then one of the rows is spread out so that it is longer than the other. The child is now asked, does one row have more marbles than the other or are they just the same? Preschool children fail this task, typically asserting that the longer row now has more marbles. These results are very robust and can be replicated by anyone working with preschoolers; if you change the length of the row, the child believes the number of items changes. These well-known results have led to the conclusion that preschoolers have no, or at best a severely deformed, concept of number. Where older children conceive of number as a mathematical property independent of length and colors—i.e., they understand number as distinct from many number-irrelevant attributes of objects—preschoolers seem to have little idea of the true nature of number. Personal experience can also confirm this impression. Preschoolers often do not count correctly ("one, two, seven, four"), often show deficient number-based behavior (as in their use and understanding of money), and lack many number skills (even elementary ones such as addition and subtraction) that must be acquired later in school.

However, consider the following recent demonstration by Gelman (1972). A three-year-old child was shown two plates. On one plate, there was a row of three small toys (two mice and a truck) and on the other a row of two toys. The plates were covered with a can and their positions were shuffled. Over the course of a number of trials, the child had to learn to identify "the winner." The winner was always the same plate, the one with three toys. After the child could identify the winner consistently, the plates were covered for one more trial and the winner was surreptitiously changed. For some children the number of items was changed, for example one item was removed from the winner plate leaving both plates with only two items. For others the number was left unchanged but some other feature was changed, say the three items were all pushed together or rearranged. What did young children then do when they had to pick "the winner?" A typical response to having an item removed was to judge that there was now no winner and to explain this by saying, "There was three animals. In the can (looks around). Took one. 'Cuz there's two now" (p. 84). However, a typical response to having the items pushed together was to insist that there was still a winner even while explaining, "These pushed together. When you turned 'em in the can" (p. 84). In short, in this situation young children seemed to adequately identify the number of items (3 vs. 2), spontaneously judged that number and not some other feature (such as length) defined the winner, understood that subtraction of an item changed the winner but pushing the items together did not, and explained occurrences in number-relevant manners (a toy was removed or added). The contrast between the results on Gelman's magic task and the classic Piaget number conservation task is striking and raises many questions. Most important, why do preschoolers look fairly sophisticated in Gelman's task yet deficient in many other tasks? What positive competencies with number are in fact possessed by very young children?

Table 7.1 contains a summary of information needed to answer these questions. This table lists many of the skills and components involved in an understanding of number. Some of the skills listed in the table are observable in preschoolers, others are acquired later. One important distinction indicated in Table 7.1, is that number knowledge can be divided into two distinct types (Gelman and Gallistel 1978). First, there are those skills that allow a person to tell how many items are in some given array. These are termed *number extraction* processes. Counting the items is a primary example of a number extraction skill. In addition to number extraction, there is *number reasoning*. Piaget's task, that requires the child to judge that two rows still have the same number in spite of changing the lengths of the rows, involves number reasoning. Notice that it is not necessary to count the items (to extract a representation of number) to reason correctly in this task; given that one starts with identical rows, all one must know is that no items have been added or removed. Number extraction and number reasoning are distinct skills.

What number knowledge does the preschool child possess? Preschoolers possess a variety of number concepts that are found within the left-hand column of

Table 7.1.
Factors involved in the acquisition of number concepts.

	Small sets of items *(approximately 4 or fewer)*	Large sets of items	Sets with no definite number
Number extraction	Counting: the one-to-one principle the stable order principle the cardinal principle the order-irrelevance principle	Counting Generative counting Estimating	$a, a + 1, a + 2 \ldots a + N$ One-to-one correspondence
Number reasoning	Equality (3=3) Number-relevant transformations: adding, subtracting Number-irrelevant transformations: rearrangement; substitution Qualitative solutions: adding to increase, subtracting to decrease Quantitative solutions (4−2=2 exactly)	Equality Number-relevant transformations Number-irrelevant transformations Qualitative solutions Quantitative solutions	Algebraic reasoning $a + b = b + a$ if $a = b$, and $b = c$ then $a = c$

Table 7.1. If the focus of their knowledge is very small sets of countable objects, then preschool children can be shown to know a surprising amount about numbers. Skill with large sets of items (the second column) or with uncountable sets (the third column) represent number knowledge to be acquired later.

First, following the order of Table 7.1, begin with preschoolers' counting skills. The following is a typical demonstration of a two- or three-year-old's counting (Gelman and Gallistel 1978). The child is given small sets of items to count. In such cases the young child may count two items as "one, two," count three items as "one, two, six," and count four items as "one, two, six, five." Though these counts are unconventional, that is the child does not use the correct sequence of standard number names, still when carefully analyzed they reveal considerable knowledge of counting. First, young children seem to know that every item to be counted should be counted just once (the one-to-one principle). In the above example two number words were used for two items, and four were used for four. Second, they know that the words used for counting should be recited in a consistent sequence (the stable order principle). The child above used "one, two, six" for three items and "one, two, six, five" for four items. The child would use "one, two, six" again if counting a different set of three. Third, children often know that the last count word that you come to in counting represents the total amount of all that you have counted (the cardinal principle). In the last example above the child would conclude there were five total items in all. Finally, they know that any set can be counted in a variety of orders—from left to right or right to left, or skipping around—and that this is irrelevant to coming up with a proper count (the order-irrelevance principle). In short, in spite of using counting systems that are not yet the same as the prescribed conventional sequence, young preschoolers' unconventional but consistent behavior indicates systematic knowledge about the goal and methods of counting.

Older children are more consistent in their counting—they make fewer errors. For example, if asked to count sets containing 4 items, approximately 60 percent of three-year-olds and 100 percent of five-year-olds consistently evidence all three of the one-to-one, stable order, and cardinal principles in their counts (Gelman and Gallistel 1978). Older children also are more conventional in their counting—they use the standard number word list to represent numbers. For example, when faced with 4 items, approximately 60 percent of three-year-olds and 90 percent of five-year-olds will say there are 4 (the conventional number) items present (Gelman and Tucker 1975). Obviously, and very importantly, older children, especially those beyond preschool, learn to make much longer counts. There would seem to be two parts to this development. First the child learns to count moderately sized arrays, arrays of from 6 to 13 or 14 items. Later yet the child learns that counting is a generative process. This occurs when children recognize and employ the rules that are used to generate larger and indefinite counts (21, 22 . . . 31, 32 . . . 41, 42 . . .). The end point is the ability to extract an exact numerical representation for very large sets of items—even item sets so large that one has never had to count to such a number before.

What of number reasoning? Are young children able to reason about the numerosity of sets that they can count? Recent research suggests that the young child can reason about numbers in certain ways that represent sizable achievements in themselves, and that also set the stage for later developments. Again Gelman's work is revealing here, especially results from her magic experiments (1972), introduced earlier.

Consider the lower left-hand cell of Table 7.1, and, first, reasoning about equality. In the magic experiments sometimes the winner was changed in number-irrelevant ways (items pushed together, a toy car substituted for a toy mouse). In these cases preschoolers typically considered the new arrangement to still be the winner. Thus they understood something of the equality of the two sets; the new set was still the winner because it had a number equal to the old winner. At other times, items were added to or subtracted from one set, sometimes resulting in equal numbered sets on the same trial. The following is a typical response to this occurrence by three- and four-year-olds: The child places the soldier on the two-mouse plate. "This is gonna be a winner plate too. Both have three things" (Gelman and Tucker 1975). This "both have three" response indicates an understanding of equality.

This "both have three" response brings up a very important point about young children's number reasoning: They seem to be able to reason only in those cases where they can compare the counted number of items directly. Thus if they can count your cookies and find three and count my cookies and find three they know that $3 = 3$ and that you and I have the same. However, if they cannot achieve a count (because there are too many items or because they are not allowed to count them), then they cannot reason about equality. For example, if each time I give Adam a cracker I also give Kathy one, an adult or older child would know that the two children must have equal amounts even if they could not count or even see the accumulated crackers. Preschoolers would not come to this conclusion. They would be able to tell this by counting both Adam's and Kathy's crackers and then comparing, but they would not know just on the basis of the obvious one-to-one correspondence of the crackers themselves.

The examples above also show the young child's understanding of number-relevant transformations—addition and subtraction of items change the winner. Similarly there is understanding of certain number-irrelevant transformation—rearrangement and item substitution (replacing a car with a mouse) does not change the winner since it does not change the number on the plate.

The reader can easily imagine how these impressive but limited abilities lead to further developments. As the child can count larger sets (column two in the table), number-reasoning can expand to more and more situations. In addition, children will eventually develop the ability to reason about numbers even when they cannot achieve a total count of the sets at all. This is what is typically referred to as *algebraic reasoning* and is represented by the last column of Table 7.1. Algebraic reasoning is numerical reasoning independent of any specific number. For example, if I know that Adam and Kathy both have the same number of crackers and each eat half of them, then I can reason that they both have the same number of crackers left. To reason in this fashion I need never appeal to specific numbers. Similarly I could know that Joshua is twice as old as Luis who is twice as old as Dylan, and therefore know that Joshua is four times as old as Dylan, without knowing anyone's specific age. This type of number reasoning is beyond the skill—and beyond the conception—of the young child who must be able to extract some specific (small) number to apply to the sets she or he reasons about.

One other skill of the young child's number reasoning deserves mention. In the magic experiments, after the winner plate was changed the child was often given an opportunity to fix the plate so it would be a winner again. In these repair situations the children evidenced a rough idea of how to solve numerical problems. For example, suppose the winner originally had five items but now appeared with three. The typical response was to *add* items to try to fix the winner. This response shows children's understanding that subtraction can be solved (repaired) by adding. Young children in this situation could not figure out exactly how many items to add; they could only approximate it with considerable trial and error (adding some and counting, then subtracting some and counting again, etc.). This type of ability is termed *qualitative solutions* in Table 7.1. This is to distinguish it from *quantitative solutions* that older children develop. Young children's solution attempts are qualitative because they understand the direction of change accurately; older children are quantitative however because they understand both the direction of change and the exact magnitude of change required for the solution ($4-2=2$ exactly, so precisely 2 items would need to be added to repair the winners).

While I have concentrated on Gelman's work because it provides the most detailed description of preschool children, there is other research that contributes to the above picture (see Gelman and Gallistel 1978, or Ginsburg 1977 for reviews). Also, I have dispensed with the numerous important cautions as to the limits of our knowledge. The above description is still tentative and bound to be revised as well as enriched by future work.

In summary, preschool children have an extensive conceptual system relevant to number. This includes an important number extraction skill, specifically counting, and many simple but fundamental number reasoning concepts. These skills lay the groundwork for later arithmetic and algebraic knowledge. These early skills also determine the child's ability to solve very real numerical problems. Young children's knowledge of small sets of numbers means that they often can and do notice whether they have their full share of small amounts of cookies or crackers, whether they have both mittens, and who is older than who (among their three-, four-, and five-year-old peers). Young children's need to make concrete counts in order to reason about number partly explains the prevalent use of their fingers in counting. Such aids help the child to "think about three" in order to solve number problems (Curcio, Robbins, and Ela 1971).

One other point should be made, not obvious in our discussion so far. Preschoolers seem genuinely and spontaneously interested in number or number-like properties. Counting objects, rehearsing the sequence of number names, attending to equality and inequality seem ubiquitous activities of the young child. Fortunately for the teacher, not only are young children interested in number but everyday classroom activities are rich in potential sources of number learning. Adults can use everyday tasks and events—such as dividing things up (carrot sticks, juice cups, scissors, etc.), accumulating things (both mittens, all the puzzles), making correspondences (a hat for every child, a jacket for every record), recording data (each child's height or age, days and dates, who is absent or present)—to increase the child's knowledge and curiosity about number (see Kamii 1982; Kamii and DeVries 1978).

The concept of thinking in the young child

All of us possess a reasonable idea of what basic number knowledge might be like, and this provides a needed background for understanding the number knowledge that develops in the preschool child. But, what of our second topic, conceptions of human thinking? What might a person know about human thinking broadly defined, about such mental activities as dreaming, remembering, or imagining? In answer to this question, consider for a moment the kinds of comments that adults make every day about mental processes and states. Statements like: "He's very *smart*. Are you *sure* about that? I *forgot* your birthday. I just *remembered* her name. I had a strange *dream* last night. It slipped my *mind*. I didn't *understand* a word of it. I *thought* I *knew* the answer." Adults frequently refer to human thinking.

The ability to think about our own thinking is a very impressive skill. Scholars have conjectured that an ability to contemplate our own selves, to reflect on our own thoughts, hopes, and knowledge is one characteristic that distinguishes humans from lower animals. Further, the development of concepts about thinking—an ability to understand one's own thought processes and the thought processes of others—is one of the important tasks of childhood. At some point children are expected to know the difference between telling a lie and telling the truth, to know the difference between pretending to do something and actually doing it (pretending to hit a friend, in play), to judge the intentions of self and others (whether something was done on purpose or accidentally), to know the difference between dreams and reality ("Don't be afraid, it was just a dream."), and to understand that others' thoughts and beliefs are different from one's own ("He didn't *know* it was yours.").

Clearly adults and older children have acquired innumerable concepts about thinking. In order to discuss the early development of this knowledge it is useful to distinguish four broad clusters of concepts in this domain (Wellman 1982):

1. *Existence*. Adults know that thoughts and internal mental states exist, that they are not the same as external acts or events. For example, consider such concepts as those of lies, hunches, guesses, and pretending. All are based on the notion of the *difference* between a mental state and external behavior. I can know that one thing is true, but say or act as if it is not. That

is, I can lie or pretend. I can be completely ignorant of the correct answer on a test, but pick the correct choice by a lucky guess. In short, as any adult knows, mental states and external behavior are not the same.

2. *Distinct processes*. People can remember or forget, they can visualize images, they can dream, they can reason, they can concentrate or daydream, they can conjecture and guess. Clearly there are a variety of distinct mental acts; thinking takes many forms. Adults know that there are many different thought processes and understand the distinctive features of different mental acts (e.g., the differences between guessing and knowing, between dreaming and daydreaming).

3. *Integration*. While there are numerous distinctions between mental processes, the different mental processes are also similar and related. For example, adults know that all mental processes reside in the brain or mind; remove the brain and all, not some, disappear. They know that thinking, dreaming, and imagining are all internal invisible events. Yet, at the same time these are very different from other internal invisible events, such as digestion or the heart pumping blood. They know that dreaming, and fantasizing, and conjuring up mental images are all related, as are remembering, learning, knowing, and understanding; and all are different from sneezing, chewing, and wiggling your toes.

4. *Variables*. Any one mental performance is influenced by a number of other factors or variables. In remembering, for example, how much one can remember depends on how hard the task is, the nature of the items, and the memory strategies used. Adults know that long lists are harder to remember than short; that meaningful items (English words for an American) are easier to remember than meaningless ones (Russian words); and that writing yourself a note is often better than rote memory.

What does the young child know about this intriguing and varied mental world that underlies and influences all human behavior? The first and primary question is about existence. Do young children realize that an internal mental world exists independent of overt behaviors and physical events? Some understanding of this independent existence is imperative for understanding mental concepts all of which are based on notions of the difference between mental states and external behavior and events.

Piaget (1929) investigated children's concepts of dreams and of thoughts. He concludes that young children do not discern the existence of mental processes. Instead preschoolers identify mental events with observable behaviors. They equate thinking with talking and believe that the organ of thinking is the mouth. They conceive of dreams as pictures flashed in the room while sleeping. In short, they do not view mental processes as different from related behavioral acts such as talking or watching.

More recent studies partly confirm this picture. Consider the following situations. Hakeem puts his coat in one of two closets. Later when he returns he looks in the correct closet and finds his coat. Alternately Philip's father hangs Philip's coat in one of two closets but Philip does not personally see which one. Later he returns to retrieve his coat and looks in one of the closets that turns out to be the correct one. The typical adult interpretation of these two scenarios would be to say that Hakeem, the first boy, *remembered* where his coat was, but that Philip only *guessed* where his was. However, when preschoolers are asked to interpret these two situations they judge that both boys remembered (Wellman and Johnson 1979). In other words they appear to think that remembering refers to a behavioral state of affairs—successfully finding the coat—not to the person's underlying knowledge. Other studies similarly show an interpretation of internal events in terms of external observable behaviors (Gordon and Flavell 1977; Misciones et al. 1978).

From these findings one is tempted to agree with Piaget that preschool children do not appreciate the fundamental existence of thinking as opposed to acting. But a study by Johnson and Wellman (1980) indicates that the situation is more complex. The key problem is one of salience. Mental processes and events are unobservable—they go on inside the head. By their very nature they are less obvious than external, observable physical actions and behaviors. We cannot see people think as we can see them smile or open a door. If mental processes were made very salient would preschoolers still ignore them? Johnson and Wellman tried to make internal events maximally salient to young children. The child was shown two boxes and an object was then hidden in one of them. After viewing the hiding, the child was asked to find the object. The boxes were constructed so that the object was *not* where it ought to have been but could be secretly changed to the other box instead. In this situation, at the behavioral level the child did not succeed in finding the object. However, four-year-olds still insisted that they did *remember* where it had been and that they *knew* where it had been even though they had not found it. That is, they used appropriate mental terms to refer to their thought state (correctly knowing where it was) and not to refer to just their observable actions (incorrectly locating the object). When Johnson and Wellman (1980) tested children in the same way as reported in Wellman and Johnson (1979) and Misciones et al. (1978) they found that children again identified mental terms with behavioral acts, e.g., remembering meant simply being correct. It was only in the trick condition, where their own state of knowledge was so obvious and discrepant from the real state of things, that four-year-olds revealed an understanding of the independent existence of the mental world.

This demonstrates an impressive, if limited, conception on the part of four- and five-year-old children. They are becoming aware that there are mental processes that are sometimes independent of the external, physical world. In addition to external, physical reality there is the realm of imagination, belief, fantasies, guessing, in short the realm of thinking.

Do children of this age also know that there are a variety of distinctly different mental processes? The data here are clear. At the very least four- and five-year-olds are able to distinguish different mental events in terms of how much those events must correspond to the real world. For example, you can *remember* only things that have actually happened, but you can *guess* anything you want, whether it could or did ever really happen or not. Similarly, to say that Laura *knows* something happened usually implies that that thing really happened (Laura knows that birds fly). But you can say that Laura *thinks* something happened whether the thing happened or not (Laura thinks birds never fly). Preschool children can distinguish *know* and *remember* as mental processes that more correctly correspond to the real state of affairs from *think* and *guess* that are less dependent on the real world (Johnson and Maratsos 1977; Johnson and Wellman 1980; Wellman and Johnson 1979) and also understand that *pretend*, and *lie* refer to denials of the true states of things (McNamara, Baker, and Olson 1976; Piaget 1965). For example, if four-year-olds know that Robert always goes to school except when he is sick and are told that "Robert is pretending he is sick," then they know Robert is not really sick at all. They also know that Robert should go to school.

The above findings are with four- and five-year-olds. What about younger preschoolers? As yet there is no evidence to show that two-and-one-half- or three-year-olds also conceive of these distinctions between different mental processes. Indeed in one study three-year-olds treated *remember* and *forget* as identical (Wellman and Johnson 1979) and in another they treated *know* and *think* as identical (Johnson and Maratsos 1977). However these data could easily underestimate the conceptions of these very young children because they may not have understood what they were supposed to do in the experimental tasks.

There are some intriguing findings with two- and three-year-olds, if a slightly different question is asked: When do children understand that different people can be thinking about different things? This conception also falls under the heading of understanding distinct processes; when do children understand that my thoughts and knowledge are often distinctly different from yours? First, four- and five-year-olds do understand that different people have different thoughts. For example, four-year-olds understand that if Heather and Brian have a secret from Jill, then the three have different knowledge: Heather and Brian know the secret but Jill does not (Marvin, Greenberg, and Mossler 1976). But the most striking demonstrations with younger preschool children concentrate on the child's concepts of knowledge through vision. Specifically, with younger children the question has been, does the child know that you and I often see different things? Seeing something is one of the simplest possible forms of knowing. If I can see the ball under the table but you cannot, I know that it is there (or that it is red) whereas you do not. It is now clear that young children know that different persons have different visual knowledge. If I hold up a card between myself and a two- or three-year-old, a card that has a dog on one side and a cat on the other, the child knows that she or he sees the cat and I see the dog (Masangkay et al. 1974). The child also knows that she or he must talk about the object differently if the listener has seen it than if the listener has not (Maratsos 1973) and if it is further away and less visible to the listener as opposed to close and clear (Wellman and Lempers 1977).

In sum, young preschoolers know the basic fact that another person need not see the same object that they see. Older children of four and five further under stand that even when another person sees the same object, that the other may have a different view of that object (Flavell 1978). I may see the front and you may see the side. Thus, young preschoolers know that different people see *different objects;* the older preschooler understands that different people can see *different views* of the same objects.

To this point we have considered children's concepts of the *existence* of thoughts and knowledge, and their concepts of *distinct* types of thinking and knowing. Older preschoolers also realize that different mental processes are *integrated* in certain ways. One thing they seem to know in this regard is that all mental processes similarly reside in the brain or mind. Johnson and Wellman (in press) asked children whether they needed their brains to engage in various activities: Do you need your brain to think; do you need your brain to wiggle your toes; do you need your brain to sneeze? In fact, four- and five-year-olds demonstrated a very mind-like view of the brain. They knew that thinking, remembering, dreaming, and knowing were all similar *mental* processes that required the brain whereas external behaviors, like wiggling toes, or involuntary acts, like sneezing, did not. In addition, young children clearly avoided certain misconceptions of the brain. They did not identify the brain just with the observable head, for example—they knew the brain was invisible and inside the head. They judged that you need your brain to think but not for all head acts, e.g., not to shake your head. They also believed that certain internal events were not mental events—feeling an ice cube in your closed mouth did not require the brain but dreaming did. Thus they discriminated internal mental events from other internal events.

A beginning understanding of the *variables* that influence human thinking is also apparent in preschool-age children. Wellman (1977) tested three-, four-, and five-year-olds' understanding of the following memory-relevant variables: number of items (that more items are harder to remember than few), interference (that noisy distractions can impede memory efforts), age (that adults often remember better than young children), help (that splitting the memory task with a friend is easier than having to do it all yourself), drawing (that drawing a picture of the item to look at later, when you have to remember, will help you), time (that a short time to study the items will detract from memory performance in comparison to having ample study time), and cues (that cued recall, where someone gives you a cue for each item to remember, is easier than free recall, where you have to remember everything on your own). The vast majority of three-, four-, and five-year-olds understood the relevance of at least some of these variables. The earliest variables understood, by three-year-olds, were the influence of number of items and the effect of interference on remembering. The last variable understood, missed by some of the five-year-olds, was cues (see also Ritter 1978).

Wellman (1977) also found that the same preschoolers knew that some potential variables did *not* affect memory. What the rememberer was wearing, her or his hair color, and if she or he was fat or skinny were all judged to have no influence on the person's memory performance.

Of course older children understand still more variables (Flavell and Wellman 1977). For example they know that related items (black-white) are easier to remember than unrelated ones (apple-black); they know that forming a mental image helps you remember, and that concentrating on one task can block out simultaneous attention to another. But the groundwork for this future development is clearly laid in the preschool years.

In conclusion, there is both a positive picture of what young children know about thinking broadly defined and also clear limitations to this early knowledge. On the positive side even two- and three-year-olds are beginning to form concepts of thinking. They use words such as *remember* and *think* in their everyday speech. They associate the brain with the head. And they know that different persons have different visual knowledge. Three-year-olds know that it is harder to think about many things than one, and that distractions interfere with thinking.

Our picture of the conceptions of older preschoolers is even clearer. Four- and five-year-olds have a rudimentary but rich conception of the mental world. They understand that an internal mental world exists independent of and apart from a person's observable behaviors and acts. Relatedly they know that two peoples' thinking might be quite different, that others may not know what you are thinking or what you know. They understand fairly well the meanings of such mental terms as *remember, forget, think, know, guess, pretend,* and can distinguish among these various cognitive acts and processes. In particular, they know that some of these mental processes are more tied to the true nature of occurrences in the world (e.g., *know*) and some can be completely unrelated to reality (e.g., *guess*). They have the beginnings of an integrated knowledge of the mental world.

This picture of competence is balanced by the preschool child's limitations. Most important, the mental world has a much less central and salient place in the child's total conception of human behavior. Unless stimulated to do so, preschoolers often avoid thinking about mental occurrences. They do not ordinarily ponder the internal mediating causes of behavior, such as one's reasons or intentions. They often misunderstand mental terms as applying to less complex but observable features of persons—e.g., forgetting just means you are wrong. They also isolate the mental world. Only older children tend to see various mental processes as being integrated into all of human behavior. All in all, the elementary school child has a more consolidated, richer, and more pervasive conception of human cognition.

The preschool child is clearly more knowledgeable about the mental world than has been asserted in the past (e.g., Piaget 1929). However, these concepts are still at the cutting edge of the child's concept development. It is appropriate for teachers and parents to expect certain things of the child—for example, to remember to do or not to do certain things if told, to begin to distinguish lies from the truth, and accidents from intended misdeeds. It is useful to instruct the child in the larger implications of one's knowledge, for example, the implications of the fact that people have different minds—"He didn't know you were playing with it," "Tell him what you want." But it is inappropriate to expect the young child to have adult mastery of these concepts, to meet these expectations consistently, or to understand relevant instructions completely.

Understanding and furthering concept development

Comparing and contrasting the concepts of number and concepts of thinking reveal some more general conclusions about concept development in the young child. The best way to organize these conclusions is by considering certain recurring themes in the investigation of concept development. The following discussion will not make clear all there is to know about concept development, but considering these themes will call attention to some larger unanswered questions (see also Flavell 1970) and to some important conclusions.

Assessment

In both areas of concept development reviewed above, the obvious major question was, what do preschool children really know? What is an accurate assessment of their conceptual accomplishments? This is an important question for both researchers and teachers. Researchers strive for an accurate understanding of the child. Teachers strive to provide information and experiences that match and build upon the child's current conceptions.

Piaget's assessment of preschoolers remains an important starting point. Both researchers and teachers have found it extremely useful. But, Piaget's description now seems incomplete. Piaget emphasizes that preschoolers see the world primarily in terms of the external, surface features of things and events such as size, shape, and color. Preschoolers are supposed to be unable to see beyond these features to more inferred, less obvious conceptions. For example, in Piaget's number conservation task preschoolers apparently focused on how long the rows looked rather than on the numbers of items present. As this chapter has shown, despite uneven performances, preschoolers do conceive of these relatively invisible aspects of the world. They attend to and understand number and they have rudimentary but impressive conceptions of unobservable mental processes. Of course, it is important not to overstate the young child's sophistication. Piaget is certainly correct that the surface features of events have a provocative pull on the thinking of the young child. Further, the young child's knowledge is often limited to only certain helpful situations. Thus preschool concepts and knowledge include a mixture of abilities and ignorance. For investigators, as well as for parents and teachers, it is embarrassingly easy to both underestimate and at the same time overestimate the preschooler.

Current advances in our assessment of preschoolers have come from studying preschoolers in their own right, not just as negative reflections of older children. This new approach to the study of young children has meant (a) looking at preschoolers of different ages, not just a group of four-year-olds to compare to older children, (b) utilizing phenomena and events with which the child has had firsthand experience, and (c) developing procedures specifically for younger subjects—methods used with older children often require too much verbal sophistication and cooperation from the younger child. Much progress is still required. We are particularly ignorant about two- and three-year-olds, an important and formative age bridging the world of the young infant with the skills and conceptions of the relatively sophisticated older preschooler. Better understanding here will depend on future careful and creative assessment techniques.

Patterns and sequences

One reason that accurate assessment is such a critical endeavor is that in general we do not merely want to find out if the child knows a single fact. Instead we want to appreciate the child's knowledge of many related facts and to understand how all of this knowledge fits together; what is known at the same time as what, what is known first, what only later? That is, we want to understand patterns and sequences.

In this regard the most important information in the above reviews is about patterns and sequences: arithmetic reasoning precedes algebraic reasoning; children first understand that different persons see different objects and only later understand that they also may have different views; the first knowledge of variables is that the number of things to think about influences thinking. The average ages cited above are *not* so important; individual children develop faster or slower.

Another aspect of sequences is that, once acquired, concepts can be utilized to aid in the accomplishment of other tasks and goals. Concepts of number aid the child in games or sports that require counting or keeping score, in earning and spending money, in making quantitative comparisons, and in all forms of computational behavior both in and out of school. Similarly early concepts of the thinking process are incorporated into later developments. The child must know of differences between the thoughts of different people in order to communicate accurately, to plan and evaluate her or his own acts by evaluating the consequences of what is done, and to understand and tolerate people from different backgrounds. In addition the child's developing ability to solve many problems depends on an understanding of the workings of one's own thoughts—for example that memory is limited and so must be assisted by using various strategies, that concentration affects what is learned, that a two-year-old brother is unlikely to be able to help you on some problem where an eight-year-old sister may.

Acquisition

As important as *what* concepts children possess is *how* the child acquires new knowledge. There are two related questions here. First, what accounts for the fact that five-year-olds know more about number and about thinking than three-year-olds, in the normal course of development? Second, what should adults do to aid the child's concept development?

To begin, consider two different possibilities about developing children and their experiences. In the first, adult teachers or parents are thought of as *training* the child and the child is a more or less *passive* trainee. In the second, experiences with or without adults are thought of as merely sources of *information* for the child who is an *active* seeker and interpreter of information. Following Piaget, most developmental psychologists believe that the second description more accurately characterizes the child's acquisition of major and fundamental conceptual systems such as concepts of number and of thinking.

Children do not wait for a teacher to teach them to count or that $3 = 3$, to first think about number. The child's development does not depend on certain specific training experiences such as being taught the conventional number words, or being told that more items to remember is harder than few. Instead the child is always actively striving to make sense of the world, to form miniature theories about how the world operates and to test these theories. In fact, if you think about it the world provides a rich source of information for the child where many different experiences lead to the same major conceptual conclusions. After all, almost any set of items—the child's toys or socks, etc.,—has a specific number, can be compared to other sets, can be counted, rearranged, and counted again. Similarly, there are many experiences contributing information about the mental world: dreams are *not* real, pretending to be sick is not the same as being sick, a child often has hopes or wishes for things (e.g., a birthday present) that do not come true, and even if a child starts out by assuming that the other person knows exactly what she or he knows, experience in miscommunication and missed expectations will eventually inform the child otherwise.

Does this picture of concept development mean that adults have no role to play in the child's development? No. Indeed, this picture points to the important role of providing information-rich experiences for children and in aiding them in the process of interpretation. Recall that young children at first understand the distinction between internal thought processes and external behaviors only in certain salient situations. Adults can and do increase the salience of important features of everyday events ("How many are there? Let's count them." "He doesn't know what you want. How can you tell him?"), and they can arrange special experiences to provoke the child's attention. Early childhood education programs attempt to provide such experiences, based on highlighting concepts when they are useful and meaningful to the child as part of the everyday life of the classroom. (For a good example of what this might mean in the case of teaching number concepts, see Kamii 1982; Kamii and DeVries 1978).

Through conversation and formal and informal instruction, adults also play an indispensable role in providing children with conventional knowledge. Children's concepts will develop to some extent without their knowing the conventional terms and names for them. Indeed, as we have seen, young children demonstrate considerable knowledge of counting even when still using unconventional number terms; and children reveal some understanding of thinking before correctly using *remember, think,* and *know.* However, eventual mastery of these conventions is also important, and requires feedback and instruction. Why is conventional number and language knowledge so important if concept development can proceed without it? The answer is that children's stimulation for concept development would be limited to their own personal experiences unless they can talk with others about *their* experiences. Imagine that all the knowledge you had ever acquired came directly from your own experiences. The wealth of information in books, in your past teachers' minds, in your parents' common sense, would be cut off from you. All you knew about mathematics, for example, was what was discovered on your own, unaided by what Euclid, Newton, and others discovered and passed along. In short, imagine that the entire world of social knowledge was erased from your mind. This gives a sense of the enormous importance of socially transmitted information, even if it is not the only source of information for children's theory building and interpretation.

In sum, children's active efforts benefit greatly from adult support and direction. Of course, as all teachers know, no child is constantly motivated to learn in an active way and certain children have special learning problems. External support is helpful to all and crucial to some. This can range from scheduling inviting activities when children are most rested (and more likely to attend to the conceptual features) all the way to instituting more controlled behavior modification programs. Varied educational techniques can be employed to provide individual children an environment within which ongoing active learning may most effectively operate.

Conclusions

Concept development in the young child is an extremely important topic. It is important to the child because it sets the stage for numerous later developments. Knowledge of the conceptions and misconceptions of preschoolers is important to adults—researchers, parents, educators—who seek to understand the child's potentials and limits, and to communicate with the child as friend, counselor, and teacher. Recent research, that concentrates on preschoolers in their own right, is creating an intriguing picture of the young child's impressive knowledge. The next few years should prove exciting in this regard as the broad outlines of concept development in the young child become clearer.

Preparation of this chapter was supported in part by a Spencer Fellowship from the National Academy of Education to the author.

References

Curcio, F.; Robbins, O.; and Ela, S. S. "The Role of Body Parts and Readiness in Acquisition of Number Conservation." *Child Development* 42 (1971): 1641–1646.

Flavell, J. H. "Concept Development." In *Carmichael's Manual of Child Psychology. Vol. 1,* ed. P. H. Mussen. New York: Wiley, 1970.

Flavell, J. H. "The Development of Knowledge about Visual Perception." In *Nebraska Symposium on Motivation. Vol. 25,* ed. C. B. Keasey. Lincoln,

Neb.: University of Nebraska Press, 1978.

Flavell, J. H., and Wellman, H. M. "Metamemory." In *Perspectives on the Development of Memory and Cognition,* ed. R. Kail and J. Hagen. Hillsdale, N.J.: Lawrence Erlbaum Associates, 1977.

Gelman, R. "Logical Capacity of Very Young Children: Number Invariance Rules." *Child Development* 43 (1972): 75–90.

Gelman, R. "Cognitive Development." *Annual Review of Psychology* 29 (1978): 297–332.

Gelman, R., and Gallistel, C. R. *The Child's Understanding of Number.* Cambridge, Mass.: Harvard University Press, 1978.

Gelman, R., and Tucker, M. F. "Further Investigations of the Young Child's Conception of Number." *Child Development* 46 (1975): 167–175.

Ginsburg, H. *Children's Arithmetic.* New York: Van Nostrand, 1977.

Gordon, F. R., and Flavell, J. H. "The Development of Intuitions about Cognitive Cueing." *Child Development* 48 (1977): 1027–1033.

Johnson, C. N., and Maratsos, N. "Early Comprehension of Mental Verbs: Think and Know." *Child Development* 48 (1977): 1743–1747.

Johnson, C. N., and Wellman, H. M. "Developing Understanding of Mental States and Mental Verbs: 'Remember,' 'Know,' and 'Guess.' " *Child Development* 51 (1980): 1095–1102.

Johnson, C. N., and Wellman, H. M. "Children's Developing Conceptions of the Mind and the Brain." *Child Development,* in press.

Kamii, C. *Number in Preschool and Kindergarten: Educational Implications of Piaget's Theory.* Washington D. C.: National Association for the Education of Young Children, 1982.

Kamii, C., and DeVries, R. *Physical Knowledge in Preschool Education: Implications of Piaget's Theory.* Englewood Cliffs, N.J.: Prentice-Hall, 1978.

Maratsos, M. "Nonegocentric Communication Abilities in Preschool Children." *Child Development* 44 (1973): 697–700.

Marvin, R. S.; Greenberg, M. T.; and Mossler, D. G. "The Early Development of Conceptual Perspective Taking: Distinguishing among Multiple Perspectives." *Child Development* 47 (1976): 511–514.

Masangkay, Z. S.; McCluskey, K. A.; McIntyre, C. W.; Sims-Knight, J.; Vaughn, B. E.; and Flavell, J. H. "The Early Development of Inferences about the Visual Percepts of Others." *Child Development* 45 (1974): 357–366.

McNamara, J.; Baker, E.; and Olson, C. L. "Four-Year-Olds' Understanding of 'Pretend,' 'Forget,' and 'Know': Evidence for Proposition Operations." *Child Development* 47 (1976): 62–70.

Misciones, J. L.; Marvin, R. S.; O'Brien, R. G.; and Greenberg, M. T. "A Developmental Study of Preschool Children's Understanding of the Words 'Know' and 'Guess.' " *Child Development* 49 (1978): 1107–1113.

Piaget, J. *The Child's Conception of the World.* New York: Harcourt, Brace, 1929.

Piaget, J. *The Child's Conception of Number.* New York: Norton, 1952.

Piaget, J. *The Moral Judgement of the Child.* New York: Harcourt, Brace, 1965.

Ritter, K. "The Development of Knowledge of an External Retrieval Cue Strategy." *Child Development* 49 (1978): 1227–1230.

Wellman, H. M. "Preschoolers' Understanding of Memory-Relevant Variables." *Child Development* 48 (1977): 1720–1723.

Wellman, H. M. "A Child's Theory of Mind: The Development of Conceptions of Cognition." In *The Growth of Reflection,* ed. S. R. Yussen. New York: Academic Press, 1982.

Wellman, H. M., and Johnson, C. N. "Understanding of Mental Processes: A Developmental Study of 'Remember' and 'Forget.' *Child Development* 50 (1979): 79–88.

Wellman, H. M., and Lempers, J. D. "The Naturalistic Communicative Abilities of Two-Year-Olds." *Child Development* 48 (1977): 1052–1057.

Cluster III

Children's social relationships: process and consequences

Children's acquisition of the values of their culture is of perennial interest to researchers and practitioners. Practitioners are in the position to use directly many of the insights from this research. As Grusec and Arnason note, recent work has focused on enhancing prosocial skills of altruism and empathy, in contrast to earlier research centering on topics such as aggression and egocentrism. Recent research points to the significance of cognitive skills in role taking and of metacognition in the early development of prosocial attitudes. As children develop in their awareness of different points of view, and in their ability to coordinate these multiple perspectives, they become increasingly able to behave empathetically. Researchers in this area are tracing the ways that the developmental level of the child influences the effectiveness of different socialization techniques.

The chapter by Asher, Renshaw, and Hymel also considers how adults can enhance children's social development, especially with children who lack the necessary skills to enjoy relationships with their age-mates. Here, too, adults may engage in direct instruction, or they may play more indirect roles, for example, by arranging toddler playgroups so that children can begin to develop social skills with their peers.

Hilliard and Vaughn-Scott alert us to the importance of remembering that when we speak of *the child*, we temporarily ignore a pressing reality in the lives of many children and their families. Each child lives in a distinctive social system—of family, ethnic, and cultural group. These social systems are nested within one another, such as a family within a community, and, at the same time, exist side by side, such as home and school. The features of social systems are sources of great variation in the lives of children. These authors express concern that labels of a child's social system may become a source of bias, stereotyping, and prejudice. In fact, children who are members of a group with one conventional label, such as Chinese-American, display great individual differences, and a Chinese-American child may resemble a Native American or Black child in her day care center more closely than she does other Chinese-Americans in the center.

Both the conscientious practitioner and researcher benefit from understanding how our expectations or attributions of children influence our behavior toward them, and their subsequent response to us. We may use such insights in positive ways, such as in telling a child about our confidence that she can master the language of the school, or in negative ways, by telling her that her low performance is about what we would expect. Research continues to document how powerful such attitudes may be as they are conveyed, implicitly or explicitly, to children.

Steven R. Asher
Peter D. Renshaw
Shelley Hymel

8 Peer relations and the development of social skills

Children's peer relations have been increasingly recognized as serving important functions in the development of competence (Asher 1978; Hartup 1980; Youniss 1980). Children provide each other with emotional support in unfamiliar or threatening circumstances (e.g., Freud and Dann 1951; Schwarz 1972), facilitate complex forms of imaginary play (e.g., Gottman and Parkhurst 1980), and provide direct instruction in various social, physical, and cognitive skills (e.g., Allen 1976; Fine 1981). Furthermore, correlational studies suggest that early difficulties in peer relations are related to adjustment problems in later life, including dropping out of school (Ullmann 1957), delinquency (Roff, Sells, and Golden 1972), mental health problems (Cowen et al. 1973; Kohn and Clausen 1955), bad conduct discharges from military service (Roff 1961), and suicide (Stengel 1971). Given the importance of peer relations and the fact that a large number of children lack friends in school (Asher and Hymel 1981; Gronlund 1959), it is essential to identify the factors that lead to satisfying social interactions among children and to develop educational strategies for helping children who are having difficulties in their peer relations.

In this chapter, children's peer relations are examined from a social-skills perspective. Thus the emphasis is on the competencies that are required to interact effectively with peers. This emphasis seems to be a valid and useful approach inasmuch as studies have consistently shown that both social knowledge and a social behavior are related to children's acceptance by the peer group (see Asher and Hymel 1981, for a review), and that intervention efforts to improve children's social skills have increased peer acceptance (Asher and Renshaw 1981; Combs and Slaby 1978). A social-skills perspective on peer relations is also an appropriate framework for teachers to adopt, because child care centers and schools are settings in which social-skill learning takes place. In this chapter we will first describe various social skills that contribute to satisfying peer relations. Our focus will be on skills that help children with three social tasks: initiating interaction with peers, maintaining ongoing relations, and resolving interpersonal conflicts. Following discussion of these skills, we will discuss the contributions that adults can make to the development of children's social skills.

Social skills as a basis of peer acceptance

The promotion of successful peer relations is a primary objective in the preschool and elementary school years, yet the decision to emphasize particular educational objectives is too frequently based on intuition, unsubstantiated theories, or the simple availability of educational materials, rather than on evidence concerning what are indeed the important skills to teach (Elardo and Elardo 1976). An alternative to nondata-based approaches is to select skills that are related to independent measures of general social adjustment and competence. This approach can be thought of as a competence-correlates approach to the identification of program objectives (Asher and Markell 1979). By identifying the skills that are empirically related to successful peer relations, it becomes possible to develop educational programs that stand a good chance of facilitating a child's social development and peer acceptance.

Fortunately, there is a long history of research aimed at identifying the social skills associated with children's acceptance by peers. Observation studies of children's social behavior (e.g., Gottman, Gonso, and Rasmussen 1975; Hartup, Glazer, and Charlesworth 1967; Koch 1933; Marshall and McCandless 1957; Moore and Updegraff 1964; Putallaz and Gottman 1981), and interview studies designed to assess children's ideas about social interaction (e.g., Asher, Renshaw, and Geraci 1980; Gottman, Gonso, and Rasmussen 1975; Ladd and Oden 1979) have produced an informative body of data. We will draw upon this literature to describe the skills that contribute to acceptance by the peer group. The focus will be on children's ability to initiate social relationships, maintain relationships, and resolve interpersonal conflicts.

Initiating interaction with peers

Children, as well as adults, are frequently faced with situations in which they must initiate contact with peers. A necessary task for all children when entering nursery school is to become acquainted with the other children. Asher and Renshaw (in preparation) interviewed 65 kindergarten children concerning their ideas about how to behave in initiation situations, as well as other social situations. On the basis of sociometric measures, 32 of the children were classified as popular, while 33 were classified as unpopular. In one initiation situation, the children were shown a picture of a new child in class and asked how the new child could get to know the other children in the class. Interesting differences existed between the strategies offered by popular vs. unpopular children. The popular children appeared more self-confident and independent than the unpopular children in the strategies they suggested. Popular children were more likely to suggest a joint activity, or suggest playing with the children, whereas the unpopular children were more likely to say that the teacher should help the new child in getting to know the children. On another initiation item, children were shown a picture of two children and were asked how one child could befriend the other. Here, too, popular children were more likely to suggest strategies such as talking to or playing with the child, or proposing a joint activity. In contrast, unpopular children were more likely to offer vague and inappropriate ideas such as "smile together" or "be it."

Unpopular elementary school children also appear to lack knowledge of how to initiate social relationships with peers. Gottman, Gonso, and Rasmussen (1975) studied the initiation skills of third- and fourth-graders using a role-playing task. Children were asked to pretend that the experimenter was a new child at school. Children's responses to this "new child" were tape-recorded and categorized. Results indicate that unpopular children were less skillful than popular children in that unpopular children were less likely to use initiation strategies such as offering a greeting, giving information, requesting information, or extending inclusion (e.g., "Wanna come over to my house sometime?").

A different sort of initiation situation arises when the child already knows the other children and is simply trying to gain entry into an ongoing peer interaction. This task is a recurring one for preschool children. Corsaro's (1981) observations of preschool children's playground interaction indicate that over 80 percent of all peer-play episodes lasted less than ten minutes. Thus, during an extended free-play session, children frequently are confronted with the task of entering a new play group. Corsaro's observations of the preschoolers' attempts to enter a play group suggest that children are often initially resisted. Accordingly, they require some social expertise to succeed. A particularly effective strategy involves approaching one's peers, observing their activities, then beginning to behave as they are behaving (Corsaro 1978). By using this sequence, children increase the likelihood of being accepted, perhaps because they integrate themselves into the ongoing activity in a nondisruptive way.

The strategies of kindergarten children for entering ongoing peer group activities were also examined by Asher and Renshaw (in preparation). The children were asked how a child might join two children already engaged in a board game. In response, both popular and unpopular children suggested the straightforward approach of asking to play, but the popular children were more likely to suggest more sophisticated strategies such as waiting until a natural break occurred in the game and then joining in. In contrast, some unpopular children's responses were vague (e.g., "He could play.") and were offered without elaboration. Not a single popular child gave this kind of vague response. Popular children, therefore, appear to be somewhat more sophisticated and to have better-defined strategies for gaining entry into ongoing activities.

Putallaz and Gottman (1981) investigated the strategies used by second- and third-grade children in entering an existing peer group. Popular and unpopular children were observed as they tried to join two children who were playing a board game. Unpopular children made more bids to enter the game but were less likely to be accepted. They were more likely to be disagreeable, to say something about themselves, to state their feelings, and to ask questions. These behaviors have the effect of calling attention to the entering child rather than to the ongoing activity, and may have caused the negative reaction from the other children. In contrast, popular children joined in the children's ongoing conversation and adopted their frame of reference. Such strategies were more likely to result in acceptance into the ongoing activity.

An important skill for initiating activity with peers, whether children are entering a newly forming peer group or an established peer group, is their ability to adapt when initial entry strategies have been unsuccessful. The majority of contacts children initiate with peers do not lead directly to sustained interaction with peers. Harold (1951) observed that about 62 percent of all initiation attempts were unsuccessful. Similarly, Beaver (1932) and Corsaro (1978; 1981) noted that children were likely to meet with resistance or no response when they attempted to initiate contact with peers. However, Corsaro (1981) reported that although half of the attempts to initiate interaction with peers met with *initial* resistance, only about half of these episodes resulted in permanent exclusion. Thus, children are likely to benefit if they can adopt alternative initiation strategies when their initial attempts fail.

The children's own perceptions of why their initial attempts at interaction failed may be critical to their adoption of alternative strategies. Goetz and Dweck (1980) examined the type of explanation elementary school children offered when their attempts to begin a new relationship with another child were rebuffed. Some children attributed their setback to a lack of effort or misunderstanding. These are temporary conditions that can be remedied by the child trying harder or clearing up the misunderstanding. However, other children consistently attributed their setback to lack of ability (e.g., "It happened because it is hard for me to make friends."). These children were less likely to make a comeback after being initially rejected because the way they perceived their situation discouraged further efforts.

Maintaining relationships

The maintenance of positive peer relationships is another important task for preschool and elementary school children. Studies have consistently shown that being accepted by peers is related to prosocial styles of interaction (Gottman, Gonso, and Rasmussen 1975; Hartup, Glazer, and Charlesworth 1967; Marshall and McCandless 1957). For example, Marshall and McCandless (1957) found that preschool children's peer acceptance, as determined by sociometric measures, was positively related to their associative play and friendly approach to peers. Hartup, Glazer, and Charlesworth (1967) also found peer acceptance to be positively related to friendly social behaviors including giving positive attention and approval, giving affection and personal acceptance, submitting to another's wishes, and giving things to another. However, negative behaviors (noncompliance, interference, derogation, or attack) were related to peer rejection. In general, then, the correlational evidence confirms the importance of adopting friendly and cooperative styles of interaction for the maintenance of positive peer relationships. Children need to feel assured that a peer can be counted on to cooperate in a game, to be a good sport, and to comply reasonably often with others' suggestions. Those children who do not consistently exhibit positive interaction styles may acquire a reputation for spoiling games and causing disruptions, and may subsequently be excluded from interaction.

In addition to a generally positive style of interaction, knowing how to be helpful to one's peers when they are in need is important in maintaining relationships. Ladd and Oden (1979) examined third and fourth graders' ideas concerning how to help another child. Children were asked to give behavioral solutions to hypothetical situations involving a child needing help (e.g., a child being teased by classmates). Children's ideas were categorized according to their content (e.g., console-comfort, solicit the aid of an adult). The most important finding was that children who were unpopular gave more responses that were unique, in that no other child gave that category of response. These unique responses were typically inappropriate to the demands of the situation (e.g., ordering the child being teased to do something vs. consoling and comforting the child). Thus, unpopular children's ideas concerning how to help appear to be ineffective and, if implemented, would in all likelihood fail to consolidate a positive relationship with other children.

Conflict management

Peer relations at all ages are riddled with the potential for disagreement or conflict, and the ability to manage or resolve interpersonal conflict is an important social task. Conflicts among preschool children often center around possession of a toy or object, whereas older children more often have disputes related to what activities to engage in, which other children to be with, or who is responsible for some negative event that just occurred. Indeed, conflict management is a difficult social task and children seem to realize this. Wheeler and Ladd (in press) asked third, fourth, and fifth graders to indicate how hard it would be for them to manage various social situations. Children reported more difficulty for the conflict than for the nonconflict situations.

Conflict situations, unlike initiation or maintenance situations, have considerable potential for evoking aggressive behavior. It is highly unusual for a child to punch, bite, or call names when faced with the task of entering a new group, or helping another child who is in distress. However, these forms of aggressive responses are relatively common ways young children have of responding to situations involving conflict. Furthermore, those children who habitually engage in physically aggressive or verbally abusive forms of behavior are far more likely than others to be disliked and rejected by the peer group (e.g., Moore 1967). Such children would benefit by learning more effective, nonaggressive ways of managing conflict situations.

Although we know that aggressive behavior is often dysfunctional, little is known about the relation between more prosocial conflict management strategies and children's success in their peer relationships. In the previously mentioned interview study with kindergarten children, Asher and Renshaw presented two different conflict situations to the children. In one, a child is shown playing with a toy when another tries to take it away. In the second situation, two children are shown watching television when one child, the guest, suddenly changes the channel to another show. The purpose was to learn about the types of strategies used by popular and unpopular children under such circumstances. Neither popular nor unpopular children acquiesced in the conflict situations, but unpopular children, compared with popular ones, were more likely to suggest aggressive strategies such as hitting the other child or destroying the toy or television.

What do children suggest when they are being neither acquiescent nor aggressive? The strategies were of four general types. First, children frequently suggested direct but nonaggressive forms of action such as "Take it back," or "Turn it back." Second, they appealed to a variety of social conventions as a means of persuading the offending child to stop. For example, they invoked the norms that one should ask first, that the person who has possession has priority, and that it is not polite simply to take something. Third, they sought compromise by suggesting that the children could take turns or share the toy or the television. Fourth, children appealed to teachers and parents quite frequently. It appears, therefore, that children, by age five, already know that their rights can be defended in peer conflicts by direct action that is not overly aggressive, by persuasion through appeals to social conventions, by seeking a compromise through sharing, and by appealing to an authority. Children's ability and willingness to use such techniques may vary for individuals and situations.

The acquisition of social skills

Research reviewed thus far indicates that unpopular children not only display less effective strategies in their observable behavior, but they also seem to lack knowledge of the kind of behavior that is most appropriate in different social situations. In this section, the focus will be on how social skills are acquired. In particular, consideration will be given to adults' roles in the development of social skills and to the types of educational approaches that are effective with children who are having difficulty in their peer relations.

The contributions of adults: setting the stage

Although recent research has increasingly recognized the unique contributions of peer interaction to children's social development (e.g., Hartup 1980; Youniss 1980), adults also play important, if not critical, roles. First, in the role of social planner, adults arrange the social and physical environment in ways that promote or undermine the development of children's social competence. Parents perform this function when they arrange occasions for children to have playmates in their home. For example, Lieberman (1977) found that parents who arranged for other children to come and visit in their homes had children who were more socially responsive in nursery school.

Teachers, too, function as social planners in the way they structure the child's school environment. For example, Quilitch and Risley (1973) and Van Alstnyne (1932) both found that social toys and materials (those designed for play involving more than one child) elicited considerably more complex social interaction among children than did isolate toys and materials (those designed for use by only one child at a time). Similarly, certain types of play activities are especially facilitative of peer interaction (Barton and Ascione 1979; Charlesworth and Hartup 1967; Parten 1933). The highest incidence of social interaction among preschool children is observed during sociodramatic activities such as house and doll play, puppet play, or play with blocks and trucks, in contrast to table activities such as puzzles, art activities, and construction work with clay or paper. Sociodramatic activities may provide children with more defined social roles and a framework in which to interact with peers (Strain and Wiegerink 1976).

The provision of toys beyond certain optimal limits may actually reduce interaction (Doke and Risley 1972; Johnson 1935). For example, Doke and Risley (1972) found that providing children with many choices of activities, increasing the amount of materials, and dismissing children individually (rather than en masse) from one activity to another resulted in greater participation with the materials. This might seem to be desirable but a second look suggests a more complicated picture. When the children worked with no activity options and were dismissed en masse, it appeared that " . . . children spent more time talking to each other" (Doke and Risley 1972, p. 416). Since conversation can lead to valuable social learning, it seems undesirable to inadvertently curtail such opportunities. An unlimited supply of materials may reduce the need for children to practice skills in sharing and managing conflict over more limited resources. Thus, it seems that peer interaction among preschoolers is most encouraged when teachers do not provide an unlimited amount of materials or equipment, and when the materials and activities provided are social rather than nonsocial in nature.

Research conducted with elementary school children suggests still other ways in which teachers can structure the school environment to facilitate positive peer interaction. For example, it appears that pairing low-accepted children with more popular peers for participation in a cooperative activity can lead to improved peer acceptance of the less popular child (e.g., Chennault 1967). Although the initial gains typically dissipate with the termination of the specially designed activity (Lilly 1971; Rucker and Vincenzo 1970), continued or repeated reliance on cooperative work activities may result in more long-term improvements in children's peer relations. This is suggested by the work of Johnson and Johnson (1974; 1978) on cooperative group learning situations.

In addition to their role as social planner, adults can also play an important role by providing verbal instruction in how to negotiate the social environment. Adults influence children by suggesting appropriate social behaviors (e.g., sharing, or playing together with other children) and by providing explicit rationales for behavior, particularly rationales that emphasize the consequences of social actions for other people. Parents who use such techniques have children who are more prosocial and who are judged by their peers to be more considerate of others (Aronfreed 1968; Hoffman and Saltzstein 1967; Sears, Maccoby, and Levin 1957; Zahn-Waxler, Radke-Yarrow, and King 1978).

A study by De Aenlle (1979) also suggests the kind of influence parents' beliefs and teaching styles may have on their children's development. Parents of popular and unpopular fourth grade children completed a questionnaire that was designed to assess parental attitudes and practices toward childhood peer relations. Although parents of both low- and high-status children were found to have strongly positive attitudes about the role of children's friendships as sources of emotional security and social learning, parents differed in how effectively they responded to four hypothetical situations (e.g., the child being invited to a party where she or he knew few of the other children; the child being bossy to playmates). Parents of low-status children were more likely to give vague responses (e.g., "Be yourself." or "Do what you feel is right."), or to sidestep the problem by saying, for example, that they would "let the problem take care of itself." Parents of high-status children appeared to have more specific and detailed ideas, and were more concerned with the feelings of other children. Furthermore, the responses of popular children's parents were rated as more appropriate and more positive in affective content.

The results of these studies clearly suggest that adults can and do function in the capacity of teacher of social skills for children. Furthermore, they imply that children who lack friends and social skills may have received inadequate modeling or social-skill instruction. If this reasoning is correct, it should be possible to help children with inadequate peer relations by providing specific social-skill training experiences. In the next section we will examine research in which children were directly taught socially adaptive behaviors. These studies not only demonstrate that teaching social skills facilitates children's peer relations, but they also provide useful procedures that could readily be adapted for use in schools and other settings.

Direct training in the acquisition of social skills

There are various ways that adults communicate with children about appropriate or desirable social behavior: by *reinforcing* children for engaging in positive behavior after the behavior has occurred, by demonstrating or *modeling* the desired behavior, and by directly *coaching* children. These three ways of informing children complement one another and are frequently used in combination by parents and teachers to affect change in children's behavior.

In this section we will review evidence concerning the extent to which each procedure results in short-term and long-term change. Although these methods will be discussed separately, most studies include more than one procedure. In particular, considerable overlap exists between studies classified here as modeling and coaching.

Positive reinforcement. Several studies have demonstrated that positive social behavior can be promoted by reinforcing desired behavior. In one of the first studies of this kind (Allen et al. 1964), the subject was a four-year-old girl who interacted frequently with her preschool teacher but much less frequently with peers. This child also showed signs of being unhappy in the school. First the child was observed during a baseline period to determine her usual level of interaction with adults and with peers. No effort was made to modify her behavior during this period. In a second phase of the study the teachers began to reinforce the child with attention whenever she stood or played near another child. Still later she was only reinforced for direct contact or interaction with her peers. This procedure of gradually reinforcing *successive approximations* of the desired behavior (known as shaping) was successful in increasing the target child's interaction with peers and, at the same time, decreasing her high level of interaction with adults. In the next phase of the experiment, the reinforcement for social interaction with peers was terminated with the result that peer interaction decreased back to the level it had been during the baseline period. Reinstatement of the reinforcement contingencies again resulted in increased peer interaction.

Reinforcement need not be only applied to a single target child. The behavior of entire groups of children can also be modified by direct reinforcement procedures. For example, Brown and Elliott (1965) modified aggressive behavior in preschool children by having teachers praise cooperative behavior in each of the children in the class and simultaneously ignore aggressive behavior. Hauserman, Walen, and Behling (1973) used a similar system to increase cross-race interaction among first grade children. In this case, children were reinforced first by both teacher praise and by tickets redeemable for candy for "sitting with a new friend" at lunch. Later, only teacher praise was used as a reinforcer. This procedure increased cross-race interaction during the lunch period and the effect was found to generalize to a subsequent free-play period. Using a similar procedure, Serbin, Tonick, and Sternglanz (1977) used teacher attention as a reinforcer to increase cross-sex play among nursery school children.

A variant of group reinforcement, called dependent group contingencies, is described by Litrow and Pumroy (1975). In this case an entire group of children is reinforced for particular behaviors shown by a given target child. A series of case studies by Hops, Walker, and Greenwood (1977) illustrates the approach. They reported that teacher praise for interacting with peers, when applied on an individual basis, was often slow to produce an effect and produced variable or inconsistent increases in interactive behavior. In contrast, when individual reward plus group reward were given, both contingent on the behavior of the target child, interaction increased more rapidly and consistently.

A study by Strain and Timm (1974) provides especially provocative results. They found both individual and dependent group reinforcement procedures to be effective in increasing the peer interaction of a three-year-old isolated girl. However, the type of contingency used differentially affected who initiated the interaction. When only the target child was reinforced for social interaction, changes in interaction were due primarily to an increase in that child's social initiations, whereas with dependent group reinforcement procedures, the target child's classmates were primarily responsible for initiating interactions with the target child; the target child's behavior did not appear to change. It is necessary, therefore, to be aware of the specific effects of any reinforcement procedure on the target behaviors of interest.

Another potential problem with dependent group contingency procedures should be noted. In two case studies reported by Kandel, Ayllon, and Rosenbaum (1977), classmates were reinforced for interacting with two socially isolated children during recess. Although the procedure successfully increased classmates' interactions with the target children, in both cases the initial reaction of those children to the resulting flood of peer interest was negative: they actually tried to escape from their peers. In one case, the initially negative reaction grew to the point where treatment was terminated because it seemed unethical and potentially harmful. Later, a modified procedure in which only two peers were reinforced for interaction with the target child was found to be successful in increasing peer interaction. The results of this study highlight a potential danger of dependent group contingencies that focus on the behavior of specific individuals. Many practitioners will be cautious about employing such procedures given the potential problem of calling undue attention to the target child and her or his problems.

Thus far, our discussion of reinforcement has focused on the immediate effects of reinforcement techniques. A major problem, however, has been their general failure to maintain initial behavior changes once reinforcement contingencies are removed. This is true of both individual and group contingencies. For example, O'Connor (1972) used reinforcement to increase individual children's rate of interaction. He produced dramatic changes that were completely reversed when reinforcement was terminated. The previously discussed group contingencies (Brown and Elliott 1965; Hauserman, Walen, and Behling 1973; Serbin, Tonick, and Sternglanz 1977) also were effective only as long as the reinforcement contingencies were used.

Several authors have attempted to specify procedures that may facilitate the maintenance of effects over time (O'Leary and Drabman 1971; Stokes and Baer 1977; Strain, Cooke, and Apolloni 1976a; 1976b). For example, maintenance over time may be facilitated by withdrawing the experimentally contrived reinforcement gradually rather than suddenly, thereby enabling the natural, spontaneous reinforcers of the peer group to take over and maintain the occurrence of the desired behavior (O'Leary and Drabman 1971; Stokes and Baer 1977). A case study by Coates (1967), reported in Baer and Wolf (1970) demonstrates the potential effectiveness of this technique in producing long-term maintenance of initial changes in social behavior. In another study, use of intermittent reinforcement procedures may have contributed to the long-term effects of a group contingency program for increasing positive peer interaction among fourth and fifth grade isolated children (Allen et al. 1975). In this study, one of the few to demonstrate long-term effects, generalization was also encouraged by reinforcing the children for interactive behavior in a variety of different activities and later reinforcing the children for interaction that occurred outside of the training situation.

Other suggestions for facilitating maintenance include training in self-reinforcement or self-management techniques (O'Leary and Drabman 1971; O'Leary and O'Leary 1976; Stokes and Baer 1977). These techniques involve instructing children to reward themselves, perhaps in a token economy system, for selected target behaviors, rather than having reinforcement provided by another individual such as the teacher. Although such procedures have not been used to date in studies of children's social interaction, their effectiveness has been suggested in studies of the modification of on-task behavior (Glynn and Thomas 1974), and inappropriate or disruptive classroom behavior (Bolstad and Johnson 1972; Johnson 1970). Finally, use of peers rather than adults as agents of reinforcement may also facilitate maintenance (Kazdin 1975; Strain, Cooke, and Apolloni 1976b), although such procedures have not been employed in research on modifying children's style of social interaction.

To summarize, the maintenance of initial gains made as a result of reinforcement procedures might be facilitated in a number of ways. Many of these possibilities, however, have not yet been systematically tested in research on children's social behavior. Thus, the problem of long-term maintenance of reinforcement effects clearly warrants further research. Other intervention strategies, however, have been shown to result in longer-term improvements in children's relations with peers. We now turn to an examination of those strategies.

Modeling. Children can be taught to engage in positive social behavior by observing others model or demonstrate the behavior. This can be accomplished through the use of live peer models (e.g., Csapo 1972), or by presenting models on television or film (e.g., Evers and Schwarz 1973; Keller and Carlson 1974; O'Connor 1969; 1972). O'Connor (1969) developed a 23-minute peer modeling film to increase the social interaction of preschool children who had relatively low rates of interaction. The film contained 11 modeling episodes involving preschool children. A narrator described the action in each episode to call children's attention to the relevant behavior. Several studies using the O'Connor film have found that increases in interactive behavior resulted from seeing the film (Evers-Pasquale 1978; Evers-Pasquale and Sherman 1975; Evers and Schwarz 1973; O'Connor 1969; 1972), and there is also evidence that the effects are maintained at one-month or two-month follow-up assessments (Evers-Pasquale and Sherman 1975; Evers and Schwarz 1973; O'Connor 1972).

It may well be the narration accompanying the O'Connor film segments accounts for the effectiveness of the film. Analyzing the script, Gottman (1976) found many examples of calling attention to the child's intention to interact, describing how to go about interacting, giving descriptions of ongoing behavioral sequences, and describing the positive consequences of interaction. For example, in one sequence the narrator said: "Now another child comes up close to watch. She wants to play too. She waits for them to see her. Now she gets a chair and she sits down with them so they will play with her. She starts to do what they are doing so they will want to play with her. . . ." This type of information-rich narration should help children to acquire general strategies that are maintained over time.

There have been two studies using the O'Connor film that have not obtained positive results and an examination of these can be instructive. In one of these studies (Gottman 1977), a sample of Head Start children were observed prior to watching the film, and again eight weeks after the film was shown, with no evidence of effects on the children's level of peer interaction. Since no assessment was made immediately after the film was shown, it is not clear whether the film had no impact or whether there were immediate effects that dissipated over time. If effects were not obtained, it could be because Head Start children are less verbally proficient than children in the middle-SES nursery schools who participated in the earlier studies; it seems plausible that the effectiveness of the film's narration would depend on the verbal and conceptual skills of the listener-viewer.

A second study by Walker et al. (1975) suggests the importance of matching the age of the models and the viewer. Elementary school children whose interaction rates were low saw the film, but showed no change in their behavior. Because the film models were preschoolers, the children viewing the film in this case may have considered it irrelevant or less applicable to their social world. There is evidence from other research that degree of perceived similarity does influence the extent to which a child imitates the behavior of a model (e.g., Rosekrans 1967); clearly, there is a need to produce more age-appropriate modeling films for use with older children.

Beside using filmed models, teachers can also have children attend to the real-life models among their classmates. Csapo (1972) had six elementary school children who were highly disruptive sit next to six classmates who were models of classroom decorum. The disruptive child was told to watch the model child and to do what that child was doing. Observations indicated that all six disruptive children improved their behavior dramatically and that follow-up data taken ten days after the intervention also showed positive results. One implication of these results is that the presence of a model in the classroom should be made explicit to the target child. Often teachers will group children together for modeling purposes but not deliberately call a target child's attention to a model's behavior. This indirect approach may be less effective than a more explicit approach.

To summarize, modeling is an effective procedure for teaching children social behavior. Particularly promising is evidence of maintenance beyond the immediate intervention period. Our discussion emphasizes the possible contribution of three factors to its effectiveness: the perceived similarity of the model to the observing child, the extent to which the presence of a model is made explicit to the child, and the extent to which the modeling display is accompanied by narration calling attention to the behavior and its underlying purposes and consequences. The next section on coaching focuses further on the contributions of this verbal component to social-skill training.

Coaching. In modeling, the defining element is showing; a number of specific instances are depicted and the learner is expected to infer a general concept or strategy. In coaching, the defining element is telling; a general concept or strategy is explicitly provided, sometimes with a few examples, and the learner is expected to use the general concept to generate appropriate behavior in a variety of future situations (Marlatt 1972). Such a procedure should be particularly useful in facilitating long-term maintenance and generalization of training across time and situations. Indeed, research shows that coaching has resulted in long-term changes in both behavior and sociometric status (Gottman, Gonso, and Schuler 1976; Ladd 1981; Oden and Asher 1977). We will now discuss several intervention programs involving coaching. It should be emphasized that just as most of the modeling studies discussed earlier contain a potentially instructive verbal narration, the coaching studies contain opportunities for children to observe a peer model. Furthermore, several of these studies introduce an additional training element, namely opportunities to rehearse, or practice, the skills being coached.

Oden and Asher's (1977) coaching procedure consisted of three components: verbal instruction, rehearsal, and postrehearsal review. This procedure was implemented with third and fourth grade children who were among the least-liked children in their class. Children first were individually instructed by an adult in four social interaction concepts: participation (e.g., getting started and paying attention), cooperation (e.g., sharing materials and taking turns), communication (e.g., talking and listening), and validation-support, referred to as being friendly, fun, and nice (e.g., offering help or encouragement). Children were told that trying out each of these ideas might make playing games with other children more fun. Children were then given an opportunity to practice the ideas during a play session with a same-sex classmate. The children played moderately competitive table games including *Blockhead,* tick-tack-toe, dominoes, and a pick-up-sticks game, as well as two table activities of a more cooperative nature (e.g., a drawing task). After a play session, the adult and the child reviewed the social interaction concepts in light of the play experience. The four-week program consisted of six sessions each involving a different game and partner.

The coaching procedure led to significant gains in peer acceptance as measured by a sociometric play-rating measure (i.e., "How much do you like to play with this person at school?"), administered a few days after the interaction ended. Particularly encouraging were results from a one-year follow-up assessment. Children who had received coaching actually continued to increase in acceptance by their peers. These results indicate that coaching had a snowball effect—perhaps because the children who were coached gained confidence, or because the new school year resulted in many new classmates and the chance to try new skills without the handicap of a negative reputation. In contrast, control children gained hardly at all in sociometric status even though a year had passed and many of their classmates were new. These results indicate that without intervention children's low acceptance in the peer group is a rather stable condition.

Ladd (1981) conducted a similar study with third grade children who were coached on three communication skills: asking positive questions, offering useful suggestions or directions, and offering supportive statements. Eight coaching sessions, lasting 40 to 50 minutes each, were conducted over a three-week period. The procedure consisted of verbally instructing children in the concepts, guiding them through rehearsal of the ideas, letting the children practice on their own while playing with a classmate, and reviewing the concepts following the practice session. The review phase included coaching in self-evaluation skills. In this phase, children were taught to evaluate their own behavior in light of the ideas they were learning about how to interact with other children.

The results of this training program were measured immediately after the training program and again four weeks later. Behavioral observations made in the classroom indicated that children improved on two of the three behaviors that were taught. Children also gained significantly on the same "play with" rating-scale sociometric measure used by Oden and Asher (1977). Control group children made no comparable gains. The results of the Ladd study are impressive because changes in both behavior and sociometric status were observed in children who received social-skill instruction.

Can coaching, relying heavily as it does on verbal instruction, be successful with much younger children? Can preschool or kindergarten children benefit from this type of cognitively based intervention strategy? The social-skill training procedures used by Oden and Asher (1977) and Ladd (1981) involve instruction in relatively abstract ideas and require extensive verbal participation from the child during instruction. Younger children may have more difficulty with such procedures. Furthermore, coaching, as employed by Oden and Asher (1977) and Ladd (1981), requires that children reflect upon their own behavior and examine their interactions in light of the concepts that are taught. It seems unlikely that younger children would be as capable of this type of self-reflective activity. Flavell (1976), in particular, discusses younger children's tendency not to monitor their own communicative behavior toward others. This failure to engage in metacommunicative activity might undermine certain types of coaching efforts with younger children.

However, several factors could make direct skill training more effective with younger than older children. Younger children may have less firmly established behavior patterns and also may be more likely to seek the advice of adults in problem-solving situations than are older children. Furthermore, the peers of an older child are likely to be more resistant; having known the child for a long time, they may less readily change their opinions or perceptions. Children's friendship selections do become more stable as children grow older (Horrocks and Buker 1951), and it seems likely that the classroom clique structure becomes less permeable in the later years. This too would make it harder for a newly trained child to become part of the group.

Two studies with preschool children suggest that coaching can be successful in teaching young children social skills. One investigation by Chittenden (1942) is an early classic in the field of social development. Chittenden's focus was on preschoolers who, compared to classmates, used a high proportion of dominative behaviors (for example, snatching toys, commanding others to do things, and hurting others), and a low proportion of cooperative behaviors. She used two dolls, Mandy and Sandy, as teaching aids to help children learn to share, take turns, and play together. In early sessions the dolls played out contrasting endings, so that the children could learn to discriminate unhappy outcomes (such as fighting over a toy) from happy outcomes (such as sharing and having a good time). Later sessions served both modeling and coaching functions. Some-times the dolls played successfully, thereby modeling appropriate behavior. On other occasions the two dolls fought and the experimenter discussed possible ways that the conflicts the dolls faced could be resolved. In still later sessions, the child was asked to show the dolls what they could do to play more successful-ly. Chittenden's training procedure was successful in changing the behavior of the children both in a specially designed game situation involving only two chil-dren, and in the everyday classroom environment.

A study by Zahavi and Asher (1978) relied exclusively on verbal instruction and discussion to teach preschool children social-interaction skills. The eight most aggressive children in a nursery school were identified using an observa-tional procedure. Half of the children then participated in a one-to-one discus-sion between the teacher and the child in which three concepts were empha-sized: (a) that aggression hurts another person and makes that person sad, (b) that aggression does not solve problems and only brings about the resent-ment of the other child, and (c) that positive ways to solve conflicts are sharing and taking turns. The discussion consisted of a question-answer format so that the child participated to some extent in developing the concepts. Children who received this intervention decreased, compared to the control group, in aggres-sive behavior and increased in positive behaviors such as cooperative play and constructive individual play. Furthermore, these improvements were main-tained at the two-week follow-up observations. Following the post-test observa-tions, the control-group children participated in the same kind of discussion with their teacher and their behavior, too, changed in positive directions. Thus, this study, like Chittenden's, provides evidence of the effect of verbal instructional training strategies with very young children.

The coaching procedures used in these two preschool studies differ in one particularly interesting respect from the procedures used by Oden and Asher (1977) and Ladd (1981) with elementary school children. Skill training with the older children included self-evaluation in which the children reflected on the concepts taught in light of their own behavior. In contrast, the preschool proce-dures did not require explicit self-reflection or self-monitoring by the child. It seems that the designers of both the preschool and elementary school training strategies were taking into account the developmental level of the child.

Ethical issues in social-skills training

Educators have long attempted to influence children's social behavior as well as their cognitive functioning, and parents seem to view the socialization func-tion of schools as second only to the teaching of reading. Still, direct attempts to teach social behavior or social values often raise ethical issues that rarely surface when the focus of interaction is on academic subjects. Is it right to alter a child's style of interaction? Might many children who have no friends prefer more solitary but nonetheless satisfying pursuits? Should we be imposing our image of the good social life on others?

The question whether children without friends prefer things that way is an empirical one that can be answered by learning more about the feelings of children who are not well accepted by the peer group. A recent study by Hymel et al. (1981) addressed this issue by surveying over 500 third through sixth grade children. The results indicated that children who had no friends in class were more likely to report being very lonely and that this trend increased as children became older. Furthermore, the survey results showed that children without friends were no more likely than those with friends to be engaged in solitary pursuits such as hobbies or reading. Thus, these children do not fit the image of well-adjusted children who simply prefer to do their own thing. Instead, many seem to be unhappy and adrift. These data also are consistent with the research discussed earlier, that early difficulties in peer relations are related to adjustment problems in later life. Thus, it appears that instead of asking "Is it right to intervene?" we might better ask "Is it right to do nothing?"

Conclusion

In this chapter, children's peer relations were examined from a social-skills perspective. Our approach emphasizes the competencies that are required by children to interact effectively with peers, highlights the crucial role played by adults in helping children form satisfying peer relationships, and is optimistic regarding the ability of teachers and parents to help children who are having peer relationship problems.

In concluding, three important qualifications should be noted. One is that a variety of factors, in addition to a child's social skillfulness, influences acceptance or rejection by the peer group (see Asher, Oden, and Gottman 1977, for a review). Children may be disliked because they are of a different race or sex, have an unusual name, are physically unattractive or disabled, or are perceived as dissimilar in attitudes or beliefs. It should be emphasized, therefore, that social skills, however important, are not the sole determinants of peer acceptance.

Second, recognition needs to be given to other important dimensions of children's social competence in addition to their ability to gain acceptance by peers. In particular, the child's ability to exert influence or leadership among peers merits attention. Although the skills underlying leadership may be related to those underlying peer acceptance, these are nonetheless conceptually distinct domains. An important issue for children, as for adults (Schutz 1960), is to manage the tension that sometimes exists between the need to have influence and the need to be included and receive affection. In this chapter we have highlighted peer acceptance not because it is the only aspect of peer relations, but because it is one of the most important.

Finally, the distinction needs to be made between being accepted by peers and being involved with peers to the exclusion of other activities. Adults have other educational goals for children that may compete with extremely high levels of peer involvement. For example, parents and teachers want children to achieve academically and to be able to engage in other more solitary pursuits. These other goals may require children to sometimes resist the pull of peers and spend task-oriented time in other directions. Although this chapter has focused on the importance of skills that promote acceptance and friendship, it should be emphasized that acquiring these skills need not mean that children sacrifice other important goals. Indeed, as we have seen, for most children positive peer relations are part of the larger pattern of successful and satisfying life adjustment.

References

Allen, K. E.; Hart, B.; Buell, J. S.; Harris, F. R.; and Wolf, M. M. "Effects of Social Reinforcement of Isolate Behavior of a Nursery School Child." *Child Development* 35 (1964): 511–518.

Allen, R. P.; Safer, D. J.; Heaton, R.; Ward, A.; and Barrell, M. "Behavior Therapy for Socially Ineffective Children." *Journal of the American Academy of Child Psychiatry* 14 (1975): 500–509.

Allen, V. L., ed. *Children As Teachers: Theory and Research on Tutoring.* New York: Academic Press, 1976.

Aronfreed, J. "The Concept of Internalization." In *Handbook of Socialization Theory and Research,* ed. D. G. Goslin. Chicago: Rand McNally, 1968.

Asher, S. R. "Children's Peer Relations." In *Social and Personality Development,* ed. M. E. Lamb. New York: Holt, Rinehart & Winston, 1978.

Asher, S. R., and Hymel, S. "Children's Social Competence in Peer Relations: Sociometric and Behavioral Assessment." In *Social Competence,* ed. J. D. Wine and M. D. Smye. New York: Guilford Press, 1981.

Asher, S. R., and Markell, R. A. *Peer Relations and Social Interaction: Assessment and Intervention.* Unpublished manuscript, University of Illinois, Urbana, 1979.

Asher, S. R.; Oden, S. L.; and Gottman, J. M. "Children's Friendships in School Settings." In *Current Topics in Early Childhood Education. Vol. 1,* ed. L. G. Katz. Norwood, N.J.: Ablex, 1977.

Asher, S. R., and Renshaw, P. D. "Children Without Friends: Social Knowledge and Social Skill Training." In *The Development of Children's Friendships,* ed. S. R. Asher and J. M. Gottman. New York: Cambridge University Press, 1981.

Asher, S. R., and Renshaw, P. D. "Social Skills and Social Knowledge of High- and Low-Status Kindergarten Children," in preparation.

Asher, S. R.; Renshaw, P. D.; and Geraci, R. L. "Children's Friendships and Social Competence." *International Journal of Psycholinguistics* 7 (1980): 27–39.

Baer, D. M., and Wolf, H. M. "Recent Examples of Behavior Modification in Preschool Settings." In *Behavior Modification in Clinical Psychology*, ed. C. Neuringer and J. L. Michael. New York: Appleton-Century-Crofts, 1970.

Barton, E. J., and Ascione, F. R. "Sharing in Preschool Children: Facilitation, Stimulus Generalization, Response Generalization and Maintenance." *Journal of Applied Behavior Analysis* 12 (1979): 417–430.

Beaver, A. P. *The Initiation of Social Contacts by Preschool Children*. New York: Teachers College, Columbia University, 1932.

Bolstad, O. D., and Johnson, S. M. "Self-Regulation in the Modification of Disruptive Classroom Behavior." *Journal of Applied Behavior Analysis* 5 (1972): 443–454.

Brown, P., and Elliott, R. "Control of Aggression in a Nursery School Class." *Journal of Experimental Child Psychology* 2 (1965): 103–107.

Charlesworth, R., and Hartup, W. W. "Positive Social Reinforcement in the Nursery School Peer Group." *Child Development* 38 (1967): 993–1003.

Chennault, M. "Improving the Social Acceptance of Unpopular Educable Mentally Retarded Pupils in Special Classes." *American Journal of Mental Deficiency* 72 (1967): 455–458.

Chittenden, M. F. "An Experimental Study in Measuring and Modifying Assertive Behavior in Young Children." *Monographs of the Society for Research in Child Development* 7 (1942). Serial No. 31.

Combs, M. L., and Slaby, D. A. "Social Skills Training with Children." In *Advances in Clinical Child Psychology. Vol. 1*, ed. B. Lahey and A. Kazdin. New York: Plenum, 1978.

Corsaro, W. A. " 'We're Friends Right?' ": *Children's Use of Access Rituals in a Nursery School*. Working Papers in Sociolinguistics. Austin, Tex.: Southwest Educational Development Laboratory, 1978.

Corsaro, W. A. "Friendship in the Nursery School: Social Organization in a Peer Environment." In *The Development of Children's Friendships*, ed. S. R. Asher and J. M. Gottman. New York: Cambridge University Press, 1981.

Cowen, E. L.; Pederson, A.; Babigian, H.; Izzo, L. D.; and Trost, M. A. "Long-Term Follow-Up of Early Detected Vulnerable Children." *Journal of Consulting and Clinical Psychology* 41 (1973): 438–446.

Csapo, M. "Peer Models Reverse the 'One Bad Apple Spoils the Barrel' Theory." *Teaching Exceptional Children* 5 (1972): 20–24.

De Aenlle, C. R. "Parental Involvement in Children's Peer Relations: Their Role As Problem Solvers and Teachers of Social Skills." Unpublished Master's thesis, University of Illinois, Urbana, 1979.

Doke, L., and Risley, T. R. "The Organization of Day-Care Environments: Required Vs. Optional Activities." *Journal of Applied Behavior Analysis* 5 (1972): 405–420.

Elardo, P. T., and Elardo, R. "A Critical Analysis of Social Development Programs in Elementary Education." *Journal of School Psychology* 14 (1976): 118–130.

Evers-Pasquale, W. "The Peer Preference Test As a Measure of Reward Value:

Item Analysis, Cross-Validation, Concurrent Validation, and Replication." *Journal of Abnormal Child Psychology* 6 (1978): 175–188.

Evers-Pasquale, W., and Sherman, M. "The Reward Value of Peers: A Variable Influencing the Efficacy of Filmed Modeling in Modifying Social Isolation in Preschoolers." *Journal of Abnormal Child Psychology* 3 (1975): 170–180.

Evers, W. L., and Schwarz, J. C. "Modifying Social Withdrawal in Preschoolers: The Effects of Filmed Modeling and Teacher Praise." *Journal of Abnormal Child Psychology* 1 (1973): 248–256.

Fine, G. A. "Friends, Impression Management, and Pre-Adolescent Behavior." In *The Development of Children's Friendships*, ed. S. R. Asher and J. M. Gottman. New York: Cambridge University Press, 1981.

Flavell, J. H. "The Development of Metacommunication." Paper presented at the Symposium on Language and Cognition, International Congress of Psychology, Paris, July 1976.

Fouts, G., and Liikanen, P. "The Effects of Age and Development Level on Imitation in Children." *Child Development* 46 (1975): 555–558.

Freud, A., and Dann, S. "An Experiment in Group Upbringing." *Psychoanalytic Study of the Child* 6 (1951): 127–168.

Furman, W. "Promoting Appropriate School Behavior: Developmental Implications for Treatment." In *Advances in Clinical Child Psychology. Vol. 3,* ed. B. Lahey and A. Kazdin. New York: Plenum, 1980.

Glynn, E. L., and Thomas, J. D. "Effect of Cueing on Self-Control of Classroom Behavior." *Journal of Applied Behavior Analysis* 7 (1974): 299–306.

Goetz, T. E., and Dweck, C. S. "Learned Helplessness in Social Situations." *Journal of Personality and Social Psychology* 39 (1980): 246–255.

Gottman, J. M. Personal communication, July 1976.

Gottman, J. M. "The Effects of a Modeling Film on Social Isolation in Preschool Children: A Methodological Investigation." *Journal of Abnormal Child Psychology* 5 (1977): 69–78.

Gottman, J. M.; Gonso, J.; and Rasmussen, B. "Social Interaction, Social Competence and Friendship in Children." *Child Development* 46 (1975): 709–718.

Gottman, J. M.; Gonso, J.; and Schuler, P. "Teaching Social Skills to Isolated Children." *Journal of Abnormal Child Psychology* 4 (1976): 179–197.

Gottman, J. M., and Parkhurst, J. T. "The Development of Friendship and Acquaintanceship Processes." In *Minnesota Symposia on Child Psychology. Vol. 13,* ed. A. Collins. Hillsdale, N.J.: Lawrence Erlbaum Associates, 1980.

Gronlund, N. W. *Sociometry in the Classroom.* New York: Harper, 1959.

Harold, E. F. "An Analysis of the Success of Methods of Initiating Social Contacts by Young Children." In *Twenty-Five Years of Child Study,* Institute of Child Study. Toronto: University of Toronto Press, 1951.

Hartup, W. W. "Peer Relations and Family Relations: Two Social Worlds." In *Scientific Foundations of Developmental Psychiatry,* ed. M. Rutter. London: Heinemann Medical Books, 1980.

Hartup, W. W.; Glazer, J. A.; and Charlesworth, R. "Peer Reinforcement and Sociometric Status." *Child Development* 38 (1967): 1017–1024.

Hauserman, N.; Walen, S. R.; and Behling, M. "Reinforced Racial Integration in the First Grade: A Study in Generalization." *Journal of Applied Behavior Analysis* 6 (1973): 193–200.

Hoffman, M. L., and Saltzstein, H. D. "Parent Discipline and the Child's Moral Development." *Journal of Personality and Social Psychology* 5 (1967): 45–57.

Hops, H.; Walker, H. M.; and Greenwood, C. R. "PEERS—A Program for Remediating Social Withdrawal in the School Setting: Aspects of a Research and Development Process." Paper presented at Banff 9: The History and Future of the Developmentally Disabled: Programmatic and Methodological Issues, Banff, Alberta, March 1977.

Horrocks, J. E., and Buker, M. E. "A Study of the Friendship Fluctuations of Preadolescents." *The Journal of Genetic Psychology* 78 (1951): 131–144.

Hymel, S.; Asher, S. R.; Renshaw, P. D.; and Geraci, R. L. "Loneliness in Children: Development of a Self-Report Measure." Paper presented at the annual meeting of the American Educational Research Association, Los Angeles, 1981.

Johnson, D. W., and Johnson, R. T. "Instructional Structure: Cooperative, Competitive and Individualistic." *Review of Educational Research* 44 (1974): 213–240.

Johnson, D. W., and Johnson, R. T. "Cooperative, Competitive, and Individualistic Learning." *Journal of Research and Development in Education* 12 (1978): 3–15.

Johnson, M. W. "The Effect on Behavior of Variation in Amount of Play Equipment." *Child Development* 6 (1935): 56–68.

Johnson, S. M. "Self-Reinforcement Versus External Reinforcement in Behavior Modification with Children." *Developmental Psychology* 3 (1970): 147–148.

Kandel, H. J.; Ayllon, T.; and Rosenbaum, R. "Flooding or Systematic Exposure in the Treatment of Extreme Social Withdrawal in Children." *Journal of Behavior Therapy and Experimental Psychiatry* 8 (1977): 75–81.

Kazdin, A. E. *Behavior Modification in Applied Settings*. Homewood, Ill.: Dorsey, 1975.

Keller, M. F., and Carlson, P. M. "The Use of Symbolic Modeling to Promote Social Skills in Preschool Children with Low Levels of Social Responsiveness." *Child Development* 45 (1974): 912–919.

Koch, H. L. "Popularity in Preschool Children: Some Related Factors and a Technique for Its Measurement." *Child Development* 4 (1933): 164–175.

Kohn, N., and Clausen, J. "Social Isolation and Schizophrenia." *American Sociological Review* 20 (1955): 265–273.

Ladd, G. W. "Effectiveness of a Social Learning Method for Enhancing Children's Social Interaction and Peer Acceptance." *Child Development* 52 (1981): 171–178.

Ladd, G. W., and Oden, S. "The Relationship Between Peer Acceptance and Children's Ideas about Helpfulness." *Child Development* 50 (1979): 402–408.

Lieberman, A. F. "Preschoolers' Competence with a Peer: Relations with

Attachment and Peer Experience." *Child Development* 48 (1977): 1277–1287.

Lilly, M. S. "Improving Social Acceptance of Low Sociometric Status, Low-Achieving Students." *Exceptional Children* 37 (1971): 341–347.

Litrow, L., and Pumroy, D. K. "A Brief Review of Classroom Group-Oriented Contingencies." *Journal of Applied Behavior Analysis* 8 (1975): 341–347.

Marlatt, G. A. "Task Structure and the Experimental Modification of Verbal Behavior." *Psychological Bulletin* 78 (1972): 335–350.

Marshall, H. R., and McCandless, B. R. "A Study in Prediction of Social Behavior of Preschool Children." *Child Development* 28 (1957): 149–159.

Moore, S. G. "Correlates of Peer Acceptance in Nursery School Children." In *The Young Child: Reviews of Research. Vol. 1*, ed. W. W. Hartup and N. L. Smothergill. Washington, D.C.: National Association for the Education of Young Children, 1967.

Moore, S. G., and Updegraff, R. "Sociometric Status of Preschool Children Related to Age, Sex, Nurturance Giving, and Dependency." *Child Development* 35 (1964): 519–524.

O'Connor, R. D. "Modification of Social Withdrawal Through Symbolic Modeling." *Journal of Applied Behavior Analysis* 2 (1969): 15–22.

O'Connor, R. D. "Relative Efficacy of Modeling, Shaping, and the Combined Procedures for Modification of Social Withdrawal." *Journal of Abnormal Psychology* 79 (1972): 327–334.

Oden, S., and Asher, S. R. "Coaching Children in Social Skills for Friendship Making." *Child Development* 48 (1977): 495–506.

O'Leary, K. D., and Drabman, R. "Token Reinforcement Programs in the Classroom: A Review." *Psychological Bulletin* 75 (1971): 379–398.

O'Leary, S. G., and O'Leary, K. D. "Behavior Modification in the School." In *Handbook of Behavior Modification*, ed. H. Leitenberg. Englewood Cliffs, N.J.: Prentice-Hall, 1976.

Parten, M. B. "Social Play among Preschool Children." *Journal of Abnormal Social Psychology* 28 (1933): 136–147.

Putallaz, M., and Gottman, J. M. "Social Skills and Group Acceptance." In *The Development of Children's Friendships*, ed. S. R. Asher and J. M. Gottman. New York: Cambridge University Press, 1981.

Quilitch, H. R., and Risley, T. R. "The Effects of Play Materials on Social Play." *Journal of Applied Behavior Analysis* 6 (1973): 573–578.

Roff, M. "Childhood Social Interactions and Young Adult Bad Conduct." *Journal of Abnormal and Social Psychology* 63 (1961): 333–337.

Roff, M.; Sells, S. B.; and Golden, M. M. *Social Adjustment and Personality Development in Children*. Minneapolis, Minn.: University of Minnesota Press, 1972.

Rosekrans, M. A. "Imitation in Children As a Function of Perceived Similarity to a Social Model and Vicarious Reinforcement." *Journal of Personality and Social Psychology* 7 (1967): 307–315.

Rucker, C. N., and Vincenzo, F. M. "Maintaining Social Acceptance Gains Made by Mentally Retarded Children." *Exceptional Children* 36 (1970): 679–680.

Schutz, W. C. *FIRO: A Three-Dimensional Theory of Interpersonal Behavior.* New York: Holt, Rinehart & Winston, 1960.

Schwarz, J. C. "Effects of Peer Familiarity on the Behavior of Preschoolers in a Novel Situation." *Journal of Personality and Social Psychology* 24 (1972): 276–284.

Sears, R. R.; Maccoby, E. E.; and Levin, H. *Patterns of Child-Rearing.* Evanston, Ill.: Row, Peterson, 1957.

Serbin, L. A.; Tonick, I. J.; and Sternglanz, S. H. "Shaping Cooperative Cross-Sex Play." *Child Development* 48 (1977): 924–929.

Stengel, E. *Suicide and Attempted Suicide.* Middlesex, Great Britain: Penguin, 1971.

Stokes, T. F., and Baer, D. M. "An Implicit Technology of Generalization." *Journal of Applied Behavior Analysis* 10 (1977): 349–367.

Strain, P. S.; Cooke, T. P.; and Apolloni, T. *Teaching Exceptional Children: Assessing and Modifying Social Behavior.* New York: Academic Press, 1976a.

Strain, P. S.; Cooke, T. P.; and Apolloni, T. "The Role of Peers in Modifying Classmates' Social Behavior." *Journal of Special Education* 10 (1976b): 351–356.

Strain, P. S., and Timm, M. "An Experimental Analysis of Social Interaction Between a Behaviorally Disordered Preschool Child and Her Classroom Peers." *Journal of Applied Behavior Analysis* 7 (1974): 583–590.

Strain, P. S., and Wiegerink, R. "The Effects of Sociodramatic Activities on Social Interaction among Behaviorally Disordered Preschool Children." *Journal of Special Education* 10 (1976): 71–75.

Ullmann, C. A. "Teachers, Peers and Tests As Predictors of Adjustment." *Journal of Educational Psychology* 48 (1957): 257–267.

Van Alstnyne, D. *Play Behavior and Choices of Play Materials of Preschool Children.* Chicago: University of Chicago Press, 1932.

Walker, H. M.; Hops, H.; Greenwood, C. R.; and Todd, N. M. *Social Interaction: Effects of Symbolic Modeling and Individual and Group Reinforcement Contingencies on the Behavior of Withdrawn Children.* (Report No. 15). Eugene, Oreg.: University of Oregon, Center at Oregon for Research in the Behavioral Education of the Handicapped, 1975.

Wheeler, V., and Ladd, G. "Assessment of Children's Self-Efficacy for Social Interactions with Peers." *Developmental Psychology,* in press.

Youniss, J. *Parents and Peers in Social Development: A Sullivan-Piaget Perspective.* Chicago: University of Chicago Press, 1980.

Zahavi, S. L., and Asher, S. R. "The Effect of Verbal Instructions on Preschool Children's Aggressive Behavior." *Journal of School Psychology* 16 (1978): 146–153.

Zahn-Waxler, C. Z.; Radke-Yarrow, M. R.; and King, R. A. "Child Rearing and the Development of Children's Altruism." Paper presented at the annual meeting of the American Psychological Association, Toronto, 1978.

Joan E. Grusec
Lynn Arnason

9 Consideration for others: approaches to enhancing altruism

Newborn infants, for all their amazing capabilities, show little in the way of consideration for others. Selfish and self-centered, occupied solely with their own needs and desires, they present a challenge to those charged with their care. For from this unpromising beginning must emerge adults who, to some degree at least, are willing to sacrifice personal interests and comfort in order to make life easier for others. The development of altruism, or consideration for others, is a topic that has been of increasing concern to psychological researchers in recent years, if only because of its practical significance. Examples of the callous disregard humans are capable of showing for each other abound in daily existence. Yet we are also capable of showing impressive compassion and care. The task for teachers and parents—those given the job of socializing children so that they become responsible members of society—is to encourage these examples of consideration for others and to suppress cold-hearted disregard. While some (e.g., Hamilton 1964) argue that human beings are naturally inclined to share and help, most research on the development of altruism has been guided by the assumption that children need to learn how to show compassion for others or, at the very least, that their naturally occurring tendencies must be encouraged.

The goal of socialization is the internalization of prosocial values; as they mature, children must adopt social values not because of external pressure but because they have accepted such values as their own. The implication then, is that parents and teachers should work actively to provide an environment that will encourage the growth of an inner desire to be helpful. For an act to be truly altruistic it must not be motivated by external hope of reward or fear of punishment.

In the last volume of this series, Rosenhan (1972) surveys research on the development of altruism. He focuses on the role of affect in promoting concern for others—on how the association of pleasurable feelings with altruism leads to its acquisition as well as how positive or negative states (feeling happy or sad) predispose a child to be more or less kind to others. Rosenhan also describes the important role of example, that is, observing altruistic behavior in parents and others, in promoting altruism. He concludes that altruistic models are more effective than the very commonly employed technique of moral exhortation or preaching.

An interest in research on altruism has continued since 1972, including a recognition of the importance of adult and peer models, instruction, and even preaching and exhortation. Interest in affect also continues, although recent research has been concerned primarily with the study of empathy—the child's ability to feel the same, or a related, emotion to that of another person—and its role in the development of altruism. Increasing emphasis on the child's cognitive capacities is evident in studies that reveal how the child's perspective-taking skills, particularly knowledge of other people's thoughts and feeling, help the child to show greater concern for others. These continuities, and changing emphases, will be reflected in the material that follows.

We will begin by discussing the onset of consideration for others and the role of empathy and role-taking in its development and enhancement. Following this, research will be presented on several other factors that encourage altruistic attitudes and increase altruistic behavior in children, including moral exhortation, adult demands for consideration for others, and the use of character attribution. The implications of the research for practice will be discussed. For more complete reviews of these topics the reader is referred to such sources as Grusec (1981), Mussen and Eisenberg-Berg (1977), and Rushton (1980).

The onset of concern for distress in others

At what point in the developmental process do children begin to show concern for the distress of other people? Zahn-Waxler, Radke-Yarrow, and their associates address this question in an interesting way. It is obviously difficult to introduce a broad range of distressing experiences into the laboratory, so they trained mothers to observe and report all situations in which their children, during the everyday course of their activities, encountered someone who was expressing distressing feelings such as anger, sorrow, or pain. By analyzing the detailed descriptions provided by mothers, Zahn-Waxler and Radke-Yarrow were able to see how it is that children develop in the ways they experience and express concern for others.

According to their mothers, children as young as 12 months exhibit strong reactions to distress in others (Zahn-Waxler and Radke-Yarrow 1979). Thus one child, when her mother was crying, ran to her, patted her face, and then buried her face in her mother's lap—a combination of providing comfort as well as requesting it. By the time she was 17 months old this same child was physically comforting another infant, without demanding comfort herself. Zahn-Waxler and Radke-Yarrow report that children between the ages of two and seven years were becoming more proficient in their reactions to emotional upset in others, dealing with more abstract kind of distresses, responding to more subtle cues, and taking into consideration the feelings of others that are not immediately observable. Thus young children responded to such events as the physical pain and obvious suffering of others. An older child, in contrast, pretended to like the present her father had given her because she did not "want him to be disappointed." Another older child sorrowfully commented about a television report of a family killed in a fire, hoping the children were not so young as to have had no chance to enjoy life before dying.

What was surprising, however, were the similarities in behavior for two- and seven-year-olds. Even the youngest children were adept at making inferences about the emotional states of others and there was no difference in the frequency with which younger and older children offered help. Moreover, there was consistency within individual children in the nature of their behavior. Children as young as two exhibited a stable and consistent response to distress in others: Some were intensely emotional and compassionate, some were intellectual and analytical, some avoided and were unable to tolerate emotion in others, some were nonresponsive or nondescript in their reactions. These modes of reacting were still evident in the children when they were seven, with approximately two-thirds of them showing the same kind of reaction as they had shown when they were two. An 18-month-old child who ran away or plugged her ears in response to crying and anger complained, at the age of seven, that she could just not take much more of someone's crying. The child who at 17 months physically comforted a crying baby, at the age of seven years spontaneously gave her sandals to a younger friend to protect her feet from burning as they walked together on the hot sidewalk. Another child who, at the age of two, had pushed a child away to protect a friend, at the age of seven confronted an adult who had pushed ahead of his grandmother in the grocery line. These consistencies led Zahn-Waxler and Radke-Yarrow to suggest that, if distinctive orientations are evident in early years, this may be an especially important time for socializing agents to strengthen or redirect existing behavior. The responses of a child who seems to be reacting to distress in others in a useful and constructive way should be supported. Evidence that a young child is not reactive to the needs of those around, however, should be a signal that parents or teachers must make extra efforts to train a sense of concern for others.

The role of empathy and role-taking ability in the development of concern for others

Empathy, as we indicated above, refers to the child's ability to feel the same emotion (or at least a related one) as someone else is experiencing. The empathic child feels unhappy when she or he observes an unhappy person: Perhaps the extent of unhappiness is not the same, but the child does experience a negative emotion rather than no emotion or an inappropriate one such as joy. Empathy has been distinguished from perspective- or role-taking ability in that the latter refers to the capability of *knowing* how others are feeling and/or thinking. Empathy, then, is primarily an affective component of awareness of others while role-taking is primarily a cognitive component.

As children mature they become increasingly capable of both empathy and role-taking. A number of researchers (e.g., Hoffman 1975a) suggest that it is through this increasing awareness of others and of their needs that the young child's altruism grows. The child's awareness leads to uncomfortable arousal at the plight of another: The act of helping lowers this arousal and thus reinforces the altruistic behavior. For example, a child who is upset when another child cries is motivated to reduce that child's distress in order to reduce her or his own state of arousal. Also knowing what another person is feeling and thinking should enable the child to respond more efficiently to that person's needs. For example, by knowing that a companion is crying because of a lost toy instead of for some other reason, a child can either find the toy or offer another in its place. In these ways, then, empathy, as well as the ability to understand the perspective of another person, are seen to be powerful determinants of at least some kinds of altruistic behavior.

If empathy and role-taking ability facilitate altruism, as investigators suggest, then certain predictions follow. First, children who show the greatest consideration for others and who help most should be those who have the greatest ability to understand the thoughts and feelings of others and to feel as others are feeling. Second, it should be possible to make children more altruistic by teaching them about the internal states of others and by training their empathic abilities.

Attempts to correlate empathy and role-taking ability with altruism have not uniformly met with success. A review of these studies suggests that age may be an important variable, with the ability to understand the perspective, thoughts, and emotions of others and to experience a similar emotion to theirs, related to altruism somewhat more often in younger children than in older ones.

The first group of studies we shall discuss has to do with role-taking ability. Rubin and Schneider (1973) found 7-year-olds' willingness to help and share with others to be positively correlated with one measure of role-taking skill—the ability to take into account other people's knowledge when communicating with them. Similarly, Buckley, Siegel, and Ness (1979) found that 3- to 8-year-old children who displayed adeptness at seeing the visual perspective of others (by rotating a display of plastic figures and buildings so that they had the same view as someone else) helped and shared more with a peer than those who were less adept at the task. [Zahn-Waxler, Radke-Yarrow, and Brady-Smith (1977) did not find the same relationship under similar circumstances and with children of a similar age. Their study differed from Buckley, Siegel, and Ness (1979), however, in that the measures of concern for others involved helping, sharing, and comforting an adult, whom children may well have perceived as quite capable of looking after herself, rather than a peer.] Using older children, ranging in age from 7 to 11 years of age, Rushton and Wiener (1975) were unable to find a relationship between a series of role-taking tasks and giving to charity or generosity to a friend.

When one considers studies assessing empathy, and the correlation between it and altruism, again there appears the suggestion of a relationship for younger children but not for older ones. Buckley, Siegel, and Ness (1979) (who studied three- to eight-year-olds) found that altruistic children were better able to identify the emotion of a character in a story than children who were not altruistic. Also Sawin (1979), who measured empathy by observing children's facial and vocal expressions of emotion while they watched slides of other children in situations that were emotion-arousing, found that this measure of empathy correlated with willingness to donate tokens to other children who could not participate in the study. The relationship held for six-year-olds, however, and not for eight-year-olds. Finally, Iannotti (1978), whose subjects were six- and nine-year-olds, found empathy to be unrelated to altruism. (He did, however, find a relationship between role-taking ability and altruism.)

From this array of studies, then, we conclude that altruism is often related to empathy and role-taking ability in children younger than seven or eight, but not in children older than ten. Perhaps, if this generalization is accurate, it holds because by seven to eight years of age, virtually all children possess the basic empathic and role-taking abilities that enable them to engage in altruism, and that individual differences in altruism *after* that age are determined more by such things as knowledge of social norms and self-concept.

Training children to understand other points of view

If the most altruistic young child is the one who is most empathic or most able to see another's perspective, then, by training children to have more of these abilities, one might be able to increase altruism. This hypothesis has been the starting point of a number of investigations. In one of the first studies to show how altruism could be facilitated in this manner, Staub (1971) gave role-playing training to pairs of kindergarten children by having them take turns acting out situations in which one child needed help and the other provided it. A day later the children were brought, individually, to a room where they heard cries of distress (actually a recording) coming from a neighboring room. Girls who had had role-playing experience responded more to the cries of distress than did girls who had not had such practice. Although boys with training did not help more, they were more altruistic in another way—they shared more candy they had been given than did those who had not had role-playing experiences. Thus both boys and girls had learned something about altruism from their role-playing sessions, but the learning was revealed in different ways. Perhaps boys felt pressured in the role-playing experience and therefore resisted direct indications that they should help but responded indirectly by giving candy in a situation where they felt less pressured. It is also possible that boys donated more candy to compensate for their stubborn resistance to being helpful. Staub (1975) reports this type of resistance in boys in other situations.

That boys do learn from role-playing experience was demonstrated again by Iannotti (1978). He had six- and nine-year-old boys role-play the characters in a series of skits. Some boys played the same role each session and others switched roles often. Training sessions lasted for 25 minutes a day for ten days. The skits revolved around finding solutions for dilemmas. In one, for instance, several boys who needed money found a wallet with money inside it, and subjects were required to act out several possible solutions to the problem. While they were acting out the skits the boys were also asked questions about the motives, feelings, and thoughts of the particular character they were playing. Although Iannotti's procedure did not work for the nine-year-olds, it did for the six-year-olds. They shared more candy than six-year-olds in a control group who had spent the same amount of time discussing the stories but had not actually acted them out. Thus it was not the consideration and solving of dilemmas alone that increased altruism among the six-year-olds who role-played (although this may have contributed). Rather, the actual experience of pretending to be someone else was effective in facilitating altruism. The boys who benefited most, in fact, were those who switched roles during each session, rather than playing just one role, thereby presumably gaining more practice in knowing what others are thinking and feeling.

Finally, Friedrich and Stein (1975) had five-year-olds watch segments of *Mister Rogers' Neighborhood*, that attempts to teach prosocial behavior. The children, using hand puppets, then rehearsed some of the prosocial events from the program. This role-playing experience increased the children's willingness to help repair a damaged collage that another child had been making for her or his mother's birthday gift, with the effect being the most pronounced for boys.

The results of all these studies indicate that children at least to the age of six years can be made more altruistic by having them actively play the role of other people. In this way young children may be educated to more clearly understand the thoughts and feelings of others. Iannotti's finding that nine-year-olds did not benefit from role-taking experience accords with our earlier suggestion that older children may have reached a level of role-taking ability sufficient for most kinds of altruism. An alternative explanation of the various findings of these training studies is that children are just beginning to learn appropriate helping techniques; therefore having repeated practice in being helpful, and being reinforced for helping during training, improves their performance. This explanation is certainly reasonable and existing evidence does not allow it to be dismissed. Furthermore, it is consistent with Iannotti's evidence since older children would already have a repertoire of helping skills and thus training would not be as effective for them. Nevertheless, whatever the explanation, it is clear that role-playing experience can be very useful in training altruism in young children.

Empathic and perspective-taking skills can be encouraged in a variety of ways. In the course of disciplining children for their misdemeanors, for example, socializing agents may use the opportunity to orient them to the effects their behavior has on others. In this way knowledge of the thoughts and feelings of others can be further promoted. Hoffman (1970) argues that parents who explain to their children the consequences of their misbehavior for others will aid them in internalizing parental values, including those of concern for others. By the use of a discipline technique that he labels other-oriented induction, he argues that parents arouse the child's natural tendency to be empathic.

Overall, the data relevant to this hypothesis are mixed. Hoffman (1963) found that mothers of preschoolers who used other-oriented discipline had children who showed greater concern for others in a nursery school setting. This finding held, however, only for mothers who made *minimal* use of "power assertive" techniques of discipline (threats, force, physical punishment). These low-power-assertive mothers, then, appeared to be teaching concern for others by using other-oriented induction as well as by modeling consideration in their own approach to childrearing. Hoffman and Saltzstein (1967) studied the discipline techniques that parents of seventh grade children reported they used with their children. Those who said they used other-oriented discipline had girls who were described by their parents as considerate. But quite a different picture emerged for boys. Boys rated as considerate had parents who used, not induction, but physical punishment, withdrawal of privileges, and verbal censure. However, in a later study, Hoffman (1975b) reports that boys and girls described as considerate by their peers had one parent (the one of the opposite sex) who expected that reparation be made after deviation (i.e., who encouraged their children to help those they had harmed), encouraged apologies after deviation, and expressed concern for the feelings of the victim. Finally, Dlugokinski and Firestone (1974) found that 10- and 13-year-olds who described their mothers as relying on other-oriented discipline were rated by classmates as considerate, and attaching more importance to other-centered values ("getting a job that helps others" rather than "having a life of pleasure and comfort"). Moreover, these same children gave more money to charity when, as part of the research procedure, they were asked to donate money to UNICEF. While it is not immediately obvious why there is not always a relationship between other-oriented induction and altruism, such a relationship seems to exist under at least some circumstances.

The role of verbal instruction, preaching, and moral exhortation in altruism

Rosenhan (1972) describes several studies that show that when adults *preach* one set of values but *act* in accord with a different set, the effect of their behavior wins out over that of their preaching (e.g., Bryan and Walbek 1970). More recently, investigators (e.g., Midlarsky and Bryan 1972; Rice and Grusec 1975; Rushton 1975) have found that exhortations alone, unconfounded by a conflicting behavioral example, can be effective in promoting altruistic behavior, particularly if the exhortations are accompanied by some kind of relatively extensive rationale. For example, telling a child "It is good to give because it makes other people happy," is more effective than the statement "It is good to give."

Having come to the conclusion that preaching, or moral exhortation, can at least occasionally modify children's altruistic behavior, researchers now have begun to consider if some *kinds* of exhortation are more effective than others. In a study conducted in our own laboratory (Grusec, Saas-Kortsaak, and Simutis

1978) children were urged to donate some of the tokens they won playing a game and that could be exchanged for toys, to help obtain toys for children less fortunate than themselves. Some of the children were given a specific exhortation to share—they were told they should *give half their winnings to the less-fortunate children* since it would be a good thing to make them happy by doing this. Other children were given a more general exhortation to share—they were told it is a good thing to make other people happy by *helping them in any way one can.* Both kinds of exhortations were equally effective in inducing children to donate to the less-fortunate children. When, at the end of the session, the children were given 12 colored pencils as rewards for helping the experimenter, and told they could leave some pencils for children who would not be able to play the game, only the specific exhortation group who previously had been told that they should share, shared pencils and then it worked only with boys.

Several weeks after they had been preached to about sharing and/or helping others, the children were visited in their classrooms by a man whom they had never seen before. He asked them to collect items such as empty milk cartons, buttons, material, and boxes that could be used by children in a local hospital to make crafts. This was a test of altruism that was far removed, then, from the original training situation, both in time and in kind. The children who showed the greatest concern for others under these conditions were those who had originally heard a *general* exhortation that it is good to help other people in any way one can.

We conclude from these findings that socializing agents who want children to be helpful in all areas of their lives should emphasize the importance of generalized helping, in addition to giving them training about specific situations. In this way they may aid children in extracting from their training a generalized principle of concern for others, rather than leaving them to do the extracting for themselves.

Another dimension of exhortation is explored by Eisenberg-Berg and Geisheker (1979). They delivered to a group of eight- and nine-year-old children either a "normative exhortation," in which they stated that people *ought* to share with less-fortunate children, or an "empathic exhortation," that emphasized how happy and excited the recipients of sharing would be. The empathic exhortation produced more donation of money to less-fortunate children than did preaching of a normative kind, perhaps by arousing the children's sensitivity to the feelings and needs of others. Here we see a link with some of the issues raised in the previous section on empathy; indeed, empathic exhortations may be one additional way of training children's empathy and hence their altruism.

People sometimes resist being pushed or forced into engaging in a behavior, even if it is one they might not ordinarily mind doing. Herein lies one of the dangers of preaching and moral exhortation which is often suspected of causing reactance—a desire to do just the opposite of what one is told is the right and virtuous thing to do. Evidence for such a suspicion is provided by Staub (1971) who found that children who were preached to about the need for helping others were less likely to help the experimenter pick up a box of paper clips that he had "accidentally" dropped than were those who had not been subjected to the experimenter's moralizing. Even if reactance does occur, however, it may dissipate with time. Certainly we found no evidence of it in the Grusec, Saas-Kortsaak, and Simutis (1978) study when children were asked, several weeks after they had been exhorted to show consideration for others, to collect craft materials for the hospitalized children. Perhaps children's memories of coercion are briefer than their memories for messages about the importance of helping. Possibly messages that focus their attention on the plight of others and thereby arouse their empathic capacities eventually overcome feelings of resistance and reactance. Perhaps reactance is specific to the exhorter or, at least, certain kinds of exhorters. Thus exhorters who are loved, admired, or with whom the child has identified, may be more effective than those who have no particular significance for the child. But here we are only speculating and must wait for clarifying research.

There may also be age differences in susceptibility to reactance. Cheyne (1972), for example, found that kindergarten children obeyed a prohibition not to play with an attractive toy but that third graders required the addition of a reason about why they should not play with it before they would conform to an adult's dictate. In fact, the older children were *more* deviant than the younger ones when a rationale for conformity was not provided.

Adult demands for consideration and altruism

Rather than exhort children to be altruistic, or attempt to make them sensitive to the needs of others, agents of socialization may simply demand consideration, backing up these demands with their greater power. Indeed, moral exhortation may acquire some of its potency by being paired with an implied or real threat of displeasure or disapproval. Baumrind (1973), in an extensive study of how parents' childrearing practices relate to a variety of behaviors in their offspring, reports that parents who were warm and reasonable, but who placed demands on their children to display prosocial behavior and who firmly enforced those demands, had children who showed consideration for others by their cooperative and friendly behavior. Zahn-Waxler, Radke-Yarrow, and King (1979), as part of the research program described earlier, assessed maternal disciplinary practices when children themselves were the cause of distress to others. They found that children who showed the greatest concern for others—who provided physical and verbal sympathy ("All better now?" or hugging), who produced bandages or other kinds of assistance and/or protection when someone was hurt or in difficulty—had mothers who responded to their deviations by explaining why they should not have done what they did. These explanations had two major components. First, they had a strong dimension of moralizing ("It's not nice to bite," "It was bad for Jim to hit Mary."). But second, the moral exhortations were delivered affectively, that is, with some degree of emotion on the mother's part. This affect may well have aroused anxiety in the children and motivated them to obey the exhortation in order to avoid future maternal social disapproval.

Earlier we argued that concern for others that is motivated by fear of external punishment is not internalized altruism. There is some evidence, however, that children who receive rewards or punishments of a *social* nature for helping (approval or disapproval, for example) are more inclined to attribute their altruistic behavior to an inner desire to be helpful—internalized concern for others—than are children who receive *material* rewards or material punishments (Smith et al. 1979). As long as adult punishment comes in the form of social disapproval, then, it should be conducive to the eventual internalization of altruistic values. Even material and physical punishment may be effective if their coerciveness is reduced by accompanying rationales for why it is important to show concern for others.

Several studies suggest that simply instructing children to behave altruistically is an effective way of obtaining concern for others. Rice and Grusec (1975) had adults suggest in a nonforceful way that altruism was appropriate ("I guess they expect us to share with the less-fortunate children. Probably that's what one had better do.") and found this to be as effective as modeling, unless children had been given explicit permission *not* to share if they did not want to. White (1972) and White and Burnham (1975) also report that instructing children to donate was more effective than telling them they could donate if they wished to but that they did not have to. Moreover, it was more effective than the modeling of altruism on an immediate test and as effective as modeling on a delayed test that took place several days after the original instruction. In all these cases, then, it would seem that adults who indicate they expect concern for others will be more effective than those who adopt a more permissive approach.

Not only does research suggest that demands for responsible behavior can be effective in promoting altruism but parents appear to act as though they are quite aware of this relationship. In one assessment of parental childrearing practices (Grusec and Kuczynski 1980) mothers of four- and seven-year-old boys and girls were played tape-recorded depictions of some common misbehaviors. The mothers were asked to imagine that it was their child who was misbehaving and to describe what their reactions to their child would be. Of the 40 mothers interviewed, 95 percent reported that on one or more occasions they would use strong verbal pressure in order to force their child to engage in appropriate behavior. For example, a large number of mothers were in agreement that they would force their children to show appropriate behavior when two children were fighting and one pushed the other off a tricycle, and when their child was given a chocolate bar to share with a friend, but did not share equally. It is worth noting that approximately one-quarter of the time these demands were accompanied with a *reason* for why the child should do what she or he had been told to do.

Why should demands for altruism be effective in developing concern for others? There is a variety of possible reasons. If direct instruction is delivered in an emotional context children may, as with moral exhortation delivered in a similar manner, be motivated to behave altruistically in order to avoid adult social disapproval. Also, following an instruction to be altruistic may provide practice in altruistic behaving that will make it easier for children to display similar behavior when it is required in the future. Finally, parental reinforcement for the altruism that follows an instruction may make it even more likely to reoccur. If pressure to perform an altruistic act is not too coercive or arbitrary (if, for example, it is accompanied by a reason) then children may eventually come to attribute their behavior to internal causes, that is, they may come to believe they have behaved altruistically because they themselves wished to. This latter explanation leads us to the next section, a discussion of the role of attribution in the growth of altruism.

Character attribution and altruism

According to attribution theory (e.g., Kelley 1967), the explanations that people give themselves to account for their own behavior are crucial in determining whether or not they will continue to behave in the same way. Children who believe they have just shared their favorite toy with a friend because they are the kind of people who like to share will continue to be more altruistic than children who do it because their mother said to share or she would take the toy away. In the first case values and beliefs about the virtues of sharing are alleged to come into line with behavior, thereby directing future behavior ("I shared. No one made me do it. Therefore I myself must believe it is good to share, and shall continue to do so."). In the case where sharing is perceived as forced by external pressures, there is less reason for it to continue when those external pressures are removed. Attribution theory, then, appears to provide an important mechanism for the internalization of concern for others.

A number of investigators demonstrate how attribution theory could account for events in the domain of socialization. Miller, Brickman, and Bolen (1975), for example, had teachers and the school principal tell a classroom of fifth grade children on several occasions that they *were* neat, clean, and ecology-conscious, an attribution condition. Another classroom was told that they *ought to be* neat, clean, and ecology-conscious, a moral exhortation condition. Finally, a control classroom received no treatment at all. Miller, Brickman, and Bolen found that the most effective of their techniques was attribution. Children who had been repeatedly reminded of how ecology-conscious they were put more wrappers from candy and gifts they had been given into wastebaskets, and picked up more wrappers thrown on the ground than children in the control group. Children in the persuasion or moral exhortation group fell midway between the attribution and control groups. Thus moral exhortation, as we have previously indicated, was an effective way of promoting consideration. Under the circumstances of this study, however, it was not as effective as attribution.

Telling children they are neat and tidy, or the kind of people who care for others, should surely not be effective if they know very well that they are messy, or that they are not altruistic, or that they have been altruistic only because someone forced them to be. That this is so was demonstrated in a study from our own laboratory (Grusec et al. 1978). In this experiment, seven- to ten-year-old children were induced to donate some of their winnings from a game so that the experimenter could obtain toys for the less-fortunate children. In one condition children were given a direct instruction—they were told to share their winnings, and an adult stood beside them to make sure that they did. In a second (modeling) condition the children had first watched an adult play the game and donate half her winnings to the less-fortunate children. When the children then took their turn, with the adult standing nearby, they virtually all shared, with only a few of them requiring informal prompts in the form of a suggestion that they might wish to give half of their winnings to the less-fortunate children. We thought that in the first condition of direct instruction the children would be quite aware of why they had shared—they had been told to. In the second, modeling, condition it should have been less clear to them why they had shared; although there was certainly external pressure on them to do so, it was of a subtle nature.

All the children in the study, after they had shared, were then assigned to an attribution condition. They were told either that they must have shared because the experimenter expected them to (an external attribution) or because they were the kind of people who liked to help others whenever possible (an internal attribution) or they were not told anything (no attribution). Each child had additional opportunities then to play the game and to share winnings or not. The results of this sharing are summarized in Table 9.1. As predicted, it was the children in the modeling condition whose sharing subsequent to the attribution was affected by these different reasons. They shared more after the internal attribution (you like helping others) than they did after the external attribution (it was expected of you). Children in the direct instruction condition subsequently donated about as many of their winnings after an external as after an internal attribution. For them, the experimenter's attribution of altruism had no effect since they were quite aware of why they had been altruistic—an adult had told them to behave that way.

While attributions of prosocial behavior help children to develop greater concern for others, this is not a technique that works at every developmental level. Five-year-old children, for example, seem to be unaffected by positive statements about their character (Grusec and Redler 1980). Some evidence suggests that it is not until the age of seven or eight years that children think of themselves as having stable and consistent patterns of behavior (Livesley and Bromley 1973; Peevers and Secord 1973). Only when they begin to believe that they possess certain attributes that affect their behavior across a variety of situations should character attributions have an impact on what they do.

Why is the attribution of positive moral characteristics successful in teaching children to show concern for others? Perry et al. (1980) argue that children anticipate and experience heightened self-criticism when they fail to live up to prosocial dispositions attributed to them. When told they possess desirable attributes, their self-image changes and they make higher demands of themselves for good behavior. Failure to meet these high expectations leads to greater dissatisfaction and self-recrimination than does failure in children who never had high expectations of themselves in the first place. Support for these views comes from Perry

Table 9.1.
Mean number of tokens shared in each condition.

Condition	External attribution N = 14	Internal attribution N = 14	No attribution N = 14
Modeling	2.72	6.07	4.14
Direct instruction	4.78	5.64	4.36

et al.'s experimental findings. They told some children that, based on their interaction with them, they believed them to be capable of carrying out instructions, following rules, working hard, and avoiding distraction. Other children were not provided with any kind of character attribution. The children were then asked to perform a boring task and not to be distracted by an exciting cartoon that was playing at the same time. The children did, of course, yield to temptation under these circumstances, and it was suggested to them (by an adult other than the one who had provided the original attribution) that they might not be deserving of all of some tokens they had been given for their participation. Children who had been told they were the kind who could resist temptation—but who had failed—kept fewer tokens for themselves than did those whose self-concept had not been subjected to influence. Perry et al. interpret this finding as an indication of increased dissatisfaction with personal performance in children who expected good behavior of themselves.

Encouraging concern for others: some final thoughts

In this review we have emphasized several processes that researchers interested in altruism have studied extensively. An important component of altruism is an awareness of the internal state of the person needing help, and it is evident that increasing sensitivity to others can be encouraged and developed by parents, teachers, and other socializing agents. In addition, verbal direction, particularly when its coerciveness is minimized (by, for example, accompanying it with good reasons for conformity) appears to be a useful tool for those who want to foster concern for others. Nor should one minimize the role of clear demands for consideration of others. Finally, concern for others can also be facilitated by encouraging children to believe that their altruism is motivated by an inner image of themselves as helpful people.

Although we have said little about it, the modeling of consideration for others is one of the most important mechanisms for the socialization of altruism. No matter how empathic the child, or how strong her or his self-concept of morality, these tendencies must be translated into action. The specific actions whereby others are helped can often be learned quite efficiently through observation. A young boy pats the head of a crying child and utters soothing words because he observes others doing that and has himself been soothed in that way. A woman hears of a destitute family and organizes food and clothing for them because once a teacher or parent did the same thing in response to the same problem.

The most successful socializing agent—parent or teacher—is probably one who uses a variety of techniques in concert. This is an individual, then, who models specific actions; attempts to sensitize a child to the feelings of others; exhorts, and even firmly demands, concern for others; and who reinforces altruism when it occurs as well as attributing it to the child's inner disposition to be kind and helpful.

References

Baumrind, D. "The Development of Instrumental Competence Through Socialization." *Minnesota Symposia on Motivation. Vol. 7*, ed. A. D. Pick. Minneapolis, Minn.: University of Minnesota Press, 1973.

Bryan, J. H., and Walbek, N. "Preaching and Practicing Generosity: Children's Actions and Reactions." *Child Development* 41 (1970): 329–353.

Buckley, N.; Siegel, L. S.; and Ness, S. "Egocentrism, Empathy, and Altruistic Behavior in Young Children." *Developmental Psychology* 15 (1979): 329–330.

Cheyne, A. J. "Punishment and Reasoning in the Development of Self-Control." In *Recent Trends in Social Learning Theory*, ed. R. D. Parke. New York: Academic Press, 1972.

Dlugokinski, E. L., and Firestone, I. J. "Other Centeredness and Susceptibility to Charitable Appeals: Effects of Perceived Discipline." *Developmental Psychology* 10 (1974): 21–28.

Eisenberg-Berg, N., and Geisheker, E. "Content of Preachings and Power of the Model/Preacher: The Effect on Children's Generosity." *Developmental Psychology* 15 (1979): 168–175.

Friedrich, L. K., and Stein, A. H. "Prosocial Television and Young Children: The Effects of Verbal Labeling and Role Playing on Learning and Behavior." *Child Development* 46 (1975): 27–38.

Grusec, J. E. "Socialization Processes in the Development of Altruism." In *Altruism and Helping Behavior*, ed. J. P. Rushton and R. M. Sorrentino. Hillsdale, N. J.: Lawrence Erlbaum Associates, 1981.

Grusec, J. E., and Kuczynski, L. "Direction of Effect in Socialization: A Comparison of the Parent Vs. the Child's Behavior As Determinants of Disciplinary Techniques." *Developmental Psychology* 16 (1980): 1–9.

Grusec, J. E.; Kuczynski, L.; Rushton, J. P.; and Simutis, Z. "Modeling, Direct Instruction, and Attributions: Effects on Altruism." *Developmental Psychol-*

ogy 14 (1978): 51–57.

Grusec, J. E., and Redler, E. "Attribution, Reinforcement, and Altruism." *Developmental Psychology* 16 (1980): 525–534.

Grusec, J. E.; Saas-Kortsaak, P.; and Simutis, Z. M. "The Role of Example and Moral Exhortation in the Training of Altruism." *Child Development* 49 (1978): 920–923.

Hamilton, W. D. "The Genetical Theory of Social Behavior, I, II." *Journal of Theoretical Biology* 7 (1964): 1–52.

Hoffman, M. L. "Parent Discipline and the Child's Consideration for Others." *Child Development* 34 (1963): 573–588.

Hoffman, M. L. "Conscience, Personality, and Socialization Techniques." *Human Development* 13 (1970): 90–126.

Hoffman, M. L. "Developmental Synthesis of Affect and Cognition and Its Implications for Altruistic Motivation." *Developmental Psychology* 11 (1975a): 607–622.

Hoffman, M. L. "Altruistic Behavior and the Parent-Child Relationship." *Journal of Personality and Social Psychology* 31 (1975b): 937–943.

Hoffman, M. L., and Saltzstein, H. D. "Parent Discipline and the Child's Moral Development." *Journal of Personality and Social Psychology* 5 (1967): 45–57.

Iannotti, R. J. "Effect of Role-Taking Experiences on Role Taking, Empathy, Altruism, and Aggression." *Developmental Psychology* 14 (1978): 119–124.

Kelley, H. H. "Attribution Theory in Social Psychology." In *Nebraska Symposium on Motivation*, ed. D. Levine. Lincoln, Nebr.: University of Nebraska Press, 1967.

Livesley, W. J., and Bromley, D. B. *Person Perception in Childhood and Adolescence*. London: Wiley, 1973.

Midlarsky, E., and Bryan, J. H. "Affect Expressions and Children's Imitative Altruism." *Journal of Experimental Research in Personality* 6 (1972): 195–203.

Miller, R. L.; Brickman, P.; and Bolen, D. "Attribution Versus Persuasion As a Means for Modifying Behavior." *Journal of Personality and Social Psychology* 31 (1975): 430–441.

Mussen, P. H., and Eisenberg-Berg, N. *Roots of Caring, Sharing, and Helping*. San Francisco: Freeman, 1977.

Peevers, B. H., and Secord, P. F. "Developmental Changes in Attribution of Descriptive Concepts to Persons." *Journal of Personality and Social Psychology* 27 (1973): 120–128.

Perry, D. G.; Perry, L. C.; Bussey, K.; English, D.; and Arnold, G. "Processes of Attribution and Children's Self-Punishment Following Misbehavior." *Child Development* 51 (1980): 545–552.

Rice, M. E., and Grusec, J. E. "Saying and Doing: Effects on Observer Performance." *Journal of Personality and Social Psychology* 32 (1975): 584–593.

Rosenhan, D. "Prosocial Behavior of Children." In *The Young Child: Reviews of Research. Vol. 2*, ed. W. W. Hartup. Washington, D.C.: National Associa-

tion for the Education of Young Children, 1972.
Rubin, K. H., and Schneider, F. W. "The Relationship Between Moral Judgment, Egocentrism, and Altruistic Behavior." *Child Development* 44 (1973): 661–665.
Rushton, J. P. "Generosity in Children: Immediate and Long-Term Effects of Modeling, Preaching, and Moral Judgment." *Journal of Personality and Social Psychology* 31 (1975): 459–466.
Rushton, J. P. *Altruism, Socialization, and Society.* Englewood Cliffs, N. J.: Prentice-Hall, 1980.
Rushton, J. P., and Wiener, J. "Altruism and Cognitive Development in Children." *British Journal of Social and Clinical Psychology* 14 (1975): 341–349.
Sawin, D. B. "Assessing Empathy in Children: A Search for an Elusive Construct." Paper presented at the biennial meeting of the Society for Research in Child Development, San Francisco, March 1979.
Smith, C. L.; Gelfand, D. M.; Hartmann, D. P.; and Partlow, M. E. Y. "Children's Causal Attributions Regarding Help Giving." *Child Development* 50 (1979): 203–210.
Staub, E. "The Use of Role Playing and Induction in Children's Learning of Helping and Sharing Behavior." *Child Development* 42 (1971): 805–816.
Staub, E. "To Rear a Prosocial Child." In *Moral Development: Current Theory and Research,* ed. D. J. DePalma and J. M. Foley. Hillsdale, N. J.: Lawrence Erlbaum Associates, 1975.
White, G. M. "Immediate and Deferred Effects of Model Observation and Guided and Unguided Rehearsal on Donating and Stealing." *Journal of Personality and Social Psychology* 21 (1972): 139–148.
White, G. M., and Burnham, M. A. "Socially Cued Altruism: Effects of Modeling, Instructions, and Age on Public and Private Donations." *Child Development* 46 (1975): 559–563.
Zahn-Waxler, C. Z., and Radke-Yarrow, M. R. "A Developmental Analysis of Children's Responses to Emotions in Others." Paper presented at the biennial meeting of the Society for Research in Child Development, San Francisco, March 1979.
Zahn-Waxler, C. Z.; Radke-Yarrow, M. R.; and Brady-Smith, J. "Perspective-Taking and Prosocial Behavior." *Developmental Psychology* 13 (1977): 87–88.
Zahn-Waxler, C. Z.; Radke-Yarrow, M. R.; and King, R. A. "Child Rearing and Children's Prosocial Initiations Toward Victims of Distress." *Child Development* 50 (1979): 319–330.

Asa G. Hilliard III
Mona Vaughn-Scott

10 The quest for the "minority" child

There are millions of children in America. They and their families have arrived here from many different places, for many different reasons, in many different ways. Since their arrival, the children and families of some cultural groups have had happy and easy experiences. The children and families of other cultural groups have not fared so well.

Sometimes the children who have not fared so well are thought of as an aggregate, despite enormous cultural diversity among the groups, and are referred to as "minority" children. Sometimes they are labeled "disadvantaged" or "inner-city" children. Regardless of the name, these children have been the object of many research studies. Yet, when the different cultural groups are studied out of their historical and cultural contexts, the identity of the child and other members of her or his cultural group is lost. Very different people are frequently treated as if they were the same, and usually as if they were but incomplete copies of a mythical middle-SES White or Western European-American (Brazziel 1973; Cohen 1969; Cross 1977; Erny 1973; Diop 1978; Kleinfeld 1973). This has created a special kind of problem for those who wish to understand these children, their families, and the teaching and learning situations in which they are involved, since so many presumably relevant research findings simply cannot be explained or interpreted meaningfully. For example, to study the "vocabulary" competence of African-American children only by using instruments such as the Stanford-Binet (Terman and Merrill 1973) or the Peabody Picture Vocabulary Test (Dunn 1965) may give a false picture of the actual vocabulary possessed by such children, since many of these children may well know many other vocabulary words that are unfamiliar to their examiners (King 1975; Labov 1970; Smith 1978; Smitherman 1977). In short, we may learn what the child does *not* know by use of certain standardized tests, but remain ignorant as to what the child *does* know. The culturally sophisticated observer knows that there are many "normal" vocabularies among groups of people.

In truth, therefore, one must question the validity of research on "minority" children, despite a widespread belief that such a label does give information about the identity of the children. In fact, the bulk of material written about children from low-status cultural groups in America is written from a perspective that tends to ignore totally *who* the children actually are (Meyers, Rana, and Harris 1979; Nobles 1978). When children of other cultural groups are not like the model White American child, they are said to be deficient, rather than simply different. This way of thinking about the performance of low-status groups is sometimes called "the deficit model." The result is that healthy and normal children are diagnosed as sick or retarded simply because they behave like members of their own cultural group.

Some valid research has been conducted about specific cultural groups. Though few in number, these studies can show what needs to be done and can help prevent misinterpretation of studies about various cultural groups. Therefore, it is our purpose in this chapter to do the following:

1. To convey information and stimulate thinking about factors in the early development of the child that may be important for understanding specific cultural groups.

2. To highlight approaches to research that correct the use of models based on the view that the behavior of White children in middle-SES America is the only behavior that is normal or desirable. Research can be and is being done that starts with the idea that there are many ways to be normal, and that we must consider the cultural experience of a given group of children if we are to understand their behavior.

3. To present examples of alternative interpretations of research findings that are assumed to be valid by many researchers. For example, Kamin (1974) reports on the views of Terman, who believed that African-American and Mexican-American children were genetically inferior to European-American children. More culturally sophisticated contemporary researchers have challenged this deficit model (Hilliard 1975; Kamin 1974; Laosa 1978; Massey, Vaughn-Scott, and Dornbusch 1975; Pearce 1965). Yet the ideas of Terman and others linger because they become fixed in the minds and models of researchers (e.g., Jensen 1969; 1980).

Even today some researchers who study various cultural groups still feel that these groups must be compared to a European-American cultural experience on such factors as vocabulary, general information, or values. Much of the research with African-Americans, Mexican-Americans, Puerto Rican-Americans, and others is conducted by those who are not fully prepared to know the subjects of their research (Ginsberg 1972; Hall 1977; Hill 1977; Hilliard 1976a; 1976b; Levi-Strauss 1966; Ramirez and Casteneda 1974). Seldom do researchers know the culture of the people whom they seek to understand. This can lead to serious errors in the interpretation of the data.

A distinction is made between the intellectual caliber of white researchers who have studied black people in the past, and those who study us today. Today's white researchers are perhaps counterproductive in black communities, not because they are white, but because they are poorly trained in culture and in appropriate cross-cultural research methodologies. While race or skin color may be highly correlated with the amount of community legitimation a researcher acquires, it is not a determinant. Equally, if not more important are the *values* which the researcher acquires as a result of his professional training. The problems associated with the influence of these values on black communities can be solved if action is taken with regard for several concrete issues. Conceivably white researchers may have the willingness and capacity to deal effectively with these. (Brazziel 1973, p. 41)

Readers of research findings must be alert to the problem. They should look for evidence of the cultural sophistication of researchers who work with particular cultural groups. That a given researcher has done many studies on a particular cultural group is not, by itself, evidence that the researcher understands the group. Special preparation is required for those who do cross-cultural research, including a study of the history and culture of each group studied.

The meaning of "minority"

It is culture that provides every group of people with its special identity and reality (Hall 1977). The *size* of one group (the minority) with respect to another (the majority) is not an *identity;* it is only an environmental condition within which a cultural group may find itself. A Mexican-American child who comes to the United States becomes a member of a numerical minority. Yet, the cultural and personal identity of the child remains essentially what it had been before the child came to a new country (Ramirez and Casteneda 1974).

Many cultural groups in the United States are actually in a numerical minority but are not commonly thought of as minorities. The French-American, German-American, Spanish-American, or Scandinavian-American are, taken separately, numerical minorities. Yet in the current use of the word, these groups do not think of themselves as minorities. Therefore, if we consider the meaning of "minority" used in the United States, it does not refer at all to the cultural experience and identity of a group, but to the *power* position of particular cultural groups in the United States. It also connotes the cultural group's experiences of exclusion, exploitation, racism, and varying forms of oppression (Rose 1974). Thus the term "minority" has come to conjure up images that are accepted as fact, such as those of the "inner city," "disadvantaged," and "culturally deprived." If a person is asked to name a group that comes to mind when the word *minority* is used, the response will almost always be African-American, American Indian, Puerto Rican-American, Mexican-American, or Asian-American. From a professional perspective, the language or label used to designate groups makes a profound difference; indeed, when a group thinks of itself or is thought of as a minority, then an observer is deprived conceptually of an awareness of reality itself!

Low-power minority status is an actual *environmental* condition. People who live in that minority condition are frequently stigmatized, stereotyped, exploited, and in general shut off from accurate information about themselves. No doubt these conditions create abnormal stress that affects individuals, families, and groups. Professionals need to generate empirical data on the experiences of specific cultural groups and the treatment of these groups by those who are in power. Professionals who treat *numerical* minority status as a significant feature of a given group would benefit from redirecting their attention more to the larger society that creates that status and less at the cultural groups who have become its victims.

This leaves us with a question: If we do not call people "minorities," what do we call them? The answer is simple. Call people by their names! "Hey, you!" would draw an angered or an annoyed response from most individuals. "Minority" is worse than "Hey, you!" But more important than how people feel is the fact that calling a group by its name alerts us to the reality that every person or group has a history and lives in a culture. To understand what has happened to a group and why it happened, one must know the history and culture of that group.

Acknowledging culture: implications for the future

A practical consequence of these ideas should now become apparent. There are so many groups, each with its own cultural integrity, that no single review of literature can be comprehensive for all groups under a heading such as *minority*. However, we can illustrate the type of approach that is necessary to understand cultural groups who have been the victims of exclusion, neglect, or abuse. We will look for examples from the literature on young children who are either African-American, American-Indian, Asian-American, Mexican-American, or Puerto Rican-American. In practice, even these groupings require further breakdowns. For example, Asian-Americans do not comprise a single cultural group. Regardless of how long the list of cultural groups is, we must try to identify for each the special qualities that we need to understand.

1. *We need to know about the cultural patterns of specific groups.* We need to know about these patterns as they pertain to child growth, childrearing and socialization practices, identity formation, and the special place occupied by the child in a particular culture's world view. For example, African children in Uganda, Johannesburg, and Dakar have been reported to have superior physical performance during their early years in studies by Evans (1970), Pearce (1977), and Stewart (1981). These researchers attribute this precocity, among other things, to certain childrearing practices such as carrying the baby in a sling close to the mother, breast-feeding on demand, and keeping the baby close to the mother most of the time.

2. *We need to know more about individual and institutional oppression and a cultural group's response to that oppression.* Stress and group identity are but two possible sources of such influence on the physical, intellectual, emotional, and social development of children (Carnoy 1974; Fanon 1965; 1967; Howard

1980; Kamin 1974; King 1975; McDermott 1972; Pearce 1965; Rist 1973; Schwartz and Disch 1970).

3. *We need to know more about the cultural patterns of dominant groups in America and how the growth of their children occurs, especially those aspects of early experience that lead to later participation, consciously or unconsciously, in a system of oppression* (Blauner 1972; Hodge, Struckman, and Trost 1975; Pearce 1965; Rosenthal and Jacobson 1968; Schwartz and Disch 1970; Tenhouten 1971).

We will focus here on the first and second points, sampling findings that describe the unique culture of specific groups, and then presenting a sample of studies that illustrates the special pressures that many African-Americans, Mexican-Americans, American Indian, and Asian-Americans endure.

Research on child development, identity, and stress in selected cultural groups

Large numbers of children in the United States are members of one cultural group while being taught or cared for by members of other cultural groups (Cohen 1969; Tenhouten 1971). Although this need not create problems, research shows that special problems can arise in many cross-cultural teaching settings. Lightfoot (1978) documents the social distance that exists among children of African-American and other non-European-American groups and many teachers and researchers who tend to be European-Americans. Four types of problems tend to develop:

1. There are problems when the *language* that is spoken by the child is not understood by caregivers from another culture.

2. There are problems when caregivers develop low *expectations* for children based largely upon the children's membership in a low-status cultural group, rather than upon the actual abilities of the children.

3. There are problems when caregivers are unprepared to deal with children whose general *behavioral style* is different from that of the caregivers.

4. There are problems when standard *testing and assessment* techniques are applied to certain cultural groups with insufficient recognition of, or respect for, the cultural patterns of the group.

Much more scientific investigation is needed on all of these topics.

Language

The language that we use is "invisible" (Shuy 1979) in that we are seldom aware of what affects the way that we speak to, and understand, one another. Therefore, it may be hard to appreciate or to understand language styles that are different from the one that we use. Moreover, some languages and variations of American English have low status, as do the people who speak the low-status language. Bikson (1977), in a study on "minority speech" as objectively measured and subjectively evaluated, reports on the investigation of spontaneous speech performance of certain cultural groups of children of elementary school age. The group was comprised of children equally divided among Blacks, Chicanos, and Whites. They were evaluated by six White teachers. The following results were reported:

> The analyses focused on whether minority children were, or were perceived as, linguistically deficient compared with white age mates. Measures indicated that minority speech performance equalled or excelled white performance, but teachers heard it as significantly inferior. . . . Teachers did not hear Chicano-Black speech differences which appeared in the objective measures. . . . (p. 42)

This study supports the work of Shuy (1979) who shows that most speakers are unaware of the rules of their own language, yet many teachers and others in education assume that they *are* aware of the language that children use. As can be seen from this example, this assumption would lead to inappropriate responses to children. If psychometrists, like teachers in general, are not skilled in cultural linguistic principles, they would not be in a position to understand or to correct inappropriate language items in the course of test construction. This misunderstanding and devaluation of the legitimate language of the child may result in major problems. Since most transactions in schools or child care centers are rooted in language, and the language that a child speaks is both a vehicle for communication and a symbol of the child's fundamental personal and social identity, the misunderstanding and misuse of a child's language will lead to errors in communication, errors in assessment, and strained interpersonal relations.

Lindfors (1980) has written comprehensively about the place of language in the learning process. She shows how some linguistically based problems may be avoided by teachers. Christian and Wolfram (1979), under the auspices of the Center for Applied Linguistics, have written an excellent series, *Dialects and Educational Equity,* to help teachers understand basic linguistic principles and to use language wisely. The series points out that an expression in a dialect and an expression in standard English can be linguistically equivalent. Therefore a standard English expression should not be regarded as intellectually superior to an equivalent expression in a less-favored dialect. The social value of a dialect may not be high, yet its intellectual meaning may be quite the same as that of an expression in common English.

Alleyne (1969), Labov (1970), Smith (1978), Smitherman (1977), and Vass (1979) are among a very small group of linguists who have looked at Ebonics, sometimes referred to as Black English or Black Language. Because of their work, it has become clear that many African-American children speak a language that is a fusion of English and African features. The grammar, phonology, and syntax are not random or arbitrary, but rule-governed. The vocabulary is culturally specific, not deficient (Smith 1979; Wofford 1978). Therefore the automatic assessment of African-American children as language-deficient by those who do not understand the language that is spoken in African-American communities is an empirical error. Perhaps one of the most sensitive and well-founded examples of understanding the language of African-Americans is the work of Vass (1979), who brings to her analysis of the speech patterns of African-Americans a special background. She lived in a Bantu-speaking area of Africa for nearly 50 years, and learned to speak the language. Moreover, she learned the history of Africa and Africans in America. Because of that background, she has been able to discover extensive Bantu retentions in the speech patterns of African-American communities. Without the historical and cultural knowledge she possesses, she would not have been able to analyze the data on African-American language in such depth.

While the need for children to learn to speak common English remains, the Ebonics that they may speak is in no way a deficient language from a linguistic perspective. To say that an Ebonics speaker "deleted" a copula (the verb *be*) or "dropped" a final consonant cluster at the end of a word ("bein' ") is an error in interpretation. These judgments ignore the fact that these common English rules are not a part of the linguistic system of some African-Americans (Smitherman 1977). Therefore when teachers or researchers diagnose the Ebonics speaker as having low intellectual ability simply on the basis of the child's use of the normal community language, a school-created problem emerges.

The critical need for linguistic compatibility between adults and children is nowhere better illustrated than in the work of Donaldson (1978). She shows that even when adults and children speak the same language, language-based communication errors can make gross differences in the outcome of testing. "This is an important set of findings. Neither perceptual contrast nor change of wording alone made a difference. The two together made a considerable one. Also it is interesting to notice that the change of wording which made such a difference when perceptual contrast was present was a very slight one: the insertion of a single adjective" (p. 42). Here Donaldson refers to a task where children were asked, "Are there more red steps to the chair or more steps to go to the table?" and another group of children who were matched with them were asked, "Are there more steps to go to the chair or more steps to go to the table?" (see Fig. 10.1). Thirty-eight percent of the first group of 32 children answered correctly, while 66 percent of a second group of 21 did so. Many other examples are given.

Clearly, greater linguistic sophistication would help teachers in their work with children. This would minimize one set of problems in the cross-cultural teaching situations in which African-American, American Indian, Mexican-American, and other cultural groups experience discrimination in school.

Low expectations and the deficit model

The position that certain cultural groups who are different from European-Americans are deficient in some special way stems from profound cultural ignorance (Bernstein 1970; Deutsch and Brown 1964; Hess et al. 1968; Jensen 1969; Moynihan 1967). Recently, more sophisticated observers have begun to correct these ethnocentric views (Hall 1977; Levi-Strauss 1966). Nevertheless, as chil-

Figure 10.1.

(Donaldson 1978, p. 42)

dren of low-status cultural groups have come to child care programs and schools, many have met caregivers who *expected* them to fail or to do poorly compared to other children. A series of studies has examined the effects of a teacher's expectations on children's learning (H. M. Cooper 1979; Rist 1973; Rosenthal and Jacobson 1968). Not only do teachers tend to hold low expectations for children from low-status cultural groups, but classroom observations document that teachers give differential treatment to children based upon those expectations. For example, Rist shows that children are often sorted into ability groups from the first few days of school, based apparently on social class indicators such as dress and speech, rather than on evidence of potential for academic achievement. The positive interactions and reinforcements for children from low-status cultural groups also are infrequent compared to reinforcements given to other children. Much of the research confuses the socioeconomic status of children with cultural group membership. Research is needed to document the treatment that children from specific cultural groups are likely to receive in school.

Some children of African-American, American Indian, Mexican-American, and other cultural groups react to oppressive school environments by learning to be helpless (McDermott 1972; Thomas 1979). For example, McDermott observes that such children gradually tend to reduce their attention span, screening out painful social feedback, and focus their attention on social interactions in the classroom or in other settings that result in positive feedback. Since so much of their social interaction with teachers in school is painful, such children learn to seek positive responses from peers outside of the school setting and teach themselves the social rules of subordinate behavior that reduce stress. The researchers describe the behavior of some of these children who do not engage in school tasks and who appear to have minimal motivation for school work as learned helplessness. Whether this is "learned helplessness" or simply the child's response based on an astute assessment of what her or his efforts might bring remains to be determined. Quite clearly, low expectations and differential treatment by adults are associated with poor performances by children. If expectations of teachers and child care workers are appropriate for individual children, their behavior is also likely to be more supportive of children from low-status cultural groups. A proper understanding of cultural principles allows cultural variations to be seen as having internal integrity.

Behavioral style

An understanding of culture results in an understanding of modal behavioral styles within specific cultural groups. We include cognitive style simply as one aspect of a general behavioral style. Among the many investigators who have studied cultural differences in behavioral styles are Cohen (1969), Cole and Scribner (1974), Hilliard (1976a), Ramirez and Casteneda (1974), and Tenhouten (1971). Behavioral styles, including cognitive style, distinguish many members of a cultural group from members of other groups. For example, some individuals and groups prefer to deal analytically with the world, comprehending it by breaking it down into small parts. Others prefer to deal with the world and with experiences in general by approaches that are more holistic. Some individuals and groups seem to prefer that work be done more by individuals rather than cooperatively. For other groups, the reverse is true. The variations in style can create problems in school settings, especially if caregivers are rigid in their own styles and are unable to accept alternative styles as legitimate.

G. Cooper (1979) illustrates the consequences of a lack of communication among teachers and children from different cultural backgrounds. She reports the experience of a teacher who was able to use verbal communication to understand the actions of American Indian students who were previously misinterpreted.

> A teacher once told a tale of how difficult a time she had in teaching American Indian pupils at a Navajo reservation. The children would not volunteer answers to questions and would not respond to questions when called upon; they were all failing their courses. When she asked her fellow white American teachers if they had suggestions to solve the problem, she was told: "These people are just slow, you can't teach them much."
>
> But when the teacher spoke to a tribal elder, she understood the reason for the pupils' behavior. In the Navajo culture, competition is frowned upon. If a student were to volunteer or even speak out in response to a class question, he would be rude to his peers; he would be flaunting his knowledge, making himself look better than they, violating a credo of his culture. By changing her teaching methods, the teacher was able to demonstrate that her pupils were indeed as capable of learning as other pupils. (G. Cooper 1979, p. 18)

Boggs (1972) conducted an ethnographic study of communication in a first grade classroom in Hawaii that also addresses the issue of alternative behavioral styles. He hypothesized that the poor school performance of the children could be due to the mismatch between the styles of the European-American teacher and the Hawaiian children. He found that the children were expressive, voluble, and spontaneous when interacting with each other. However, when they were questioned in public by the teacher as individuals, or when the observer asked probing, private questions, they became reticent. As the children felt safe with adults, their responses became more spontaneous.

Finally, Kagan and Madsen (1971) report that European-American, Mexican, and Mexican-American children performed quite differently on simple tasks depending upon whether cooperation or competition was required. They found that tasks requiring *cooperation* were performed best by Mexican children, then by Mexican-American children, and least well by European-American children. Where *competition* was required, the order was reversed.

Schools not only teach certain subjects, but the subjects tend to be taught in certain ways or with certain styles. Since schools are for the most part managed by European-Americans, school experience reflects that cultural tradition and style. A problem occurs when both a special content and a special style that may be incompatible with the behavioral styles of many children are presented in school settings.

Standardized testing and cultural diversity

Increasingly, educators have come to rely upon widely used standardized tests as a way of obtaining information about the cognitive functioning of young children. The Peabody Picture Vocabulary Test (Dunn 1965) and the Preschool Inventory (Cooperative Preschool Inventory Handbook 1970) are two examples. Young children are also given more general developmental inventories that have been standardized. Most of the tests and developmental inventories rely heavily upon a common form of English; there is little doubt that the language of the tests is less familiar to many children from other cultural groups than it is to European-Americans; yet the children from all groups are compared with each other as if there were a universal language in America (Shuy 1976; 1979). Some of the most widely used tests and inventories are presented with no indication that they have been evaluated by linguists, even though they rely heavily on language. This can lead to serious error. It is also an error to use tests that are designed for one cultural group with members of another group when it is clear that cultural differences exist. For example, anthropologists show that children may learn to see and to manipulate their environment in ways that are both quite appropriate and culturally unique (Cole and Scribner 1974; Erny 1973; Howard 1980). The use of tests that are constructed in ignorance of such principles has grave consequences for many children. Children from some cultural groups are said to be mentally impaired when they are simply following the rules of their language and culture.

> A great deal of cross-cultural psychological research is based on notions and theories about non-Western thinking that are centered about a *deficiency hypothesis*. This line of thinking typically engenders generalizations such as the following: "In respect to such-and-such a cognitive skill, X tribe fails to perform as well as (American) (German) (English) groups." But when we turn to the area of memory, the picture is reversed. The severest critics of "primitive mentality" unite in extolling the superlative quality of primitive *memory*, and find Europeans wanting by comparison. (Cole and Scribner 1974, p. 123)

Cole and Scribner go on to discuss the need for memory as a function of the cultural and environmental conditions within which learners are located. They also show that cognitive skills which other cultures may have developed more fully can be taught to so called "primitive" groups.

Mercer (1979) has developed an alternative to standardized tests for intelligence called the System of Multicultural and Pluralistic Assessment (SOMPA). With the SOMPA, children are asked questions about things that occur in their own environment, such as asking directions to the local store. The SOMPA was developed as a substitute for traditional tests of intelligence. It is said to measure adaptive behavior that can be used by any cultural group. Although it is still not clear what basic skills the SOMPA actually measures, it is one of the few attempts to make testing responsive to specific cultural experiences. Future research is needed to clarify how the SOMPA will help in enhancing children's school learning experiences.

The problem with traditional tests may lie not so much in what they measure as in how the scores are used. Thus, it is not enough to demonstrate that a given test predicts future school achievement. The question must be answered as to *why* it does. If children with high test scores receive different and higher quality instruction than children with low test scores, then the prediction is based upon nonequivalent situations. High-scoring children are treated better in school. Therefore, predictive validity should not be seen as a justification for testing, unless it can be shown that a high quality of instruction *cannot* change the achievement outcomes for children.

Test use has caused many competent children to be labeled falsely as inherently incompetent, especially African-American, American Indian, Mexican-American, and certain other cultural groups. Yet, this error could be corrected easily if a simple scientific precaution were taken when validation studies are done. *We need to evaluate whether children who are being compared to other children have had an equivalent opportunity to learn and are equally motivated to learn the required test content.* There is no evidence that test makers are able to show users how to take this crucial step.

The importance of an opportunity to learn is demonstrated in the work of Fuller (1977). Fuller's *Ball-Stick-Bird* method was initially designed for superior children. Yet when this method for teaching reading was used with children who according to their IQ scores were said to be retarded, even children with very low IQ scores learned to read.

> Quite unexpectedly, severely retarded students, IQ's in the 30's, learned to read with comprehension and perform academically with the system intended for superior students. By doing so, these low IQ students raised basic questions about the meaning of IQ tests and the concept of intelligence. These results should not have been obtainable if today's conceptualizations of intelligence, abstract learning and IQ are correct. The initial results and their continued replication represent concrete data that something is wrong, not only with our IQ tests, not only with our concept of intelligence, but with our basic philosophy of education. (Fuller 1977, p. 14)

The children in Fuller's example were from two different cultural groups. *The thing that they had in common was instruction of a known quality.* We know of no other cultural comparison studies of the relationship between IQ and school success that ensure that the cultural groups that are being compared have had an equal opportunity to learn. It is amazing that after so many years of use, there should be so few studies of IQ measures that address this obvious problem.

Conclusion

Cultural reality or experience is a medium in which action takes place for all people. No one, for the sake of convenience, tidiness, or economy, can ignore this basic reality where children are concerned. Though the "minority" child does not exist, every child lives deeply rooted in a specific cultural milieu. That reality must be acknowledged, respected, and used as a basis for child care and education.

All cultures represent the creativities of people, and each culture is quite as "good" as the next culture. An intolerance for cultural diversity may be a symptom of an inexperienced or naïve frame of reference. Professionals have long been admonished to "start with the child where she or he is." We must recognize the child's experience as the base from which learning proceeds.

References

Alleyne, M. C. "The Linguistic Continuity of Africa in the Caribbean." In *Topics in African American Studies*, ed. H. J. Richard. New York: Black Academic Press, 1969.

Bernstein, B. "A Sociolinguistic Approach to Socialization: With Some References to Educatability." In *Language and Poverty*, ed. F. Williams. Chicago: Markham, 1970.

Bikson, T. K. "Minority Speech As Objectively Measured and Subjectively Evaluated." ERIC Documents, Bibliographic Retrieval Services, Corporation Park, Building 702, Scotia, NY 12302, 1977.

Blauner, R. *Racial Oppression in America*. New York: Harper & Row, 1972.

Boggs, S. "The Meaning of Questions and Narratives to Hawaiian Children." In *Functions of Language in the Classroom*, ed. C. Cazden, V. John, and D. Hymes. New York: Teachers College Press, 1972.

Brazziel, W. F. "White Research in Black Communities: When Solutions Become a Part of the Problem." *Journal of Social Issues* 29 (November 1973): 41–44.

Carnoy, M. *Education As Cultural Imperialism*. New York: McKay, 1974.

Christian, D., and Wolfram, W. *Dialects and Education Equity*. Arlington, Va.: Center for Applied Linguistics, 1979.

Cohen, R. "Conceptual Styles, Culture Conflict, and Non-Verbal Tests of Intelligence." *American Anthropologist* 71, no. 5 (1969): 828–857.

Cole, M., and Scribner, S. *Culture and Thought*. New York: Wiley, 1974.

Cooper, G. "Issues in Cross-Cultural Communications." *New Directions* (April 1979): 18–19.

Cooper, H. M. "Pygmalion Grows Up: A Model for Teacher Expectation, Communication and Performance Influence." *Review of Educational Research* 49 (1979): 389–410.

Cooperative Preschool Inventory Handbook. Rev. ed. Reading, Mass.: Addison-Wesley, 1970.

Cross, W. E. "Black Family and Black Identity: A Literature Review." Unpublished manuscript, 1977.

Deutsch, M., and Brown, B. R. "Social Influences in Negro-White Intelligence Differences." *Journal of Social Issues* 20 (1964): 24–35.

Diop, C. A. *The Cultural Unity of Black Africa.* Chicago: Third World Press, 1978.

Donaldson, M. *Children's Minds.* New York: Norton, 1978.

Dunn, L. M. *Peabody Picture Vocabulary Test: Manual.* Circle Pines, Minn.: American Guidance Service, 1965.

Erny, P. *Childhood and the Cosmos: The Social Psychology of the Black African Child.* New York: Black Orpheus Press, 1973.

Evans, J. *Children in Africa: A Review of Psychological Research.* New York: Teachers College Press, 1970.

Fanon, F. *A Dying Colonialism.* New York: Evergreen, 1965.

Fanon, F. *Black Skin, White Masks.* New York: Grove, 1967.

Fuller, R. *In Search of the IQ Correlation: A Scientific Whodunit.* Stonybrook, N.Y.: Ball-Stick-Bird, 1977.

Ginsberg, H. *The Myth of the Deprived Child: Poor Children's Intellect and Education.* Englewood Cliffs, N.J.: Prentice-Hall, 1972.

Hall, E. T. *Beyond Culture.* New York: Anchor, 1977.

Hess, R.; Shipman, V.; Barr, R. M.; and Brophy, J. *The Cognitive Environments of Urban Pre-School Children.* Chicago: University of Chicago Press, 1968.

Hill, R. *Informal Adoption among Black Families.* Washington, D.C.: National Urban League, 1977.

Hilliard, A. G. "The Strengths and Weaknesses of Cognitive Tests for Young Children." In *One Child Indivisible,* ed. J. D. Andrews. Washington, D.C.: National Association for the Education of Young Children, 1975.

Hilliard, A. G. *Alternatives to IQ Testing: An Approach to the Identification of Gifted "Minority" Children.* Final report to California State Department of Education, ERIC Clearinghouse on Early Childhood Education, ED 147 009, College of Education, University of Illinois, Urbana, IL 61801, 1976a.

Hilliard, A. G. "The Education of 'Inner-City' Children." In *Demythologizing the Inner-City Child,* ed. R. C. Granger and J. C. Young. Washington, D.C.: National Association for the Education of Young Children, 1976b.

Hodge, J. L.; Struckman, D. K.; and Trost, L. D. *Cultural Basis for Racism and Group Oppression: An Examination of Traditional "Western" Concepts, Values, and Institutional Structures Which Support Racism, Sexism, and Elitism.* Berkeley, Calif.: Two Riders Press, 1975.

Howard, J. "Toward a Social Psychology of Colonialism." In *Black Psycholo-*

gy, ed. R. L. Jones. New York: Harper & Row, 1980.

Jensen, A. "How Much Can We Boost IQ and Scholastic Achievement?" *Harvard Educational Review* 30 (1969): 1–123.

Jensen, A. *Bias in Mental Testing*. New York: Free Press, 1980.

Kagan, S., and Madsen, M. C. "Cooperation and Competition of Mexican and Anglo-American Children of Two Years under Instructional Sets." *Developmental Psychology* 5, no. 5 (1971): 32–39.

Kamın, L. *The Science and Politics of IQ*. New York: Lawrence Erlbaum Associates, 1974.

King, L. M. "Blonde Wig, Black Child: On the Nature of Social Science Paradigms Affecting the Legitimate Study of the Black Child." Unpublished manuscript, 1975.

Kleinfeld, J. S. "Intellectual Strengths in Culturally Different Groups: An Eskimo Illustration." *Review of Educational Research* 43 (1973): 341–359.

Labov, W. "The Logic of Non-Standard English." In *Language and Poverty*, ed. F. Williams. Chicago: Markham, 1970.

Laosa, L. M. "Maternal Teaching Strategies in Chicano Families of Varied Educational and Socio-Economic Levels." *Child Development* 49 (1978): 1129–1135.

Levi-Strauss, C. *The Savage Mind*. Chicago: University of Chicago Press, 1966.

Lightfoot, S. L. *Worlds Apart*. New York: Basic Books, 1978.

Lindfors, J. W. *Children's Language and Learning*. Englewood Cliffs, N.J.: Prentice-Hall, 1980.

Massey, G.; Vaughn-Scott, M.; and Dornbusch, S. "Racism Without Racists: Institutional Racism in Urban Schools." Stanford University Center for Research and Development in Teaching, Occasional Paper #8, 1975.

McDermott, R. "Selective Attention and the Politics of Everyday Life: An Inquiry into the Causes of Reading Failure." Unpublished manuscript, Stanford University, 1972.

Mercer, J. *Systems of Multicultural Pluralistic Assessment Technical Manual*. New York: The Psychological Corporation, 1979.

Meyers, H. F.; Rana, P. G.; and Harris, M. *Black Child Development in America 1927–1977: An Annotated Bibliography*. Westport, Conn.: Greenwood Press, 1979.

Moynihan, D. P. "The Negro Family, the Case for National Action." In *The Moynihan Report and the Politics of Controversy*, ed. L. Rainwater and W. Yancy. Cambridge, Mass.: MIT Press, 1967.

Nobles, W. "The Black Family and Its Children: The Survival of Humaneness." *Black Books Bulletin* 6, no. 2 (1978): 6–14.

Pearce, J. C. *Magical Child*. New York: Dutton, 1977.

Pearce, R. H. *Savagism and Civilization: A Study of the Indian and the American Mind*. Baltimore, Md.: Johns Hopkins University Press, 1965.

Ramirez, M., and Casteneda, A. *Cultural Democracy, Bicognitive Development, and Education*. New York: Academic Press, 1974.

Rist, R. C. *The Urban School a Factory for Failure: A Study of Education in American Society.* Cambridge, Mass.: MIT Press, 1973.

Rose, P. I. *They and We.* New York: Random House, 1974.

Rosenthal, R., and Jacobson, L. *Pygmalion in the Classroom.* New York: Holt, Rinehart & Winston, 1968.

Schwartz, B., and Disch, R. *White Racism: Its History, Pathology and Practice.* New York: Dell, 1970.

Shuy, R. "Quantitative Language Data: A Case For and Some Warnings Against." Unpublished manuscript, 1976.

Shuy, R. "Is the Construct Intelligence a Twentieth Century Myth?" Paper presented at the annual convention of the American Psychological Association, New York, 1979.

Smith, E. "The Retention of the Phonological, Phonemic, and Morpho-Phonemic Features of Africa in Afro-American Ebonics." Seminar Series Paper, Department of Linguistics, California State University at Fullerton, 1978.

Smith, E. "A Diagnostic Instrument for Assessing the Phonological Competence and Performance of the Inner City Afro-American Child." Seminar Series, Paper No. 41, Department of Linguistics, California State University at Fullerton, 1979.

Smitherman, G. *Talkin and Testifyin: The Language of Black America.* Boston: Houghton Mifflin, 1977.

Stewart, M. "Sensori-Motor Abilities of the Afrikan-American Infant: Implications for Developmental Screening." Dissertation, George Peabody College for Teachers, Vanderbilt University, 1981.

Tenhouten, W. *Cognitive Styles and the Social Order.* Los Angeles: University of California at Los Angeles, 1971. (Distributed by National Technical Information Service, U.S. Department of Commerce, 5285 Port Royal Rd., Springfield, VA 22151.)

Terman, L. M., and Merrill, M. A. *Stanford-Binet Intelligence Scale: 1972 Norms Edition.* Boston: Houghton Mifflin, 1973.

Thomas, A. "Learned Helplessness and Expectancy Factors: Implications for Research in Learning Disabilities." *Review of Educational Research* 49 (1979): 208–221.

Vass, W. K. *The Bantu Speaking Heritage of the United States.* Los Angeles: University of California, Center for Afro-American Studies, 1979.

Wofford, J. E. "Code-Switching in Black Third Grade Low-Socioeconomic Status Children in Formal and Informal Situations." Doctoral dissertation, San Francisco State University, 1978.

Cluster IV

Biological factors in development: the issue of malleability

11 **Sex differences: biological and social factors influencing the behavior of young boys and girls**

Beverly I. Fagot and Sandra J. Kronsberg

12 **Motor development in the early years**

Robert M. Malina

As long as we have studied biological aspects of development, dramatic individual differences in children have been evident. In the chapters by Fagot and Kronsberg and by Malina, we see a clear picture of the origin of these differences in sex differences and in motor development; practitioners can use this information in reflecting upon and perhaps modifying their work with children and families. For example, studies of sex differences in physical and motor development continue to demonstrate the power of socializing influences, often in nonconscious ways.

In the areas of sex differences in development, Fagot and Kronsberg describe how biologically originating prenatal patterns continue to be documented during the neonatal period. But the importance of the attitudes and expectations of adults in shaping later sex-role behavior has also been emphasized by much recent work both in infancy and later childhood. The distinction between sex-appropriate attitudes and sex-appropriate behavior is an important one, and research indicates that we can trace different learning patterns for each.

Malina discusses how physical and motor development have also received increasing attention as links to school learning, peer acceptance, and self-esteem. Efforts to improve our ability to predict later physical development have revealed how some areas seem stable, while others appear responsive or vulnerable to environmental facilitation or insult. Research has documented the range of effects of different environments, and offers specified ways of enhancing children's development.

These chapters illustrate how societal values interact with our scientific interests. In recent years, for example, interest in sex-role stereotyping has motivated researchers in motor skills to identify areas of difference in girls' and boys' competencies, and possible socialization experiences that might account for these differences.

Beverly I. Fagot
Sandra J. Kronsberg

11 Sex differences: biological and social factors influencing the behavior of young boys and girls

"If I had a magic wand and I could make you a boy or girl right now, would you like to be a boy or a girl?" When more than 150 young children were asked this question during the years from two to four, with techniques adapted from De-Vries (1969) and Slaby and Frey (1975), over one-half of the girls at some time said they would like to be a boy, yet none of the boys over the age of two ever said he had wanted to be a girl. Although these were very young children, they clearly reflected the cultural message that being a boy is somehow preferable. Moreover, the parents of these children said that they placed a high value on equality and tried to practice these beliefs within their child's home environment (Fagot, in preparation).

Many parents and teachers are puzzled that their attempts to minimize sex differences in the behavior and attitudes of young children fail. Parents and teachers, however, are not alone in their concern with the development of differences in behavior between boys and girls; researchers ask many of the same questions.

In this chapter, we will discuss three major theories designed to account for sex differences. We will also provide a broad overview of the research literature on the effects of biological and social factors that influence the development of these differences. In a concluding section, consideration will be given to the implications these research findings have for understanding the interactive process that produces sex differences in behavior, and a set of problems will be outlined that should be addressed in the future.

Recent theoretical approaches and research investigations concerning sex-role development have generated a variety of terms and concepts, and so to avoid confusion, before proceeding we will provide definitions of the terms that will be used in this chapter.

Terminology

Sex-role development is the overall process, both biological and social, of becoming male or female. Money and Ehrhardt (1972) have developed a useful terminology to describe the two major outcomes of the process. *Gender identity* is the individual's understanding of her or his own sex, one's definition of oneself as male or female, while *gender role* is everything the person does and says to indicate to others the degree to which one is either male or female. Gender role also has two components, observable *behaviors* and sex-role *attitudes*. Actual sex differences in behaviors or preferences have been considered in the research literature in several ways: sex preferred (Fagot 1977), sex-typed behaviors (Lynn 1969), or sex-role adoptions (Fling and Manosevitz 1972). Although these terms all have slightly different meanings, all refer to differences in behavior that are relative because there is always an overlap of behavior styles between the sexes. In this chapter, we will speak of these behavioral differences between males and females as *sex-typical behaviors*. That is, they are more typical of one sex than the other, although not exclusive of one sex. For example, both boys and girls show aggressive behaviors, but boys typically show more aggression. Such sex differences can be forms of play activities or broader categories of behavior categories such as aggression or dependency.

In addition to observed behavior, a second measure of gender role is the individual's *attitudes* concerning the appropriateness of activities and/or behaviors for males and females. We will speak of these attitudes as *sex stereotypes*, and it should be clear that both children and the adults who socialize them show sex stereotypes.

Theoretical approaches

Three major theoretical approaches have influenced recent work in the study of sex differences: a *biological* approach, a *cognitive-developmental* approach, and a *social learning* approach. Most of the research concerning the biological explanations of sex differences has focused upon animals other than humans, although recently more work has been done using human newborns and individuals with hormonal anomalies. The research of Money and Ehrhardt (1972) on early hormonal influences on a broad range of intellectual and social behaviors has been the most influential biological approach and will therefore be discussed in the section on prenatal development. In addition, the theoretical work of Wilson (1978) has stimulated a rethinking of the biological underpinnings of sex differences. From this perspective, much of human nature, including the existence of sex roles, is considered biological processes that have evolved within an evolutionary context. Both Money and Ehrhardt, and Wilson take care to emphasize, however, that it is the interaction of these biological underpinnings with social-cultural factors that creates the sex differences that have been observed.

The second approach involves a cognitive-developmental perspective. It was first developed by Kohlberg (1966), and focuses largely upon gender identity, that is, an individual's self-identification as either male or female. Kohlberg maintains that sex-role development proceeds in a regular progression, or series of stages, as a function of the child's level of cognitive development. As a first step, children appear to learn to label themselves as either male or female (in Kohlberg's terms, to have some form of gender identity). Then, as a second step, they understand that one's sex is stable over the life cycle; that is, little boys become men, not women (gender stability). Finally, in a third step, children come to understand that sex is constant despite perceptual transformations (such as the length or style of hair) of the self or another person (gender constancy). There is general agreement about this developmental sequence, with the final step of gender constancy occurring sometime between five and seven years of age for most children. However, there is still controversy over the extent to which cognitive structures (such as the child's understanding of the self as a boy or girl) organize or guide the child's sex-role development.

The third approach, social learning, has been most thoroughly outlined by Mischel (1966; 1970), and it emphasizes environmental and social influences on observable behaviors. The research based on this approach has sought to reveal the importance of social reinforcement and modeling by the key people in the child's environment (e.g., parents, peers, and teachers) in shaping appropriate sex-role behaviors.

More recently, all of these theoretical approaches have been criticized because none by itself explains the observed sex differences very well. We believe that this is because the theories rely on a unidimensional perspective that assumes either that social agents, especially parents, shape children's development or that biological processes control this development. These theories fail to recognize that children are an ever-changing and active agent in their own socialization and development. The picture is, however, beginning to change and a far more sophisticated and interesting perspective is emerging in which the interactive nature of children's development is acknowledged (Bell 1968). Although recognition of children's effect upon the environment, as well as the effect of the environment upon children, presents a more realistic picture, it poses some difficult problems for researchers to untangle.

Sex-role development

Prenatal sexual differentiation

Chromosomal sex is determined at conception, but for a period of six weeks, the female (XX) and the male (XY) fetus are indistinguishable except for this chromosomal difference. However, by the seventh week of life, primitive forms of the reproductive systems of both the female (Müllerian ducts) and the male (Wolffian ducts) are present in *both* the female and male fetus. The female Müllerian system does not require hormonal stimulation to direct its development. The male Wolffian system, however, will not develop without hormones. This differentiation of reproductive systems begins around the eighth week of prenatal development when the Y chromosome in the male fetus causes the secretion of a substance called the H-Y antigen, that in turn stimulates the production of two hormones in the primitive testes. One hormone, MIS (Müllerian Inhibiting Substance), is as yet chemically unidentified and is named for its effect in inhibiting the growth of the female reproductive system. The second hormone, an androgen, stimulates the development of the male system.

It is important to note, however, that these hormones will act upon the fetus regardless of the actual chromosomal sex of the fetus. In a very small percentage of cases, a hormonal malfunctioning does occur. Prenatal overexposure to androgen in a female fetus can be caused by two different problems. In Adrenal Genital Syndrome (AGS), the fetus's own adrenal cortex malfunctions. In other cases, when mothers were given progestin during pregnancy to prevent miscarriage, abnormal androgen production has also resulted. There has been extensive study of these females who were exposed prenatally to androgen. Any abnormalities, such as enlarged clitoris or fused labia, can be surgically corrected shortly after birth, and the children given suitable hormone treatment when necessary. These children can then develop as females capable of producing offspring.

An interesting question that has been studied is how these physiological anomalies and their treatment relate to gender identity and gender role. Studies seem to show that neither chromosomal sex nor the prenatal hormone levels necessarily determine gender identity. Instead, it is the child's sex of rearing (whether the child is treated as a boy or girl by the family members and others) that appears to be the crucial variable that determines the child's gender identity. Nevertheless, there is some evidence that prenatally androgenized females do show more sex-typical male behaviors and fewer female behaviors than control girls, even when surgically corrected. For instance, the androgenized females are more active, more likely to be classified as tomboys, and more interested in careers than the control children. Children without this medical history show more female sex-typical behaviors such as doll play and interest in dressing up (Baker and Ehrhardt 1974; Ehrhardt and Baker 1974). Yet follow-up studies of these children as adults show them to be successful mothers (Money 1978).

The newborn period

In trying to separate the biological contributions of sex differences from the social contributions, it seems logical to investigate differences in the behavior of newborn boys and girls, because the impact of social and cultural events on development is surely less at birth than at any other time in the child's life.

Korner (1973) reviewed the available studies on neonates in the first two weeks of life, and concludes sex differences are evident at birth. The most consistent findings indicate that newborn girls appear to be more sensitive than newborn boys to both tactile stimulation and certain types of oral stimulation, such as a sweet formula. There is also some suggestion that boys' ability to lift their heads higher from a prone position may indicate greater muscular strength. However, there are no differences between girls and boys on a variety of other expected dimensions, such as responsiveness to auditory or visual stimulation, spontaneous activity level, or crying.

Furthermore, the sex differences in newborns that have been consistently noted here in the United States have not been found in similar studies conducted in Europe. It has been suggested (Richards, Bernal, and Brackbill 1976) that perhaps the reason for this discrepancy in findings between countries might have to do with the custom of circumcision. While boys in the United States are routinely circumcised immediately after birth, this is rarely done in Europe and, therefore, perhaps the sex differences that have been reported in this country are an artifact of the boys' side-effect reaction to circumcision.

This possibility was investigated in a carefully controlled study of the spontaneous behavior of a small sample of newborn Jewish boys and girls who were observed for two days after birth (Phillips, King, and DuBois 1978). Jewish children were chosen because religious custom dictates that boys not be circumcised until the eighth day after birth. The results showed that for the large numbers of behaviors that were observed, there were only a few differences between the boys and girls; boys were awake more often and made more facial grimaces and low-intensity body motions (e.g., slight turn of the head, slow wave of the hand).

In sum, this brief overview suggests that there are few, if any, differences between the behavior of newborn boys and girls. While there may be sex differences due to prenatal hormonal differences, as the biological approach suggests, they do not seem to appear in newborns. However, this does not exclude the possibility that there may be biologically programmed sex differences (e.g., activity level) that manifest themselves later during early childhood, just as marked differences in size and strength manifest themselves in adolescence.

Parent behavior with newborns. A good deal of evidence indicates that from birth parents respond to boys differently than girls, although this differential treatment is probably not in response to any differences in the newborn's behavior. Mothers and fathers were asked to rate their newborns during the first 24 hours after birth, when actual contact with their child was minimal (Rubin, Provenzano, and Luria 1974). The children were all full-term and equivalent in length, weight, and Apgar Scale scores (an assessment of neonate functioning made a few minutes after birth that includes pulse, breathing, muscle tone, reflex responses, and color). Yet the parents, and especially fathers, tended to use very stereotypic ratings. Daughters were more often described as soft, fine-featured, little, awkward, and weak, while sons were usually described as firm, large-featured, big, well-coordinated, and strong.

The differential treatment by parents might be related to their expectations of what boys and girls are like, since mothers appear to have more social interaction with their daughters and more physical involvement with their sons. A study of mother-neonate interaction (Thoman, Leiderman, and Olson 1972) showed that the mother's behavior during breast-feeding while still in the hospital varied depending on the sex of the newborn. Mothers of boys spent more time breast-feeding, whereas mothers of girls spent more of their time talking to their daughters.

Lewis (1974) and Moss (1967) also found that mothers spent more time talking to their daughters, while mothers of sons spent more time physically stimulating their children by rocking, touching, and holding them, and that the differences were observed for infants up to three months of age (Lewis 1974; Moss 1967; 1974). Lewis tries to separate out the child effects from the parent effects. He analyzes the sequences of interaction between mothers and their infants and concludes that mothers' differential responses to sons and daughters occur even in the absence of any behavior differences in the infants themselves.

The infant and toddler period

Sex differences in child behavior do not begin to appear with any regularity until about the first birthday, and even these differences are few in comparison with the similarities observed between boys and girls at this age. Goldberg and Lewis (1969) reveal several sex differences in the behavior of one-year-olds when they were individually observed with their mothers during a free play situation. Girls appeared to be more restricted in their style of play; they tended to sit and play with a combination of toys that required fine-motor control such as a pegboard. They also tended to look at, talk to, touch, and stay near their mothers. By contrast, the boys' style of play was more active; they played with toys requiring large-motor control, such as a plastic lawnmower, and they tended to manipulate these toys by banging, hitting, and throwing them. Boys were also more likely to explore the playroom which resulted in play with non-toys, such as the doorknob and electrical outlets. However, the most striking difference between the boys and girls was in response to the barrier frustration test, a plastic mesh barrier behind which their mothers put them toward the end of the session. The boys tended to rush to either end of the barrier attempting to move it or get out. The girls, on the other hand, tended to stand where they had been placed, crying and motioning for help.

The infants' behavior in this study seemed to parallel sex-stereotypic descriptions of older children and adults, and correspond to the sex-stereotyped ratings made by parents of their newborn sons and daughters (Rubin, Provenzano, and Luria 1974). This suggests that parental expectations might have some influence on the sex-typical behaviors that eventually develop in children.

It is important to note, however, that although Goldberg and Lewis's study is frequently cited, most of the replication studies that followed have not found such extensive sex differences in style of play or behavior of the mother (Brooks and Lewis 1974; Clarke-Stewart 1973; Jacklin, Maccoby, and Dick 1973; Maccoby and Jacklin 1973; Messer and Lewis 1972). Furthermore, a follow-up study of the original Goldberg and Lewis sample one year later, using the barrier frustration test, also found sex differences in behavior, but not necessarily in the expected direction. Feiring and Lewis (1979) report that at age two, the girls vocalized to their mothers for help and made more attempts at problem solving, while the boys spent more time fretting, crying, and looking at their mothers. Such results suggest that girls may develop and use instrumental behaviors sooner than boys, especially the instrumental use of adults as an aid to problem solving.

While sex differences in the behavior of infant boys and girls are minimal, by the time children approach their second birthday, there is substantial evidence for consistent differences that would appear to be an extension of those occasionally observed during the first year of life. For example, a frequent finding involves differences in the toy preferences of toddler girls and boys observed during play at home. Girls tend to play with soft toys and dolls, and they dress up and dance; whereas boys tend to play with transportation toys and blocks, to actively manipulate objects, and to play more often with toys forbidden by parents (Fagot 1974; 1978b; Fein et al. 1975; Smith and Daglish 1977). Also consistent with the expected or stereotyped social expressive orientation of girls and the object orientation of boys, girls tend to begin to talk earlier than boys (Schachter et al. 1978) and to use this ability to their advantage in problem situations such as the barrier frustration task (Feiring and Lewis 1979).

Parent behaviors with infants and toddlers. Many parents provide different socialization experiences for their daughters and their sons at the same time that sex-typical toddler behaviors are emerging. Parents tend to buy their sons more transportation toys, sports equipment, and military toys while they buy their daughters dolls, stuffed animals, and domestic toys (Rheingold and Cook 1975). In addition, parents often react more positively to both boys and girls when the children are engaged in sex-stereotypical behaviors and activities (e.g., girls with dolls, boys with blocks) (Fagot 1978b).

There is also some indication that parents are more inclined to interact verbally with their daughters and physically with their sons. For example, the tendency for mothers to talk more to their daughters during the newborn period continues to be observed with one-year-olds (Kronsberg 1975), and with two-year-olds (Cherry and Lewis 1976; Clarke-Stewart 1973). Fagot (1978b), studying toddlers in the home, found that both mothers and fathers were more likely to interact with their daughters' appropriate play by giving positive comments, while they physically joined the play of their sons. If parents considered play inappropriate, they criticized girls, but intervened physically with boys and stopped their play.

In an attempt to untangle some of the sex-of-parent by sex-of-child interaction findings, Kronsberg (1981) developed a set of video clips with children who were equally likely to be rated as boys or girls. These children then engaged in simulated risky or mischievous behaviors. Fathers and mothers of boys or girls were asked to view the tape and told they could press a verbal or physical intervention response button or allow the child to continue the taped activity without intervention. Parents of boys pressed the physical intervention button much quicker and on more behaviors than parents of girls who tended to use verbal intervention. The gender manipulation (half of the parents were told a child was a boy and the other half that the child was a girl) was not effective. The parents reacted to all children on the tape as if they were the same sex as their own child. One might think that this study suggests that children teach their parents a style of intervention; however, many of these parents had very young infants. The parents of infants did not differ in style of response from the parents of toddlers which suggests that stereotypes of boys' and girls' behaviors were present before the child had a chance to teach the parent a particular style. A similar study is now being completed on expectant parents. Our prediction is that the gender manipulation should be effective for this group, and that the expectant parents will verbally intervene when told the child is a girl, and physically intervene when told the child is a boy.

Do parents buy their sons and daughters sex-stereotypic toys because they think children should play with "appropriate" toys, or do they buy them because the child requests them? Do mothers talk more to their young daughters because girls learn to talk sooner and are therefore more responsive and skilled at communication, or conversely, do girls learn to talk sooner than boys because mothers talk more to daughters?

Unfortunately, once interactions are started, each participant affects the other person's response and it becomes almost impossible to untangle the origins of differential treatment. Perhaps the differential treatment of boys and girls begins as a function of parental expectations about sex-stereotypic child behavior, that in turn promotes sex-typical behavior in their children, that in turn elicits further differential treatment from parents (Condry and Condry 1976; Fagot 1973a; Rubin, Provenzano, and Luria 1974; Seavey, Katz, and Zalk 1975; Will, Self, and Datan 1976). An interesting case in point was an attempt to assess differential treatment by parents while keeping the effect of the child relatively constant (Frisch 1977). Both men and women who were parents had opportunities to play with a 14-month-old infant in a laboratory playroom, while the child's mother sat unobtrusively in the background. The actual sex of the infant was never revealed, and each child was introduced on different occasions as being "a boy" or "a girl." As might be expected for both the men and women, when the infant was introduced as a girl, it received more interpersonal stimulation and nurturant play, but when the infant was introduced as a boy, there was more encouragement for activity and male sex-typical toy choice. No sex differences were observed in the infants' actual play, so the differential treatment provided by these parents resulted from their own projections as to what was appropriate play behavior.

The preschool and early school years

The same kinds of sex differences in toddler toy preferences and play styles observed at home that were reviewed in the previous section seem to be firmly established among three-year-old children observed in preschool settings. Fagot and Patterson (1969) in the United States, and Clark, Wyon, and Richards (1969) in England found very similar differences in children's play; their behaviors are what one would expect from the sexual stereotypes. Girls engage in more doll play, domestic rehearsal, art activities, and dancing, while boys play with transportation toys, woodworking materials, and blocks. Boys also engage in more rough-and-tumble play and are more aggressive in their interchanges with peers, especially other boys (Pedersen and Bell 1970). These results have been replicated many times since 1969 and little change in sex differences in three-year-olds' play has occurred during that time (Etaugh, Collins, and Gerson 1975; Fagot 1977; Serbin et al. 1973). As noted in Hartup (1970), observation studies in the 1930s also document the same sex differences. It is important to note that both these recent studies and those conducted in the 1930s were based on observing children in natural settings and involved techniques that evolved from behavioral and ecological studies. In contrast to these naturalistic observations, most research concerning sex differences from 1940 through the late 1960s came from laboratory studies of children using tests that required a verbal response. The conclusion most often drawn from the verbal tests is that consistent sex-typical behaviors do not develop until age five or six (Spencer 1967). It is now generally accepted that the inconsistent laboratory findings with three- and four-year-olds are due to the difficulties of obtaining reliable test (verbal) responses from such young children.

Tests of sex stereotypes. In order to measure the child's knowledge concerning the perceived appropriateness of any particular activity for males or females (sex stereotypes), several different tests have been devised. The It Scale (Brown 1956) has been used extensively to study the child's knowledge of sex stereotypes, and such results have often been used to make inferences concerning the child's underlying gender identity. In this scale, *It* is an abstract stick figure that is essentially "sexless," allowing the child to project her or his own sex to the figure. The child is asked to select, from among pictures of masculine and feminine objects, the ones that It would prefer. Although most boys make more masculine choices for It and most girls make more feminine choices, when children are asked whether It is actually a boy or a girl, a substantial number of girls feel that It is a boy, and that they are choosing toys that a boy would like. While children's ability to make such choices suggests at least the beginnings of sex stereotypes, it is inappropriate to use the test as a measure of gender identity for individual children (Thompson and McCandless 1970).

Williams, Bennett, and Best (1975) have developed a series of 24 stories designed to test the child's knowledge of sex stereotypes. The child is told a story representing male or female sex-stereotypic behavior and is then shown a drawing of a male and female and asked to point out which figure is the main character of the story. Williams, Bennett, and Best find that five-year-olds have some knowledge of sex stereotypes and by age seven, children's responses are very similar to adults'. Unfortunately, this test is too difficult for three- and four-year-old children and it is unclear whether this is due to a lack of understanding of the instructions or the lack of a knowledge of sex stereotypes.

Edelbrock and Sugawara (1978) have constructed a Sex Role Learning Index for preschool children that allows children to rate pictures according to the cultural sex-role stereotypes and their own ideas as to appropriate activities for children and adults. This test appears to be a promising way of measuring a child's understanding of sex stereotyping and avoids the methodological flaws of earlier tests. It is apparent that sex stereotypes start to be formed very young and that children as young as two have some rudimentary knowledge of cultural sex stereotypes (Haugh, Hoffman, and Cowan 1980; Kuhn, Nash, and Brucken 1978).

Studies specifically designed to test Kohlberg's theory of gender identity help in understanding the cognitive component in sex-role development. Slaby and Frey (1975) asked children from 26 to 68 months of age a set of questions designed to tap their cognitive understanding of gender identity, and of the fact that gender is stable over the life span, and constant over changes in appearance, clothing, etc. They found that children conformed to Kohlberg's predicted sequence of stages (in which gender identity comes first) with only a few children showing evidence of the highest stage (constancy) prior to the other two.

Marcus and Overton (1978) also found that children progress through the gender stages in the sequence predicted by Kohlberg. However, they were also interested in Kohlberg's prediction that the attainment of gender constancy is an organizer of sex-role behavior. Therefore, one important question in their study is how the child's gender stage relates to the performance of, or understanding of, sex-typical behaviors. Marcus and Overton found no significant relationship between gender constancy and actual sex-typical behaviors such as preferences of TV shows. Fagot (in preparation) also found that gender stage and sex-typical behaviors in free play are not significantly related. In both the Marcus and Overton, and Fagot studies, there is an indication that the child who has achieved gender constancy may actually be *more* likely rather than *less* likely to try out a broader range of behaviors, perhaps because these children understand that sex is not dependent on physical characteristics such as long hair or particular play behaviors.

Influences beyond parents: peer and teacher behavior. From ages three to seven children enter a much more complex world than toddlers encounter. The child is exposed to a broader range of social reactions from more people. While parents and other members of the family still hold a large place in the child's life, most children during this time become members of various peer groups (such as neighborhood, school, or children of parents' friends) and encounter teachers as they enter school. What does this mean to the child in terms of gender development?

In the last few years, there has been a great deal of interest in the question of differential socialization by early childhood teachers. Fagot and Patterson (1969) found that unlike parents, female preschool teachers tend to respond positively to feminine sex-typical behaviors in both sexes, while not responding to male sex-typical behavior, regardless of the sex of the child. There has been some speculation that male teachers react more positively to male-typical behaviors in boys, and some early studies confirm this (Etaugh, Collins, and Gerson 1975; McCandless, Bush, and Carden 1975). However, when amount of experience of the teacher is controlled, both male and female teachers react more positively to both boys and girls involved in female-typical behaviors such as art activities and helping behaviors (Fagot 1978a). The results are best seen as due to overlap between expectations for appropriate pupil behavior and the feminine sex-stereotypic behavior (Lee and Voivodas 1977).

There are other differences in the ways preschool teachers (who are mostly women) react to boys and girls. Girls tend to receive more instructions from teachers than boys receive (Biber, Miller, and Dyer 1972; Fagot 1973b), and their speech tends to be acknowledged more often (Cherry 1975). However, to a great extent, the differences in teacher response appear to be a function of the girls' tendency to stay within close proximity to teachers, presumably inviting teacher interaction (Fagot 1978a; Serbin et al. 1973). During the times that boys are participating appropriately in class activities, they too receive positive attention, in fact, more than girls. Teachers also react more negatively to aggressive behaviors in boys than in girls, indicated by the fact that boys receive more negative feedback from the teacher than seems warranted by the amount of aggression actually observed (Serbin et al. 1973).

Teachers of young children see their job as encouraging behaviors that will help the child in school (Lee and Gropper 1974) and they perceive that boys have more difficulty than girls in conforming to school pressures. Hence, they attend to both the positive and negative behaviors of boys more, and monitor them more closely. Even though few preschool teachers feel that girls' femininity and their lack of participation in male sex-typical behaviors might have a negative effect on school performance, studies indicate that girls' early participation in male sex-typical behavior is *positively* correlated with an interest in science during the later school years and with high performance in both math and science subjects (Fagot and Littman 1976; Tyler 1964).

In fairness to teachers, one additional comment should be made concerning their responses to young children. Studies of young children show that both boys and girls receive overwhelmingly more positive feedback than negative feedback from teachers, and that the children themselves engage in far more prosocial behavior than negative behavior. Observational studies also suggest that for most children the preschool environment is extremely supportive and very positive, although in slightly different ways for boys and girls.

The influence of peers in maintaining sex-typical behaviors has always been acknowledged, but only recently has there been an attempt to look at just how age-mates influence sex differences. As early as age three, children play in same-sex groups (Charlesworth and Hartup 1967; Fagot and Patterson 1969), and children receive most of their social reactions from same-sex peers. Fagot (1977) found that peers tend to regard children positively when they engage in appropriate sex-typical behaviors and negatively when they engage in typical behaviors of the opposite sex. She also found that boys who consistently prefer female sex-typical behaviors have far less positive and far more negative peer interaction than the average for the class, but girls with male-behavior preferences are treated no differently than the rest of the class. Lamb and Roopnarine (1979) found that boys play longer in male sex-typical situations when given positive reactions by other boys than if they are treated positively by girls.

Children also behave as though they expect their peers to reinforce them for conventional behaviors. Burchardt and Serbin (1977) found that children explore opposite-sex-typical behaviors more when alone than in the presence of a peer, particularly an opposite-sex peer. In all, the information suggests that peers do interact with children on the basis of both the child's sex and the sex stereotype of the activity in which the child is engaged. Indications are that not only is the preschool peer group, especially boys, quite conservative in terms of their sex-role values, but they do not hesitate to let their companions know when they are crossing into the other sex's "territory."

In summary, for children from two to seven there is good evidence that boys and girls engage in quite different activities and that parents and peers tend to encourage differential participation. Teachers make some attempt to encourage boys to sample a wider range of behaviors, but they do not similarly encourage girls. At these ages there are not yet any large differences in personality or cognitive performance in boys and girls (Maccoby and Jacklin 1974), although by the time children start school at six, boys exceed girls in difficulty adjusting both emotionally and cognitively (Eme 1979). However, by early adolescence, consistent mean differences in intellectual activities, such as higher math scores for boys and higher verbal scores for girls, are evident.

Block (1979) suggests that the play experiences of young boys and girls differ on several dimensions that actually result in the personality and intellectual styles of men and women. She feels that the kinds of toys girls are given (e.g., dolls, household items) encourage imitative play and the learning of existing social roles. Boys are given toys that encourage the child to explore new directions and to find new solutions (e.g., puzzles, tools). In this way, both boys and girls fail to learn valuable skills because of the sex-typed nature of their toys and resulting play.

Implications

The major concerns of this chapter have been the relative contributions of biological and social factors to the process of sex-role development. Social influences have been discussed in greater detail than biological influences, in part, due to the lack of studies with humans and especially with young children. However, this emphasis also represents the authors' conviction that the biological components of gender identity and sex-role behavior, while definitely of consequence, are relatively small by comparison with cultural influences. Blurton-Jones and Konner, after conducting research with young children in London and in the Bushman culture, conclude that while sex differences have some biological component, cultures burden children with unnecessary paraphernalia that go well beyond the dictates of biology (Blurton-Jones and Konner 1973, p. 734).

To understand sex differences and why girls and boys develop different competencies and deficiencies, it is important to pay close attention to the interactions that children experience, both as initiators and as recipients of social responses, with parents, teachers, peers, and other members of their culture. Since it appears that for the toddler and preschool child, options are still open, the content of early learning environments is important. For example, early childhood programs should scrutinize their curricula and educational practices for their contribution to the process of sex-role development. On close inspection, one finds that it is widely recognized that boys have more difficulty than girls in school during the early years. Consequently, early school programs have tried to remediate the problem by broadening the boys' repertoires and giving them the verbal and fine-motor experiences necessary for success. However, very few teachers think to try to provide girls practice in activities that call for restructuring the environment or that involve active, gross-motor coordination (i.e., looking beyond obvious solutions). Instead, it is considered natural that girls should fall behind on tasks that call for such abilities; no problem is perceived when they do. This imbalance in adult perceptions of what is problematical for boys vs. girls needs to be rectified so that appropriate learning experiences are provided for all children.

Indeed, it is quite possible to design activities that teach boys fine-motor coordination and verbal skills but that are not necessarily identified as female-sex typical. It is also possible to teach boys to be caring and nurturant without feminizing them. Furthermore, it is possible to encourage spatial skills in girls by encouraging them to build with blocks, to play vigorously, and to be assertive without threatening the child's gender identity. In general then, teachers can design activities that are not gender-related but that teach both boys and girls the skills necessary for being a capable human being. These suggestions are not only applicable to preschool environments, but are also relevant to the kinds of activities and interactions parents provide within the home. More extensive suggestions and guidelines for developing these environments are now available in several sources and the interested reader is encouraged to pursue them (e.g., Sprung 1975).

We are, however, aware that suggesting the development of an early environment that minimizes sex typing may be met with skepticism or resistance by parents and teachers alike. While most parents do not seem overly concerned that their daughter's style of play or toy choices may result in their child being labeled a tomboy, many parents are very concerned that their son might be labeled a sissy. These parents, particularly fathers, believe that the practice of opposite-sex-role behavior by boys, such as nurturance play with dolls, for example, will lead to problems in heterosexual adjustment later. Our information concerning the development of sexual attraction is meager, but it appears that sexual attraction develops as a different system than either gender identity or gender-role behavior (Green 1976). Therefore, when we suggest that children should be given the opportunity to learn the skills of both sexes (an androgynous point of view), we are saying that children should not be excessively sex stereotyped in either direction.

In conclusion, it is our suggestion that children should be reared with the opportunity to explore as many capabilities and interests as possible, so that they will be able to function successfully and competently in a broad range of situations. Home and school environments designed to teach the strong points of both the male and female roles will ultimately result in happier, more competent children and adults.

References

Baker, S. W., and Ehrhardt, A. A. "Prenatal Androgen, Intelligence, and Cognitive Sex Differences." In *Sex Differences in Behavior*, ed. R. C. Friedman, R. M. Richart, and R. L. Van de Wiele. New York: Wiley, 1974.

Bell, R. Q. "A Reinterpretation of the Direction of Effects in Studies of Socialization." *Psychological Review* 75 (1968): 81–95.

Biber, H.; Miller, L. B.; and Dyer, J. L. "Feminization in Preschool." *Developmental Psychology* 7 (1972): 86.

Block, J. H. "Socialization Influences on Personality Development in Males and Females." In *APA Master Lecture Series on Issues of Sex and Gender in Psychology*, ed. M. M. Parks. Washington, D.C.: American Psychological Association, 1979.

Blurton-Jones, N. G., and Konner, M. J. "Sex Differences in Behaviour of London and Bushman Children." In *Comparative Ecology and Behaviour of Primates*, ed. R. P. Michael and J. H. Crook. London: Academic Press, 1973.

Brooks, J., and Lewis, M. "Attachment Behavior in Thirteen-Month-Old Opposite Sex Twins." *Child Development* 45 (1974): 243–247.

Brown, D. G. "Sex Role Preference in Young Children." *Psychological Monographs* 70 (1956). No. 421.

Burchardt, C. J., and Serbin, L. A. "Effects of Peer Presence on Sex-Typing of Children's Toy Choices." Paper presented at the biennial meeting of the Society for Research in Child Development, New Orleans, March 1979.

Charlesworth, R., and Hartup, W. W. "Positive Social Reinforcement in the Nursery School Peer Group." *Child Development* 38 (1967): 315–320.

Cherry, L. "The Preschool Teacher-Child Dyad: Sex Differences in Verbal Interaction." *Child Development* 46 (1975): 532–535.

Cherry, L., and Lewis, M. "Mothers and Two-Year-Olds: A Study of Sex-Differentiated Aspects of Verbal Interaction." *Developmental Psychology* 12 (1976): 278–282.

Clark, A. H.; Wyon, S. M.; and Richards, M. P. M. "Freeplay in Nursery

School Children." *Journal of Child Psychology and Psychiatry* 10 (1969): 205–216.

Clarke-Stewart, K. A. "Interactions Between Mothers and Their Young Children: Characteristics and Consequences." *Monographs of the Society for Research in Child Development* 38 (1973). Serial No. 153.

Condry, J., and Condry, S. "Sex Differences: A Study of the Eye of the Beholder." *Child Development* 47 (1976): 812–819.

DeVries, R. "Constancy of Generic Identity in the Years Three to Six." *Monographs of the Society for Research in Child Development* 34 (1969). Serial No. 127.

Edelbrock, C. S., and Sugawara, A. I. "Acquisition of Sex-Typed Preferences in Preschool-Aged Children." *Developmental Psychology* 14 (1978): 614–623.

Ehrhardt, A. A., and Baker, S. W. "Fetal Androgens, Human Central Nervous System Differentiation, and Behavior Sex Differences." In *Sex Differences in Behavior,* ed. R. C. Friedman, R. M. Richart, and R. L. Van de Wiele. New York: Wiley, 1974.

Eme, R. J. "Sex Differences in Childhood Psychopathology: A Review." *Psychological Bulletin* 86 (1979): 574–595.

Etaugh, C.; Collins, G.; and Gerson, A. "Reinforcement of Sex-Typed Behaviors of Two-Year-Old Children in a Nursery School Setting." *Developmental Psychology* 11 (1975): 255.

Fagot, B. I. "Sex-Related Stereotyping of Toddlers' Behaviors." *Developmental Psychology* 9 (1973a): 429.

Fagot, B. I. "Influence of Teacher Behavior in the Preschool." *Developmental Psychology* 9 (1973b): 198–206.

Fagot, B. I. "Sex Differences in Toddlers' Behavior and Parental Reaction." *Developmental Psychology* 10 (1974): 554–558.

Fagot, B. I. "Consequences of Moderate Cross-Gender Behavior in Preschool Children." *Child Development* 48 (1977): 902–907.

Fagot, B. I. "Reinforcing Contingencies for Sex-Role Behaviors: Effect of Experience with Children." *Child Development* 49 (1978a): 30–36.

Fagot, B. I. "The Influence of Sex of Child on Parental Reactions to Toddler Children." *Child Development* 49 (1978b): 459–465.

Fagot, B. I. "Male and Female Teachers: Do They Treat Boys and Girls Differently?" *Sex Roles* 7 (1981): 263–272.

Fagot, B. I. "Sex Role Preferences and Cognitive Gender Identity." Eugene, Oreg.: University of Oregon, paper in preparation.

Fagot, B. I., and Littman, I. "Relation of Preschool Sex Typing to Intellectual Performance in Elementary School." *Psychological Reports* 39 (1976): 699–704.

Fagot, B. I., and Patterson, G. R. "An In Vivo Analysis of Reinforcing Contingencies for Sex-Role Behaviors in the Preschool Child." *Developmental Psychology* 1 (1969): 563–568.

Fein, G.; Johnson, D.; Kosson, N.; Stork, L.; and Wasserman, L. "Sex Stereotypes and Preferences in the Toy Choices of 20-Month-Old Boys and

Girls." *Developmental Psychology* 11 (1975): 527–528.

Feiring, C., and Lewis, M. "Sex and Age Differences in Young Children's Reactions to Frustration: A Further Look at the Goldberg and Lewis Subjects." *Child Development* 50 (1979): 848–853.

Fling, S., and Manosevitz, M. "Sex Typing in Nursery School Children's Play Interests." *Developmental Psychology* 7 (1972): 146–152.

Frisch, H. L. "Sex Stereotypes in Adult-Infant Play." *Child Development* 48 (1977): 1671–1675.

Goldberg, S., and Lewis, M. "Play Behavior in the Year-Old Infant: Early Sex Differences." *Child Development* 40 (1969): 21–31.

Green, R. "One Hundred Ten Feminine and Masculine Boys: Behavioral Contrasts and Demographic Similarities." *Archives of Sexual Behavior* 5 (1976): 425–446.

Hartup, W. W. "Peer Interaction and Social Organization." In *Carmichael's Manual of Child Psychology. Vol. II,* ed. P. H. Mussen. New York: Wiley, 1970.

Haugh, S.; Hoffman, C.; and Cowan, G. "The Eye of the Very Young Beholder: Sex Typing of Infants by Young Children." *Child Development* 51 (1980): 598–600.

Jacklin, C.; Maccoby, E.; and Dick, A. "Barrier Behavior and Toy Preferences: Sex Differences (and Their Absence) in the Year-Old Child." *Child Development* 44 (1973): 196–200.

Kohlberg, L. "A Cognitive-Developmental Analysis of Children's Sex-Role Concepts and Attitudes." In *The Development of Sex Differences,* ed. E. Maccoby. Stanford, Calif.: Stanford University Press, 1966.

Korner, A. F. "Sex Differences in Newborns with Special Reference to Differences in the Organization of Oral Behavior." *Journal of Child Psychology and Psychiatry* 14 (1973): 19–29.

Kronsberg, S. J. "Maternal Behavior and the Development of Sex Differences in Infants." Unpublished Master's thesis, University of Connecticut, 1975.

Kronsberg, S. J. "An Investigation of Parent Intervention Behavior with Toddler Boys and Girls." Doctoral dissertation, University of Oregon, 1981.

Kuhn, D.; Nash, S. C.; and Brucken, L. "Sex Role Concepts of Two- and Three-Year Olds." *Child Development* 49 (1978): 445–451.

Lamb, M., and Roopnarine, J. "Peer Influences on Sex Role Development in Pre-Schoolers." *Child Development* 50 (1979): 1219–1222.

Lee, P. C., and Gropper, N. B. "Sex-Role Culture and Educational Practice." *Harvard Educational Review* 44 (1974): 369–410.

Lee, P. C., and Voivodas, G. K. "Sex Role and Pupil Role in Early Childhood Education." In *Current Topics in Early Childhood Education. Vol. 1,* ed. L. G. Katz. Norwood, N. J.: Ablex, 1977.

Lewis, M. "State As an Infant-Environment Interaction: An Analysis of Mother-Infant Interactions As a Function of Sex." *Merrill-Palmer Quarterly* 20 (1974): 195–204.

Lynn, D. B. *Parental and Sex-Role Identification: A Theoretical Formulation.*

Berkeley, Calif.: McCutchan, 1969.

Maccoby, E. E., and Jacklin, C. N. "Stress, Activity, and Proximity Seeking: Sex Differences in the Year-Old Child." *Child Development* 44 (1973): 34–42.

Maccoby, E. E., and Jacklin, C. N. *The Psychology of Sex Differences.* Stanford, Calif.: Stanford University Press, 1974.

Marcus, D. E., and Overton, W. F. "The Development of Cognitive Gender Constancy and Sex Role Preferences." *Child Development* 49 (1978): 434–444.

McCandless, B. R.; Bush, C.; and Carden, A. I. "Reinforcing Contingencies for Sex Role Behaviors in Preschool Children." Unpublished manuscript, Emory University, Atlanta, 1975.

Messer, S., and Lewis, M. "Social Class and Sex Differences in the Attachment and Play Behavior of the Year-Old Infant." *Merrill-Palmer Quarterly* 18 (1972): 295–306.

Mischel, W. "A Social-Learning View of Sex Differences in Behavior." In *The Development of Sex Differences,* ed. E. Maccoby. Stanford, Calif.: Stanford University Press, 1966.

Mischel, W. "Sex-Typing and Socialization." In *Carmichael's Manual of Child Psychology. Vol. II,* ed. P. H. Mussen. New York: Wiley, 1970.

Money, J. "Sex Determination and Sex Stereotyping: Aristotle to H-Y Antigen." Address to the Western Psychological Association, San Francisco, April 1978.

Money, J., and Ehrhardt, A. A. *Man & Woman, Boy & Girl.* Baltimore, Md.: Johns Hopkins University Press, 1972.

Moss, H. A. "Sex, Age, and State As Determinants of Mother-Infant Interaction." *Merrill-Palmer Quarterly* 13 (1967): 19–36.

Moss, H. A. "Early Sex Differences and Mother-Infant Interaction." In *Sex Differences in Behavior,* ed. R. Friedman, R. Richart, and R. Van de Wiele. New York: Wiley, 1974.

Pedersen, F. A., and Bell, R. Q. "Sex Differences in Preschool Children Without Histories of Complications of Pregnancy and Delivery." *Developmental Psychology* 3 (1970): 10–15.

Phillips, S.; King, S.; and DuBois, L. "Spontaneous Activities of Female Versus Male Newborns." *Child Development* 49 (1978): 590–597.

Rheingold, H. L., and Cook, K. V. "The Content of Boys' and Girls' Rooms As an Index of Parents' Behavior." *Child Development* 46 (1975): 459–463.

Richards, M. P.; Bernal, J. F.; and Brackbill, Y. "Early Behavioral Differences: Gender or Circumcision?" *Developmental Psychobiology* 9 (1976): 89–95.

Rubin, J. Z.; Provenzano, F. J.; and Luria, Z. "The Eye of the Beholder: Parents' Views on Sex of Newborns." *American Journal of Orthopsychiatry* 44 (1974): 512–519.

Schachter, F. F.; Shore, E.; Hodapp, R.; Chalfin, S.; and Bundy, C. "Do Girls Talk Earlier?: Mean Length of Utterance in Toddlers." *Developmental Psychology* 14 (1978): 388–392.

Seavey, C. A.; Katz, P. A.; and Zalk, S. R. "Baby X: The Effect of Gender

Labels on Adult Responses to Infants." *Sex Roles* 1 (1975): 103–109.

Serbin, L. A.; O'Leary, K. D.; Kent, R. N.; and Tonick, I. J. "A Comparison of Teacher Response to the Preacademic and Problem Behavior of Boys and Girls." *Child Development* 44 (1973): 796–804.

Slaby, R. G., and Frey, K. S. "Development of Gender Constancy and Selective Attention to Same-Sex Models." *Child Development* 46 (1975): 849–856.

Smith, P. K., and Daglish, L. "Sex Differences in Parent and Infant Behavior." *Child Development* 48 (1977): 1250–1254.

Spencer, T. D. "Sex-Role Learning in Early Childhood." In *The Young Child: Reviews of Research. Vol. 1,* ed. W. W. Hartup and N. L. Smothergill. Washington, D.C.: National Association for the Education of Young Children, 1967.

Sprung, B. *Non-Sexist Education for Young Children: A Practical Guide.* New York: Citation Press, 1975.

Thoman, E.; Leiderman, P.; and Olson, J. "Neonate-Mother Interaction During Breast Feeding." *Developmental Psychology* 6 (1972): 110–118.

Thompson, N. L., and McCandless, B. R. "It Score Variations by Instructional Style." *Child Development* 41 (1970): 425–436.

Tyler, L. E. "The Antecedents of Two Varieties of Vocational Interests." *Genetic Psychology Monographs* 70 (1964): 177–227.

Will, J. A.; Self, P. A.; and Datan, N. "Maternal Behavior and Perceived Sex of Infant." *American Journal of Orthopsychiatry* 46 (1976): 135–139.

Williams, J. E.; Bennett, S. M.; and Best, D. L. "Awareness and Expression of Sex Stereotypes in Young Children." *Developmental Psychology* 5 (1975): 635–642.

Wilson, E. O. *On Human Nature.* Cambridge, Mass.: Harvard University Press, 1978.

Robert M. Malina

12 Motor development in the early years

"To comprehend a landscape one must look at it from varied angles." (Gesell and Ilg 1946, p. 6)

The development and refinement of skillful performance in motor activities is a major task of childhood. All children, barring significant developmental retardation, have the potential to acquire fundamental and special movement patterns and skills that comprise an integral part of their behavioral repertoire. Through the medium of movement activities, many childhood experiences, especially early learning experiences, are mediated. In this chapter, motor development during infancy and early childhood will be examined, and a number of factors that influence motor development will be considered, including genetic factors, status at birth, nutrition, sex differences, childrearing experiences, social class, and ethnicity. Finally, implications for early childhood educators will be discussed.

Classifications of motor activities

Motor activities are frequently categorized as fine and gross. The former refers to movements requiring precision and dexterity as in manipulative tasks, the latter to movements of the entire body and/or major segments of the body, as in locomotor activities. Many tasks incorporate both gross- and fine-motor elements, for example, the precision necessary for projecting an object (such as a ball) accurately and with sufficient speed.

Fundamental motor patterns are the elementary forms of movement that can be classified as *locomotor* (e.g., walk, run, jump, gallop, hop, skip, etc.), *nonlocomotor* (e.g., push, pull, bend, swing, curl, and so on), and *manipulative* (e.g., throw, catch, strike, kick, dribble, and related activities involving the projection and reception of objects). Locomotor, nonlocomotor, and manipulative activities can occur in various combinations, e.g., skipping is a combination of hopping and walking, a hop being interspaced in the walking pattern. Running and reaching to catch a thrown ball combine all three categories of fundamental motor patterns. Motor development involves the acquisition and refinement of fundamental motor patterns and motor skills. In most cases, these can be objectively observed and reliably tested.

The concepts of motor pattern and motor skill differ in degree rather than kind. A motor pattern is the basic movement or movements involved in the performance of a particular task. Emphasis is on the movements comprising the act. Thus, a child can perform a basic movement pattern, but may not be very skillful. In a motor skill, emphasis is upon the accuracy, precision, and economy of performance. The motor pattern is the more general concept; motor skill, however, is a more specialized one. Skillful performance is built upon the substrate of fundamental motor patterns. The degree of skill demonstrated in a movement pattern can vary considerably within the individual as well as among children.

Fundamental motor skills can be assessed in terms of the process and the product of the motor activity. The process deals with the performance of the component movements of an act (e.g., hip rotation, arm action, leg action) or specific mechanical elements (e.g., angle of take-off, lengths of lever arms, angles of inclination at specific joints). The product of movement concerns the result or outcome of the act (e.g., the distance jumped, the time elapsed, the target score, and other similar measures of the end products of performance). The process and product of motor performance are, in general, positively related. Good performers in terms of the product demonstrate good movement patterns, i.e., proficiency in the movement process underlying the act, and vice versa. Presumably, if the process is improved through normal growth and maturation, or through instruction and practice, the product of performance also improves. This relationship between process and product is especially evident at the extremes of the motor performance continuum, while the midportion of the continuum is characterized by considerable individuality of performance. As with most performance tasks, motivation is a significant factor. With a low level of motivation, a good motor process can yield a poor product, while under heightened motivation conditions, a poor process can yield a good product.

What is motor development?

Motor development is the process through which a child acquires movement patterns and skills. It is a process of continuous modification based upon the interaction of (1) the maturational process, i.e., the genetically controlled rate of neuromuscular maturation, (2) residual effects of prior experiences, and (3) the new motor experience. To study the process more effectively, stages of development are arbitrarily imposed for each movement pattern and skill. It is thus necessary to first describe the mature motor pattern for each basic skill, and then to identify and describe the stages leading to the development of the mature pattern. The mature pattern can be viewed as an intermediate level between the minimal level evident in a young child and the level of performance shown by highly skilled performers (Wickstrom 1977).

When a basic skill is developing, the essential components are initially rather discrete, and are subsequently gradually combined into a continuous pattern. This is shown, for example, in the developmental sequence of overarm throwing (right-handed):

1. Arm and body movements occur in a posterior-anterior plane (back-to-front), with no trunk rotation and the feet fixed (ages two to three years).

2. Arm and body movements occur in a horizontal plane as a rotation component is added. The child rotates the trunk to the right in preparation to throw and then to the left in delivery. The feet still remain fixed (ages three-and-one-half to five years).

3. A forward step with the leg on the same side of the body as the throwing arm is added to the pattern. Trunk rotation may decrease somewhat, but hip flexion is increased (ages five to six years).

4. There is now opposition of movement as a contralateral step is added. The foot opposite the throwing arm steps forward (strides) in the preparatory phase. Weight is transferred forward from the right to the left foot as the hips, trunk, and shoulders rotate to the left in delivery (six-and-one-half years and older in boys; developed to a lesser extent in girls) (Wild 1938).

In contrast to motor development, motor performance is viewed in the context of tasks that are performed under specified conditions and that are amenable to precise measurement. Performance- or product-oriented studies of motor behavior of young children are ordinarily directed toward documenting their motor achievements, for example, the number of consecutive hops at three years of age, or the percentage of an age group proficient in skipping. For jumping and throwing tasks, distance measures are introduced as early as three years of age.

Motor development during infancy and early childhood

Motor development concerns primarily the voluntary control of motor activity in the form of specific movement patterns. The motor activity of the neonate is characterized by an absence of voluntary activity and a lack of inhibition of the lower brain centers indicating a lack of cerebral control. However, as the central nervous system gradually matures, cortical inhibitory functions begin to operate, reflex movements gradually diminish, and voluntary motor control commences. Evidence suggests that the reflexes are not lost; rather, they are inhibited by the higher brain centers. This becomes apparent in cases of central nervous system pathology, during the administration of drugs, under conditions of stress, and in the aged, when these reflexes can be demonstrated again.

The motor responses of the newborn are extensions of motor patterns established during fetal development. Certain noticeable reflexes are either present at birth or appear during infancy; many of these enable the child to adapt to the extrauterine environment. Some reflexes are mediated at the spinal cord level (e.g., grasping reflex, tonic neck reflex), whereas others require the integration of brain stem centers, the labyrinths, and other immature nervous centers (e.g., righting reflexes).

There is a wide range of variation in reflex responsiveness among infants as well as within the same infant, depending upon the behavioral states of the infants being investigated. The reflexes of infancy are expressions of the immaturity of the infant's nervous system, and provide an important means of assessing the integrity of the developing neuromuscular system early in life. The absence, delayed appearance or disappearance, persistence, or reappearance of certain reflexes may be indicative of neurological disorders (e.g., spastic cerebral palsy).

Approaches to the study of motor development during infancy and childhood generally take two forms. The first is concerned with general motor development during the first few years of life. This approach deals with the motor unfolding of the child as a part of overall behavioral development, and is well exemplified in the widely used developmental scales of Bayley (1935; 1969), Gesell and Amatruda (1947; see also Knobloch and Pasamanick 1974), and Frankenburg and Dodds (1967), as well as in modifications of these scales (Knobloch, Pasamanick, and Sherard 1966). Such scales indicate age placement and normal variation in a number of motor tasks. For example, in the Bayley scale infants roll from their backs to their stomachs on the average by 6.4 months, with a range of variation of 4 to 10 months. Other motor items include holding the head steady, sitting with and without support, pulling to a standing position, etc.

The second approach to motor development is concerned with the development of specific postural states and movement patterns, for example, the progression from prone to upright posture and then to walking; the sequence of development leading to mature patterns of jumping, throwing, and running; and so on. There is, of course, considerable overlap between the two approaches, as is illustrated in the observation that many of the items used in general motor development scales (e.g., the Bayley and Denver scales) are concerned with the attainment of the milestones leading to independent walking.

The sequence of motor attainments is generally the same for all children, although considerable individual variation in developmental rate and proficiency exists. The literature on motor development contains many descriptions and timetables for the attainment of postural, locomotor, and prehensile (grasping) control during the preschool years. The data are largely descriptive and are primarily "stage and age" oriented, i.e., children are expected to demonstrate certain levels of motor competence at certain chronological ages. Although individual differences are considered in early motor development, the traditional and most frequently cited studies have the inherent, sequential motor unfolding of the child as the central theme, either implicitly or explicitly. This sequential development is viewed as representing the gradual pattern of neuromuscular maturation in the child. There is a need, however, for further study of individual differences in motor abilities and their interrelationships during infancy and early childhood.

Independent walking is the major motor development task of infancy. The developmental changes leading to walking behavior are essentially a series of postural changes through which the infant gains the control necessary for maintaining upright posture and then for locomotion. The general sequence of developmental changes leading to walking is described in detail (see, for example, Gesell 1954; McGraw 1945; Pikler 1968; Shirley 1931). The infant gradually attains control of the head, upper trunk, and upper extremities. Control of the entire trunk follows, first in the development of sitting posture with support and then alone. This is followed by active efforts at locomotion by means of prone progression, whether by crawling, scooting while keeping the trunk on the floor, or other patterns. Active efforts at upright posture follow, the child standing first with support and then without support. Finally, independent walking develops, the initial efforts being rather stiff-legged and generally flat-footed, with the legs spread apart for a wide base of support and the arms outstretched for balance.

The significance of upright posture and independent locomotion cannot be overemphasized. It is a distinctly human trait, that requires the ability to support and balance the upright body and to execute stepping movements. Walking is the foundation upon which other motor skills develop or are learned. The ability to walk allows the developing child a new and more rapid means of locomotion, with many possible variations. It also frees the hands from their role as supports, so that a variety of manipulative experiences and skills are possible.

The attainment of independent walking does not indicate achievement of the mature walking pattern. The latter develops gradually; as stride length, walking speed, and cadence increase, the width of the stepping base decreases, and movement patterns show greater reproducibility.

The preschool years are a time of increasing experimentation with a variety of motor tasks, and a period of gradual and progressive motor development and learning. The development of proficiency in fundamental motor skills is one of the basic tasks of the preschool years. Fundamental motor skills ordinarily develop by six or seven years of age, and it is generally agreed that after these ages no new basic skills appear in the child's movement repertoire (Espenschade and Eckert 1974). Rather, the quality of performance continues to improve as the fundamental patterns are refined and integrated into more complex movement sequences. There are, however, a number of normal children five through eight years of age who still do not have sufficient coordination and control to accomplish certain fundamental motor tasks.

In an early study by Gutteridge (1939) children two to seven years of age were rated in terms of the proficiency of their performance in ten fundamental skills on a ten-point scale, ranging from "withdraws or retreats when opportunity is given" to "evidence of accuracy, poise, and grace." The number rated as proficient increased with age, but by six or seven years of age some children were not yet proficient in the fundamental motor skills. Similar results are shown in more recent data presented in Table 12.1 for the Hamm-Marburg Body Control Test for children (Kiphard and Schilling 1970). From five through eight years of age, there are children who do not have sufficient coordination and control to accomplish the specified task.

Wickstrom (1977) summarizes a considerable amount of information on the

Table 12.1.
Percentage of children at each age (30 per group) successfully performing each task of the Hamm-Marburg Body Control Test (criteria of successful performance vary from age to age).

Task	Age in years			
	5	6	7	8
Balloon striking	78	77	80	84
Hopping up and down steps	79	83	75	76
Hopping over blocks	85	87	84	98
Balance-beam walk	90	97	100	85
Side step	82	97	85	83
Box placing	78	83	79	77

Adapted from Kiphard and Schilling (1970)

development and refinement of running, jumping, throwing, catching, striking, and kicking movement patterns, while the achievements of children three to seven years of age in fundamental motor skills are discussed in detail by Rarick (1961) and by De Oreo (1974). Although there are no generally agreed upon reference data for the development of motor patterns and skills, these sources offer a guide as to the level of proficiency expected at certain ages as well as the normal range of individual variation.

During the preschool years motor proficiency improves with age, though not necessarily in a smooth progression. Variation in performance within an age group, from age to age, and within individual children is considerable. Preschool children often show a tendency to perform well at one occasion only to perform poorly at the next. This tendency is suggestive of Gesell's (1954) concept of development as "reciprocal interweaving," i.e., alternating from mature stages to less mature stages, and then back to mature stages. Such seemingly irregular developmental trends may be related to the fact that preschool children are learning many new activities, so that when a mature pattern is attained in one task, children might attempt other movements that detract from the mature pattern originally demonstrated. For example, a child may have mastered the overhand throw from a stationary position, but reverts to an underhand pattern when trying to throw while running.

Influences on early motor development
Many factors influence the motor development and activity of children during

infancy and childhood. Such factors as genotype, size, physique, rate of maturation, childrearing atmosphere, SES, ethnicity, nutritional status, and birth order, though not mutually exclusive, may affect the course of motor development. In this discussion consideration will be given to a number of factors that are related to motor development and performance during infancy and childhood. It is not intended as an exhaustive review of these factors. Rather it is hoped that the reader will have a better awareness of the many factors that may influence or modify a child's motor progress, and the difficulties involved in understanding the process. The available data are derived from many disciplines that address different questions and use different methods; frequently the study of the child's motor development is not the primary objective in these studies. Specific references for some of the observations reported are omitted. The citations are included in another review by the author (Malina 1980).

Genetics. Studies of twins during the first two years with the Bayley Scales of motor development indicate greater similarity between monozygotic (identical) twins who share the same genetic makeup than between dizygotic (fraternal) twins who do not. Although twin data on subsequent motor development during early childhood are not extensive, they do indicate a close correspondence in the development of motor activities among monozygotic twins early in life (see Gesell 1954). Monozygotic and dizygotic twins, however, do not differ significantly from each other in motor attainment, nor does the first-born of twins differ as a rule from the second born in early motor development. Twins, however, do show a consistent developmental lag in motor development as measured by the developmental scales cited earlier compared to singletons from three months to three years of age. Data for specific motor behaviors are ordinarily not reported, and comparisons of twins and singletons in motor performance at older ages are not available. However, some evidence for school age twins suggests that the speed of running and explosive power as in the jump and throw are more influenced by genetic factors than other motor tasks, such as errors in a coordination task.

Genetic factors thus appear to be important in motor development. This genetic basis can perhaps be viewed in terms of either a predisposition toward motor skills or the capacity to acquire them. Whether this potential is attained or developed is dependent upon the environments in which the child is reared.

Status at birth. Since birth marks the transition from a uterine to an extrauterine existence, it is of interest to view the relationship between status before, at, and shortly after birth, and subsequent motor development. Fetal movements during the last trimester are, for example, significantly related to postnatal motor development during the first year. Rosenblith (1966) reports a highly significant prognostic relationship between a neonatal assessment of motor status and fine- and gross-motor development as assessed by the Bayley Scales at eight months of age, while Black, Steinschneider, and Sheehe (1979) report delayed motor development at about nine months of age in full-term infants who experienced neonatal respiratory instability. Edwards (1968) reports significant relationships between Apgar Scores (assessments of heart rate, respiratory effort, muscle tone, reflex irritability, and color) taken at one and five minutes after birth and both fine- and gross-motor performance at four years of age.

An infant's status at birth, especially birth weight, is strongly related to maternal factors such as size, physique, health and nutritional status, and parity. Birth weight, if one excludes abnormally low-birth-weight infants (see below), is, however, not consistently related to motor development status at four months of age (Solomons and Solomons 1964), to the age of walking alone (Pineau 1961), and to gross-motor coordination at four years of age (Edwards 1968). A related factor to status at birth is the mode of delivery, i.e., spontaneous, forceps, Caesarean, and breech. The data of Silva, Buckfield, and Spears (1979), however, show no differences in the age at sitting and walking, and fine- and gross-motor coordination at three years of age among children grouped by the mode of delivery.

It is thus apparent that a number of factors are already operating before birth and at this early stage of life, and perhaps bear a significant relationship to later motor development. The significance of such observations as well as the specific operation of such influences in mediating or modifying motor development are not always clear.

Low birth weight and prematurity. There is much concern for the growth of low-birth-weight (birth weight 2500 grams or less) and premature (gestational age 37 weeks or less) infants. Low birth weight is generally assumed to be due to a shortened gestational period (i.e., prematurity), a reduced rate of intrauterine growth, or both. Low birth weight and prematurity generally occur concomitantly, especially in infants weighing less than 1500 grams.

Prematurity and/or low birth weight are associated with delayed motor development. Infants classified as such are not only smaller, but also perform consistently poorer on developmental tests, most of which include gross- and fine-motor development scales. This depression in early motor development is frequently related to the delayed physical and neurological development of these infants, although some may have experienced neurological damage due to complications of pregnancy or delivery.

Drillien (1948) relates the age of attainment of three motor development milestones to birth weight, noting a later attainment of sitting, standing, and walking behavior in low-birth-weight infants. Cutler et al. (1965) note significantly lower gross-motor scores in premature boys and girls at two-and-one-half years of age compared to full-term children. The foregoing would seem to indicate a persistence of early gross-motor deficiencies in low-birth-weight children at later ages. In some cases, however, the apparent differences would be reduced if corrections were made for gestational age. Further, follow-up studies of low-birth-weight and premature infants at school ages generally do not include motor items; they are more concerned with mental development and school performance.

Size, physique, and composition. Although available data suggest an independence of early motor development and birth weight within the normal range, the relationship of motor development to other physical characteristics needs to be examined. Studies including measures of size, build, and composition indicate some relationship between these indexes and motor development in infancy (see Malina and Rarick 1973). The relationship, as expected, is not simple, and is most apparent at the extremes of the physique continuum, i.e., the very linear and the very heavy, the long-legged and the short-legged. Muscular and small-boned infants and those of linear frame for example, tend to walk at an earlier age. Other evidence suggests that infants with a greater lean body mass (i.e., body weight minus fat) attain superior scores on gross-motor tasks, and that leg muscle mass at six months of age is predictive of walking unaided at one year (Garn 1966).

Analyses of physique and body composition relative to motor development during the preschool years are lacking (see Malina and Rarick 1973; Malina 1975). Both this gap and the limited observations on infants indicate the need to extend studies of size, physique, and body composition to motor development of infancy and the preschool ages. Behavioral correlates of size, physique, and composition also need to be investigated. Do parents expect and/or encourage certain forms of behavior from children differing in physique, for example, the fat infant as opposed to the thin, muscular infant? Conversely, how does the motor progress of the child influence parental rearing attitudes and expectations?

Nutrition. Interest in nutrition as a critical correlate of psychomotor development is considerable. An adequate nutritional intake is essential to support the needs of normal growth and development, including of course motor development. Severely undernourished infants and young children are retarded in motor development and show neuromuscular involvement (e.g., reduced nerve-conduction velocities). Severe undernutrition is accompanied by stunted physical growth and skeletal maturation, muscle wasting, general psychomotor change, and reduced levels of physical activity. Retarded motor development is also indicated as one of the "constant" signs of kwashiorkor (Jelliffe 1966), a form of severe protein-energy malnutrition.

When nutritional stress is considered, the role of organic changes in the central nervous system as it relates to retarded development is usually emphasized. However, disturbances in social experiences also accompany malnutrition, and may interact with organic changes. For example, a malnourished child may not receive the social and kinesthetic stimulation necessary to support the developing nervous system. There is thus more to the relationship of malnutrition and retarded development than food alone.

The persistence of detrimental changes associated with severe undernutrition may be dependent upon the timing, severity, and duration of the nutritional stress. Children put on nutritionally adequate diets show some catch-up in growth and development. Nevertheless, it is difficult to assess how much of the child's potential is affected by the nutritional stress. In a follow up of 14 severely malnourished children after nutritional recovery, Monckeberg (1968) noted that motor development was still retarded three to six years later. Two long-term follow-up studies of infants hospitalized for severe protein-energy malnutrition during the first two or three years of life indicated persistent effects on perceptual-motor development into adolescence. Stoch and Smythe (1976) note deficits in visual-motor perception, that reflected deficits at the central neurosensory integration level, in 13- to 18-year-old Cape Town youths (N=20) followed since hospitalization for marasmus during infancy. Hoorweg and Stanfield (1976) report lower Lincoln-Oseretsky motor development scores in 11- to 17-year-old Kampala children (N=60) who were hospitalized for protein-energy malnutrition between 8 and 27 months of age. Interestingly, there was no relationship between subsequent motor performance and the age at hospital admission. Both acute malnutrition (developing over a short time) and chronic undernutrition (developing over a longer period) had similar relationships to motor development.

The preceding discussion refers to severe nutritional inadequacy early in life, primarily due to the widespread prevalence of protein-energy malnutrition. What level of development might we expect from children reared at marginally adequate nutritional levels, as compared to those who have been hospitalized for severe nutritional inadequacy? Such specific data, are not yet available (see cross-cultural considerations below).

The influence of nutritional inadequacy early in life on motor development may be related to the brain growth spurt described by Dobbing and Sands (1973). This spurt is a period of rapid brain growth that begins at about mid-pregnancy and continues through three or four years of age. The early part of the spurt, from mid-pregnancy to about 18 months, is characterized by rapid multiplication of glial cells, while the latter part that lasts to three or four years is characterized by myelinization. The extent of the spurt, however, varies with the region of the brain.

The unique pattern characteristic of the cerebellum is relevant to motor development. The cerebellum starts its growth spurt later than the other parts (forebrain and stem), but completes the spurt earlier. Functions of the cerebellum include the development and maintenance of neuromuscular coordination, balance, and muscle tone. Hence, potential interference with the growth spurt of the cerebellum through nutritional inadequacy prenatally and early postnatally might possibly interfere with normal motor development. Studies of adult rats undernourished during most of gestation and all of lactation indicate poor motor performance, that was attributable to impaired motor coordination. The undernourished rats also had smaller cerebella (Lynch, Smart, and Dobbing 1975). These data thus suggest a differential vulnerability of the cerebellum to early nutritional stress, with resulting impairments in motor coordination. Although extrapolation from animal experiments to humans requires cautious interpretation, the data are at least suggestive.

The preceding remarks have concerned undernutrition and its effects on motor development. At the other end of the nutritional continuum is overnutrition, that ordinarily manifests itself in the form of a gross overweight condition and obesity. Excess fat represents dead weight that must be moved, and studies of elementary school children indicate a negative effect of excess fatness on performance (Malina 1975). Although data for preschool children are not available, a similar effect might be expected at these ages. Overweight and/or obesity may also function to limit the physical activity pursuits of infants and young children, and thus indirectly influence their developing motor capacities.

Sex differences. Sex differences in motor development during infancy are not systematically apparent, although sex differences in rearing practices and play behavior have been consistently reported. Mothers treat sons differently than daughters, and this sex difference begins early in infancy (Maccoby and Jacklin 1974; Teitelbaum 1976). Behavioral differences are also apparent early in life; one-year-old boys, for example, already spend more time in gross-motor activity, while girls of the same age spend more time in fine-motor activity. Boys are also more vigorous in their play and show more exploratory behavior than girls, who prefer a more quiet style of play. Observations of nursery school children two to five years of age offer similar evidence. Boys spend more time in rough-and-tumble gross-motor activities, while girls spend more time in activities requiring fine-motor manipulation.

Walker (1962) compared behavior of mesomorphic (muscular) boys and girls. Although similar in physique, mesomorphic girls tend to channel their energies into social activities, while mesomorphic boys channel their energies into gross-motor activities. Walker suggests that variations in physical energy and in body sensitivity to energy needs may thus be important mediating links between physique and behavior. It would appear, however, that at these early ages, the expectations of our culture already have an impact on what children sense is appropriate behavior for each sex.

In contrast to the first year or two of life, sex differences in motor development and performance are apparent during early childhood. From about two to five years of age, girls, on the average, excel in tasks requiring jumping, hopping, rhythmic locomotion, and balance, while boys generally perform better in tasks requiring strength and speed (Sinclair 1971; Espenschade and Eckert 1974). From the age of five or six years, boys generally perform better in running, jumping, and throwing activities, while girls excel in hopping (Keogh 1965; Espenschade and Eckert 1974). Keogh (1965), for example, included the time taken to hop 50 feet in his test battery. The data indicate that 34 percent and 23 percent of the six- and seven-year-old boys were unable to hop 50 feet, while only 7 percent and 5 percent of the six- and seven-year-old girls were unable to hop this distance.

Balancing activities show no consistent pattern of sex difference after the preschool years, although girls continue to show better performances at some ages (Keogh 1965). There is, however, considerable overlap in motor achievements of boys and girls in many tasks. For example, in Keogh's sample, the average standing-long-jump distance was 42.9 inches for six-year-old boys with about 68 percent of the boys jumping between 33.7 and 50.1 inches. Six-year-old girls jumped on the average 41.2 inches, with about 68 percent jumping between 35.2 and 46.2 inches. The degree of overlap between the sexes in this task is considerable, as many six-year-old girls perform as well as or better than boys of the same age. In contrast to jumping, sex differences in the ball throw for distance are remarkable. Six-year-old boys threw a softball on the average 34.1 feet. Girls of the same age threw the ball on the average only 19.0 feet and less than 5 percent of the girls had throws exceeding the average distance of the boys.

Observations of sex differences in motor development should be related to sex differences in activity interests, opportunity for practice, opportunity for and frequency of participation, and the availability of role models. The cultural socialization of both boys and girls, as well as the exclusion of young girls from some activities requiring physical strength and skill may be important factors in establishing and maintaining sex differences.

Rearing and birth order. A child's position in the family and sibling-sex status are also factors that influence early motor development. Some data suggest that first-born children perform slightly better on motor tasks early in life, an observation generally related to greater maternal involvement and therefore stimulation of the first born compared to later-born children. However, rearing studies of single-child families suggest overprotection, greater restriction on physical mobility, and a strong tendency to keep close track of the child on the part of mothers. In contrast to an only child, children with opposite-sex siblings have more of the characteristics of the opposite sex than children with siblings of the same sex.

It would be interesting to relate such observations to the motor development and performance of children. For example, does a girl with an older brother develop differently in motor activities or have different activity interests than a girl who has an older sister as a sibling? The same question can be raised for boys with female and male siblings respectively. However, the possible role of a younger sibling in influencing the motor behavior of an older child also warrants study.

Although the data are limited, one can inquire as to the effects of child care practices on motor development and motor activity during infancy and childhood. More specifically, how are childrearing practices translated into different motor development levels or performance styles? Do children reared in overprotective or restrictive atmospheres develop and behave differently in motor activities than children reared in permissive, less-protective atmospheres? Some observations, for example, suggest a relationship between a permissive, nonrestrictive childrearing environment and enhanced early motor development (Blank 1964; Williams and Scott 1953). Such an environment may provide for greater levels of interaction with people and objects, perhaps stimulating early motor progress. Mothers of infants rated as competent on the Bayley developmental scales and other behavioral measures do in fact interact more with their infants in a manner that focuses on the child's abilities and interests (Moore 1977). Data at older ages are limited.

Social class. Several studies have examined social class criteria relative to early motor development. Neligan and Prudham (1969) report a social class difference in the age of independent walking among a sample of Newcastle (England) children, the social class difference favoring the lower-SES children. The data were interpreted as possibly reflecting "deprivation of the opportunity to learn resulting from overprotection . . . " in the upper-SES families (Neligan and Prudham 1969, p. 417). In an earlier study, Bayley and Jones (1937) report no relationship between socioeconomic variables and age of first walking independently. There was, however, a tendency in their data for a high incidence of slightly negative correlations between motor scores and socioeconomic variables during the first year of life, implying somewhat more rapid motor development in children from the lower social strata. Hindley et al. (1966), however, did not find any social class difference in the age of walking among five European longitudinal samples. There were, however, significant differences between the five samples in the mean age of walking alone. The authors suggest genetic, nutritional, and maternal handling factors as possibly underlying the observed differences, but were not able to identify a specific role for each factor.

Data considering social class and motor achievements at other ages than the first or second year are not extensive. However, socioeconomic background is often implicated as an important factor affecting the activity pursuits of children and presumably their motor development (Malina 1973). In general, the findings suggest greater freedom to move about the neighborhood among children from lower socioeconomic backgrounds. Such an atmosphere might be conducive to greater freedom of motor activity and opportunity for practice. It should be noted, however, that most studies of social class and/or ethnic variation in rearing, life style, and patterns of socialization, have not chosen to assess motor development and motor activity.

Ethnic considerations. Available data comparing the early motor development of American Black and White children indicate advanced motor development in Black children during the first two or three years of life with the differences being most apparent during the first year. Superiority in any one type of motor behavior is not responsible for the Black motor precocity (Bayley 1965; Malina 1973). These generalizations are not, however, without exception, as several studies indicate minor or inconsistent differences in early motor development of Black and White children. Explanations offered for the observations vary. Some implicate genetic factors, while others indicate socioeconomic and childrearing variables as affecting the results.

The socioeconomic hypothesis suggests that a more permissive rearing atmosphere characterizes lower socioeconomic classes and in turn enhances motor development. This is generally, but not always, the case. When ethnic and socioeconomic differences are controlled, higher class children perform better than lower socioeconomic class children on the Bayley Scales of motor development. It should also be noted that Black infants are also advanced in the appearance of the dentition and skeletal ossification centers compared to reference data derived from White children (Malina 1969). It may be that Black infants are simply more biologically mature at birth and during infancy compared to White infants. It should be noted that these observations are limited to infancy only. More detailed considerations of motor development and performance of American Black and White children are discussed elsewhere (Malina 1969; 1973).

Comparisons of motor development and performance of children with Spanish surnames (Mexican-American, Puerto Rican) are quite limited. Using the Denver Developmental Screening Test, Frankenburg, Dick, and Carland (1975) noted few differences in fine-motor-adaptive and gross-motor items between Anglo (White) and Spanish-surnamed children when controlling for social class (all fathers were unskilled workers).

Anglo children were significantly advanced on two fine-motor-adaptive (follows to midline and pincer grasp) and two gross-motor (walks holding furniture and stands alone) tasks in the Denver Scale in the first year of life, while Spanish-surnamed children did not show advancement in any motor items of the scale. Comparisons of Spanish-surnamed and Black children showed the Black children significantly advanced in four fine-motor-adaptive and six gross-motor test items measured during the first year of life. However, after about three years of age, the Spanish-surnamed children excelled in two fine-motor-adaptive and one gross-motor task compared to Black children. Interpretation of the results is difficult, and may be related to ethnic differences in rearing style, approach to the test situation, and related factors.

Cross-cultural considerations. Cross-cultural observations of early motor development are available for a number of cultural groups. These generally include data from developmental tests and are available for sub-Saharan African populations, with less extensive data for Jamaica, Mexico, Guatemala, and Japan (Malina 1977; see also Leiderman, Tulkin, and Rosenfeld 1977). After the age of two, the cross-cultural motor development data are scanty at best, with little systematically collected motor ability information. This probably reflects the orientation of the researchers, who commonly focus on cognitive development, mother-infant attachment, and infant-caregiver interactions. Although observed differences in motor development are generally related to societal variation in mothering and caregiving practices, such relationships do not imply a cause-effect sequence. Children in developing areas of the world often progress reasonably well in early motor development during the first year of life. A developmental lag toward the end of the first year and during the second and third years of life may be related to the break in continuity of rearing at weaning and to the effects of undernutrition. Also, delayed motor development and reduced levels of physical activity accompany protein-energy malnutrition. It is after infancy that stunting in physical growth becomes especially apparent.

Summary

Motor development is a plastic process, showing individual variation in timing, rate, and proficiency. This variation is related to a number of biological, environmental, and/or cultural factors, but the specific effects of such correlates on motor development are in most cases not known with a high degree of certainty. At this point, much is based upon conjecture and inference, especially regarding the factors associated with the rearing environment of the child.

The motor activity of the infant and young child presumably represents the foundation upon which subsequent motor proficiency is built. However, the predictive significance of early motor assessments for later, more mature motor patterns is not clear, and not ordinarily investigated. One may ask whether differences in timing and sequence during the first year or two of life lead to parallel differences at later ages. Such data are not available. It is thus difficult to extend observations from infancy and early childhood to older ages. However, it is reasonably safe to state that severe or extreme insults to the developing organism, such as severe protein-energy malnutrition, very low birth weight, and perhaps neurological damage can seriously delay or impede motor development, while the less severe forms of deprivation or insults (e.g., mild to moderate undernutrition) are not so easily detected and are perhaps overcome.

Recent research efforts in early childhood education highlight the importance of early learning. Although cognitive development is emphasized, the significance of motor development in providing experiences affecting the child's cognitive development, the child's own self-discovery, and the child's ability to communicate is becoming increasingly more apparent (see Engstrom 1971). Implications of the current emphasis on early childhood education for motor development should not be overlooked.

Parents and teachers should recognize the central role of movement experiences in the overall development of the young child and the many factors that can influence proficiency in motor activities. To this end, different kinds of opportunities for movement exploration, discovery, and practice should be provided (see Seefeldt 1979). These can take several forms. One can be a more or less planned free-choice situation for the child, i.e., permitting the child to explore and choose any number of motor activities within a playground or playroom. Another situation could focus on directed or guided movement activities, i.e., providing an environment that requires specific movements in the form of a problem to be solved (how to get to a certain spot, requiring the child to cross several obstacles) or in the form of movement concepts to be discovered (the meaning of *over* or *under* or *across*). Through such activities, the child's spatial awareness and vocabulary can be expanded with the help of movement activities. Finally, structured movement opportunities should not be overlooked. Such situations require the teaching and practice of skills or components of a skill.

Motor activities constitute an essential component of the child as a developing and growing biological organism. They also are an important component of the child's social, cognitive, and personal development. Because motor activities are an integral part of the developing child, it is important for each child to meet some degree of success in the motor domain. If success is to be facilitated and aided, an understanding of the factors underlying and modifying motor processes is essential.

References

Bayley, N. "The Development of Motor Abilities During the First Three Years." *Monographs of the Society for Research in Child Development* (1935). Serial No. 1.

Bayley, N. "Comparisons of Mental and Motor Test Scores for Ages 1–15 Months by Sex, Birth Order, Race, Geographical Location, and Education of Parents." *Child Development* 36 (1965): 379–411.

Bayley, N. *Manual for the Bayley Scales of Infant Development.* Berkeley, Calif.: Psychological Corporation, 1969.

Bayley, N., and Jones, H. E. "Environmental Correlates of Mental and Motor Development: A Cumulative Study from Infancy to Six Years." *Child Development* 8 (1937): 329–341.

Black, L.; Steinschneider, A.; and Sheehe, P. R. "Neonatal Respiratory Instability and Infant Development." *Child Development* 50 (1979): 561–564.

Blank, M. "Some Maternal Influences on Infants' Rates of Sensorimotor Development." *Journal of the American Academy of Child Psychiatry* 3 (1964): 668–687.

Cutler, R.; Heimer, C. B.; Wortis, H.; and Freedman, A. M. "The Effects of Prenatal and Neonatal Complications on the Development of Premature Children at Two-and-One-Half Years of Age." *Journal of Genetic Psychology* 107 (1965): 261–276.

De Oreo, K. L. "The Performance and Development of Fundamental Motor Skills in Preschool Children." In *Psychology of Motor Behavior and Sport*, ed. M. G. Wade and R. Martens. Urbana, Ill.: Human Kinetics Publishers, 1974.

Dobbing, J., and Sands, J. "Quantitative Growth and Development of the Human Brain." *Archives of Disease in Childhood* 48 (1973): 757–767.

Drillien, C. M. "Development and Progress of Prematurely Born Children in the Preschool Period." *Archives of Disease in Childhood* 23 (1948): 69–83.

Edwards, N. "The Relationship Between Physical Condition Immediately After Birth and Mental and Motor Performance at Age Four." *Genetic Psychology Monographs* 78 (1968): 257–289.

Engstrom, G., ed. *The Significance of the Young Child's Motor Development.* Washington, D.C.: National Association for the Education of Young Children, 1971.

Espenschade, A., and Eckert, H. "Motor Development." In *Science and Medicine of Exercise and Sport.* 2nd ed., ed. W. R. Johnson and E. R. Buskirk. New York: Harper & Row, 1974.

Frankenburg, W. K.; Dick, N. P.; and Carland, J. "Development of Preschool-Aged Children of Different Social and Ethnic Groups: Implications for Developmental Screening." *Journal of Pediatrics* 87 (1975): 125–132.

Frankenburg, W. K., and Dodds, J. B. "The Denver Developmental Screening Test." *Journal of Pediatrics* 71 (1967): 181–191.

Garn, S. M. "Body Size and Its Implications." In *Review of Child Development*

Research, ed. L. W. Hoffman and M. L. Hoffman. New York: Russell Sage Foundation, 1966.

Gesell, A. "The Ontogenesis of Infant Behavior." In *Manual of Child Psychology*. 2nd ed., ed. L. Carmichael. New York: Wiley, 1954.

Gesell, A., and Amatruda, C. S. *Developmental Diagnosis*. 2nd ed. New York: Harper & Row, 1947.

Gesell, A., and Ilg, F. *The Child from Five to Ten*. New York: Harper, 1946.

Gutteridge, M. V. "A Study of Motor Achievements of Young Children." *Archives of Psychology* no. 244 (1939).

Hindley, C. B.; Filliozat, A. M.; Klackenberg, G.; Nicolet-Meister, D.; and Sand, E. A. "Differences in Age of Walking in Five European Longitudinal Samples." *Human Biology* 38 (1966): 364–379.

Hoorweg, J., and Stanfield, J. P. "The Effects of Protein Energy Malnutrition in Early Childhood on Intellectual and Motor Abilities in Later Childhood and Adolescence." *Developmental Medicine and Child Neurology* 18 (1976): 330–350.

Jelliffe, D. B. *The Assessment of the Nutritional Status of the Community*. Geneva: World Health Organization, 1966.

Keogh, J. *Motor Performance of Elementary School Children*. Los Angeles: University of California, Department of Physical Education, 1965.

Kiphard, E. J., and Schilling, F. "Der Hamm-Marburger Köperkoordinationtest für Kinder." *Monatzeitschrift Kinderheilkunde* 118 (1970): 473–479.

Knobloch, H., and Pasamanick, B., eds. *Gesell and Amatruda's Developmental Diagnosis*. 3rd ed. New York: Harper & Row, 1974.

Knobloch, H.; Pasamanick, B.; and Sherard, E. S. "A Developmental Screening Inventory for Infants." *Pediatrics* Supplement 38 (1966): 1095–1109.

Leiderman, P. H.; Tulkin, S. R.; and Rosenfeld, A., eds. *Culture and Infancy: Variations in the Human Experience*. New York: Academic Press, 1977.

Lynch, A.; Smart, J. L.; and Dobbing, J. "Motor Coordination and Cerebellar Size in Adult Rats Undernourished in Early Life." *Brain Research* 83 (1975): 249–259.

Maccoby, E. E., and Jacklin, C. N. *The Psychology of Sex Differences*. Stanford, Calif.: Stanford University Press, 1974.

Malina, R. M. "Growth and Physical Performance of American Negro and White Children." *Clinical Pediatrics* 8 (1969): 476–483.

Malina, R. M. "Ethnic and Cultural Factors in the Development of Motor Abilities and Strength in American Children." In *Physical Activity: Human Growth and Development*, ed. G. L. Rarick. New York: Academic Press, 1973.

Malina, R. M. "Anthropometric Correlates of Strength and Motor Performance." *Exercise and Sport Sciences Reviews* 3 (1975): 249–274.

Malina, R. M. "Motor Development in a Cross-Cultural Perspective." In *Psychology of Motor Behavior and Sport. Vol. 2*, ed. R. W. Christina and D. M. Landers. Champaign, Ill.: Human Kinetics Publishers, 1977.

Malina, R. M. "Biosocial Correlates of Motor Development During Infancy and

Early Childhood." In *Social and Biological Predictors of Nutritional Status, Physical Growth, and Neurological Development*, ed. L. S. Greene and F. E. Johnston. New York: Academic Press, 1980.

Malina, R. M., and Rarick, G. L. "Growth, Physique, and Motor Performance." In *Physical Activity: Human Growth and Development*, ed. G. L. Rarick. New York: Academic Press, 1973.

McGraw, M. B. *The Neuromuscular Maturation of the Human Infant*. New York: Hafner, 1945. Reprinted by Columbia University Press, 1963.

Monckeberg, F. "Effect of Early Marasmic Malnutrition on Subsequent Physical and Psychological Development." In *Malnutrition, Learning, and Behavior*, ed. N. S. Scrimshaw and J. E. Gordon. Cambridge, Mass.: MIT Press, 1968.

Moore, S. "Mother-Child Interactions and Competence in Infants and Toddlers." *Young Children* 32, no. 3 (March 1977): 64–69.

Neligan, G., and Prudham, D. "Norms for Four Standard Developmental Milestones by Sex, Social Class and Place in Family." *Developmental Medicine and Child Neurology* 11 (1969): 413–422.

Pikler, E. "Some Contributions to the Study of the Gross Motor Development of Children." *Journal of Genetic Psychology* 113 (1968): 27–39.

Pineau, M. "Developpement de l'Enfant et Dimension de la Famille." *Biotypologie* 22 (1961): 25–53.

Rarick, G. L. *Motor Development During Infancy and Childhood*. Revised ed. Madison, Wis.: College Printing and Typing Co., 1961.

Rosenblith, J. F. "Prognostic Values of Neonatal Assessment." *Child Development* 37 (1966): 623–631.

Seefeldt, V. "Developmental Motor Patterns: Implications for Elementary School Physical Education." In *Psychology of Motor Behavior and Sport*, ed. M. G. Wade and R. Martens. Champaign, Ill.: Human Kinetics Publishers, 1979.

Shirley, M. M. *The First Two Years: A Study of Twenty-Five Babies. Vol. 1, Postural and Locomotor Development*. Minneapolis, Minn.: University of Minnesota Press, 1931.

Silva, P. A.; Buckfield, P.; and Spears, G. F. "Mode of Delivery and Developmental Characteristics in a Thousand Dunedin Three Year Olds." *New Zealand Medical Journal* 89 (1979): 79–81.

Sinclair, C. B. *Movement and Movement Patterns of Early Childhood*. Richmond, Va.: State Department of Education, 1971.

Solomons, G., and Solomons, H. C. "Factors Affecting Motor Performance in Four-Month-Old Infants." *Child Development* 35 (1964): 1283–1295.

Stoch, M. B., and Smythe, P. M. "Fifteen Year Developmental Study on Effects of Severe Undernutrition During Infancy on Subsequent Physical Growth and Intellectual Functioning." *Archives of Disease in Childhood* 51 (1976): 327–336.

Teitelbaum, M. S., ed. *Sex Differences: Social and Biological Perspectives*. Garden City, N.Y.: Doubleday, 1976.

Walker, R. N. "Body Build and Behavior in Young Children: I. Body Build and Nursery School Teachers' Ratings." *Monographs of the Society for Research in Child Development* (1962). No. 84.

Wickstrom, R. L. *Fundamental Motor Patterns*. 2nd ed. Philadelphia: Lea & Febiger, 1977.

Wild, M. "The Behavior Pattern of Throwing and Some Observations Concerning Its Course of Development in Children." *Research Quarterly* 9 (1938): 20–24.

Williams, J. R., and Scott, R. B. "Growth and Development of Negro Infants: IV. Motor Development and Its Relationship to Child Rearing Practices in Two Groups of Negro Infants." *Child Development* 24 (1953): 103–121.

Cluster V

Special needs of children: labels, prediction, and intervention

13 **Psychopathology in early development**

Catherine Lord

14 **The risks of prediction: relationships between etiology, handicapping conditions, and developmental outcomes**

Samuel J. Meisels and Nicholas J. Anastasiow

"What is wrong with my child?" A parent asking this question is seeking many different kinds of information: an explanation for the cause of an unusual or disturbing behavior, a prediction of the extent of future difficulty with the child, and, inevitably, reassurance about the parent's own role in both the past and the future. Very frequently, such a parent is given some label for the problem. Such labels as hyperactive, mentally retarded, or autistic are frequently meant to explain and reassure, yet recent research indicates that they may be more harmful than we have suspected, as the chapters in this cluster show.

Lord and Meisels and Anastasiow, emphasize one of the problems with labels: they convey a sense of permanence about the condition they describe. These authors document how malleable many of these labeled problems may be, and explore the role of parental and professional expectations in the development of children bearing such labels.

A second problem the authors discuss concerning labels is that they seem to concentrate the responsibility for change solely with the child. As previous chapters have stressed, the individual develops within a system of social relationships, and each person in a child's network may influence one another. Consequently, any effort to alter the behavior of a child must take this network into account. Perhaps we have taken this for granted in situations in which children have been quite similar in their intellectual and physical skills. But the integration of exceptional children into classrooms has challenged us to see how the development of children's potential depends upon the support of the peers and adults.

A final point concerns short- versus long-term gains in children's development. These authors explore strategies to achieve rapid control over a difficult problem, or to induce precocious behavior, such as athletic skill. Lord discusses some of the unanticipated costs of such a focus on short-term gains, and attempts to identify the specific qualities of these experiences that can be harmful.

Catherine Lord

13 Psychopathology in early development

Although the majority of young children are healthy in mind and spirit, it is evident, from screening and child find efforts and from clinic reports, that psychological disorders do affect the well-being of many children during the first few years of life. Yet the diagnosis and treatment of psychopathology in the toddler and preschool child are two of the least explored areas of child development (Richman 1978). One reason for this omission is that young children have been seen primarily as reacting to their parents' pathology; thus, professionals have typically studied and treated the parents while often ignoring the troubled child. Second, understandable concern about the negative effects of early labeling, especially given the good prognosis of many childhood disorders, has also affected research with very young children. Consequently, research often has been limited to case reports or studies that identify normal children who are on one end or another of a continuum (such as shyness or impulsiveness) but who really should not be considered pathological. These research efforts cannot provide all of the answers needed to assess, treat, or prevent childhood disorders of a more serious magnitude.

However, research in this area recently has been expanding. With increasing numbers of early screening and intervention programs, young children with problems have become much more accessible for identification, treatment, and study. In addition, procedures for diagnosis and treatment that are more appropriate to the skills and problems of the very young child are being developed.

One of the most difficult aspects of working with child-clients is the reconciliation of the fact that these are still-maturing children with the goal of their becoming psychologically healthy adults (Wolman 1978). That children are developing organisms makes their treatment different from adults in a number of ways (Rutter 1975). Maturational changes, whether physical, social, or cognitive, frequently allow children to grow out of psychological problems that would typically be much more long-lasting in an adult. Childhood fears, sleeping and eating problems, many psychosomatic disorders, and some habit disturbances (e.g., thumb sucking) all fall into this category (Rutter 1975). In the case of these and other relatively minor problems, it is sometimes difficult to know whether to intervene, thus calling attention to the problem and possibly making matters worse, or to ignore or work around the problem while hoping it goes away. The risk of doing nothing is that if a childhood disorder is sufficiently potent or occurs in combination with other disturbing circumstances (e.g., family discord, presence of other disabilities), it may actually impede development. Berlin (1974) refers to this phenomenon as "growing into" the problem.

Young children's psychological disorders do not fit easily into the traditional diagnostic framework that has been useful in work with adolescents and adults (Achenbach and Edelbrock 1981; Kohn and Rosman 1972). Few children brought for treatment for example, would be considered neurotic; obsessive-compulsive behavior and clinical depression in children are very rare (Wolff 1971). Children with autism, a childhood psychosis, are not out of touch with reality in the same way as psychotic adults. The distinction between delay and deviance can also be difficult to resolve with very young children. Thus, predicting whether an immature child will grow out of her or his problems or will be held back by them is often complex.

In the following sections, five representative psychological disorders that occur during early childhood will be described. Three of the problems—negative behavior, fears, and bed-wetting in children over four years of age—are frequent reasons for referral of young children to mental health professionals. The fourth behavior, hyperactivity, though most often diagnosed when a child is older, is discussed here because it affects children during the preschool years even though it is often not yet treated. Autism, the most severe psychological disorder of early childhood, is the final syndrome presented. These sections will be followed by a discussion of advances in the treatment of young children's disorders and a brief summary.

Specific psychological disorders in young children

Negative behavior

Three recent studies investigated the reasons for which two- to six-year-old children were referred for psychological services to a pediatric psychologist (Schroeder 1979), a school psychologist (Lorion, Cowen, and Caldwell 1974), and a child psychiatrist (Rutter 1975). In all three cases a variant of negative behavior was the most common cause for referral. The term negative behavior has been used to refer to acting-out, antisocial behavior, disobedience, aggression, and temper tantrums. In her classic study, Goodenough (1931) found that tantrums (i.e., intense crying accompanied by flailing limbs, clenched fists, and a red face) were the most common expression of negative behavior in very young children. Tantrums decreased in frequency during the second year of life while negative verbal statements and specific, more controlled motor behaviors (i.e., stamping, hitting, and other attack behaviors) increased until about age three. From ages two to six years, verbal aggression has also been shown to increase, as have after reactions such as sulking or brooding following a negative encounter (Hartup 1974).

Not only do the behaviors associated with aggression change during the early years, but so do the situations in which the negative acts typically occur. For infants and toddlers, most negative behaviors are elicited by physical discomfort or by a desire for attention, while young preschoolers' negative actions are typically reported as occurring around socialization issues related to toilet training, eating, and sleeping (Goodenough 1931). From about age four, most negative episodes involve peers and often concern possessions (Goodenough 1931; Hartup 1974). As children enter kindergarten and early elementary school, the *proportion* of more hostile, person-oriented aggression (e.g., rejection, insults) increases while the *proportion* of instrumental, or object-oriented negative behavior decreases, though possessions remain the major single source of disagreement (Hartup 1974). One explanation for this age difference is that as children grow older they learn ways other than negative acts to accomplish object-oriented goals (e.g., to persuade another child to trade toys rather than to push him and grab the desired object). At the same time, children become more subject to hurt feelings and are able to attribute bad intentions to other people. Consequently, school age children are likely to direct their aggression at the particular person perceived to be the agent of their difficulties (Hartup 1974). Thus, one can conceptualize the development of negative behavior from the tantrum of an exhausted toddler to the foot stamping of a young preschool child who, put to bed, throws her stuffed animals across the room, to the shoving of the same preschooler who pushes her friend off a tricycle, to the cry of the older child who yells "You can't come to my birthday party," when he is not chosen for a game.

Group and individual differences in aggressive behavior have been studied with increasing frequency (de Wit and Hartup 1974). When sex differences have been identified, boys have always been found to be more physically aggressive than girls. However, at least one study of aggressive behavior among preschool children showed that, while the two or three most aggressive children in a class were always boys, there were no other sex differences (Smith 1974). Therefore, it may be incorrect to assume that *most* preschool boys are more aggressive than *most* preschool girls.

Environmental factors related to negative behavior are another important consideration. Goodenough (1931) found that in toddlers, negative behavior was most likely to occur when particular demands or restraints were made upon them (e.g., toileting, restrictive clothing, bedtime) and when they were tired, hungry, or ill. Smith (1974) studied aspects of the nursery school environment that affected the incidence of aggression. While limited space had no effect on the number of aggressive episodes, limited availability of play equipment was associated with more aggression. Thumb sucking also increased with fewer toys and more conflicts. Aggression was most frequent during the time when the children were just getting acquainted with each other. Also, aggression tended to increase in the course of a morning. The implications of this work for the design of programs for aggression-prone children may not be as simple as one would like to think, but the modifications implied (e.g., sufficient play equipment, stable groups of children, breaks or shorter playtimes) seem worth some experimentation.

Researchers have also explored the relationship between how adults respond to negative behavior and its likelihood of reoccurrence. Studies by numerous investigators including Sears (1961), Bandura and Walters (1959), and Patterson and his colleagues (Patterson and Cobb 1971; Patterson, Littman, and Bricker 1967) show that adult behaviors that result in the rapid termination of a single episode of negative behavior are often associated with an overall higher incidence of aggression in the child. For example, Goodenough (1931) showed that children were most likely to stop a tantrum if the parents granted their desire. However, children whose parents frequently gave into their tantrums, or to other negative behavior, had the greater number of tantrums over time. Isolating the children or diverting their attention were the two parental behaviors that were most consistently effective in both stopping the particular tantrum and preventing a reoccurrence.

Similarly, aggressive adult behaviors that initially act to stop children's aggressive acts may actually increase the likelihood of more aggression. Although mild punishment may be effective with low to moderately aggressive children (for whom aggression is not a serious problem) physical punishment used with highly aggressive children does not appear to be effective over the long run. Typically parents escalate punishment with such children until it becomes a battle of wills, or until the child learns to inhibit aggression in the presence of the punitive parent while she or he continues to act-out when away from the parent (Bandura and Walters 1959). Parental punishment in these cases may be viewed not only as a response to the child's behavior but also as a model of aggressive behavior. Consistent with this analysis, Bandura and Walters (1959) note that parents of aggressive teenage boys tended to show more aggressive behavior themselves than parents of other children. In addition, parents of aggressive children are more likely to maintain a permissive attitude about aggressive behavior outside of the home than are other parents (Sears 1961); punishment for such children may not have the same deterrent effect that it has on most children (Patterson 1976).

The most common treatment methods of negative behavior in preschool children involve behavioral techniques. One successful technique is to give a child praise and attention contingent upon acceptable prosocial behaviors that provide the child with alternative ways of accomplishing ones goals (Maloney, Fixsen, and Maloney 1978; Patterson 1976). With older children, praise and attention given by peers as well as adults have been particularly effective (Maloney, Fixsen, and Maloney 1978). Behavioral contracts in which a child agrees to behave in a certain way in order to earn a clearly defined privilege have been successful, especially when the contracts also include mild sanctions for failure to meet responsibilities, regular feedback, and a bonus for complying with the contract itself (Stuart 1971). Directly teaching the desired or appropriate behavior in a positive context may also be sufficient to cause behavior to change in some cases (Spivack and Shure 1974). See Chapters 8 and 9 of this volume for related discussions on this topic.

Brief time-outs (i.e., time away from pleasurable activity) can be very effective in some situations in decreasing negative behaviors. Time-outs do not necessarily imply physical removal from the group, but can include the teacher ignoring the child for even a few seconds or having the child sit on a chair away from toys or other people. However, these methods do not guarantee replacement of the inappropriate behavior by a more appropriate one. With very young children who may actually not possess or understand alternative ways of behaving, behavioral techniques that function primarily by eliminating the undesired behavior (as opposed to helping the child to learn a new, acceptable alternative) may make the problem even worse (Gelfand 1978; Maloney, Fixsen, and Maloney 1978).

Catharsis (i.e., the release of tension, often in the specialized context of play therapy or intensive psychotherapy) has been proposed as an important aspect of the treatment of aggression. The rationale for this treatment is that if children give vent to their aggressive impulses in play or through fantasy, their motivation to be aggressive in interpersonal situations will be reduced. However, at this point there is no solid evidence that catharsis reduces aggression or has any other productive effect (Achenbach 1974).

Finally, drugs can be used as a treatment for aggression. Very little is known, however, about the direct effect of drugs on aggressive or negative behavior in preschool or school-age children. In any case, because of unknown side effects, medication would seldom be an appropriate treatment for behavior problems in young children.

Research with older children shows that antisocial, aggressive behavior is one of the most stable psychological problems of later childhood (Bandura and Walters 1959; Quay 1979) and that school-age children who act-out in one way are more likely to be negative or aggressive in other ways as well (Achenbach 1966). Furthermore, as adults, children treated for aggressive behavior are far more likely to have serious psychological problems, including antisocial behavior, than are children with other kind of disorders. The prognosis is particularly poor if children have many different negative behaviors and these behaviors occurred most often outside the home (Robins 1966).

However, little continuity seems to exist between simple measures of preschool children's negative behavior and their psychiatric status as adults (Achenbach and Edelbrock 1981). One reason for this apparent contradiction to the research with older children is that much of the negative behavior of preschool children is probably a reflection of the child's social naiveté rather than evidence of psychopathology. Research shows that preschool children who are more aggressive than average often are also more friendly, empathetic, and willing to share materials than other children (see Moore 1978). It is important to note that this finding is not evident in older aggressive children. Thus, a moderate degree of disobedience to parents by preschool children seems to be a characteristic of the age group and has not been linked to later psychopathology. The distinction between normal aggression in children and pathological aggression may lie in the other kinds of behavior the child exhibits. That is, aggressive or negative behavior in preschool children who are sociable and well-liked by other children, may be as much a product of such things as amount of experience with other children, access to toys, family demands, or general activity level, than an indicator of any serious disorder.

Nevertheless, one might seriously consider referral or intervention for a child who repeatedly shows several different kinds of negative behaviors in various situations, particularly if the child has unusual or eccentric ways of behaving and has difficulty relating to peers (Westman, Rice, and Bermann 1967). Since the treatment of negative behavior has been shown to be most effective at earlier ages (Rutter 1975), the possibility of avoiding what Patterson (1976) calls the "coercive cycle" (i.e., negative feedback for negative behavior that, in turn, breeds more negative behavior) should encourage early intervention in some cases. The difficulty for the early educator lies in recognizing the difference between a child's normal experimentation with aggression and patterns of negative behavior with more serious implications.

Hyperactivity

Excessive activity is also a major cause of referral of children to psychological and psychiatric services (Rutter 1975). In a recent series of epidemiological studies, pervasive overactivity at age three was the strongest predictor of behavior-emotional problems at age eight (Richman, Stevenson, and Graham, in press; Schachar, Rutter, and Smith, in press). Estimates of how many children should actually be defined as hyperactive or hyperkinetic (Stewart and Olds 1973; Sroufe 1975) range from about 4 to 10 percent of the school-age population (Ross and Ross 1976). However, these estimates vary according to the diagnostic criteria, the method of data collection, and the informant. For example, teachers tend to describe more children as hyperactive than unfamiliar adults observing the same children (Kenny et al. 1971). It is worth noting that in one study, almost one-half of the mothers of a normal sample of five-year-old boys and over one-third of the mothers of normal five-year-old girls described their children as exhibiting excessive activity to a degree where the mothers considered it a problem (Macfarlane, Allen, and Honzik 1954). Apparently adults frequently find normally active children difficult to handle.

Ross and Ross (1976) suggest differentiating between overactivity and hyperactivity by identifying school-age children as hyperactive only when (1) the overactivity occurs frequently in situations where it is clearly inappropriate, (2) the child is unable to inhibit her or his activity despite social pressure to do so, (3) the child often appears to be capable of only one speed of response even when the child is clearly motivated to exhibit other response speeds, and (4) the overactivity is accompanied by related behavioral and/or physiological symptoms including short attention span, high distractibility, impulsivity, anti-social behavior, emotional immaturity, and problems with peers (Stewart and Olds 1973).

While the above criteria discriminate overactivity from hyperactivity, there is still an enormous range for variation within the category hyperactivity. No two hyperactive children are the same even in terms of the symptoms that make us call them hyperactive (Sroufe 1975). Yet they do share enough characteristics to be worth considering as a possible diagnostic group. Hyperactive children usually show some symptoms before age five, and are more often male than female. They frequently have language problems in preschool and have reading problems later on (Richman, Stevenson, and Graham, in press; Stevenson and Richman 1978). Like aggressive children, children diagnosed as hyperactive have more of most psychological problems as adults than other children (Rutter 1975).

Many researchers believe that the major manifestations of hyperactivity begin in infancy and the preschool years; however, the most common time for mental health referrals concerning hyperactivity is after a child starts elementary school (Ross and Ross 1976). The belief that most hyperactive children show early signs of the disorder stems in part from clinical experience and in part from piecing together information from retrospective studies and from studies identifying infants and preschoolers as showing behaviors similar to those shown by older children diagnosed as hyperactive (Ross and Ross 1976). The general picture of the hyperactive preschooler is of a child who is hard to manage at home, who has unpredictable moods and irregular sleeping and eating habits, who has a low tolerance for frustration, who touches things more often than other children, who is accident-prone as well as having a high level of motor activity (Stewart and Olds 1973; Ross and Ross 1976). Direct observation of children in a nursery school indicated that, unlike their school-age counterparts, preschoolers labeled hyperactive did not have more problems with peers than other children (Schleifer et al. 1975). Similarly, the younger hyperactive children were not different from a control group during free play. However, when assigned a structured table task, they were more often aggressive, out of their chairs, and completely away from their table than other children.

A child's hyperactivity may not be recognized until she or he starts school for a number of reasons. Going to school may exacerbate problems that have been relatively mild for young children who spend most of their time at home or in an undemanding, relatively calm nursery school. Also behaviors associated with hyperactivity in preschoolers may have occurred but have gone relatively unnoticed by very tolerant or inexperienced parents (Ross and Ross 1976). Finally, since many of the differences between normal and hyperactive children at this age are differences in degree, parents' attempts to get help for their young children through physicians may have been perceived as parental exaggeration or overexpectation (Brazelton 1961). With more and more young children attending day care centers and nursery schools, one might expect to see children being referred for hyperactivity at increasingly younger ages, in part because group situations may place greater demands on the children and in part because experienced teachers may recognize or confirm the severity of the problem suspected by parents. Given the tendency of adults to describe a very high proportion of young children as overly active, care must be taken to distinguish that very small number of truly hyperactive children (where individual treatment may be appropriate) from the larger group of children with high activity levels for whom modification of the environment or lessening of expectations may be much more helpful than direct treatment of the child.

Research has still not provided many clear answers concerning the etiology of hyperactivity (Sroufe 1975). Many investigators now feel that its causes in any particular child are probably multiple and interacting with each other. Allergens (e.g., additives, particular foods), lead poisoning, radiation, metabolic abnormalities, documented minimal brain damage, and general delays in maturation have all been linked to hyperactivity (Wender 1971; Sroufe 1975). Inappropriate parental expectations, modeling, reinforcement, and family discord have also been shown to at least exacerbate hyperactivity, if not cause it (Ross and Ross 1976).

The use of medication in treating hyperactivity is a controversial topic (Ross and Ross 1976; Sroufe 1975). Though drugs are often the treatment of choice for older children, many investigators question their effectiveness and appropriateness in treating preschool children (Schleifer et al. 1975; Wender 1971). Research shows that the most serious side effects of medication, including insomnia, interference with speech, eating problems, and decreased cognitive abilities occur more often with very young children than their older counterparts (Schleifer et al. 1975). Because little knowledge exists about the long-term effects of psychoactive drugs on physical or mental development, most medical texts recommend that medication be considered only *after* other treatments have been tried and then only in conjunction with a systematic program of therapy (Ross and Ross 1976). In any case, given the problems and uncertain effectiveness of drugs for children younger than six years, the benefits vs. drawbacks of using medication need to be weighed with particular care (Solomons 1973).

As with aggression, the most common psychological treatments of school-age hyperactive children are behavioral in design. These methods, including modeling and the use of reinforcement, have been shown to be effective in changing specific behaviors of hyperactive children in relatively short periods of time (Patterson, Littman, and Bricker 1967). An avalanche effect of general improvement on other nontarget behaviors is fairly common as well (Patterson, Littman, and Bricker 1967). Cognitive behavior therapies where children are taught to instruct themselves in appropriate behavior (Meichenbaum and Goodman 1971) have also been shown to reduce impulsive behaviors in carefully controlled situations. For example, children have been taught to say "I have to go slowly," as they put together puzzles (Meichenbaum and Goodman 1971). These techniques have been used to modify children's behavior both at home and at school with parents and teachers actually carrying out the plans. Many of the same methods may be modifiable for use with preschool children.

As with treatments of other problems, a first step in working with very young children is to ascertain that the child understands what is expected and knows how to perform the required behavior. Once this is established, factors such as the immediacy of reinforcement and the careful selection of reinforcers have been found to be particularly significant in treating hyperactive young children (Patterson, Littman, and Bricker 1967). For example, some children may welcome (or be reinforced by) a hug or a pat on the back while other children would be made uncomfortable by affection of that kind. Eventual use of peers and adults other than the head teacher or parent as givers of reinforcement, deliberate shifts from food or money to more natural reinforcers like attention and praise, varied schedules of rewards, and the gradual diminution of the size and frequency of reinforcement are critical features of behavioral programs that produce the most generalized effects (Ross and Ross 1976). Presumably, these modifications provide a systematic transition from treatment to a time when the desired behavior is automatic and is sufficiently reinforced in natural ways in the normal environment so that the child no longer needs such intense rewards.

The use of treatments other than medication or behavioral management with hyperactive children has received relatively little attention in the research literature. While typically psychotherapy has been shown to be ineffective when used by itself with older hyperactive children, brief family-oriented psychotherapeutic techniques have been used to provide support and insight to families where children are also receiving medical or behavioral treatment (Watzlawick, Weakland, and Fisch 1974). Family therapy or play therapy may also be helpful with younger children when used in conjunction with the other approaches.

Hyperactivity was once considered a transient disorder of middle childhood; however, follow-up studies show it to be a problem with lifelong implications (Ross and Ross 1976; Schachar, Rutter, and Smith, in press). Many researchers and clinicians are optimistic that, with treatment, the diminished activity level often seen in hyperactive children as adolescents and adults will allow most such children to lead productive adult lives (Stewart and Olds 1973). However, at this point, the evidence from follow-up studies of untreated children and from studies of mental patients (who more often report histories of hyperactivity as children than would be expected in the population) is quite sobering (Laufer 1971). Adults who were hyperactive as children and were not helped show more of almost every kind of psychiatric problem than expected, including alcoholism, personality disorders, and schizophrenia (Morrison and Stewart 1973; Cantwell 1975).

While the distance between a hyperactive four-year-old and a schizophrenic adult seems great, these data have serious implications for the treatment of very young children. Research with hyperactive children and other difficult-to-manage children suggests that the most significant factors in a given child's prognosis are not necessarily the child's primary symptoms but how these symptoms interact with her or his environment (Ross and Ross 1976). Studies suggest that overactivity and other behaviors associated with hyperactivity can be particularly hard on parent-child relations when children are very young, while later, these behaviors may particularly interfere with peer interactions and academic achievement (Schachar, Rutter, and Smith, in press). Early intervention that enhances children's family interactions, supports their beginning peer interactions, and facilitates their initial academic attempts would seem particularly relevant. Discovering ways to ease routines that often lead to conflict at home or school (e.g., dressing, going to bed, extreme restlessness), helping parents find competent child care, and providing support, information, and behavior management techniques to parents and teachers may prevent exacerbation of a hyperactive child's underlying problem (Ross and Ross 1976). A number of the suggestions made by Ross and Ross (1976) to elementary teachers seems useful in maximizing the hyperactive preschool child's social and intellectual opportunities. These suggestions include use of small group activities, high-status peers who deliberately model appropriate behaviors for the hyperactive child, and the introduction of novel, exciting, or competitive activities with enough structure and predictability to reduce stress and distractibility. Ross and Ross (1976) also emphasize the importance of kindergarten as a transition from the less demanding atmosphere of the nursery school to the more formal academic first grade classroom. Highly academic kindergartens may be less appropriate for overactive five-year-olds than more socially oriented classes. Also, some hyperactive children, particularly those who are less physically and/or cognitively mature, may benefit from an extra year in a socialization-based kindergarten or transition program.

Fears and shyness

Intense, irrational fears of specific objects or events are extremely common during early childhood. It is estimated that at some point between ages 2 and 12 years, over 90 percent of children will experience intense fear of some kind (Macfarlane, Allen, and Honzik 1954). During the preschool years children seem to be particularly prone to such fears (Gelfand 1978). In many ways, childhood fears are not evidence of psychopathology at all, but are a normal part of growing. Most childhood fears or phobias (the terms will be used interchangeably, although they have somewhat different connotations) disappear within five years or less without treatment (Agras, Chapin, and Oliveau 1972). Unlike those of adults or adolescents, fears in the early years are not usually associated with other psychological problems, nor are they predictive of emotional disorder in adulthood (Rutter 1975). However, childhood phobias can still cause a great deal of pain and disruption for the child and family. Given the brevity and effectiveness of available treatment, intervention may be a reasonable option, even though most fears in childhood eventually dissipate without it.

The most common phobias experienced by toddlers and preschool children are fears of animals, especially dogs and snakes, storms and darkness, doctors, strange people, unfamiliar situations, and imaginary creatures (Miller et al. 1972). While fears of animals tend to persist for longer periods of time, the other typical fears of early childhood are more transient (Miller et al. 1972).

The best documented treatment of fears is desensitization, a procedure that consists of teaching a child to relax and then, while in a relaxed state, to tolerate a graded series of presentations of the feared object that gradually become more fear-producing. There is a great deal of evidence that desensitization can be a brief, inexpensive, and effective treatment of specific phobias in adolescents and adults (Lazarus 1960; Wolpe 1958). While it has been assumed that the same techniques would be equally effective with young children (Achenbach 1974), this may not be the case. Desensitization procedures are based on the assumption that the client knows how to behave in the presence of the feared object but that her or his adaptive skills are inhibited because of the fear. In fact, the very young child may not have such skills at all (Rimm and Masters 1974). For example, a preschool child may not know what to do when encountering a large, barking dog or when placed in the lap of a strange, bearded, white-haired man. The child also may not understand the very small chance of real danger from certain events (e.g., thunder, helicopters). Emotive imagery, one aspect of some desensitization programs that involves the child imagining specific frightening or unpleasant events, also has been found to be difficult for preschool-age children to understand (Tasto 1969).

Relapses following desensitization are fairly common among young children (Gelfand 1978). Consequently, desensitization alone, especially those programs requiring complex imagery, does not seem to be the optimal treatment for very young children. Investigators suggest alternative or additional behavioral methods that are especially suited to the needs and limitations of very young clients. Research shows that modeling can be a particularly effective method for teaching preschoolers specific behaviors needed to cope with fears (Bandura, Grusec, and Menlove 1967). Role-playing and direct teaching of the desired behaviors would seem to be appropriate for the treatment of fears as well. Gelfand (1978) suggests that if kindergartners know what to do in the presence of a feared event or object, they can benefit from instructions to act like particularly competent people they know or to think to themselves, "I am brave."

Another technique found useful in helping children cope with fears is reinforced practice (Leitenberg and Callahan 1973). This method goes beyond more traditional desensitization procedures by repeatedly reinforcing appropriate behavior in a maximally fearful situation. For example, rather than pronouncing a child cured the first time he can finally pet a real garter snake, a program of reinforced practice would give the child reinforcement for petting a number of different snakes. Reinforced practice can be used by itself or following a desensitization program. The purpose of the procedure is to help the child overlearn what to do in the fear-provoking situation and thus enhance the likelihood that the fear will not return once treatment is over.

Like phobias, shyness or fear of interacting with unfamiliar people is very common in childhood. Frequently, like other fears, shyness disappears without treatment. In a study of adolescents and college students, Zimbardo, Pilkonis, and Norwood (1974 as cited in Gelfand 1978) found that 30 percent of the students identified themselves as presently shy and 25 percent stated that they had been timid most of their lives. Another 40 percent of the students stated that they had been shy as young children but had grown out of it. Although the typical onset of shyness has not really been studied, investigators have found it relatively easy to identify withdrawn children in groups of preschoolers (Furman, Rahe, and Hartup 1979). It can probably be assumed that at least some other children who are not perceived as withdrawn would also identify themselves as shy if they could tell us so.

Shyness, like other childhood fears, is not, on its own, evidence of psychopathology. During school age, many children who are anxious and who have somatic complaints (e.g., stomachaches, headaches) are also shy (Achenbach 1966). However, the reverse does not necessarily hold true. There is no evidence that most shy children are more often anxious or more neurotic overall than gregarious children. It is *not* true, for example, that schizophrenics or highly disturbed adults were identified as being shy as children (Robins 1966). In fact, recent research suggests that children who are most likely to have later serious psychological problems are more typically antisocial, eccentric, or negative during their early years rather than shy (Rutter 1975). This does not imply that educators and clinicians should ignore children who are painfully shy or timid. However, it does mean that in most cases shyness can be treated for the current problems it presents to the child, rather than as a manifestation of serious psychological disturbance.

Considerations in planning treatment programs to encourage social interaction in shy children are very similar to those in treating other fears in preschool children. The one major difference is that shyness is by definition a social problem that requires the involvement of people other than the child in treatment. Because other people have their own habits and patterns of behavior, treatment of shyness in very young children needs to take into account the social environment in which the timidity usually occurs. Observations suggest that teachers and parents often unwittingly reinforce social withdrawal in the preschool child simply by paying more attention to a child when she or he is alone than when the child is with other children. In a study by Allen et al. (1964) the contingencies were reversed and the teachers attended to a very shy child only when she played with others. The results were that the child became much more interactive.

As in the case of other fears, modeling is shown to be a very effective treatment for shyness in young children (O'Connor 1972). One interesting finding is that treatment is most successful when shy children perceive the models to be like themselves; very shy preschool children may reject live or filmed suave "child-about-town" models and actually come to feel worse about their own incompetence (Gelfand 1978). One creative approach to this problem is to show timid children films of other shy children who have become progressively more interactive with more and more positive results (O'Connor 1969). Other aspects of the use of filmed models such as the size of the group watching the film (i.e., smaller groups were more effective) and the presence of a first-person narrator also influence the effectiveness of this kind of treatment (see Gelfand 1978). The source of these effects seems to lie in gradual exposure of children to clear examples of the appropriate behavior so as not to overwhelm them. Extremely withdrawn children may need to learn and practice new behaviors in relatively isolated situations before being required to produce them in the classroom or other public settings (Jackson and Wallace 1974). One study shows that giving isolated children a chance to play in dyads with peer "therapists" (i.e., a child with adequate social skills) for a short period each day increases the children's social interactiveness with their own classmates (Furman, Rahe, and Hartup 1979). Peers who are somewhat younger than the isolated children are slightly more effective playmate therapists, perhaps because they give the withdrawn children a chance to practice taking the initiative.

Teaching social skills as part of the school curriculum is also shown to be an effective method in changing children's behavior (Spivack and Shure 1974), although most typically skill teaching has not been aimed at shy children. These programs involve procedures such as teaching children to generate many different solutions to problem situations (e.g., think of three ways to respond to being pushed by a peer) and then to anticipate the social consequences of each solution. More indirect methods, where withdrawn children are given the opportunity to interact positively with other children by passing out food or using group-oriented play equipment, have increased the number of positive social interactions shown by the timid children (Buell et al. 1968; Kirby and Toler 1970). Explicit statements of the social behavior desired by the teacher or parent (e.g., "I want you to play with Johnny on the teeter-totter.") also are used to increase shy children's participation in group activities. In many cases, use of several methods at once can be maximally effective (Gelfand 1978).

Follow-up studies show that treatment of shyness tends to have less lasting effects than treatment of other fears (Keller and Carlson 1974). One reason this may occur is that the environment outside the treatment program may continue to encourage the original behavior. (Companions, for example, may continue to ignore a child who has refused to join them in the past.) In addition, the transition away from a successful treatment to environmental rewards can be particularly difficult in the treatment of shyness. If rewards and attention for participation are withdrawn too suddenly from a formerly timid child, the child may feel confused, uncertain how to behave, and even punished. As much care should be taken to plan this shift as in planning the original treatment. Cutting down the frequency of reinforcement, gradually shifting from materials (e.g., food, charts, stickers) to social rewards (such as attention and approval), and regularly checking that the child and the social environment are maintaining the desired interactions can enhance the likelihood of lasting improvement (Gelfand 1978).

There are numerous effective methods to treat children who have particular fears or shyness; however, to be truly successful, treatment in very young children must be carefully planned and executed around the needs and abilities of very young children in general and of the individual child-client in particular. Major advances include not only increasingly refined treatment methods, but also the recognition of the relative normality of shyness and childhood fears and the avoidance of overinterpretation and overtreatment of these problems.

Developmental problems

In a recent survey, concerns about toileting, eating, and sleeping were the most common problems for which parents of two-year-olds sought help in a pediatric setting (Schroeder 1979). For three- and four-year-olds, such develop- -mental problems were second only to negative behavior in the frequency of parent-initiated referral. While psychologists acknowledge that problems in these areas are very common (Erickson 1978), both clinical description and systematic research on eating and sleeping problems are very rare. The assumption seems to be that since most adults develop reasonable eating and sleeping habits, children's difficulties in this area are more problems to the parents than disorders of the children. Inappropriate parental expectations (e.g., that all children must eat all foods, that all two-year-olds need two naps a day) and poor management (e.g., having no quiet bedtime routine, allowing children to snack before meals) are often named as the major sources of these problems (Erickson 1978; Knopf 1979). However, the relationship between such problems and parental behavior is often inference on the part of writers and is seldom based on research.

Nevertheless, research has made significant contributions to the treatment of enuresis, or failure in voluntary bladder control. Data are much more limited on the treatment of encopresis or failure in voluntary bowel control. (Since encopresis is quite rare and requires careful medical management, it will not be considered here.)

While bladder accidents are usually considered to be a problem for children by four years of age, the greatest number of psychiatric referrals for enuresis are made during the early grade school years (Knopf 1979). Yet, in most cases these children have never attained consistent control of toileting (Kanner 1972). Estimates of the number of school-age children who fall into this category range from 5 to 15 percent of the total population, with a sex ratio of 2 or 3 males to 1 female (Bakwin and Bakwin 1966; Kaffman and Elizur 1977). Although some cases of enuresis will disappear by age seven with or without treatment (Kaffman and Elizur 1977), the secondary problems associated with the disorder (e.g., parental frustration, social restriction and embarrassment, health concerns) can be very disruptive. Thus, enuresis is a reasonable target for early psychological intervention, given that organic causes have been ruled out and it is clear that the child has the necessary physiological and social maturity to control the bladder.

Most cases of enuresis involve nighttime wetting only. Although there are children who have frequent daytime accidents, daytime enuresis almost always accompanies nocturnal problems. The reverse is not true. Because nocturnal enuresis is much more common and better-researched, this discussion will be limited to children who wet only at night. Episodes of nocturnal enuresis are very common among children who have undergone some kind of major change (e.g., a move, loss of a parent due to death or divorce, changes in school, a new sibling). However, *if* complete bladder control has been established once, children in this situation tend to recover very rapidly on their own (Knopf 1979).

Treatment is more generally warranted for children who have always had toileting accidents.

No single cause has been identified for enuresis in later preschool and early-school-age children. However, as more research is undertaken, some patterns are emerging: unlike childhood fears, enuresis is rarely an isolated symptom. It is usually accompanied by at least one other psychological symptom and, particularly for girls, about one-third of the time it is associated with several other problems (Young and Morgan 1973). Other childhood disorders that frequently accompany enuresis in young children are irritability, restlessness, moodiness, multiple fears, temper tantrums, bad habits (e.g., thumbsucking after age five, head-banging), acting-out, and eating problems. Enuresis can occur in children of all intellectual levels, but it is often associated with general physical and social immaturity. A number of studies show that school-age enuretic children experienced more major stresses (e.g., hospitalization, illness, injury, birth of sibling) when they were toddlers and preschoolers than most children (Young and Morgan 1973). Also enuresis is more common in children of poorly educated, low-SES parents than in upper-middle-SES children, and children with enuresis are more likely than other children to have parents who are involved in discordant marriages or who have emotional problems themselves (Achenbach and Edelbrock 1981). Although enuresis tends to occur more often in some families than others, investigators have hypothesized that enuresis is seldom directly due to genetic causes nor is it related in a simple way to immediate stress. Rather, in many cases family circumstances, including cultural factors (e.g., concern about modesty or cleanliness), general childrearing style, attitudes toward toilet training, and the experiences the parents had as children being toilet trained are believed to interact with specific stresses experienced by the child during the preschool years. The result is that the enuretic child never really acquires nocturnal bladder control (Knopf 1979).

Research shows behavioral methods to be most effective in the treatment of enuresis. One such method involves a child sleeping on a pad laid over the bed. The pad is moisture-sensitive so that when the child first starts to urinate, a bell rings to wake the child. The bell and pad system (Mowrer and Mowrer 1938) is shown to be more effective than no treatment or than psychotherapy for preschool and school-age children who have nocturnal enuresis. Yet, there are serious problems in followup, with up to 40 percent relapse rates within two years (Lovibond 1963). The durability of the bell and pad system has been improved by simply increasing the child's fluid intake immediately before bed so that the child learns to control even a very full bladder (Young and Morgan 1973). Yet, given the association of enuresis with other problems, it is important for clinicians and educators not to treat the bell and pad as a panacea for all of the child's needs and to be aware of the potential for relapse if the total problem is not addressed.

Another treatment involves the use of imipramine, (tradename, Tofranil), a drug that stops nocturnal enuresis almost immediately by increasing bladder capacity at the same time lightening sleep. Because it has a high rate of relapse over very short periods of time, a number of investigators conclude that imipramine should not be used as the sole treatment for enuresis and question its use except when other treatments have failed, or when the immediate need to eliminate the problem is great.

Early childhood autism and severe social impairment

While autism is a rare condition, its characteristics are so marked and its implications for development so devastating that it is appropriate to discuss it among the major psychological disorders affecting young children. Major advances have been made in our understanding of autism over the last few years. Nevertheless, it continues to be one of the most puzzling and the most controversial disorders in the study of childhood psychopathology.

Recent definitions of autism list three necessary behavioral criteria for a child to be considered autistic: (1) a profound and general failure to develop social relations, (2) language retardation with impaired comprehension, and (3) ritualistic or compulsive insistence on sameness (Rutter 1978a). Other behaviors that often, but not always accompany these problems in autistic children are stereotypic movements (e.g., hand-flapping, ear-pulling), short attention span, self-injurious behavior, limitations in play, and delayed bowel control (Rutter 1978a). Most autistic children play in a stereotyped, repetitive fashion (e.g., repeatedly dropping things from a fixed distance above the ground, spinning or rolling small objects, lining toys up) (Wing and Gould 1979). As they get older, some autistic children develop interests in elaborate but highly repetitious activities (e.g., copying names from phone books, drawing maps or railroad systems). Insistence on routines may also characterize younger autistic children who demand to say goodbye to each teacher before leaving school or who become very upset if all the window shades are not pulled down exactly to the windowsill (Wing and Gould 1979).

Most, but not all, autistic children are mentally retarded (Lotter 1978). For the autistic child, mental retardation simply means that all of the child's skills are significantly below her or his chronological age and that these delays will never be completely overcome with development or treatment (Rutter 1978a). However, it should be kept in mind that there are some autistic children of average or above average intelligence and that most mildly to moderately retarded children are not at all autistic. Diagnoses can be confusing because many profoundly retarded children and children with multiple sensory handicaps show some autistic-like behaviors. For example, young children with undiagnosed profound hearing loss may look autistic; by the same token, young autistic children, because they frequently do not attend to speech, may appear to be deaf (Wing 1976). Young children with very severe language disorders may sometimes appear autistic as well. However, children with specific developmental language disorders can usually be differentiated from autistic children because the language-handicapped children can use gestures, show some creative play, and have more normal-appearing relationships with familiar adults (Wing 1976).

Contrary to early speculation, autism has little to do with schizophrenia. Autistic children do not behave like adult schizophrenics nor do they grow up to be adult schizophrenics (DeMyer et al. 1973). In an attempt to differentiate it from a childhood form of schizophrenia even more rare than autism, the term *autism* is restricted to disorders that develop before the age of 30 months (Wing 1976).

Motor milestones may be delayed in autistic children, but often early motor skills are within the normal range. The typical preschool-age autistic child walks, drinks from a cup, and can ride a tricycle (Wing 1976). The child's failure to talk or loss of speech (that may have been at a one-word level) often precipitates the child's first contact with a mental health professional (Chess and Rosenberg 1974). In fact, from infancy, the child probably failed to master the language comprehension shown by most children when they are toddlers and young preschoolers. This is an important point because what is now recognized as a lack of comprehension has been often misinterpreted in the past as a lack of cooperation or motivation. The misinterpretation has been due in part to the fact that people who have frequent contact with young autistic children often unwittingly derive complicated methods of cuing through gestures, gaze, and use of objects so that the children appear to the speaker to understand language when, in fact, they do not (Wing 1976). Watching how a parent communicates with an autistic child can provide the clinician or teacher with information about the extent to which the child may need nonverbal cues in order to comprehend. Also, observing parents can help others learn some possible communication methods that are effective with such children (Lord and Baker 1978).

Some autistic children repeat long sentences or entire paragraphs that they have memorized from someone else's speech. While not always completely meaningless, this kind of speech, called echolalia seldom means the same thing to the child as to the adult who hears it. For example, an autistic child may use the phrase "Let's make a deal," memorized from a television show, to ask people to give her things. However, in this case, the child may actually be producing language that she would not understand if someone else said the same words. Use of real, spontaneous language (not echolalia) in young autistic children is related to intelligence; autistic children who have developed some spontaneous language by age five also have a much better prognosis than children who remain mute (Rutter 1978b).

The social impairments of the young autistic child include the tendency to use peripheral vision (that can look like the avoidance of eye contact), failure to approach or initiate interaction with familiar people, failure to act differently with unfamiliar and familiar adults, and greater attention to sensory stimuli (e.g., lights, lines) than to people (Wing 1976). Autistic children often act more normally with adults than with other children. Their social behavior can range from uniformly inappropriate cuddliness or friendliness to complete aloofness. The latter behavior was originally interpreted as an indication of the autistic child's intense withdrawal or wish to avoid people (Kanner 1943). However, more recently, many researchers and clinicians have come to feel that the social problems of autistic children stem at least in part from their not knowing what to do (e.g., how to talk, how to gesture, how to play) rather than in choosing not to do things (Rutter 1978a; Wing 1976).

Recent advances in the understanding of the cause of autism have served primarily to eliminate some hypotheses and to provide rather indirect evidence in support of other general theories. A number of studies over the past few years have refuted the suggestion that autism is a psychogenic disorder, caused by psychological trauma or faulty parenting (Schopler 1971). With proper control groups, research concludes that parents of autistic children are not significantly different from parents of children with other handicaps (Cox et al. 1975). Research also provides evidence that links autism in numerous ways to brain dysfunction and other organic disorders (Coleman 1978; DeLong 1978), although specific causes have not been identified.

Structured treatments based on behavioral and educational methods similar to those used with fears and phobias are shown to be more successful in eliminating specific undesired behaviors (Lovaas et al. 1965) and in teaching very simple skills than psychotherapy or therapeutic nursery school programs (Bartak 1978). The introduction of signing (as in the treatment of deaf children) provides a communication system for some nonverbal children and even enhances acquisition of speech for some autistic children (Carr 1979). Use of parents as therapists with their own children is being increasingly emphasized (Schopler and Reichler 1971).

Although children in treatment may show specific improvements, overall generalization across tasks and settings is very poor and the prognosis for most autistic children remains bleak (Lotter 1978). Even though the behavior problems of many autistic children improve in later school age and adolescence, the cognitive impairments and the social impairments remain, often seeming even more obvious in older children and adolescents (Wing 1976). Unless there are community-based group living situations, most autistic adults eventually live in institutions. Like hyperactivity, the recent years have seen growing recognition that autism is most often a lifelong disorder (Schopler, Rutter, and Chess 1979). At this point, hope seems to lie in the search for specific organic causes and subsequent attempts at treatment or prevention.

Advances in therapy

One recurring theme throughout the discussion of children's disorders is the gradual refinement of treatment methods appropriate to the needs and abilities of the young child. While behavioral methods have received the clearest documentation in research, play therapy and treatments that involve modifying the social and physical environment (sometimes called milieu therapy) are also interventions employed more and more frequently with very young children (Mahon and Battin 1978). At this time, there is very little well-controlled research indicating whether these methods are effective and if so, with what populations. Evidence does exist, however, that brief, somewhat structured psychotherapy can be an effective treatment for general emotional problems in older children when it is performed by a competent therapist (Graham 1974). Research concerning the comparative effectiveness of these different methods with very young children is needed.

Although research has not yet given many clear ideas about the usefulness of one treatment over another for many psychological problems in young children, there is a growing body of literature on specific ways in which traditional therapies have been modified to be more appropriate for young clients. These modifications often have been truly eclectic, in that they occurred for different kinds of interventions and for different kinds of problems. The adjustments include: (1) deliberately considering how the child perceives her or his problem and others' attempts to remediate it, (2) investigating the relationship of the specific problem to other aspects of the child's life and skills, especially peer and family relations, (3) confirming that the child knows how to perform the appropriate behavior before expecting or demanding it and, if not, teaching the behavior through modeling or shaping, (4) requiring only very gradual changes, (5) providing opportunities to overlearn the new behaviors in the initial situation, (6) planning specifically for the generalization of the appropriate behavior and providing opportunities to practice it in new situations, (7) gradually weaning the child from reliance on frequent tangible reinforcement, (8) using several different treatment methods at once, and (9) including peers and parents in the treatment as colleagues or for support whenever possible.

A final issue is the importance of secondary factors in the psychopathology of young children. These factors include aspects of a child's life, such as characteristics of the family, the child's academic skills, or physical health, that affect and are affected by the primary psychological problem. In many cases these factors, particularly the parents' marital relationship and emotional status, are more predictive of a child's mental health as an adult than knowledge about the child (Ross and Ross 1976; Rutter 1975). In addition, many treatments for the more serious childhood disorders (e.g., autism, hyperactivity) are really designed to help the child and the family avoid secondary problems. Although at this point we cannot prevent or stop children from being autistic, we can at least help them to be more comfortable, less aggressive or self-abusive, and to become a more accepted member of their families. Though hyperactivity is seldom cured, we can increase the child's ability to get along with family members and friends and minimize the child's chance of educational failure (Ross and Ross 1976). Though we cannot yet prevent most kinds of childhood psychopathology, we can identify children who are at risk because of secondary factors (e.g., chronic illness, discordant families, low SES, large families) that make them potentially more vulnerable to other problems and treat or provide support for these aspects of the child's life that may have the greatest impact on psychological development in the long run.

Summary

In this chapter we have discussed issues in the diagnosis and treatment of psychopathological disorders in the preschool child. In particular, we reviewed five representative psychological problems seen in young children: negative behavior, fears, enuresis, hyperactivity, and autism.

Perhaps with greater knowledge, we will be able to ensure that usually minor short-term problems such as childhood fears and eating disturbances remain minor and transient for everyone; perhaps we will also be able to keep more serious problems from interfering with young children's development, at least until we can prevent or cure the original disorder.

References

Achenbach, T. M. "The Classification of Children's Psychiatric Symptoms: A Factor-Analytic Study." *Psychological Monographs* 80 (1966).

Achenbach, T. M. *Developmental Psychopathology*. New York: Ronald Press, 1974.

Achenbach, T. M., and Edelbrock, C. S. "Behavioral Problems and Competencies Reported by Parents of Normal and Disturbed Children Aged 4 Through 16." *Monographs of the Society for Research in Child Development* 46 (1981).

Agras, W. S.; Chapin, H. H.; and Oliveau, D. C. "The Natural History of Phobia." *Archives of General Psychiatry* 26 (1972): 315–317.

Allen, K.; Hart, B.; Buell, S.; Harris, R.; and Wolf, M. "Effects of Social Reinforcement on Isolate Behavior of a Nursery School Child." *Child Development* 35, no. 19 (1964): 511–518.

Bakwin, H., and Bakwin, R. *Clinical Management of Behavior Disorders in Children*. Philadelphia: Saunders, 1966.

Bandura, A.; Grusec, E.; and Menlove, F. L. "Vicarious Extinction of Avoidance Behavior." *Journal of Personality and Social Psychology* 5 (1967): 16–23.

Bandura, A., and Walters, R. *Adolescent Aggression*. New York: Ronald Press, 1959.

Bartak, L. "Educational Approaches." In *Autism: A Reappraisal of Concepts and Treatment*, ed. M. Rutter and E. Schopler. New York: Plenum, 1978.

Berlin, T. "Minimal Brain Dysfunction: Management of Family Distress." *Journal of the American Medical Association* 229, no. 11 (1974): 1454–1456.

Brazelton, T. B. "Psychophysiologic Reactions of the Neonate." *Journal of Pediatrics* 58 (1961): 508–512.

Buell, J.; Stoddard, P.; Harris, F. R.; and Baer, D. M. "Collateral Social Development Accompanying Reinforcement of Outdoor Play in a Preschool Child." *Journal of Applied Behavior Analysis* 1 (1968): 167–173.

Cantwell, D. P. "Natural History and Prognosis in the Hyperactive Child Syndrome." In *The Hyperactive Child*, ed. D. P. Cantwell. New York: Spectrum, 1975.

Carr, E. G. "Teaching Autistic Children to Use Sign Language: Some Research

Issues." *Journal of Autism and Developmental Disorders* 9, no. 4 (1979): 345–360.

Chess, S., and Rosenberg, M. "Clinical Differentiation Between Children with Initial Language Complaints." *Journal of Autism and Childhood Schizophrenia* 4 (1974): 99–109.

Clement, P. W.; Roberts, P. V.; and Lantz, C. E. "Social Models and Token Reinforcement in the Treatment of Shy Withdrawn Boys." *Proceedings of the 78th Annual Convention of the American Psychological Association* 5 (1970): 515–516.

Coleman, M. "The Autistic Syndromes." In *Autism: A Reappraisal of Concepts and Treatment*, ed. M. Rutter and E. Schopler. New York: Plenum, 1978.

Cox, A.; Rutter, M.; Newman, S.; and Bartak, L. "A Comparative Study of Infantile Autism and Specific Developmental Receptive Language Disorder, II. Parental Characteristics." *British Journal of Psychiatry* 126 (1975): 146–159.

DeLong, G. R. "A Neuropsychologic Interpretation of Infantile Autism." In *Autism: A Reappraisal of Concepts and Treatment*, ed. M. Rutter and E. Schopler. New York: Plenum, 1978.

DeMyer, M. K.; Barton, S.; DeMyer, W. E.; Norton, J. A.; Allen, J.; and Steele, R. "Prognosis in Autism: A Follow-Up Study." *Journal of Autism and Childhood Schizophrenia* 3 (1973): 199–210.

de Wit, J., and Hartup, W. W., eds. *Determinants and Origins of Aggression.* The Hague: Mouton, 1974.

Erickson, M. T. *Child Psychopathology.* Englewood Cliffs, N.J.: Prentice-Hall, 1978.

Furman, W.; Rahe, D.; and Hartup, W. W. "Social Rehabilitation of Low-Interactive Preschool Children by Peer Intervention." *Child Development* 50 (1979): 915–922.

Gelfand, D. M. "Social Withdrawal and Negative Emotional States: Behavior Therapy." In *Handbook of Treatment of Mental Disorders in Childhood and Adolescence*, ed. B. B. Wolman, J. Egan, and A. O. Ross. Englewood Cliffs, N.J.: Prentice-Hall, 1978.

Goodenough, F. L. *Anger in Young Children.* Minneapolis, Minn.: University of Minnesota Press, 1931.

Graham, P. "Child Psychiatry and Psychotherapy." *Journal of Child Psychology and Psychiatry and Allied Disciplines* 15 (1974): 59–66.

Hartup, W. W. "Aggression and Childhood: Developmental Perspectives." *American Psychologist* 29 (1974): 336–341.

Jackson, D. A., and Wallace, R. F. "The Modification and Generalization of Voice Loudness in a Fifteen-Year-Old Retarded Girl." *Journal of Applied Behavior Analysis* 7 (1974): 461–471.

Kaffman, M., and Elizur, E. "Infants Who Become Enuretics: A Longitudinal Study of 161 Kibbutz Children." *Monographs of the Society for Research in Child Development* 42 (1977).

Kanner, L. "Autistic Disturbances of Affective Contact." *Nervous Child* 2 (1943): 217–250.

Kanner, L. *Child Psychiatry.* 4th ed. Springfield, Ill.: Charles C. Thomas, 1972.

Keller, M. F., and Carlson, P. M. "The Use of Symbolic Modeling to Promote Social Skills in Preschool Children with Low Levels of Social Responsiveness." *Child Development* 45 (1974): 912–919.

Kenny, T. J.; Clemens, R. L.; Hudson, B.; Lentz, G. A.; Circi, R.; and Nair, P. "Characteristics of Children Referred Because of Hyperactivity." *Journal of Pediatrics* 79 (1971): 618–622.

Kirby, F. D., and Toler, H. C., Jr. "Modification of Preschool Isolate Behavior: A Case Study." *Journal of Applied Behavior Analysis* 3 (1970): 309–314.

Knopf, I. J. *Childhood Psychopathology: A Developmental Approach.* Englewood Cliffs, N.J.: Prentice-Hall, 1979.

Kohn, M., and Rosman, L. "A Social Competence Scale and Symptom Checklist for the Preschool Child: Factor Dimensions, Their Cross Instrument Generality and Longitudinal Persistence." *Developmental Psychology* 6 (1972): 430–444.

Laufer, M. W. "Long-Term Management and Some Follow-Up Findings on the Use of Drugs with Minimal Cerebral Syndromes." *Journal of Learning Disabilities* 4 (1971): 55–58.

Lazarus, A. A. "The Elimination of Children's Phobias by Deconditioning." In *Behavior Therapy and the Neuroses,* ed. H. J. Eysenek. New York: Pergamon Press, 1960.

Leitenberg, H., and Callahan, E. G. "Reinforced Practice and Reduction of Different Kinds of Fears in Adults and Children." *Behavior Research and Therapy* 11 (1973): 19–30.

Lord, C., and Baker, A. B. "Communicating with Autistic Children." *Journal of Pediatric Psychology* 3, no. 3 (1978): 181–186.

Lorion, R. P.; Cowen, E. L.; and Caldwell, R. A. "Problem Types of Children Referred to a School-Based Mental Health Program." *Journal of Consulting and Clinical Psychology* 42 (1974): 491–496.

Lotter, V. "Follow-Up Studies." In *Autism: A Reappraisal of Concepts and Treatment,* ed. M. Rutter and E. Schopler. New York: Plenum, 1978.

Lovaas, O. I.; Freitag, G.; Gold, W.; and Kassorla, I. C. "Experimental Studies in Childhood Schizophrenia." *Journal of Experimental Child Psychology* 2 (1965): 67–75.

Lovibond, S. H. "The Mechanism of Conditioning Treatment of Enuresis." *Behavior Research and Therapy* 1 (1963): 17–24.

Maccoby, E., and Jacklin, C. N. *The Psychology of Sex Differences.* Stanford, Calif.: Stanford University Press, 1974.

Macfarlane, J. W.; Allen, L.; and Honzik, M. *A Developmental Study of the Behavior Problems of Normal Children.* Berkeley, Calif.: University of California Press, 1954.

Mahon, E., and Battin, D. "Therapeutic Nurseries." In *Handbook of Treatment of Mental Disorders in Childhood and Adolescence,* ed. B. B. Wolman,

J. Egan, and A. O. Ross. Englewood Cliffs, N.J.: Prentice-Hall, 1978.

Maloney, D. M.; Fixsen, D. L.; and Maloney, K. B. "Anti-Social Behavior: Behavior Modification." In *Handbook of Treatment of Mental Disorders in Childhood and Adolescence,* ed. B. B. Wolman, J. Egan, and A. O. Ross. Englewood Cliffs, N.J.: Prentice-Hall, 1978.

Meichenbaum, D. H., and Goodman, J. "Training Impulsive Children to Talk to Themselves." *Journal of Abnormal Psychology* 77, no. 2 (1971): 115–126.

Miller, L. C.; Barrett, C. L.; Hampe, E.; and Noble, H. "Factor Structure of Children's Fears." *Journal of Consulting and Clinical Psychology* 39 (1972): 264–268.

Moore, S. G. "The Social Interaction of Young Children: Friend and Foe." In *Research Reviews for Practitioners and Parents,* ed. J. Schick and J. Klayman. Minneapolis, Minn.: University of Minnesota, Center for Early Education and Development, no. 1 (1978): 11–23.

Morrison, J. R., and Stewart, M. A. "A Family Study of the Hyperactive Child Syndrome." *Biological Psychiatry* 3 (1973): 189–195.

Mowrer, O. H., and Mowrer, W. A. "Enuresis: A Method for Its Study and Treatment." *American Journal of Orthopsychiatry* 8 (1938): 436–459.

O'Connor, R. D. "Modification of Social Withdrawal Through Symbolic Modeling." *Journal of Applied Behavior Analysis* 2 (1969): 15–22.

O'Connor, R. D. "Relative Efficacy of Modeling, Shaping and the Combined Procedures for Modification of Social Withdrawal." *Journal of Abnormal Psychology* 79 (1972): 327–334.

Patterson, G. R. "The Aggressive Child: Victim and Architect of a Coercive System." In *Behavior Modification and Families,* ed. E. J. Mash, L. A. Hamerlynck, and L. C. Handy. New York: Brunner/Mazel, 1976.

Patterson, G. R., and Cobb, J. "A Dyadic Analysis of Aggressive Behaviors." In *Minnesota Symposia on Child Psychology. Vol. 5,* ed. J. P. Hill. Minneapolis, Minn.: University of Minnesota Press, 1971.

Patterson, G. R.; Littman, R. A.; and Bricker, W. "Assertive Behavior in Children: A Step Toward a Theory of Aggression." *Monographs of the Society for Research in Child Development* 32 (1967).

Quay, H. C. "Classification." In *Psychopathological Disorders of Childhood,* ed. H. C. Quay and J. S. Werry. New York: Wiley, 1979.

Richman, N. "Disorders in Preschool Children." In *Child Psychiatry: Modern Approaches,* ed. M. Rutter and L. Hersov. New York: Plenum, 1978.

Richman, N.; Stevenson, J. E.; and Graham, P. "Upset and Upsetting: A Longitudinal Study of Preschool Children." In press.

Rimm, D. C., and Masters, J. C. *Behavior Therapy: Techniques and Empirical Findings.* New York: Academic Press, 1974.

Robins, L. N. *Deviant Children Grown Up.* Baltimore, Md.: Williams & Wilkins, 1966.

Ross, D. M., and Ross, S. A. *Hyperactivity: Research, Theory, Action.* New York: Wiley, 1976.

Rutter, M. *Helping Troubled Children.* New York: Penguin Books, 1975.

Rutter, M. "Diagnosis and Definition." In *Autism: A Reappraisal of Concepts and Treatment,* ed. M. Rutter and E. Schopler. New York: Plenum, 1978a.

Rutter, M. "Language Disorder and Infantile Autism." In *Autism: A Reappraisal of Concepts and Treatment,* ed. M. Rutter and E. Schopler. New York: Plenum, 1978b.

Schachar, R.; Rutter, M.; and Smith, A. "The Characteristics of Situationally and Pervasively Hyperactive Children: Implications for Syndrome Definition." *Journal of Child Psychology and Psychiatry,* in press.

Schleifer, M.; Weiss, G.; Cohen, N.; Elman, M.; Cvejic, H.; and Kruger, E. "Hyperactivity in Preschoolers and the Effect of Methylphenedate." *American Journal of Orthopsychiatry* 21 (1975): 77–88.

Schopler, E. "Parents of Psychotic Children As Scapegoats." *Journal of Contemporary Psychotherapy* 4 (1971): 17–20.

Schopler, E., and Reichler, R. "Parents As Co-Therapists in the Treatment of Psychotic Children." *Journal of Autism and Childhood Schizophrenia* 4 (1971): 17–20.

Schopler, E.; Rutter, M.; and Chess, S. "Editorial Change in Journal Scope and Title." *Journal of Autism and Developmental Disorders* 9 (1979): 1–10.

Schroeder, C. "Psychologists in a Private Pediatric Practice." *Journal of Pediatric Psychology* 4, no. 1 (1979): 8–18.

Sears, R. R. "Relation of Early Socialization Experiences to Aggression in Middle Childhood." *Journal of Abnormal and Social Psychology* 63 (1961): 466–492.

Smith, P. K. "Aggression in a Preschool Playgroup: Effects of Varying Physical Resources." In *Determinants and Origins of Aggressive Behavior,* ed. J. de Wit and W. W. Hartup. The Hague: Mouton, 1974.

Solomons, G. "Drug Therapy: Initiation and Follow-Up." *Annals of the New York Academy of Sciences* 205 (1973): 335–344.

Spivack, G., and Shure, M. B. *Social Adjustment of Young Children.* San Francisco: Jossey-Bass, 1974.

Sroufe, L. A. "Drug Treatment of Children with Behavior Problems." In *Review of Child Development Research. Vol. 4,* ed. F. Horowitz. Chicago: University of Chicago Press, 1975.

Stevenson, J., and Richman, N. "Behavior, Language and Development in Three-Year-Old Children." *Journal of Autism and Childhood Schizophrenia* 8 (1978): 299–314.

Stewart, M. A., and Olds, I. *Raising a Hyperactive Child.* New York: Harper & Row, 1973.

Stuart, R. B. "Behavioral Contracting Within the Families of Delinquents." *Journal of Behavior Therapy and Experimental Psychiatry* 2 (1971): 1–11.

Tasto, D. L. "Systematic Desensitization, Muscle Relaxation and Visual Imagery in the Counter-Conditioning of a Four-Year-Old Phobic Child." *Behavior Research and Therapy* 7 (1969): 409–411.

Watzlawick, P.; Weakland, J. H.; and Fisch, R. *Change: Principles of Problem Formation and Problem Resolution.* New York: Norton, 1974.

Wender, P. H. *Minimal Brain Dysfunction in Children*. New York: Wiley Interscience, 1971.

Westman, J. C.; Rice, D. L.; and Bermann, E. "Nursery School Behavior and Later School Adjustment." *American Journal of Orthopsychiatry* 37 (1967): 725–731.

Wing, L. *Early Childhood Autism*. Oxford: Pergamon Press, 1976.

Wing, L., and Gould, J. "Severe Impairments of Social Interaction and Associated Abnormalities in Children: Epidemiology and Classification." *Journal of Autism and Developmental Disorders* 9, no. 1 (1979): 11–29.

Wolff, S. "Dimensions and Clusters of Symptoms in Disturbed Children." *British Journal of Psychiatry* 118 (1971): 421–427.

Wolman, B. B. "The Rationale of Child Therapy." In *Handbook of Treatment of Mental Disorders in Childhood and Adolescence,* ed. B. B. Wolman, J. Egan, and A. O. Ross. Englewood Cliffs, N.J.: Prentice-Hall, 1978.

Wolpe, J. *Psychotherapy by Reciprocal Inhibition*. Stanford, Calif.: Stanford University Press, 1958.

Young, G. C., and Morgan, R. T. T. "Rapidity of Response to the Treatment of Enuresis." *Developmental Medicine and Child Neurology* 15 (1973): 488–496.

Zimbardo, P.; Pilkonis, P.; and Norwood, R. "The Silent Prison of Shyness." Unpublished manuscript, Stanford University, 1974.

Samuel J. Meisels
Nicholas J. Anastasiow

14 The risks of prediction: relationships between etiology, handicapping conditions, and developmental outcomes

The problems of prediction

Most parents, and a substantial proportion of professionals, view the relationship between causes of handicapping conditions (i.e., etiology) and developmental outcomes in childhood (i.e., prognosis) as regular, repetitive, and predictable. A child born with Down syndrome will be retarded, children who have myelomeningocele will have a number of motor and neurological impairments, most infants who have the condition known as retrolental fibroplasia will become blind. For many individuals establishing the cause of a handicapping condition leads directly to a prediction of developmental outcomes of delay or impairment.

In the personal accounts written by parents of handicapped children, their reactions to the birth or diagnosis of a disabled child strongly reflect the attitudes and practices of professionals who subscribe to this perspective (Darling 1979; Kaufman 1976; Massie and Massie 1976; Murray and Murray 1975; Park 1967; Roskies 1972; Turnbull and Turnbull 1978). Judgments concerning the presence of a handicapping condition seem typically to be accompanied by predictions

259

regarding overall developmental achievement and potential. One mother describes her experience as follows:

> (In the recovery room) the head of pediatrics asked where my husband was. I said I didn't know, and he said, "Maybe I should come back." I said, "You might as well discuss it with me now. . . . " He said, "Well, there's a problem, and it's serious, but as an alternative, the child could be institutionalized."—and that's how Danny's birth was first explained. . . . I didn't want to see him; I thought it was so bad. (The child had Down's syndrome.) (Darling 1979, p. 133)

Another example demonstrates how the diagnosis of a handicapping condition is taken to imply that a child's developmental outcomes are fixed. This mother had believed that her child's problems were largely physical and were amenable to surgical correction. She had just been told that her child might also be retarded.

> Dr. Smith was the first one to really go into detail about (the syndrome). What really got me upset was the book with those really ugly pictures and the fact that I saw "Mental Retardation" on the cover. . . . He asked me, "What do you think of mental retardation?" When I think of mental retardation I think of a kid that is real bad, you know. . . . I wasn't ready for it. . . . When I came home I cried all afternoon. (Darling 1979, p. 137)

These examples graphically illustrate the sorrow, confusion, and anxiety experienced by most parents when they learn that their child is disabled. However, they also illustrate a conceptual problem that confounds a great deal of the research, treatment, and teaching of handicapped children. The confusion is that of moving precipitously from *etiology,* i.e., cause or origin of handicapping condition, to *prognosis,* or prediction regarding the child's developmental potential. In most instances etiology predicts handicapping conditions, but etiology bears only a potentially uncertain relationship to developmental outcome.

Developmental outcome refers to such varied indicators as level of intellectual functioning or adaptiveness, ability to communicate, quality and range of interpersonal relations, or extent of independent functioning. By definition, such outcomes are separated in time from the onset of a disability or from the identification of a handicapping condition. It is this period of time in which the child is functioning with parents, peers, and other human and physical agents of stimulation, that potentially alters the predictive relationship between etiology and prognosis or developmental outcome. The thesis of this chapter is that the predictive relationship between the origins of a disability and the outcomes associated with that disability are profoundly affected by the reciprocal transactions that take place over time between the child and her or his environment. To take a transactional perspective, is to recognize that development results from a continuous interaction between a dynamic organism and a dynamic environment.

In this chapter we will discuss the occurrence of handicapping conditions in young children, and alternative models of the course of development of such children. We will then review the research in four categories of handicapped young children: children with established (diagnosed) medical disorders, children who are biologically vulnerable and at-risk, children who are environmentally at-risk, and children with handicapping conditions of unknown origin. Diagnosis, remediation, and prediction of developmental outcomes will be considered for each category. Finally, a transactional model of development will be presented advancing the notion that only when there exists an appreciation of the complex intermediate steps between cause and outcome can we begin to make confident predictions concerning a child's overall development.

Histories of exceptionalities

According to U.S. government computation, 12 percent of all children between ages 3 and 19 are handicapped (State Program Implementation Studies Branch 1979). This percentage translates to approximately 10 million children and young adults. This number can be rendered somewhat more realistic by realizing that every 73 seconds a child is born in this country who is chronically ill or physically handicapped. Massie and Massie (1976) have calculated that this statistic means that there are "1,177 more of these children every day, 8,241 every week, 428,571 every year" (p. xi).

Traditional epidemiological studies assign the order of specific types of handicapping conditions, from most to least common, as follows: speech impairment, learning disabilities, mental retardation, emotional disturbance, crippling conditions and other health impairments, hard of hearing, visual impairment, deafness, and multihandicapped (National Advisory Committee on the Handicapped 1976). These labels can, in turn, be grouped in terms of a variety of etiological (causal) considerations. These groupings are adapted from Tjossem's (1976) categories of vulnerable infants.

1. *Established diagnosis* refers to children whose early developmental disabilities are presumed to be related to diagnosed medical disorders. Examples of such disorders include Down syndrome, inborn errors of metabolism (e.g., untreated PKU and other disorders of the body's chemical system), multiple congenital anomalies (e.g., spina bifida) and morphological anomalies (e.g., cleft palate, extra digits).
2. *Biologically vulnerable* refers to children who present a history of high-risk factors during their prenatal, perinatal, or neonatal periods. Such factors include metabolic disease and nutritional deficiencies in the mother, obstetrical complications, low birth weight, anoxia, or prematurity among many others. These factors, or early developmental events, are suggestive of possible impaired development or biological injury to the infant's developing central nervous system.
3. *Environmentally at-risk* refers to children whose experiences are significantly limited during early childhood in areas of maternal attachment, family and health care, and in opportunities for physical, social, and adaptive stimulation. Such factors are highly correlated with a probability of delayed development.
4. *Unknown origin* refers to children whose symptoms are recognizable but

cannot be clearly associated with one or more specific generative (causal) factors. Such children may demonstrate disabilities in any area of functioning.

The first three of these groupings are not mutually exclusive categories. A child may have an established diagnosis, may be biologically vulnerable because of birth trauma, and may also be at risk environmentally. Such a combination of unfortunate events illustrates the problematic course of some children's lives and also indicates how complex the diagnostic process can be (Johnston and Magrab 1976).

The four etiological groupings presented above can be conceptualized through a series of models of development. These models balance chronological age against some appropriate measure of developmental level (e.g., psychomotor rating, mental, or developmental age). Crocker (1977) proposes that these models can be considered deviations from a theoretically smooth developmental course as illustrated in Figure 14.1. Different types of developmental courses, each based on information from "the course to date, and the best understanding possible about the biologic issues which will affect the future" (Crocker 1977, p. 3), result in different developmental curves. For example, Figure 14.2 depicts an established, or "fixed" diagnosis; Figure 14.3 shows another form of established diagnosis, but one in which near-normal development is succeeded by progressive difficulty such as neuronal cell death, myelination handicap, or cerebral maturational failure. Such increasing dysfunction often accompanies metabolic disorders such as Tay-Sachs disease, Niemann-Pick disease, or Hurler disease.

Figure 14.4 represents a curve associated with an "acquired" modification of development. This developmental course is analogous to that of biologically vulnerable infants, as well as children who have suffered severe injury or a disease such as encephalitis early in life. In these conditions there may be a temporary arrest of development and then a recovery that leads to a return to normal function.

The development of the child who is environmentally at-risk is depicted in Figure 14.5. This child's development may be compromised by inadequate or inconsistent social and environmental supports, by caregiving that is confounded by parental psychosis or sudden separation, or by other forms of abuse and neglect.

Finally, in Figure 14.6 these theoretical models of development are superimposed on one another, thus demonstrating that although particular individuals may appear similar to one another at a specific time, "there can be varying dynamics in the developmental course, dependent on etiology" (Crocker 1977, p. 5). This is one of the critical reasons that a search for causes should be undertaken and can be practically justified. However, it is rare that etiology implies developmental outcomes in rigid and inevitable terms. Most of the developmental courses described above are accessible to modification, remediation, or amelioration. Consequently, these theoretical curves or models would not depict development following intervention nor are they designed to reflect the

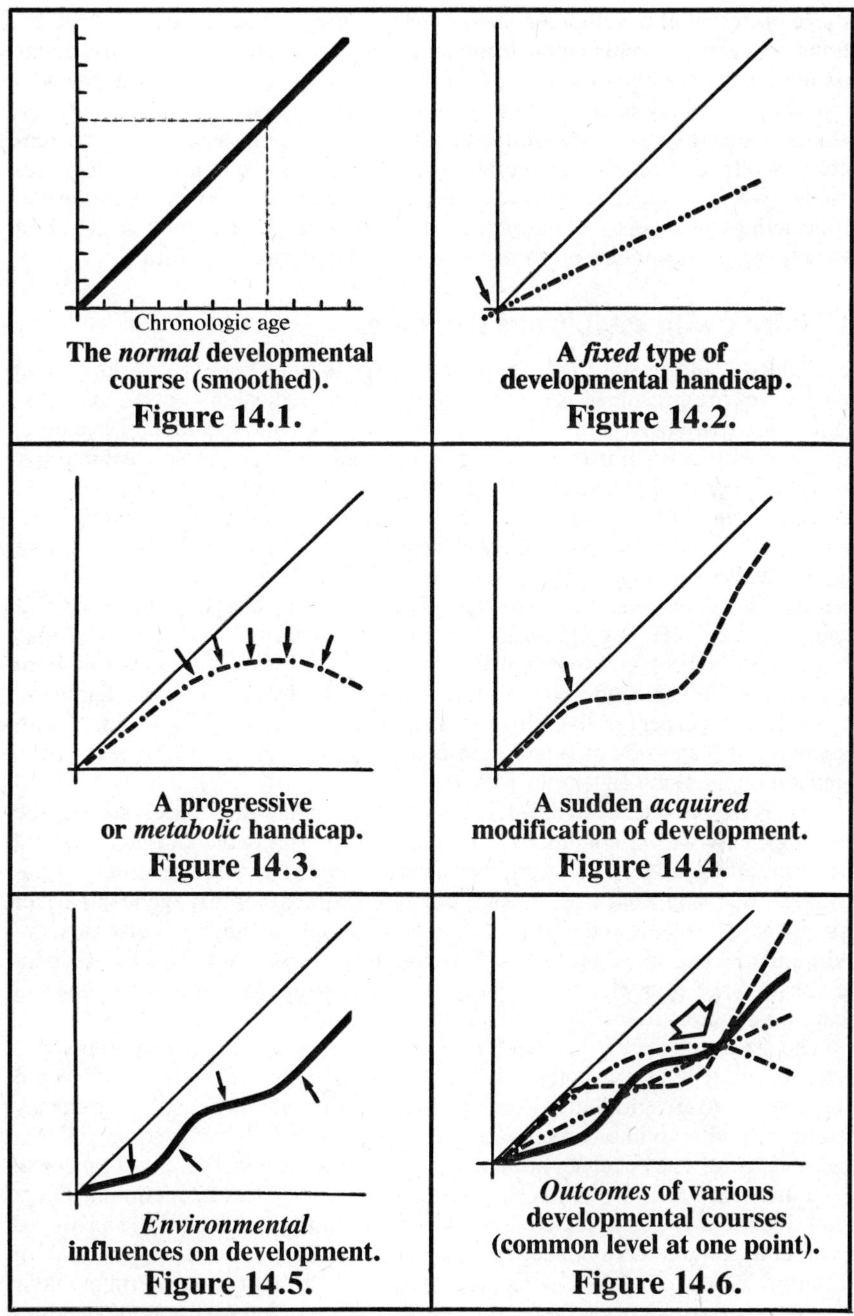

The *normal* developmental course (smoothed).
Figure 14.1.

A *fixed* type of developmental handicap.
Figure 14.2.

A progressive or *metabolic* handicap.
Figure 14.3.

A sudden *acquired* modification of development.
Figure 14.4.

***Environmental* influences on development.**
Figure 14.5.

***Outcomes* of various developmental courses (common level at one point).**
Figure 14.6.

From Crocker (1977)

range of potential developmental outcomes as they are influenced by transactions between the child and environment. Indeed, it is only by means of a focus on the effects of intervention and the effects of child-environment transactions that the facts of etiological determinism under which many parents and profes- -sionals labor may be modified. In the following sections, recent research concerning remediation and amelioration of handicapping conditions will be reviewed with particular attention devoted to the factors of early intervention and transactions between the environment and the developing individual. Each of the etiological groupings presented above will be discussed in turn.

Children with established diagnoses

Children with established diagnoses are those whose early developmental disabilities are presumed to be related to known medical disorders. Such disorders are extremely varied (Downey and Low 1974) and include, for example, children with cystic fibrosis, juvenile rheumatoid arthritis, chronic asthma, spina bifida, cerebral palsy, childhood orthopedic syndromes, psychopathology, and other hereditary syndromes. Each of these handicapping conditions is characterized by different levels of prevalence. For example, in a recent study of 18,155 newborns, 2 percent, or 357 of the children, demonstrated one or more serious morphological malformations (Holmes 1976). These inborn errors of morphogenesis (Holmes 1974) include physical abnormalities such as cardiac anomalies, cleft lip and palate, and extra fingers or toes. Children with inborn errors of metabolism and other anomalies of the body's chemical system comprise only .6 percent of live births (Friedrich and Nielson 1973). Children with established diagnoses of retardation constitute only about .75 percent of the general population (Zigler 1967; 1969).

Just as the prevalence of different handicapping conditions varies, so does the etiology vary within conditions. For example, the probable causes of mental retardation include hereditary issues such as genetic syndromes and chromosomal abnormalities, aberrations occurring during embryogenesis, other pregnancy problems and perinatal morbidity, acquired childhood diseases, environmental and social problems, as well as unknown causes. This list, that encompasses all four etiological groupings, clearly displays the wide range of causative factors associated with mental retardation.

The severity of disability resulting from these handicapping conditions also varies greatly. For example, children with PKU imbalance who are detected early and who are enrolled in a therapeutic medical and nutritional program may suffer virtually no ill effects later in life (Levy 1973). Similarly, some children with significant physical abnormalities can undergo remedial surgical or medical treatment that permits the development of virtually complete functioning (Katz and Challenor 1974). In these cases the questions of prediction can be answered with considerable confidence. In many other instances, however, the task of accurately predicting developmental outcomes is difficult and uncertain, and is apparently dependent on the extent and type of early intervention the child receives, as well as the type of environment in which the child lives. Children born with profound sensorineural hearing loss will probably never hear as a result of early intervention, and children with cerebral palsy will always have some form of brain lesion or damage. However, the developmental potential of these children is neither described nor determined by the mere identification of their problem.

Support for these statements emerges from a variety of sources. Horton (1974) found that intervention with deaf children before the age of two resulted in their adaptation to normal classrooms, whereas deaf children who were not in intervention programs until the age of three did not make these adaptations. Northcott (1971) reports that early intervention with hearing-impaired children prevents the development of negative behaviors such as excessive bodily contact, grimaces, and other stereotypic behaviors that tend to limit the acceptance of the deaf child by the normally hearing population.

Other dramatic results have been demonstrated with visually impaired children. Fraiberg (1977) notes that when congenitally blind children are not provided with environmental stimulation to compensate for loss of sight, they may develop stereotyped hand behavior, rocking, swaying, mutism, or echolalic speech. Fraiberg notes that in a group of blind infants that she studied, the behavior patterns of some of the children were so strikingly uniform, that brain damage and/or infantile autism were among the suspected etiologies. Fraiberg and her colleagues found, in their sample of blind-from-birth babies, that there were severe problems of attachment and an insufficiency of stimuli for the infants' tactile-kinesthetic-auditory development. Thus, they embarked upon an intervention program designed to maximize these infants' potentials for adaptation in the areas of human attachments, grasping, locomotion, and language development. The effects of this intervention were such as to bring these educationally advantaged blind infants closer to sighted-child behavioral ranges than to blind-child ranges (Fraiberg 1977, p. 283).

Some of the strongest evidence concerning the impact of early stimulation on developmental outcomes emerges from inferences that can be drawn from recent neurological research with animals. The justification for these inferences lies with two assumptions. First, it is assumed that the basic processes of genes and cells function similarly across species. Thus, if one were able to show a cellular basis for the storage of memory in rats or primates, it could be taken as support for a cellular basis for memory in humans. Second, the brain of the human species has evolved from the brains of less complex species (Mac Lean 1978) and has retained all of the lower structures while evolving new ones as well.

In a study of the function of the cortical area (orbital prefrontal cortex) of 7–24-month-old monkeys, Goldman (1976) found that, following cortical damage, recovery of the ability to perform a delayed-response task is related to the experience prior to brain maturation and not to the maturation of brain structures alone. It is not known whether training promotes recovery of function by developing specific learning or simply through a generalized enriching of experience (Rudel 1978). In any case, the finding supports the fact that experience promotes recovery. This finding is of major importance when one considers that some brain-damaged children exhibit a potential for recovery of some functions as they grow older (Goldman 1976). Goldman's data suggest that what may appear to be initially unsuccessful training at one stage of development might be critical if these children are to recover at a later stage. It is a strong argument for intervening early rather than waiting until the organism matures.

Environmental stimulation is closely tied to full maturation of functions. Normally sighted chimpanzees raised in the dark for a period of time fail to see when brought into the light (Ganz and Fitch 1968). White rats raised in a stimulating environment in the first days of life have larger brains than those raised in a deprived environment (Rosenzweig et al. 1972). Kittens carried around a room on a moving carrousel fail to make the depth perceptions that kittens who were permitted to move through the environment on their own are able to make easily (Held and Hein 1963). Thus, it has been clearly demonstrated with animals that early experience and stimulation modify the brain in terms of its size, structure, and functioning (Chall and Mirsky 1978).

Floeter and Greenough (1979) speculate that the sensitivity of the brain to experience may be related to the degree of maturation of the structure at the time of the experience. That is, environmental effects may be greatest on those structures of the brain that are yet to mature. As the brain structures reach maturity, the effects of the environment are minimized in terms of modifying that structure. In Rudel's studies, cited above, it was the section of the brain that had not fully matured that was influenced by the training sessions. Once the structure was mature biologically, the training experience did not result in learning. Further support for this notion has appeared in the work of Spinelli and Jensen (1979).

It is assumed that similar principles hold for the human central nervous system. There is abundant anatomical and behavioral evidence that indicates that if neural circuits are not brought into play at certain critical times of development, they may never be capable of functioning (Mac Lean 1978). The human brain does not add brain cells after the second year of life. The major additions between the second and the fifteenth or sixteenth years of age, when growth is complete, are more extended and branched axons and dendrites of brain cells, the myelin sheath, and increased arterial blood supply. These increases do not appear in a gradual sequence but manifest themselves in five growth spurts (Epstein 1978). The spurts are initially accompanied by dramatic changes in the intellectual and social functioning of the infant. The first brain spurt is at 2 to 3 months of age and is accompanied by the appearance of the social smile and changes in sleep and brain wave patterns (Emde, Gaensbauer, and Harmon 1976). The second brain growth spurt occurs between 6 and 8 months and signals, in some children, at least, the appearance of "stranger anxiety" or infant fear of strangers. The third brain growth spurt takes place between 18 to 24 months, a time when language and speech accelerate rapidly. The next brain growth spurts accompanied by bio-behavioral shifts occur between 6 to 8, 10 to

12, and 14 to 16 years of age.

These spurts in brain growth appear to signal maturation of structures and represent either periods of rapid learning (Epstein 1978) or, as noted above, periods when previous learnings make their appearance in child performances (Goldman 1976). The latter position is taken in this chapter. Thus, the inference that can be drawn from the impact of experience on brain development is that stimulation or intervention should occur *before* the maturation of structures, even though the effects of training and learning are not felt until sometime after the structure matures. As we shall see below, parents who provide emotional support and appropriately organized and structured environments for their infants can help offset the potentially devastating effects of perinatal stress, thus altering the presumed link between etiology and developmental outcome.

Biologically vulnerable children

Biologically vulnerable children are infants who are at-risk for developmental delay, disability, or even death as a result of a number of factors occurring during pregnancy, at birth, or in the neonatal period. Numerous studies and reviews have been conducted seeking to link perinatal events to a variety of subsequent conditions (Balow, Rubin, and Rosen 1975–76; Kawi and Pasamanick 1959; Pasamanick and Lilienfeld 1955). Recently, a number of investigators have reinterpreted these data and have offered alternative explanations of the relationship between perinatal events or conditions and developmental potential (Broman, Nichols, and Kennedy 1975; Caputo and Mandell 1970; Field et al. 1979; Gottfried 1973; Rubin and Balow 1977; 1979; Sameroff and Chandler 1975; Werner and Smith 1979).

The principal variables that have been most extensively studied include low birth weight, prematurity, and anoxia. However, the range of prenatal, perinatal (at birth), and neonatal (after birth) variables that contribute to an infant's risk status may include the following:

1. Prenatal variables: factors suggestive of an abnormal fetus, prenatal strain, or accident.
2. The general birth process: abnormal delivery, instrumental delivery, baby held back, unusual presentation, premature separation of placenta, cord around neck, induced labor.
3. The neonate: serum bilirubin levels, minimal brain damage (organic damage), convulsions, absent cry or sucking, fractures, intracranial hemorrhage, head misshapen or marked, jaundice, paralysis, pupillary abnormalities, abnormal reflexes, projectile vomiting, comatose state.
4. The mother: illness, weight gain, blood pressure, smoking, severe effects of delivery, weight loss, history of rubella, virus infection during pregnancy, influenza, abnormal or contracted pelvis. (Rubin and Balow 1977, pp. 125–126)

These factors were combined by Lilienfeld and Parkhurst (1951) and Pasamanick and Knobloch (1961) under the expression "continuum of reproductive casualty." This expression was meant to describe the complete range of deviant pregnancy outcomes. The view that abnormal antecedent events or conditions, such as those enumerated above and included in the reproductive risk continuum, result in abnormal outcomes is an inherently causal view. It focuses on "discovering missing links in a chain of efficient causality leading from early traumas to later abnormality" (Sameroff and Chandler 1975, p. 236).

A major problem with the research that culminated in the continuum of biological risk is that it was based on retrospective rather than prospective methodology. In a retrospective approach, only the children whose early vulnerability actually led to a handicap are studied. Then, in retrospect, the researcher looks back to see what risk factors characterized those children during the early months of life. In a prospective approach the investigator studies *all* of the children who were at-risk during the early months of life and identifies how many, and which ones, actually did develop a significant handicap (Sameroff and Chandler 1975).

Extensive prospective studies have now been completed. The results of these studies do not uniformly support the implication of the early risk factors as a cause of later disorders. One of the most comprehensive studies is known as the Collaborative Perinatal Project (Broman, Nichols, and Kennedy 1975). This national project studied the relationship between 169 prenatal and postnatal variables and the overall development of more than 53,000 children. Broman, Nichols, and Kennedy reviewed the intellectual performance at age four of 26,760 children whose mothers enrolled during pregnancy in the Collaborative Perinatal Project. Their findings are that social class variables have a much greater effect on intellectual development than do the presence of perinatal complications. Moreover, they determined that "prior to birth the most consistent predictor of intellectual retardation at four years of age was years of education completed by the mother."

Another study based on the Collaborative Project data, but designed to follow a subsample of children through their teens and early adolescence, came to a similar conclusion. In this study it was found that "the single best predictor of all developmental, educational, and behavioral outcomes is the socioeconomic status of the child's family" (Rubin and Balow 1977, p. 151).

In another major longitudinal study, Werner, Bierman, and French (1971) studied all of the children who were born and raised on the Hawaiian island of Kauai. They also conclude that the family, social, and environmental conditions are of greater influence on developmental outcomes than any but the most severe perinatal and neonatal abnormalities.

Thus, for children who are biologically vulnerable, the most potent single predictive variable appears to be the characteristics of the family and the caretaking environment. In recognition of the role that reproductive risk factors may play in predetermining an initial negative caretaking environment, Sameroff and Chandler (1975) propose a variation of the "continuum of reproductive casualty" called a "continuum of caretaking casualty." In this transactional model, the child and her or his caretaking environment tend to mutually alter one another. To the extent that the child elicits or is provided with nurturance from the environment, positive outcomes are a likely consequence. To the extent that the child elicits negative responses from the environment, the child is likely to be at high risk for later difficulties. Thus, in Sameroff's terms, "although reproductive casualties may play an initiating role in the production of later problems, it is the caretaking environment that will determine the ultimate outcome" (Sameroff 1975b, p. 274).

With the exceptions of gross insults that lead to serious brain damage, perinatal disorders are not consistently related to later childhood disorders. It is the quality of the subsequent transactions that take place between the child and her or his caretaking environment that serves to create or to obviate the linkage between earlier trauma and later disability. This transactional model will be explored more fully in the succeeding sections of this paper.

Children at-risk environmentally

Children who are environmentally at-risk are children whose experiences in early childhood, including maternal attachment and family and health care, as well as opportunities for physical, social, and adaptive stimulation are significantly limited. Such factors are highly correlated with a probability of delayed development. Such children may demonstrate mild mental retardation, delayed motor milestones, restricted expressive and receptive language abilities, or serious emotional disturbance, among other problematic conditions.

From the vantage point of the data presented in the preceding section on biological vulnerability, it would appear that, to some extent, every child born into a low-SES family is at-risk. However, such a conclusion is unwarranted. The studies noted earlier include SES, educational level of the mother, and the quality of transactions between the child and the environment as all being significant variables to review in predicting developmental outcomes.

In a study designed to focus on the predictive quality of these conditions, Ramey et al. (1978) demonstrate that it is possible to identify children at birth who, presumably for sociocultural reasons, are likely to need special services before or during elementary school. Using only information available from birth certificates, Ramey and his colleagues determined that "the children who appeared to be most severely at risk for retarded development were third or later born siblings whose mother had a tenth grade or less educational level and who, herself, had a previous live birth now dead and who began care for the target child in the third or later month of pregnancy" (p. 533). Although it is important to note that these characteristics do not, themselves, "cause" poor child performance, that is, they do not necessarily imply that negative consequences will follow, they are highly correlated with developmental outcome. SES and its concomitants play a critical role in development.

However, environmental deprivation may take many forms. In their 18-year longitudinal study of the children of Kauai, Werner and Smith (1977) note that "poverty alone was not a sufficient condition for the likelihood of significant coping problems" (p. 218). Rather, they identify the interaction of early biological stress and early family instability as leading to a high risk of developing serious and persistent learning and behavior problems in middle-SES children as well as in lower-SES children.

In other words, in reviewing the effects on children of environmental risk, it is critical to note that the *caregiving environment* is not sufficiently described by SES (Ramey, Farran, and Campbell 1979); adequate development is not a middle-SES phenomenon. Furthermore, development is a concept that is subject to change. Clarke and Clarke (1976) report a number of studies of children who began their lives amidst great adversity, but, with a radical change in the quality of the environment, were able to lead more normal lives. Winick, Meyer, and Harris (1975) found that even the effects of severe malnutrition could at times be mitigated by the environmental enrichment of adoptive homes. Similarly, IQ scores have been shown to change significantly as a function of intervention and environmental supports over time (Murphy and Moriarty 1976). In Hunt's words, "A major share of early losses can be made up if the development-fostering quality of experience improves, and a great deal of early gain can be lost if the quality of experience depreciates" (Hunt 1979, p. 136).

Several longitudinal studies conclusively demonstrate that the quality of the transactions that take place between a caregiver (usually the mother) and an infant can either facilitate or retard development (Bradley and Caldwell 1978; Broman, Nichols, and Kennedy 1975; Elardo, Bradley, and Caldwell 1975; 1977; Neligan, Prudham, and Steiner 1974; Thomas and Chess 1977; Thomas, Chess, and Birch 1968; Werner, Bierman, and French 1971). The findings of more than 60 studies report a consistent pattern of childrearing attitudes that relate to, and probably facilitate the child's IQ and achievement development (Martin 1975). These attitudes include a moderate degree of warmth, low use of physical punishment, high levels of verbalization, moderate response to a child's needs, and a press for the child to make age-appropriate developmental attainment. Further, caregivers who respond to the child, talk with the child, and present stimulating experiences such as providing toys in the home and taking the child out of the home, have children who learn to speak earlier and more competently (Nelson 1973).

It can be surmised that a biologically intact organism plays a key role in eliciting particular environmental responses. Some of these behavior patterns are genetic in base and have strong survival value. Thus, the infant who enacts these patterns more rapidly, that is, an infant who is more active and more alert, and who is usually described as brighter or more intelligent, elicits greater maternal involvement (Bradley, Caldwell, and Elardo 1979; Rheingold and Eckerman 1975). In contrast, the infant who is less alert, or who is passive and quiet, receives less attention and stimulation.

The impact of this failure to stimulate and, in turn, to receive stimulation is graphically displayed in the syndrome of learned incompetence labeled "iatrogenic retardation" by Kearsley (1979). Kearsley's position is that "children's inherent capacity to attain and maintain an overall state of well being requires an environment that not only makes available the essential physical and psychological nutrients, but also provides the constraints and challenges necessary for the actualization of those processes that support physical growth and psychological development" (p. 165). In his clinical research, Kearsley has identified a number of children with apparently normal cognitive abilities who nevertheless display significant motoric, linguistic, and socioemotional delay. The development of these infants and children has taken place in an environment of "prolonged parental anxiety and inappropriate caretaking practices" (p. 155). Moreover, the maintenance of this level of anxiety is attributed by Kearsley to the manner in which the child's physician or other influential professionals adjust the prognosis to accommodate the possibility of an unfavorable outcome. This continuing negative influence on the parents affects their motivation and ability to alter the state of psychological malnutrition in which they and their child find themselves.

Thus, the transactional model that suggests that development takes place as a result of the interplay between the child and the environment is a double-edged sword. In the case of children who are environmentally at-risk, environment-organism interactions have the potential of either *reducing* or *magnifying* early developmental difficulties. Kearsley notes that parents, although directly involved in the genesis of iatrogenic retardation, "are the primary therapeutic resource available to the children to overcome their developmental handicap" (Kearsley 1979, p. 177). The causal link between environmental etiology and developmental outcomes is neither necessary nor sufficient, but the relationship between the environment and outcomes is extremely complex and highly influential.

Handicapping conditions of unknown origin

This discussion will be brief, in contrast to the other etiological groupings. Children who have handicapping conditions of unknown origin present symptoms that are recognizable, but that cannot be clearly associated with one or more specific generative factors. Unknown origin may be associated with any handicapping condition. Intervention techniques with children who have problems of unknown origin focus on the behavioral concomitants of the handicapping condition. The effects of transactions between these children and their parents would not be expected to differ significantly from the situations that are associated with other disabled children, although the absence of a cause may have transactional effects of its own.

There may be more children with unknown etiologies than is commonly accepted. In a sample of more than 1000 cases of developmental delay, 31 percent of the causes of retardation in that group were of unknown origin (Milunsky 1975). From another perspective, excellent developmental outcomes in the face of extremely negative early life experiences are also sometimes of apparently unknown origins, and have given rise to the construct of invulnerability or resiliency (Anthony and Koupernik 1974; Anthony 1974a; 1974c; Garmezy 1974; Werner and Smith 1979). Although the causes of some children's invulnerability cannot be conclusively identified, several researchers (Anthony 1974b; Garmezy 1974; Werner and Smith 1979; Wertheim 1975) identify a variety of experiential conditions that contribute to this resiliency such as emotional support from outside the home provided by other adults, friends, or peers.

Nevertheless, the research on invulnerability demonstrates that the effort to relate the quality of the caregiving environment to the child's perceived developmental outcomes is not always successful. Thomas and Chess (1977) note that "even when there is an excellent fit between a child's temperament, and the characteristics of his or her caretaking environment, it may be impossible to make a direct correlation between environmental influences, such as parental attitudes and practices, and the child's psychological development" (p. 4). Thomas and Chess are not questioning the effects of transactional relationships between parents and children. Rather, they are noting the presence of psychopathology independent of good parenting, as well as the healthy development of personality in children growing up in families with severe disorganization, parental disturbance, and social stress. The causes of some outcomes are apparently both unknown and unintuitive—and sometimes quite unpredictable.

The transactional model

Without simply redefining an environmentalist position, it can be asserted that the contribution of the social environment is critical to the development of young children, particularly children who are born with handicapping conditions. Research demonstrates that even newborn infants are synergistically related to their environments (Als 1978; Beckwith 1976; Sander 1969). That is, a variety of infant characteristics have been identified (temperament; sex; birth order; state and responsiveness to visual, auditory, and tactile stimuli) that affect the infant-caregiver relationship. Many of these characteristics are influenced in turn by maternal attitudes and behavior (Osofsky and Connors 1979). Indeed, as we have seen, judgments concerning developmental outcomes must be withheld until both the etiology and the caregiving environment have been closely scrutinized. As Murphy and Moriarty (1976) suggest, "development is not merely due to the effect of either simple hereditary or environmental forces" (p. 150). At any time the child's way of responding to and coping with constitutional and environmental forces, as well as the complex interactions between these forces, is difficult if not impossible to predict.

The transactional view of development owes much to the research of Werner, Bierman, and French (1971) and Thomas, Chess, and Birch (1968), and has been well defined by Sameroff and Chandler (1975), Thomas and Chess (1977), and by Sameroff (1975a; 1979). It stands in contrast to linear and unidirectional models of causation and development such as that of Gesell (Anastasiow and Stengel 1980), and is consistent with the theories of Dewey and Piaget (Meisels 1979). It implies that each element in the transaction may have reciprocal effects—either positive or negative—upon each other.

Thus, although the effects of positive caregiving and environmental support in the presence of a good fit with the child's temperament and abilities facilitate development (Cohen and Beckwith 1979), the long-term impact of less-facilitating environments can have markedly persistent effects on a child's developmental progress. As in the case of extreme child abuse exemplified by holding children captive in basements or in attics, the child may eventually be helped, but will probably never function as a normal child (Bourne and Newberger 1979; Clarke and Clarke 1976; Curtiss 1977).

Recently, theorists propounding a life span position have made important observations concerning the malleability of development throughout the life span (Goldhaber 1979). Clarke and Clarke (1976) propose the model of a wedge theory of development, "representing at the thick 'young' end maximal responsiveness to the environment and at the extreme 'older' end, no responsiveness at all" (p. 18). They argue that the thin end lies well into the chronological age range; thus, the possibilities for alteration in response to a changing environment remain open longer into the life span than is typically expected. Nevertheless, the likelihood remains that although much can be done for a disabled child later in development, early intervention might accomplish much more. This conclusion is supported by Werner and Smith (1979), as well as by Sameroff (1975b) and Kagan et al. (1979). When children are exposed to a positive environment and facilitating parenting skills, they will usually develop normally, even if they may have suffered some form of stress at birth, such as anoxia. Conversely, if the environment is not facilitating, and the parenting skills are not responsive, normal children achieve low levels of cognitive functioning and stressed children do not usually achieve normal developmental levels. The long-term effects of such deprivation are significant and pronounced and they seem to be related, in part, to the accumulated sequence of negative transactions.

Research has given us clues as to how development is facilitated or distorted. The early interventionists have given us hope of how to ameliorate significant disabilities. Nevertheless, it is our contention that there is a need for studies of the development of handicapped children in a variety of adaptive caregiving environments, examining the ongoing feedback between the caregiver and the infant or young child. Such studies hold the promise of elucidating the manner in which bonding and attachment can be established in impaired children in the first years of life, how caregivers can encourage independence, competence, and self-reliance, and in general, how the transactional process actually facilitates development.

In addition, such studies may contribute to the education of both parents and professionals concerning the potential developmental outcomes of their handicapped children. Even the initial experience of learning that one's child is disabled can contribute to a sequence of negative (or positive) caregiving transactions. Two parents of a retarded child reflect on this experience as follows:

> Dr. Eldridge tried to get Little John to do all sorts of things. . . . He cried a lot, and succeeded at very little. She wants him to go for tests to her medical school, where she can arrange for the head of Pediatrics, her old professor, to take his case. When I asked if that was really necessary . . . She answered caustically, "Why, he's *way*

behind!'' Then she sat down and lectured us with a horribly false cheerfulness, in an overconfidential tone: ''I was visiting an institution recently, and the children were all so happy because there wasn't any competition. They do such wonderful things with them. He would be much better off there.''

> Everything in our lives is being chopped down ruthlessly. I don't even want to look at Little John. In my imagination I see him already deformed, behaving grossly, his features ugly, and I wish he hadn't been born. (Murray and Murray 1975, pp. 22–23)

Events such as these play critical roles in a child's development. It has been the thesis of this chapter that within certain ranges, the boundaries of etiological causation can be broken and reformed or at least reviewed and revised. Human understanding regarding the developmental potential of handicapped children is intricately involved in this process of reformulation. For just as the child cannot be understood in isolation from her or his environment, so an understanding of developmental outcomes in handicapped children requires a knowledge and appreciation of the importance of the interactions of that child with the environment.

Conclusion

The basic argument presented in this chapter is that the social environment greatly facilitates or interferes with human organisms in realizing their genetic potential. Development is a transactional process involving the integrity of the organism, the environment, and the skills of the interactive agent in the environment. Recent research regarding the infant's central nervous system suggests that it may be flexible enough to provide alternative structures in the case of sensory or physical impairments. However, these impairments, whether real or suspected, must be identified and treated before the maturation of the alternative structures occurs. Moreover, when the treatment is provided by persons who have daily interaction with the infant or young child, the treatment itself is likely to contribute to a transactional effect that may offset the impairment, regardless of whether the cause of the impairment is biological or environmental. Although the link between etiology, handicapping conditions, and developmental outcomes is not severed by the approach and perspective presented in this chapter, evidence exists that most handicapped children can lead richer and more fulfilling lives than would otherwise be the case—if their environments are dynamic and responsive, and if they are arranged so as to permit the children to develop to the fullest their physical, emotional, and intellectual abilities.

References

Als, H. "Assessing an Assessment: Conceptual Considerations, Methodological Issues, and a Perspective on the Future of the Neonatal Behavioral Assessment Scale." In *Organization and Stability of Newborn Behavior: A Commentary on the Brazelton Neonatal Behavior Assessment Scale. Monographs of the Society for Research in Child Development* 43 (1978). Serial No. 177.

Anastasiow, N. J., and Stengel, A. H. "Educating Physicians in Child Development: Why, What and How." In *Pediatric Education and the Needs of Exceptional Children,* ed. M. J. Guralnick and H. B. Richardson, Jr. Baltimore, Md.: University Park Press, 1980.

Anthony, E. J., and Koupernik, C., eds. *The Child in His Family: Children at Psychiatric Risk. Vol. III.* New York: Wiley, 1974.

Anthony, E. J. "Introduction: The Syndrome of the Psychologically Invulnerable Child." In *The Child in His Family: Children at Psychiatric Risk. Vol. III,* ed. E. J. Anthony and C. Koupernik. New York: Wiley, 1974a.

Anthony, E. J. "A Risk-Vulnerability Intervention Model for Children of Psychotic Parents." In *The Child in His Family: Children at Psychiatric Risk. Vol. III,* ed. E. J. Anthony and C. Koupernik. New York: Wiley, 1974b.

Anthony, E. J. "The Syndrome of the Psychologically Invulnerable Child." In *The Child in His Family: Children at Psychiatric Risk. Vol. III,* ed. E. J. Anthony and C. Koupernik. New York: Wiley, 1974c.

Balow, B.; Rubin, R.; and Rosen, M. "Perinatal Events As Precursors of Reading Disability." *Reading Research Quarterly* 11, no. 1 (1975–76): 36–71.

Beckwith, L. "Caregiver-Infant Interaction and the Development of the High Risk Infant." In *Intervention Strategies for High Risk Infants and Young Children,* ed. T. Tjossem. Baltimore, Md.: University Park Press, 1976.

Bourne, R., and Newberger, E. H. *Critical Perspectives on Child Abuse.* Lexington, Mass.: D. C. Heath, 1979.

Bradley, R. H., and Caldwell, B. M. "Screening the Environment." *American Journal of Orthopsychiatry* 48, no. 1 (1978): 114–130.

Bradley, R. H.; Caldwell, B. M.; and Elardo, R. "Home Environment and Cognitive Development in the First 2 Years: A Cross-Lagged Panel Analysis." *Developmental Psychology* 15, no. 3 (1979): 246–250.

Broman, S. H.; Nichols, P. L.; and Kennedy, W. A. *Preschool IQ: Prenatal and Early Development Correlates.* Hillsdale, N.J.: Lawrence Erlbaum Associates, 1975.

Caputo, D., and Mandell, W. "Consequences of Low Birth Weight." *Developmental Psychology* 3 (1970): 363–383.

Chall, J., and Mirsky, A., eds. *Education and the Brain.* Chicago: University of Chicago Press, 1978.

Clarke, A. M., and Clarke, A. D. B. *Early Experience: Myth and Evidence.* New York: Free Press, 1976.

Cohen, S. E., and Beckwith, L. "Preterm Infant Interaction with the Caregiver in the First Year of Life and Competence at Age Two." *Child Development* 50 (1979): 767–776.

Crocker, A. C. "Application of Assessment Data to Personal and Educational Planning." Paper presented at the Annual Meeting of the American Association for the Advancement of Science, Denver, 1977.

Curtiss, S., ed. *Genie: A Psycholinguistic Study of a Modern-Day "Wild Child."* New York: Academic Press, 1977.

Darling, R. B. *Families Against Society: A Study of Reactions to Children with Birth Defects.* Beverly Hills, Calif.: Sage Publications, 1979.

Downey, J. A., and Low, N. L. *The Child with Disabling Illness: Principles of Rehabilitation.* Philadelphia: Saunders, 1974.

Elardo, R.; Bradley, R.; and Caldwell, B. M. "The Relation of Infants' Home Environment to Mental Tests Performance from Six to Thirty-Six Months: A Longitudinal Analysis." *Child Development* 46 (1975): 71–76.

Elardo, R.; Bradley, R.; and Caldwell, B. M. "A Longitudinal Study of the Relation of Infants' Home Environment to Language Development at Age Three." *Child Development* 48 (1977): 595–603.

Emde, R. N.; Gaensbauer, T. J.; and Harmon, R. J. *Emotional Expression in Infancy: A Biobehavioral Study.* New York: International Universities Press, 1976.

Epstein, H. T. "Growth Spurts During Brain Development: Implications for Educational Policy and Practice." In *Education and the Brain,* ed. J. S. Chall and A. F. Mirsky. Chicago: University of Chicago Press, 1978.

Field, T. M.; Sostek, A.; Goldberg, S.; Shuman, H., eds. *Infants Born at Risk: Behavior and Development.* New York: Spectrum, 1979.

Floeter, M. K., and Greenough, W. T. "Cerebellar Plasticity: Modification of Purkinje Cell Structure by Differential Rearing in Monkeys." *Science* 206, no. 12 (1979): 227–232.

Fraiberg, S. *Insights from the Blind.* New York: Basic Books, 1977.

Friedrich, U., and Nielson, J. "Chromosome Studies in 5,049 Consecutive Newborn Children." *Clinical Genetics* 4 (1973): 333–343.

Ganz, L., and Fitch, M. "The Effect of Visual Deprivation on Perceptual Behavior." *Experimental Neurology* 22 (1968): 638–680.

Garmezy, N. "The Study of Competence in Children at Risk for Severe Psychopathology." In *The Child in His Family: Children at Psychiatric Risk. Vol. III,* ed. E. J. Anthony and C. Koupernik. New York: Wiley, 1974.

Goldhaber, D. "Does the Changing View of Early Experience Imply a Changing View of Early Development?" In *Current Topics in Early Childhood Education. Vol. II,* ed. L. Katz et al. Norwood, N.J.: Ablex, 1979.

Goldman, P. S. "The Role of Experience in Recovery of Function Following Orbital Prefrontal Lesions in Infant Monkeys." *Neuropsychologia* 14 (1976): 401–411.

Gottfried, A. W. "Intellectual Consequences of Perinatal Anoxia." *Psychology Bulletin* 80 (1973): 231–242.

Held, R., and Hein, A. "Movement-Produced Stimulation in the Development of Visually Guided Behavior." *Journal of Comparative and Physiological Psychology* 56 (1963): 872–876.

Holmes, L. B. "Inborn Errors of Morphogenesis: A Review of Localized Hereditary Malformations." *New England Journal of Medicine* 291 (1974): 763–773.

Holmes, L. B. *The Malformed Newborn: Practical Perspectives*. Boston: Massachusetts General Hospital, Genetics Unit, Children's Service, 1976.

Horton, K. B. "Infant Intervention and Language Learning." In *Language Perspectives: Acquisition, Retardation, and Intervention*, ed. R. L. Schiefelbusch and L. L. Lloyd. Baltimore, Md.: University Park Press, 1974.

Hunt, J. M. "Psychological Development: Early Experience." In *Annual Review of Psychology*, ed. M. R. Rosenzweig and L. W. Porter. Palo Alto, Calif.: Annual Reviews, 1979. (Vol. 30, pp. 103–143.)

Johnston, R. B., and Magrab, P. R. *Developmental Disorders: Assessment, Treatment, Education*. Baltimore, Md.: University Park Press, 1976.

Kagan, J.; Klein, R. F.; Finley, G. E.; Rogoff, B.; and Nolan, E. "A Cross-Cultural Study of Cognitive Development." *Monographs of the Society for Research in Child Development* 44 (1979). Serial No. 180.

Katz, J. F., and Challenor, Y. B. "Childhood Orthopedic Syndromes." In *The Child with Disabling Illness: Principles of Rehabilitation*, ed. J. A. Downey and N. L. Low. Philadelphia: Saunders, 1974.

Kaufman, B. *Son-Rise*. New York: Harper & Row, 1976.

Kawi, A. A., and Pasamanick, B. "Prenatal and Paranatal Factors in the Development of Childhood Reading Disorders." *Monographs of the Society for Research in Child Development* 24 (1959). Serial No. 73.

Kearsley, R. B. "Iatrogenic Retardation: A Syndrome of Learned Incompetence." In *Infants at Risk: Assessment of Cognitive Functioning*, ed. R. B. Kearsley and I. E. Sigel. Hillsdale, N. J.: Lawrence Erlbaum Associates, 1979.

Levy, H. L. "Newborn Screening for Metabolic Disorders." *New England Journal of Medicine* 288 (1973): 1299–1300.

Lilienfeld, A. M., and Parkhurst, E. "A Study of the Association of Factors of Pregnancy and Parturition with the Development of Cerebral Palsy: A Preliminary Report." *American Journal of Hygiene* 53 (1951): 262–282.

Mac Lean, P. D. "A Mind of Three Minds: Educating the Triune Brain." In *Education and the Brain*, ed. J. S. Chall and A. F. Mirsky. Chicago: University of Chicago Press, 1978.

Martin, B. "Parent-Child Relations." In *Review of Child Development Research. Vol. 4*, ed. F. D. Horowitz et al. Chicago: University of Chicago Press, 1975.

Massie, R., and Massie, S. *Journey*. New York: Knopf, 1976.

Meisels, S. J., ed. *Special Education and Development: Perspectives on Young Children with Special Needs*. Baltimore, Md.: University Park Press, 1979.

Milunsky, A., ed. *The Prevention of Genetic Disease and Mental Retardation*. Philadelphia: Saunders, 1975.

Murphy, L. B., and Moriarty, A. E. *Vulnerability, Coping and Growth*. New Haven, Conn.: Yale University Press, 1976.

Murray, J. B., and Murray, E. *And Say What He Is: The Life of a Special Child*. Cambridge, Mass.: MIT Press, 1975.

National Advisory Committee on the Handicapped. *The Unfinished Revolution: Education for the Handicapped, 1976 Annual Report*. Washington, D.C.: U.S. Government Printing Office, 1976.

Neligan, G.; Prudham, D.; and Steiner, H. *Formative Years: Birth, Family and Development in Newcastle upon Tyne*. London: Oxford University Press, 1974.

Nelson, K. "Structure and Strategy in Learning to Talk." *Monographs of the Society for Research in Child Development* 38 (1973). Serial No. 149.

Northcott, W. N. "The Integration of Young Deaf Children into Ordinary Educational Programs." *Exceptional Children* 38 (1971): 29–32.

Osofsky, J. D., and Connors, K. "Mother-Infant Interaction: An Integrative View of a Complex System." In *Handbook of Infant Development*, ed. J. D. Osofsky. New York: Wiley, 1979.

Park, C. C. *The Siege*. New York: Harcourt Brace Jovanovich, 1967.

Pasamanick, B., and Knobloch, H. "Epidemiologic Studies on the Complications of Pregnancy and the Birth Process." In *Prevention of Mental Disorders in Children*, ed. G. Caplan. New York: Basic Books, 1961.

Pasamanick, B., and Lilienfeld, A. "Association of Maternal and Fetal Factors with Development of Mental Deficiency: I. Abnormalities in the Prenatal and Paranatal Periods." *Journal of the American Medical Association* 159, no. 3 (1955): 155–160.

Ramey, C. T.; Farran, D. C.; and Campbell, F. A. "Predicting I.Q. from Mother-Infant Interactions." *Child Development* 50 (1979): 804–814.

Ramey, C. T.; Stedman, D. J.; Borders-Patterson, A.; and Mengel, W. "Predicting School Failure from Information Available at Birth." *American Journal of Mental Deficiency* 82, no. 6 (1978): 525–534.

Rheingold, H., and Eckerman, C. "Some Proposals for Unifying the Study of Social Development." In *Friendship and Peer Relations*, ed. M. Lewis and M. Rosenblum. New York: Wiley, 1975.

Rosenzweig, M. R. et al. "Brain Changes in Response to Experience." *Scientific American* 226 (1972): 22–29.

Roskies, E. *Abnormality and Normality: The Mothering of Thalidomide Children*. Ithaca, N.Y.: Cornell University Press, 1972.

Rubin, R. A., and Balow, B. "Perinatal Influences on the Behavior and Learning Problems of Children." In *Advances in Clinical Child Psychology. Vol. I*, ed. B. B. Lahey and A. E. Kazdin. New York: Plenum, 1977.

Rubin, R. A., and Balow, B. "Measures of Infant Development and Socioeconomic Status As Predictors of Later Intelligence and School Achievement." *Developmental Psychology* 15, no. 1 (1979): 225–227.

Rudel, R. G. "Neuroplasticity: Implications for Development and Education."

In *Education and the Brain*, ed. J. S. Chall and A. F. Mirsky. Chicago: University of Chicago Press, 1978.

Sameroff, A. J. "Concepts of Humanity in Primary Prevention." Paper presented at the Vermont Conference on the Primary Prevention of Psychopathology, Burlington, Vermont, 1975a.

Sameroff, A. J. "Early Influences on Development: Fact or Fancy?" *Merrill-Palmer Quarterly of Behavior and Development* 21, no. 4 (1975b): 267–294.

Sameroff, A. J. "The Etiology of Cognitive Competence: A Systems Perspective." In *Infants at Risk: Assessment of Cognitive Functioning*, ed. R. B. Kearsley and I. E. Sigel. New York: Lawrence Erlbaum Associates, 1979.

Sameroff, A. J., and Chandler, M. J. "Perinatal Risk and the Continuum of Caretaking Casualty." In *Review of Child Development Research. Vol. 4*, ed. F. Horowitz et al. Chicago: University of Chicago Press, 1975.

Sander, L. W. "The Longitudinal Course of Early Mother-Child Interaction: Cross-Case Comparisons in a Sample of Mother-Child Pairs." In *Determinants of Infant Behavior IV*, ed. B. M. Foss. London: Methuen, 1969.

Spinelli, D. N., and Jensen, F. E. "Plasticity: The Mirror of Experience." *Science* 203, no. 5 (1979): 75–78.

State Program Implementation Studies Branch. *Progress Toward a Free Appropriate Public Education: A Report to Congress on the Implementation of P. L. 94-142*. Washington, D.C.: Bureau of Education for the Handicapped, U.S. Office of Education, 1979.

Thomas, A., and Chess, S. *Temperament and Development*. New York: Brunner/Mazel, 1977.

Thomas, A.; Chess, S.; and Birch, H. G. *Temperament and Behavior Disorders in Children*. New York: New York University Press, 1968.

Tjossem, T. D. *Intervention Strategies for High Risk Infants and Young Children*. Baltimore, Md.: University Park Press, 1976.

Turnbull, A. P., and Turnbull, H. R. *Parents Speak Out: Views from the Other Side of the Two-Way Mirror*. Columbus, Ohio: Merrill, 1978.

Werner, E. E.; Bierman, J. M.; and French, F. E. *The Children of Kauai*. Honolulu: University of Hawaii Press, 1971.

Werner, E. E., and Smith, R. S. *Kauai's Children Come of Age*. Honolulu: University of Hawaii Press, 1977.

Werner, E. E., and Smith, R. S. "Vulnerable But Invincible: A Longitudinal Study of Resilient Children and Youth." Final report submitted to the Foundation for Child Development, September 30, 1979.

Wertheim, E. S. "Person-Environment Interaction: The Epigenesis of Autonomy and Competence." *British Journal of Medical Psychology* 48 (1975): 1–8(a), 95–111(b), 237–256(c), 391–402(d).

Winick, M.; Meyer, K. K.; and Harris, R. C. "Malnutrition and Environmental Enrichment by Early Adoption." *Science* 190 (1975): 1173–1175.

Zigler, E. "Familial Mental Retardation: A Continuing Dilemma." *Science* 155 (1967): 292–298.

Zigler, E. "Developmental Versus Difference Theories of Mental Retardation and the Problem of Motivation." *American Journal of Mental Deficiency* 73 (1969): 536–556.

Acknowledgments

We would like to thank Allen Crocker for permission to reprint Figures 14.1–14.6. Earlier versions of this chapter were read and commented on by Allen Crocker, Bruce Pennington, Susan Swap, Emmy Werner, and Jean Zadig. We are grateful to them for their comments and suggestions.

Index

List of contributors

Nicholas J. Anastasiow
Department of Special Education
Hunter College
New York, NY 10021

Lynn Arnason
Department of Applied Psychology
Ontario Institute for Studies in
    Education
Toronto, Ontario
Canada M5S 1V6

Steven R. Asher
210 Education Bldg.
University of Illinois
Urbana, IL 61801

Catherine R. Cooper
3403 Rosefinch Trail
Austin, TX 78746

Barbara Everett
Washington Liaison Office
Society for Research in
    Child Development
2025 Eye Street, N.W., Room 905
Washington, DC 20006

Beverly I. Fagot
Department of Psychology
University of Oregon
Eugene, OR 97403

Susan Goldberg
Psychiatric Research Unit
The Hospital for Sick Children
Toronto, Ontario
Canada M5G 1X8

Joan E. Grusec
Department of Psychology
University of Toronto
Toronto, Ontario
Canada M5S 1A1

Asa G. Hilliard III
628 Urban Life Bldg.
Georgia State University
Atlanta, GA 30303

Frances Degen Horowitz
Department of Human
    Development
University of Kansas
Lawrence, KS 66045

Shelley Hymel
Department of Psychology
University of Waterloo
Waterloo, Ontario
Canada N2L 3G1

Sandra J. Kronsberg
Washington, D.C.

Catherine Lord
Department of Psychology
Glenrose Hospital
10230 111th Avenue
Edmonton, Alberta
Canada T5G 0B7

Robert M. Malina
Department of Anthropology
University of Texas
Austin, TX 78712

Samuel J. Meisels
University of Michigan
Institute for the Study of
   Mental Retardation
   and Related Disabilities
130 S. First Street
Ann Arbor, MI 48109

Shirley G. Moore
Institute of Child Development
University of Minnesota—
   Twin Cities
Minneapolis, MN 55455

Norma Radin
School of Social Work
University of Michigan
Ann Arbor, MI 48104

Peter D. Renshaw
Riverina College of
   Advanced Education
School of Education
P.O. Box 588
Wagga Wagga,
   New South Wales 2650
Australia

Kenneth H. Rubin
Department of Psychology
University of Waterloo
Waterloo, Ontario
Canada N2L 3G1

Frances Fuchs Schachter
Department of Psychology
Barnard College
Columbia University
New York, NY 10027

Amy A. Strage
Department of Psychology
University of California at
   Berkeley
Berkeley, CA 94709

Mona Vaughn-Scott
University of San Francisco
   Medical Center
SIRECO
3641 Sacramento Street, Suite E
San Francisco, CA 84118

Henry M. Wellman
Department of Psychology
University of Michigan
Ann Arbor, MI 48104

Other NAEYC Publications of Interest

If this book is helpful to you—

1. NAEYC's journal *Young Children* is available through membership or by subscription. Write to NAEYC for further information.
2. Many other teaching ideas are included in the books listed below. Order your copies today.
3. Order ten or more copies each of this or other NAEYC books as texts for classes or workshops and receive a ten percent discount.

Code

	Title	Price
315	Administration: Making Programs Work	$6.60
318	The American Family: Myth and Reality	$2.20
106	Art: Basic for Young Children	$5.00
132	The Block Book	$3.85
111	Brain and Learning: Directions in Early Childhood Education	$3.00
200	Careers with Young Children: Making Your Decision	$4.40
121	Developmental Screening in Early Childhood: A Guide	$2.75
112	Ethical Behavior in Early Childhood Education	$2.00
212	A Good Beginning for Babies: Guidelines for Group Care	$5.75
317	Group Games in Early Education	$9.35
302	A Guide to Discipline	$1.65
105	Ideas That Work with Young Children, Vol. 2	$4.75
319	Infants: Their Social Environments	$7.70
131	Language in Early Childhood Education, Revised Edition	$5.50
114	Mainstreaming: Ideas for Teaching Young Children	$5.50
316	More Than Graham Crackers: Nutrition Education and Food Preparation with Young Children	$4.20
312	Mother/Child, Father/Child Relationships	$5.20
107	Music in Our Lives: The Early Years	$2.75
135	Parent Involvement in Early Childhood Education, Rev. Ed.	$3.30
115	Planning Environments for Young Children: Physical Space	$2.00
306	Play as a Learning Medium	$3.00
309	Science with Young Children	$3.55
128	The Significance of the Young Child's Motor Development	$2.45
402E	Some Ways of Distinguishing a Good Early Childhood Program	$ .30

All prices include postage and handling. Please enclose full payment for orders under $10.

For information about these and other NAEYC publications, write for a free publications brochure, or call 202-232-8777, toll free 800-424-2460.

Order from: NAEYC
1834 Connecticut Avenue, N.W.
Washington, DC 20009